INTRODUCTION TO COMPUTER ORGANIZATION

DIGITAL SYSTEM DESIGN SERIES

Arthur D. Friedman, Editor
George Washington University

S. Imtiaz Ahmad and Kwok T. Fung
Introduction to Computer Design and Implementation

Michael Andrews
Principles of Firmware Engineering in Microprogram Control

J.E. Arsenault and J.A. Roberts
Reliability and Maintainability of Electronic Systems

Jean-Loup Baer
Computer Systems Architecture

Melvin A. Breuer
Digital System Design Automation:
Languages, Simulation and Data Base

Melvin A. Breuer and Arthur D. Friedman
Diagnosis and Reliable Design of Digital Systems

Arthur D. Friedman
Logical Design of Digital Systems

Arthur D. Friedman and Premachandran R. Menon
Theory and Design of Switching Circuits

Ivan Tomek
Introduction to Computer Organization

Ivan Tomek
Introduction to Computer Organization Workbook

INTRODUCTION TO
COMPUTER
ORGANIZATION

Ivan Tomek
Acadia University
Wolfville, Nova Scotia

WITHDRAWN

PITMAN

PITMAN PUBLISHING LIMITED
39 Parker Street, London WC2B 5PB

Associated Companies
Pitman Publishing Pty Ltd., Melbourne
Pitman Publishing New Zealand Ltd., Wellington

First published in Great Britain in 1981
First published in USA in 1981

Copyright © in 1981 Computer Science Press, Inc.
11 Taft Court.
Rockville, Maryland 20850

This book was first published in 1981 by Computer Science Press, Inc., 11 Taft Ct., Rockville, Maryland 20850 U.S.A.

Tomek, Ivan.
    Introduction to computer organization.

    Bibliography: p.
    Includes index.
    1. Computer architecture. I. Title
QA76.9.A73T65   621.3819'52   80-24238
US ISBN 0-914894-08-0
UK ISBN 0-273-01710-1

This book is dedicated to my parents
Mrs. Olga Tomková
and
JUDR Pavel Tomek
with profound appreciation and gratitude.

PREFACE

The primary purpose of this text is to provide a beginning student of computer science (or anybody else interested in computers) with a solid and realistic understanding of the operation of modern computer hardware without going into the operation of its electronic components. It is written to give sufficient background for those students of computer science who will not take any other hardware courses but also to provide a basis on which to build a deeper knowledge and understanding. Those who want to get involved with computer engineering (design of computers and related systems) will have to supplement this text with the study of electronics and other subjects.

The text will also be useful to engineers and engineering students interested in digital systems even though it is not intended as a self-contained textbook on digital design: it covers concepts and methods complementary to those studied in electronics courses and presents an alternative view without overlap. It does not require any previous knowledge of computer science.

It is hoped that the book will also reach the quickly growing community of computer hobbyists and laymen interested in the principles of computer operation. The coverage is rigorous yet accessible to anybody with high school background and will provide him or her with a sound understanding of the subject.

The text covers the material recommended for course CS4, "An Introduction to Computer Organization," in the ACM '78 Curriculum Proposal. (CS4 is a one-semester course to be required of *all* students of computer science.) The text is, in this respect, unique among existing textbooks on hardware.

The description of CS4 specifies that it should provide fundamentals of logic design, teach the mechanics of information transfer and control, and introduce the organization and structuring of the major hardware components of computers. It is recommended to supplement the course by laboratory experiments and study in detail a simple microcomputer or minicomputer.

This brief description makes it clear that the course proposal sets it apart from traditional introductory courses on hardware for computer scientists by grouping logic design, computer organization, investigation of a real computer, and laboratory experiments. The time allotted to it is too short for the detailed study of any of the subjects. In particular digital design cannot be covered in the usual depth—and need not be since this is a course for all computer science students and not specifically for computer engineers. The goal is to introduce them to the principles of hardware components of computer systems. A similar reasoning applies to the subject of computer organization which is expected to be studied in more detail in a more advanced course designed for those computer science students who need it.

The existing textbooks touching on the required topics mostly fall into one of the following categories:

1. Books on digital circuits which cover the topic at a level appropriate for digital designers, i.e. overly detailed for the purpose of CS4, and whose coverage of computer organization is minimal, if any.
2. Books on computer organization often written for specialized courses of a more advanced character. Since these courses usually have a digital design prerequisite their treatment of logic circuits is minimal or non-existent. These books do not encourage a digital laboratory as a part of the material. They also tend to present general principles rather than the details of an existing simple computer system. This is probably because small systems are somewhat marginal to the subject of general computer architecture.

The ACM outline is the first realistic attempt to summarize what students of computer science need to know about digital systems. This is in contrast to the previous idea that they should be exposed to material basically identical to that taught to engineering students or (the other extreme) that they need not study hardware at all. The ACM attempt to set a specific computer science perspective is typical for the overall emergence of computer science as an independent coherent field.

This text covers all the recommended topics in the same order and depth as the ACM outline recommends. The main text is accompanied by a Workbook containing a section with an outline of laboratory experiments designed for a simple and inexpensive breadboarding system. They are performed with standard TTL integrated circuits and in this way give the student a realistic appreciation of the physical realities of hardware. They do not require any knowledge of electronics.

The main text has a restricted number of solved problems to prevent the fragmentation of the presented concepts. Solved problems on topics which require more examples are collected into another section of the Workbook. The reader will be well advised to read all solved problems in parallel with the textbook since some of them contain very important material not presented in the main text. A number of them contain unusual examples which, in the author's opinion, provide a much more realistic insight into the function of some of the most important digital circuits than is usually available from similar textbooks.

The basic recommendations of ACM are augmented in a few directions:

1. The topic of hardware simulation is introduced. This addition has been considered essential and useful for several reasons: it allows accurate description of circuits and system organization in a formalized way familiar to students of computer science, it presents a non-trivial alternative use of computers and computer languages, it also provides an alternative approach to experimentation and introduces the important concept of simulation. In addition, hardware simulation is an increasingly important part of digital design and a realistic appreciation of the design process is impossible without it.

   Hardware simulation is not essential to the method of presentation used in this text. It can be treated simply as an aid in formulating accurate descriptions of hardware. The coverage of the subject is based on a simulation language designed specifically for the needs of this course by the author. This language, called HARD, is being implemented in Pascal and is thus very portable. For more information on the language and its implementation contact the author.

2. The discussion of a concrete computer system is always a problem in a textbook. The main reason is that discussion of a specific system tends to limit the audience to those who have access to the computer. This book attempts to eliminate this problem by discussing several computers. Two popular and inexpensive systems accessible to most institutions are chosen as representative of microcomputers: the Heathkit Microprocessor

Trainer and the TRS-80 (Radio Shack) system. The PDP-11 family architecture is outlined to introduce minicomputers, the UNIVAC 1100/60 and the CDC Cyber 170 series are presented to provide an insight into the architecture of large computers.

The Trainer which is discussed in considerable detail is not as popular as the TRS-80. Its popularity is limited because it is a rather specialized system intended to be used by people who want to study mainly the hardware aspects of computers. It is equipped for simple implementation of experiments and is in this sense ideal for the needs of the CS4 course. It is also so simple that it can be discussed at the level of its logic diagram which is unrealistic for any more complex systems. This makes it possible to demonstrate how the principles presented in the preceding chapters can be applied to the building of a working system. Those who do not have access to the Trainer can obtain an assembler and simulator written in Pascal from the author. The TRS-80 is a much more complicated system which can be expanded into a practical and realistic system including all typical subsystems such as disk and tape storage and typical I/O devices. This system cannot be studied in complete detail but its description gives an idea of the configuration of a useful and more typical system.

The PDP-11 family was chosen because it is very widely used and generally accepted as a prototype minicomputer family.

The UNIVAC and CDC families are described because they contain elements typical for some modern and probably even future computers. They are also sufficiently different to justify simultaneous presentation. In a departure from other books IBM computers are not discussed. This is because practically every other book on computer hardware contains an outline of the major IBM products and yet another discussion would be redundant.

3. A very brief outline of certain unusual or non-standard approaches and technologies deals with topics such as pipelining, multiprocessing, associative memories, etc. This introductory coverage in Chapter 9 is accompanied by an outline of currently successful and prospectively attractive processor and memory technologies.

4. Several other extensions of the basic material include reliable design, testing, malfunctions of digital circuits, etc.

The presentation is conversational and emphasis is placed on justification. An attempt is made to assume the creative perspective of a designer rather than to present dogmata. The text also tries to present a realistic, up-to-date picture of the current technological state and strengthen this practical perspective by illustrative laboratory experiments. A set of computerized drills to accompany the text is under development.

A glossary of frequently encountered terms is given at the end of the book.

The text covers a considerable amount of material, probably at least 50 percent more than required for a typical introductory course. Combined with suitable references it could be used for a two-semester course. This was judged necessary to provide a self-contained and complete introductory coverage of the topic. This justified, for example, the introduction of digital design in addition to analysis, and the extension of description of computer systems since it was felt that presentation of only a simple microcomputer system would give a very distorted picture of actual systems. The coverage in the class may exclude some of this extra material. An example of a manageable program for an introductory one-semester course for students of computer science could cover or introduce the following topics corresponding to the description of CS4: the function and basic structure of digital systems, the binary system and functions, their description by truth tables and Boolean expressions, canonical formulas, physical implementation and diagrams. Karnaugh maps and their use in the design of simple circuits, don't care conditions, PLA, ROM, physical behavior of components, hazards and faults, reliable design. Hardware simulation. Description of sequential circuits (tables and diagrams), flip-flops and their behavior. Analysis of simple sequential circuits. Counters and design with them. Races. Registers. Transfer of data between registers, the bus. Coding and handling of errors. Pure binary, fixed-point, sign-magnitude, 2's complement, floating-point representation, arithmetic and implementation. Formulation of the basic organization of a simple computer, the CPU, programming, description of function by a control sequence, an outline of its hardwired and microprogrammed implementation. Tracing the details of the execution of a short sequence of instructions. The ALU, types of I/O implementation, I/O and memory devices. Differences of implementation on large computers—I/O channels, parallelism, pipelining, computer families. This sequence can be accompanied by relevant experiments almost from the start of the course. A tour of a computer center is very instructive at an appropriate time. It was found very helpful to give frequent and regular tests which encourage students to keep up with the wide range of topics presented in the course.

This book is based on a set of progressively evolving lecture notes for a course that I taught for several years. It grew out of my own dissatisfaction with the fact that much of what I learned about hardware was largely irrelevant and that many practically important topics were not covered in traditional hardware courses at all. This text will, I hope, help to bridge this gap between needs and traditional course contents and make it easier to teach and study a modern hardware course along the lines of ACM's CS4.

In conclusion I would like to thank Vladimir Berka, Glenn Tillotson, and Bill Wilder for reading parts of the manuscript and making valuable suggestions. Several students helped to finalize the syntax of HARD and write the simulator. Most of the programming was done by Doug Currie. Dr. Wayne Davis introduced me to hardware in his well-organized and enjoyable lectures. My colleague Dr. Wayne Brehaut has not participated directly in the preparation of the text but his indirect influence must be acknowledged. A closer cooperation would probably have resulted in a better text. The patience of my family and particularly my wife Jana is gratefully appreciated.

After having typed and retyped the manuscript at least fifty times, I am beginning to understand why every author thanks the typist in so many words. Yet I would also like to thank the editors whose permanent dissatisfaction helped me a lot and made the text more readable.

Contents

Chapter 1

INTRODUCTION

1.1 WHY STUDY HARDWARE

Computer systems consist of the *hardware* which includes all the physical components required to execute programs and the *software* which includes the information stored in the system, programs and data.

The main subject of study of the large majority of students of computer science is software: how to write programs to solve problems from various application areas, how the software of the system itself works. Included in this category is the study of various programming languages, representations of data, methods of creation of efficient programs and their evaluation, etc.

Students of computer science sometimes question the requirement to also study hardware. They argue that most of them will never participate in the design of a computer and their job will be to write programs. This argument is correct, but it does not imply that they should only study the software aspects of computer science. The following are some reasons in support of the need for the study of hardware:

1. Many programmers never have to write programs which require a good understanding of hardware. They will, however, be involved with hardware in indirect ways; their programs will be designed to make good use of the configuration of the system, and as graduates of computer science programs, they will be expected to be the experts on matters related to computers. In this capacity they may be consulted on questions related to hardware—system configurations, purchase of new hardware, comparison of various models and even relative advantages of various technologies and design approaches. Many of these

questions can be superficially answered without a sound understanding of hardware but without it a full understanding of all
implications is impossible.

2. Software cannot be fully understood without some understanding
    of hardware. A substantial part of software is very much
    hardware dependent.
3. Computer organization is based on some very general principles
    (to be presented in this text) and its scope is not only the inter-
    nal workings of standard and specialized computers but also the
    way in which individual subsystems such as terminals, card
    readers and other input/output devices, etc., are connected
    together, etc. These topics are of essential importance to many
    users of computers and cannot be understood properly without at
    least an elementary knowledge of hardware.
4. A significant proportion of programmers are involved with
    "low-level" programming and some of the problems they may
    encounter require a certain understanding of hardware.
5. Computer scientists as computer users should be qualified to
    investigate in what ways computers could be made more efficient
    and better suited to fulfill the functions that computer users
    require of them.
6. Anybody who wants to be considered an expert must understand
    the methods and tools of his specialty. Consider again program-
    ming languages: almost anybody can learn a programming
    language and write programs. But why are programming
    languages the way they are? Their structure must look rather
    arbitrary to anybody who does not understand computer organi-
    zation. One can "understand" computer organization sufficiently
    to understand the development of programming languages
    without any deeper knowledge of hardware. But why is the com-
    puter organized the way it is? To understand this one must go
    deeper. All this is a part of computer science and without at least
    an elementary knowledge of this aspect one's understanding of it
    is superficial.

1.2 DIGITAL AND ANALOG

This text is concerned with digital systems and culminates in the
study of digital computers. Today the qualification "digital" is often
dropped and the word computer is automatically interpreted as digital
computer. In the past this was not so.

Computers can be generally classified into several categories: digital, analog and hybrid. Hybrid computers are combinations of digital and analog ones. In the 1940's and early 1950's analog computers were more common than the digital ones and the qualification digital was necessary. For reasons related to the development of technology and the growing understanding of the capabilities and relative merits of digital versus analog devices, this situation has completely changed and today it is the digital computer which is much more common. Analog computers are still being built and used, particularly in engineering applications, but their use is very limited compared to that of digital computers. In fact in many applications analog devices are being replaced by digital ones.

It can be said that digital devices work on the principle of coded messages while analog devices work with more or less smooth continuous signals. Digital devices also work with signals which can be roughly interpreted as discontinuous (quantized) and treat them as representing discrete levels. The discrete levels, in turn, represent codes. Note in the example shown in Figure 1.1 how the digital signal can be idealized so as to always have one of two discrete levels.

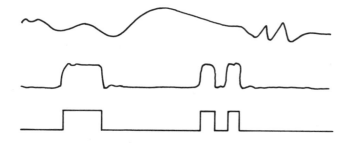

Figure 1.1   An analog signal, a digital signal, and its idealization.

In most systems both digital and analog signals occur and are converted from one form to the other in several places in the system. Consider, for example, a system consisting of two communicating digital subsystems (Figure 1.2). The transmission of the signal is by electric current of variable frequency. This current is a smooth, continuous, analog signal. At the receiver end of the line this signal is decoded (demodulated) on the basis of the following key: if the frequency of the signal is around 1000 Hertz (cycles/second) the signal is interpreted as a 0, if the frequency is around 1200 Hz it is interpreted as a 1. At the transmitting end the digital signal is encoded (modulated) to become an analog signal using the same key. We thus have an analog signal and its digital interpretation. The demodulator converts the oscillating signal into discrete levels as shown in the diagram. The modulator performs the inverse function.

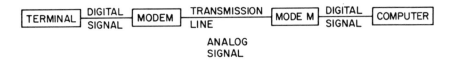

Figure 1.2   An example of a typical system employing both analog and digital signals.

It can be seen from this example that a digital signal is one which has the following two properties:

1. Its amplitude is interpreted as representing two or more discrete levels.
2. The sequence of discrete levels (the signal waveform) is interpreted as a code. The transmission signal in our example can be interpreted as a code but it does not consist of discrete amplitude levels and is therefore an analog and not a digital signal.

Digital circuits in a strict sense are systems which work only with digital signals. They can be perceived as systems processing codes representing information. They constitute devices which process information coded into discrete signals. The study of these devices and methods of combining them into larger systems is the main subject of this text.

It would be cumbersome to represent signals by waveforms (graphs). This is, fortunately, not necessary since levels in a digital signal represent codes. They can thus be represented by symbols, for example 0 for the low amplitude level (L), 1 for the high amplitude level (H). Or just the opposite: 0 for H, 1 for L. The symbol is irrelevant; it could be ? for L and ! for H. Any symbol assigned to each level will do. In practice the 0 and 1 code is the most common. This and the fact that many digital devices actually process numbers explain why the signals and devices are called digital.

As an example of a more specific system illustrating the distinction between analog and digital consider a hypothetical temperature display controller of a three engine airplane (Figure 1.3).

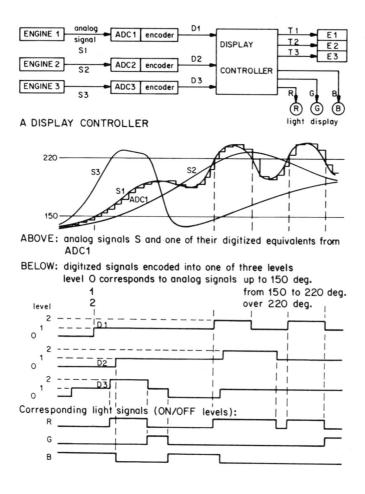

A DISPLAY CONTROLLER

ABOVE: analog signals S and one of their digitized equivalents from ADC1

BELOW: digitized signals encoded into one of three levels
level 0 corresponds to analog signals up to 150 deg.
from 150 to 220 deg.
over 220 deg.

Corresponding light signals (ON/OFF levels):

Figure 1.3   A display controller.

Each motor is equipped with a temperature sensing device which sends electric current to a simple display controller. The display is digital and shows the temperature of individual engines in degrees Celsius. When the temperature of at least one engine is below 150 C the blue light goes on. If all three temperatures are between 150 C and 220 C the green light is on. If at least one of the temperatures is over 220 C the red light goes on. The signal coming from temperature sensors is analog. It is decoded in the display controller by an Analog to Digital Converter (ADC) and displayed. It is also encoded into a 3-level digital signal: level 0 corresponds to the message "temperature up to 150 C," 1 to "temperature from 150 to 220," and 2 to "temperature over 220." This discrete (digital) signal is processed by individual light controllers and the lights turned ON or OFF as required. Note that the light signal also has the two properties of a digital signal. This simple system incorporates:

1. Analog signals (the signals coming from the three engines).
2. Digital signals (the signals from ADC and encoder to temperature displays and light controllers, from light controllers to lights are on/off. The visual signals—lights and readings—are also digital).
3. Analog devices (the temperature sensors generate analog signals).
4. Digital devices (e.g., the blue light controller produces an ON signal if any of the three input digital signals it receives is the code for a number smaller than 150, and produces an OFF signal for all other combinations).
5. Converters (which in our case are ADC).

Note how a digital device operates: any value of the temperature signal is treated in one way as long as it is below a certain value and in another way if it is above the same value. For example the blue light controller produces the same signal (ON) for all the following combinations of engine temperature signals: (100, 70, 110), (100, 170, 210), (130, 400, 300). It produces the same signal (OFF) for the following combinations: (200, 200, 200), (200, 160, 180), (300, 500, 400). If the temperature of one engine changes from 140 to 145 and the corresponding analog signal reflects this change, the output of the digital blue light controller will not change (in both cases it will be ON). This sensitivity to specific *levels* in the signal is characteristic of digital devices. Contrast this with the behavior of the temperature sensor (an analog device): if the temperature of the engine changes (even very little, e.g., from 140 to 141) the sensor's output voltage will also change (and every small change of temperature will correspond to a small change in the generated current).

The recent trend in many applications has been from analog to digital function and devices. This can be observed in the increasing use of digital watches and other measuring devices, communication technology and, of course, computers. Even gramophone records are beginning to be recorded digitally. This development has a number of reasons. The most important ones are:

1. Smaller sensitivity of digital devices to environment, internal parameters and "aging." This implies better reliability and often better accuracy. This property is the direct consequence of the discrete principle. A digital component has to be able to sense a certain number of levels with relatively restricted accuracy. An analog component must respond very accurately to every small change in its input signal and a small change of parameters may cause the system to fail.

2. Progress in technology (which made the mass production of digital devices possible at very low costs, very high quality and large density of function packed into a very small component). There has also been a significant progress in the technology of analog (often called "linear") components but not nearly as large as in the area of digital components. This is because many analog components include electric elements which cannot be produced with the revolutionary technology used for digital components. Another reason is that analog components are often used in applications which require relatively large amounts of power and this makes them unsuitable for miniaturization, which is the basis of the success of digital technologies. Digital systems work with minimal amounts of power since they only process information and this does not require any specific levels of power.

3. Another more basic reason is that most sophisticated equipment is primarily used for the processing of signals representing information. Consider our controller, a digital thermometer, a programmable stove, etc. The processed information is represented by encoded messages. Much of what the more sophisticated devices do is thus reception, processing, and output of information. We are living in a time in which the level of technology permits digital processing to be performed much more efficiently, economically and accurately than analog processing. We can thus expect that digital devices will replace analog ones in most applications involved with information processing.

1.3   A BRIEF OUTLINE OF THE HISTORY OF THE FIELD

The understanding of the directions in the development of theory and the changes in methodologies is difficult without the knowledge of the corresponding history of technology. This is perhaps especially true for the theory and practice of digital systems: there have been a number of rather abrupt changes in the direction of research in this field, and they are all related to the advancement of digital devices and their production. These advances were, of course, closely related to advances in theory, but in this case mostly theory of other fields, particularly electronics.

More generally the direction of the evolution in technology and theory is largely determined by economic considerations: we will see that attention is always directed towards improving those methods which best satisfy such economical factors as cost of production, reliability, and efficiency in answering the user's requirements. Most research is always directed to those problems whose solution promises the most drastic improvements in these economic factors. New developments lead to complete abandonment of accepted methods, change of direction of research, and new discoveries.

The following is a brief outline of the history of the very general field of information processing with attention directed particularly towards the underlying technology. This survey will be helpful in the building of a perspective in which the various approaches described in the following chapters can be viewed.

The first available technology was mechanical—levers, wheels, etc. The first significant developments in information processing by machines occurred in the seventeenth century with work on mechanical calculators capable of performing the basic arithmetic operations. The name of the French philosopher and mathematician Blaise Pascal is usually quoted in this context although a number of other people worked on similar machines at the same time. These machines were not produced commercially for another two centuries since the technology was not available for their economical manufacture. Calculators thus remained an academic curiosity, and no progress was made until the nineteenth century when the technology made it possible to produce them on a larger scale.

The next major advance is closely related with the name of the English inventor, Charles Babbage. Babbage first intended to build a machine to replace manual calculation of values for mathematical tables. He designed a "Difference Machine" which worked like a mechanical calculator capable of performing simple sequences of operations without user intervention. Then he realized that these and other sequences could be "programmed" by the user and entered into the machine in a coded form punched into paper cards. The much more sophisticated machine designed on this principle was called the "Analytical Machine." By processing the input data according to the program, the machine was to generate the desired results and print them out. The Analytical Machine was, in principle, equivalent to modern digital computers. Babbage never completely implemented his inventions; they were much too complicated for the technology available at the beginning of the nineteenth century. His machine, produced some time later, never gained wide popularity, mainly because of the inherent deficiencies of mechanical machines: communication, processing, and storage of codes were performed via moving mechanical parts. Because mechanical parts have to be relatively large, the machine must also be large. The processing is therefore very slow because the mechanical inertia and the power consumption are very large. The reliability of this machine is quite limited. As a result, the economic "gain" obtained by replacing humans with such a machine is negative, and there was no reason for the production of this machine other than curiosity. In this respect the mechanical computer followed the history of its predecessor, the mechanical calculator. This first "computer" had another major drawback: a highly qualified person was required to use it, adding to the cost of the device itself.

It is important to note what criteria determine the viability of a computer-like information processing device: speed, reliability, power consumption, cost of production, and use, ease of use, and to a lesser degree the size of the machine which is in general closely related to some of the previous criteria. We will see that these criteria, which determined the failure of the attempt to introduce a mechanical computer, also determine transitions between various stages of development ("generations") of modern computers.

The next stage arrived with progress in the understanding and use of electricity. Among other innovations, this led to progress in communication and, in the 1930's, to the building of the first analog computer. Shortly thereafter came the design of the first digital computers in Germany, England, and the United States. The designers had at their disposal both suitable technologies (they used relays and vacuum tubes developed mainly for communication) and theory (Babbage developed a considerable body of theory, but many of the designers were not aware of his work. A number of digital design techniques were developed in connection with communication technology). The progress was thus relatively fast, and by the end of the 1940's several digital computers were functional. They were developed mainly to satisfy some pressing practical needs for large military and scientific calculations. These computers were much better when measured by our criteria of speed, power consumption, reliability, cost of production and use, and size than the mechanical computers of the previous generation. They attained parameters which justified their limited production and use. By today's standards, however, they were still very inadequate. The basic reason for their limited performance was the inadequacy of technology: relays (which were soon abandoned) are electromechanical and have all of the disadvantages of mechanical devices. Vacuum tubes are relatively large components based on the motion of electrons over considerable distances. The generation of a sufficiently strong stream of electrons requires a large amount of power. The functional capabilities of individual tubes are quite elementary. These factors lead to limited processing speed and reliability, large power consumption, and related difficulties with cooling, costly production, a large number of components, connections, and space. It should be noted, however, that most of today's concepts related to the use and organization of computers were known in this period. The main difference between computers of this generation and today's machines is in technology.

The next generation of digital devices arrived with the discovery of semiconductors in the 1950's. The functional principle of semiconductor components is similar to that of vacuum tubes: their function is based on electronically controlled flow of current. The major difference between vacuum tubes and semiconductor components is that the scale at which the control current takes place is microscopic in semiconductors and macroscopic in vacuum tubes. Semiconductor devices therefore surpass vacuum tubes in their high speed and low power consumption. During the research period, reliability and production presented problems, but they were quickly solved, and semiconductors (particularly transistors) soon replaced vacuum tubes. Computers built with these components became commercially available in the late 1950's in large quantities but at high costs. They began to be used in business applications which became the principal application of computers. IBM (International Business Machines) became the best known manufacturer. Although most computers were produced in the United States (by IBM), significant research, development, and production continued to be done abroad, particularly in Europe.

Semiconductor components replaced vacuum tubes almost on a one for one basis, one new component for one old component although the circuits had to be somewhat modified. In other words the processing power of a single semiconductor component was still very limited, equivalent to that of the vacuum tube. Considering the fact that even a small computer contained tens of thousands of vacuum tubes it was clearly essential to reduce their number as much as possible. (This was, of course, also true for the previous generation of digital systems.) Thus, one of the important goals of the designer was to equip the computer to perform the given function with as few components as possible (to minimize the number of components), to reduce cost, and to improve reliability. This was the major research problem of the 1950's and early 1960's, accompanied by investigations of faster circuits, etc. More components mean not only larger size and power consumption but also larger cost of production due to the number of components and the greater complexity of interconnections; decreased reliability due to the number of components as well as the number of connections since imperfect connections constitute the most common source of failure; increased maintenance cost due to increased failure rate; increased complexity of maintenance, and often reduced speed.

Further research in electronics resulted in the development of methods allowing the placement of the equivalent of several "discrete" semiconductor components (transistors, etc.) on one "chip" of semiconductor (silicon) material. The resulting device is usually called an integrated circuit (IC) or a chip (also a "bug"). This development was the beginning of a new generation of computers. It has to be realized again what the consequences of such a technology are: increased speed (partially because of decreased distances between components) and reliability (most connections are built into the chip during its production and are much more reliable than external connections between components), smaller maintenance (due to the smaller number of components and increased reliability of the components themselves), decreased cost of production (the assembly is considerably simplified and the components are cheaper than the equivalent circuit built from discrete components). Power consumption drops significantly, and space occupied by an IC-based system is a fraction of one built with discrete semiconductor components. It took, of course, some time to develop appropriate technologies from the basic discoveries made in laboratories, but the progress in technology never slowed during the last 15 or 20 years. The result is that ICs are built which are cheaper every year, more complex and faster every year, consume less power, and are more reliable. Given these facts, it is obvious that the critical issues of 20 years ago are not necessarily so important today. In particular the predominant concern of the 1950's and early 1960's with minimization of the number of elementary components lost much of its importance because it lost its economical justification—today's components are not elementary in their function. Note that minimization is still important, particularly at the level of internal component minimization where a minimized circuit can be much simpler than a non-minimized one. As a result of changed components, design methodologies also had to change—the designer today builds from components which used to be subsystems or complete systems as recently as five years ago. We will see the changed perspectives in the following chapters.

In the last few years sophistication of technology reached a level at which it is possible to put all the processing circuits of a computer on a single chip (smaller than one square centimeter) and package it in a plastic box of about one square inch in size. Figure 1.4 shows one of the earliest "microprocessors" developed in the early 1970's by Motorola.

The cost of these microprocessor or microcomputer chips is typically between $10 and $20. This type of extremely powerful component began to appear in various products (e.g., pocket calculators, various TV games, cars, etc.) in the mid-1970's, and there is no doubt that they will soon become common in most devices requiring control of some complexity. They will also be built into simple appliances and thus provide them with additional flexibility and new functions. New products will be developed incorporating microprocessors or microcomputers. An example of the new possibilities offered by IC technologies is the portable language translator announced at the end of the 1970's. In the near future there will be thousands of products using microcomputers, and millions of them will be present in our everyday life. In this sense, it can be said that the main application of computers will very soon shift from business data processing to device control.

1.4 DIGITAL SYSTEMS

The rest of the text can be broadly divided into two parts: one dealing with digital systems in general and the other dealing with a special category of digital systems—digital computers.

A digital system can be defined as one which accepts digital information (the input part of the system), processes it according to its

Reprinted by Permission of Motorola Inc.

Figure 1.4   The MC 6800 microprocessor integrated circuit produced by Motorola.

required function and external specification (the processor) and outputs the result of this processing (the output part of the system). This basic structure is depicted in Figure 1.5.

Figure 1.5 The structure of a digital system.

This is a very general definition and for the purpose of systematic study of principles and design methods it is useful to make it more specific by pointing out some generally valid facts about the internal structure of all digital systems. In order to derive such a structural description we begin with the characterization of the internal components making up all digital systems and then study the way in which these components are interconnected. Such a model can best be developed in reference to a specific system.

Consider again the temperature display controller: the red light warns that an engine reached a dangerous temperature. If this condition persists for a long time (perhaps because the pilot overlooked the red light and has not taken an appropriate corrective action) the situation becomes dangerous and another warning signal should be generated. Let us add a buzzer which is turned ON by the controller if the red light remains ON for at least five seconds.

Examine the new system and compare the function of the red light controller and the buzzer controller: the red light controller turns the red light ON as soon as it detects that the temperature limit of at least one engine has been exceeded. In other words its output responds "immediately" to the combination of input signals. (There is, of course, a certain delay due to the physical parameters of the device but its value is negligible in this case. The delay is typically of the order of 10 nanoseconds, 10 billionths of a second.) The buzzer controller is different (Figure 1.6). It probably has two inputs: one from the red light controller and one from a digital "clock" (a device which generates regularly timed pulses, e.g., 1 pulse/second).

The output of the buzzer controller goes ON when two conditions are satisfied: the red light is ON and five clock pulses have been counted since it went ON. Counting implies remembering—when a pulse arrives, a 1 is added to the previous (remembered) value and the new value must be remembered ("stored in memory"). The buzzer controller must have a memory, a device capable of storing informaton supplied from the outside. The red light controller on the other hand does not require memory.

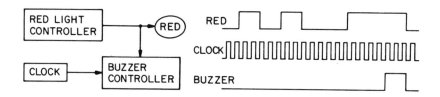

Figure 1.6   The buzzer subsystem of the controller and a sample waveform illustrating its function.

Components without memory, whose output is an "immediate" reaction to the combination of their input signals, are called *combinational* or *switching* devices (they essentially function as, and used to be implemented by, switches).

Devices capable of storing (retaining) information are called *memory* elements. Digital systems with such components are also called *sequential* systems (and this name is generally used in the study of the traditional approaches to digital systems, particularly of restricted complexity). This name reflects the fact that their output depends not only on their current inputs but also on the "memorized" previous inputs, in other words the sequence of previous inputs.

All sequential systems consist of combinational and memory elements. The study and design of digital systems is greatly simplified if they are viewed as composed of a collection of combinational elements (a combinational circuit) and a collection of memory elements (memory), appropriately connected. The block diagram of a general sequential circuit (Figure 1.7) showing its major components and interconnections can be easily derived by the following reasoning:

1. The output of a sequential circuit generally depends on the combination of the current inputs and the current contents of the memory elements (the memory).
2. What is to be remembered generally depends on what is currently stored in the memory (the current *state* of the memory) and the combination of current inputs.

Most sequential circuits work under the control of a clock of the type described above.

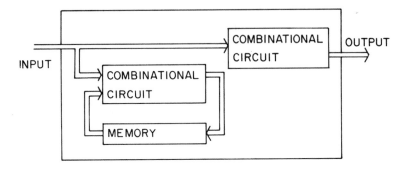

Figure 1.7   The block diagram of the internal structure of a digital system.

In our specific example this means:

1. The output of the buzzer controller is given by the contents of the counter and the red light signal.
2. What is remembered (stored) in the memory (counter) is the count. The count is continuously updated according to the following rules:
    a. The new count is the old count plus one if the red light is ON and a clock pulse is received and the old count is less than 5.
    b. The new count is the same as the old count if the red light is ON and there is no clock pulse or the count is already 5.
    c. The new count is 0 if the red light is OFF.

Note how this example fits the pattern of the general description given before.

Combinational circuits are, as can be expected, simpler and easier to understand and design than sequential circuits. They will be presented first. Sequential circuits will be studied later. Their understanding is considerably simplified by the previously gained knowledge of combinational circuits.

REFERENCES

The material presented in this chapter is very introductory and most of it will be expanded later. An interesting treatment of the economic considerations underlying digital technology is given in Blakeslee. A more detailed treatment of computer history is in the books by Hayes and Kuck and other more advanced books on computer organization.

PROBLEMS

In the following examples of digital systems identify analog and digital signals, combinational and sequential subsystems, inputs and outputs. Identify the need for AD and DA converters. Supply further details where necessary. Draw a block diagram showing the major components and their connections.

1. A controller of a solar energy collector could consist of two subsystems: the position controller and the flow controller:

   a. The position controller maintains the correct orientation of collecting panels with respect to the sun. It compares the current orientation of the panel and the position of the sun (if not obscured by a cloud) and activates a positioning motor to align the panel. The motor is a "stepping" motor which rotates its shaft by 0.1 degree for every pulse sent to it by the controller. Positioning is attempted every five minutes.

   b. The flow controller compares the temperature of the heat transporting fluid in the panel and the temperature of air in the basement of the heated house. It turns ON a pump to circulate the fluid through the panel and a heat exchanger in the basement if desirable: the pump is turned ON if the liquid is at least two degrees C warmer than the air in the basement. It is turned OFF when the difference in temperatures drops below one degree C. The pump is not turned ON if the basement is more than 22 degrees C. Indicate how the system could be expanded to provide cooling in the summer.

2. A traffic light controller at an intersection of four streets is activated by counters placed 20 meters before the intersection which count the passing vehicles. Its function is to turn the whole light system ON or OFF and switch between the two directions. One possible strategy (algorithm) could be as follows:

   a. If the counters identify fewer than three passing cars/minute (e.g. at night), turn all lights OFF otherwise turn lights ON.
   b. If lights are to remain ON, then change directions if
      (1) The current direction has been open for at least 10 seconds and at least seven cars accumulated in the closed direction in the meantime, OR
      (2) the current direction has been open for at least 30 seconds and at least one car is waiting in the closed direction.

3. A signaling system in a computer terminal room is to be used to prevent terminal users from occupying a terminal for lengthy periods while other users are waiting. The following system could be implemented. A red light is placed above each terminal. The light goes ON when all terminals are occupied and there is at least one user waiting and the current user of this terminal has been using it for at least 20 minutes.

Chapter 2

COMBINATIONAL CIRCUITS

2.1 INTRODUCTION

Combinational (switching) circuits are circuits which respond to current inputs without taking into account previous inputs. As an example, recollect the lights controller (a switching circuit) as opposed to the buzzer controller (not a switching circuit).

Consider a typical pocket calculator: when its "clear" key is depressed the dareplay and the internal accumulator are "cleared" to 0. The result of this action is independent of any keys depressed previously. On the other hand the depression of the "+" key adds the value of the number entered previously to the contents of the accumulator and displays the result. The result of this action thus depends on the currently depressed key (for + the action is other than for −, etc.) and also the sequence of all keys depressed since the last clear. The "clear" function can be implemented by a combinational circuit: the complete + function cannot.

Before discussing the analysis and synthesis (design) of combinational circuits, we have to establish some formalism for their description and understand some basic theory. This is presented in the following section.

2.2 THE BINARY SYSTEM OF VALUES

Inputs and outputs of digital systems can assume any of a number of previously chosen values. We have seen this on the example of the output of the decoder in the display controller system which produces output in one of three levels. If we chose to allow any number of input and output levels in each circuit for any single input/output line, the result would be a proliferation of substantially different components which could not be economically manufactured. In general, each application would require a different set of codes. Fortunately, any set of codes can be very easily coded using a fixed number of at least two levels. As a result, it is possible to use a standard basic set of values in all digital systems.

In order to be able to transmit information, we have to be able to distinguish at least two different levels since no information can possibly be transmitted by always sending the same signal. There is also no way of processing information if the only allowed input/output value is the same single signal. On the other hand, because of the possibility of coding mentioned above, any desired number of different messages can be coded using any fixed set of symbols. In particular the set of values consisting of just two different values—the *binary* system—is sufficient to allow transmission and processing of any coded information. The binary system is thus the minimal sufficient system of values. It is ideal for digital systems since a two-valued system corresponds to the two natural interpretations ON/OFF, used in engineering, and TRUE/FALSE, used in logic. Remember that it makes no difference what symbols or names we associate with the two values. Since most human reasoning operates with these interpretations, it is also very well suited for design considerations. The ON/OFF interpretation also allows the easiest physical interpretation: presence or absence of a physical phenomenon—current, voltage, magnetic field, etc. In summary, the binary system provides an efficient system which can be used to build digital devices from standard, uniform basic components. Most existing digital systems are based on it. It will be used exclusively in the rest of this text.

The symbols and names associated with the two binary values are 0 (also OFF, FALSE) and 1 (also ON, TRUE). We will use primarily the most common 0/1 notation. The TRUE/FALSE notation has its historical origin in classical logic and is very useful in understanding the basic functions studied in Section 2.4.

2.3 POSITIONAL REPRESENTATION

Very often it is convenient to think of codewords as representing numbers. Most codes are, in fact, used to represent numbers. The common representation of decimal numbers is also an example of a coding system.

The standard decimal representation of numbers is an example of a *positional* system: it has a fixed *base* (which is 10 and the system is thus called decimal) and a set of 10 basic symbols (their number is the same as the value of the base: 0, 1, ..., 9). Codewords are strings of digits and their value is obtained by adding together values of individual digits multiplied by fixed values (weights) corresponding to individual positions (hence "positional" system) counted from the right:

$$135 = 1*10**2 + 3*10**1 + 5*10**0 = 1*100 + 3*10 + 5*1$$

$10**2$ represents 10 to the power of 2, etc. The weight of the third digit from the right is $10**2$, etc. In general the weight of the N-th position from the right is $10**(N-1)$.

The choice of 10 as the base of the most popular system is due to the fact that humans used fingers for counting. We have established that our system should have only two basic values and two symbols representing them—the binary digits, *bits*, 0,1.

How are values of binary numbers (i.e., strings of binary digits) calculated from binary codes? The rule is the same as for any positional system, as given above. The base is 2 and the weights are powers of 2. As an example, consider the following binary numbers and their decimal equivalents:

$$111 = 1*2**2 + 1*2**1 + 1*2**0 = 1*4 + 1*2 + 1*1 = 7$$
$$101 = 1*2**2 + 0*2**1 + 1*2**0 = 1*4 + 0*2 + 1*1 = 5$$

For more examples of conversion see the Workbook.

We will consider other binary codes used to represent numbers later. First we proceed to a consideration of combinational circuits which are used to process binary codes.

2.4   DESCRIPTION OF COMBINATIONAL CIRCUITS

2.4.1   Introduction

Consider a combinational circuit as a "black box" with inputs controlled by switches and output values observed on a set of lights. Assume that the internal arrangement of the black box is unknown or inaccessible. For our purpose it is irrelevant since we are now interested in the description of the function of the device. The function of the device is characterized by its response to external conditions—the input values. Assume that the switches have two positions (ON/OFF is convenient) and the lights two states (ON/OFF). If the circuit is combinational then each combination of switch positions causes the lights to display a certain configuration independent of the previous inputs. If we assume that the circuit is *deterministic* (i.e., its behavior is not subject to variations from time to time), then all we have to do to describe its behavior is to draw a table with all possible combinations of input values on the left, try these combinations by appropriately setting input switches and fill in the observed values of output (lights). The result is a *truth table*. The origin of this term stems from the use of similar tables in mathematical logic. The truth table is a tabular representation of the function of the device, which under the previously stated assumptions contains all information about its behavior (Figure 2.1).

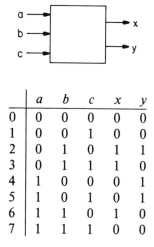

	a	b	c	x	y
0	0	0	0	0	0
1	0	0	1	0	0
2	0	1	0	1	1
3	0	1	1	1	0
4	1	0	0	0	1
5	1	0	1	0	1
6	1	1	0	1	0
7	1	1	1	0	0

Figure 2.1   An example of the description of a black box (inputs a, b, c and outputs x, y) by a truth table.

Definition: A truth table is a table whose lines are labeled with all possible combinations of values of input variables. The function column contains function values corresponding to the individual input combinations.

Several points are worth noting with regard to this simple example:

1. The output values are presumably obtained by observation. In this example they are chosen quite arbitrarily.

2. Logic values are represented by 0, 1. We could also use OFF or FALSE for 0, ON or TRUE for 1.

3. Note the order in which the column of input values is arranged: the first row is all 0's; then the last (rightmost) value is changed to 1 in the second row, etc. In summary, the last value periodically changes 010101..., the second last changes with one half of the frequency of the last one 001100110011..., etc. This labeling of rows in truth tables is not necessary but makes the construction systematic and guarantees that no combination is left out. It will always be used in this text. We can think of individual input combinations as representations of binary numbers. Their decimal equivalents are shown in the leftmost column of the table. The given arrangement of binary combinations can be seen to correspond to the natural order of decimal values. In this sense the ordering of lines is not arbitrary.

4. The fact that in our table the value of x for input combination 0,0,0 is 0 can be written $x(0,0,0)=0)$ Similarly, $y(1,0,1)=1$ means that the output value y corresponding to input combination 1,0,1 is 1, etc.

5. Note that there are eight lines in the table, numbered 0 to 7. This is because there are eight possible different combinations of three zeros and ones. Similarly, there are 16 combinations of four zeros and ones, etc. In general, for N input binary variables there are $2**N$ different combinations of zeros and ones. The output x in Figure 2.1 is one possible function of three binary variables; y is another. There are $2**(2**N)$ different binary functions of N binary variables altogether. In our case $(N=3)$ this means that 256 different binary functions of three variables are possible. For $N=4$ we have 65,536 different binary functions of four variables, etc.

Traditional and mathematical logic defines certain basic *logic (Boolean) functions*. (The name Boolean functions is used in honor of the British mathematician G. Boole who made major contributions to the development of formal logic.) We will shortly see the truth tables of some of the more important ones. After reading the last of the previous comments, you may wonder if we need a name and a device for every possible logic function; after all, a device can have any number of inputs, and we must be able to implement any required function. Fortunately, new functions do not require a different type of building component since very few types of elementary functions can be used to build any combinational device. The price is, of course, that we have to connect several basic components to build one more complicated circuit. This is, however, a very small price when we realize how many possible functions of even a very limited number of inputs there are. We will see later that certain elementary logic functions are sufficient to build any combinational circuit. In other words, enough copies of the same single basic component and appropriate interconnections can build any logic device.

The standard functions, of which we will name only the most important ones, can be divided into two basic categories: functions of one variable (*unary*) and functions of two variables (*binary*).

1. *Unary* functions. The only important one is the inverse (also called the complement or negation or simply *not*). It is denoted by any one of

NOT x, x', $\sim x$, $\overline{x}$

We will use the x' (x prime) notation. Its truth table is shown in Figure 2.2.

input	output
x	x'
0	1
1	0

Figure 2.2 The truth table of the not function.

The meaning is obvious: if x is a statement, then x' is the inverse statement. If

x: IT RAINS

then

x': IT DOES NOT RAIN (IT IS NOT TRUE THAT IT RAINS)

If x is TRUE, then x' is FALSE and vice versa. This way of remembering the interpretation of logic functions on the basis of their natural meaning is useful and allows us to avoid memorizing the corresponding truth tables. It applies also to the binary functions of the following paragraph.

There is a useful rule concerning inversion: $x'' = x$

Its validity can be established by considering again statement x above. x' can be reformulated as

x': IT IS NOT TRUE THAT (IT RAINS)
x'' can be stated as
x'': IT IS NOT TRUE THAT x'
IT IS NOT TRUE THAT (IT IS NOT TRUE THAT
(IT RAINS))

It is obvious that x'' expresses the same statement as x.

2. *Binary* functions. As we know, there are 16 different binary (i.e., 2-variable) functions altogether, but we will only need five (and of these two are just combinations of others). Binary functions important in digital design are

AND (also called logical product or conjunction) denoted x AND y or $x.y$ or x y or $AND(x,y)$
OR (logical sum or disjunction) x OR y or $x+y$ or $OR(x,y)$
Exclusive OR (also called *logical difference*) denoted
x XOR y or x y

The remaining two—NAND ($=$NOT AND) and NOR ($=$NOT OR) do not have any generally accepted special symbols and so the common representation is

$NAND(x,y) = (x\ y)'\ NOR(x,y) = (x+y)'$

The truth tables are shown in Figure 2.3.

x	y	AND	NAND	OR	NOR	XOR
0	0	0	1	0	1	0
0	1	0	1	1	0	1
1	0	0	1	1	0	1
1	1	1	0	1	0	0

Figure 2.3   Truth tables of the most useful binary logic functions.

Note that

1. $AND(x,y)$ is 1 if and only if ("iff") x is 1 and y is 1
2. OR is 0 iff $x=y=0$

3. NAND is the inverse of AND, NOR is the inverse of OR
4. XOR(x,y) is 1 iff the value of x is different from the value of y.

The functions that we just defined form the basis of a subject known as Boolean algebra.

Since Boolean functions can be thought of as formulas representing truth tables, they can also be thought of as representing black boxes implementing such truth tables. For example

$y=a.b$

can be interpreted as a formal description of the diagram in Figure 2.4.

Figure 2.4   The black box representation of a combined device.

Black boxes can be connected together to form more complicated boxes (Figure 2.5).

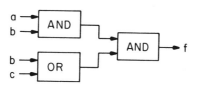

Figure 2.5   A more complicated combined device made from black boxes labeled by their functions.

In this diagram input b is connected to both the AND and the OR box. We need a way of describing such combined devices based on the notation introduced for Boolean functions. The natural approach is to use parentheses as in arithmetic. With this extension we can represent the above combined diagram as

$y = a.b$
$z = b + c$
$f = y.z = (a.b).(b+c)$

This notation and the process of combining simpler black boxes into more complicated ones allows us to generate functions of any complexity and any number of arguments such as

$$h = ((a.b).c) + ((a + b) + (a'.d))$$
$$g = (x + y).((x.z') + ((u + v).(u' + z)))$$

(Draw the corresponding combined boxes as an exercise.)

We will see shortly that this notation can be significantly simplified due to certain properties of Boolean functions.

Boolean functions have certain properties similar to arithmetic operations. A few of the rules are slightly different from those valid for arithmetic operations. Some of the rules are shown in Figure 2.6.

	AND		OR	
a	$x.0$	$= 0$	$x+1$	$= 1$
b	$x.x'$	$= 0$	$x+x'$	$= 1$
c	$x.1$	$= x$	$x+0$	$= x$
d	$x.x$	$= x$	$x+x$	$= x$
e	$(xy)z$	$= x(yz)$	$(x+y)+z$	$= x+(y+z)$
f	$x(y+z)$	$= xy+xz$	$x+(yz)$	$= (x+y)(x+z)$
g	$(xy)'$	$= x'+y'$	$(x+y)'$	$= x'y'$
h	xy	$= yx$	$x+y$	$= y+x$

Figure 2.6   Important logical identities.

A few notes:

1. $x+x' = 1$ can be interpreted as "one of x and x' is always true."
2. Property e is called associativity, f is distributivity (note the difference compared to arithmetic operations), rules g are De Morgan's rules (they relate NAND, OR, NOT and NOR, AND, NOT), h establishes commutativity. Parentheses establish the order in which logical operations are to be performed just as in arithmetic.
3. Associativity allows us to extend the definition of AND, OR to several input variables: AND, OR are by original definitions functions of two variables. But since, e.g.,

   $$a(bc) = (ab)c$$

   (functions of two variables), no confusion can arise by writing simply

   $$abc$$

and performing the operation as $(ab)c$ or $a(bc)$. The result will be the same. The same extension can be applied to four and more variables. In general we can conclude that

$$a(1).a(2).a(3).....a(N) = 1$$
$$\text{iff } a(1) = a(2) = a(3) = ... = a(N) = 1$$

This may be considered as an alternative definition of the AND function. A similar definition can be derived for the OR function.

4. Note that these rules have implications for circuit design. For example, if we have only 2-input AND devices and need the function abc, we can implement it by using two 2-input devices and associativity: $abc = a(bc)$.

5. How can we verify that the rules given above are indeed correct? We know that each formula can be thought of as representing the function of a black box. We can translate the question of correctness of a rule (identity) into the question of proving that the box represented by the formula on the left behaves identically with the box represented by the formula on the right. This naturally means that both boxes should generate identical outputs when presented with the same inputs, for all possible combinations of inputs:

    Identity
    $$f(a,b) = g(a,b)$$

    means identical behavior of outputs f and g for all possible values of a,b in the circuit in Figure 2.7. We can thus conclude that formula $f(a,b)$ is functionally identical to formula $g(a,b)$ if for any combination of values a, b the corresponding functional values in the truth tables of f and g are identical. This argument can, of course, be extended to functions of any number of variables.

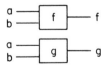

Figure 2.7   Formal identity of two logical formulas means functional equivalence of devices implementing the functions.

This approach to proving a Boolean identity is called proof **by** *perfect induction.* It consists of building the truth table for the Left Hand Side (LHS) and the truth table for the Right Hand Side (RHS), the comparison of these tables, and a check of their identity. If the tables are identical, then the LHS and the RHS are just two formally different representations of the same function, and the identity is established. Otherwise, the expressions represent different functions.

As an example, consider the associativity rule for the logical product, the first column of rule e. To prove that it holds, we need to construct the truth table for LHS and so we construct the truth table for bc and then the truth table for $a(bc)$. This is the LHS. We similarly construct the truth table for RHS (Figure 2.8).

a	b	c	ab	$(ab)c$	bc	$a(bc)$
0	0	0	0	0	0	0
0	0	1	0	0	0	0
0	1	0	0	0	0	0
0	1	1	0	0	1	0
1	0	0	0	0	0	0
1	0	1	0	0	0	0
1	1	0	1	0	0	0
1	1	1	1	1	1	1

Figure 2.8   Proof of identity $(ab)c = a(bc)$ by perfect induction.

Comparison of columns $(ab)c$ and $a(bc)$ shows their identity and proves the validity of the rule. To see how the table was constructed, consider, for example, row $(a,b,c) = (1,1,0)$. For this combination $ab = 1.1 = 1$ (according to the truth table for the AND function) and then $(ab)c = 10 = 0$ according to the definition of AND. Other columns and rows are derived similarly. For more examples of the proof by perfect induction see the Workbook.

6. Note that the left column rules in the summary of identities, and the right column rules are very closely related: replacing AND by OR (and vice versa) and 0 by 1 (and vice versa) converts rules from one column into rules from the other column. The corresponding rules are called "dual."

2.4.2 Canonical Formulas

The formalism that we developed allows us to make the important next step, namely to describe any truth table with any number of input variables by a function using only the binary functions defined so far. Consider, for example, the black box in the first example whose truth table is repeated in Figure 2.9.

	a	b	c	x	y
0	0	0	0	0	0
1	0	0	1	0	0
2	0	1	0	1	1
3	0	1	1	1	0
4	1	0	0	0	1
5	1	0	1	0	1
6	1	1	0	1	0
7	1	1	1	0	0

Figure 2.9   Truth tables of $x = a'bc' + a'bc + abc'$ and $y = a'bc'$ $+ ab'c' + ab'c$.

The x column of the table can be described in words as follows:

$x = 1$ iff ($a = 0$ AND $b = 1$ AND $c = 0$) OR ($a = 0$ AND $b = 1$ AND $c = 1$) OR ($a = 1$ AND $b = 1$ AND $c = 0$). But $a = 0$ AND $b = 1$ AND $c = 0$ is the same as $a' = 1$ AND $b = 1$ AND $c' = 1$. Let us denote the statement ($a' = 1$ AND $b = 1$ AND $c' = 1$) by $f(a,b,c)$. We claim that

$$f(a,b,c) = a'bc'$$

Indeed, $f = 1$ (TRUE) iff $a' = b = c' = 1$ according to our extended definition of the AND function given above and so our claim is proved by perfect induction.

Similar reasoning can be applied to the other two statements. As a result, we can conclude that

$$x = a'bc' + a'bc + abc'$$

To prove that this is correct, we only need to apply the method of perfect induction and construct the truth table of this function. When this function is constructed, it is found to be identical to the original truth table.

The reasoning followed for x applies also to y to give $y = a'bc' + ab'c' + ab'c$. Both expressions obtained above have the form of a (logical) sum of (logical) products.

The general method of construction of the *sum of products* formula is as follows:

ALGORITHM SP:

1. For each line with a 1 in the output column construct a term which is the AND function of all input variables. Variable a appears as a if its value on this line is 1; it appears as a' if its value on this line is 0.
2. OR all the terms obtained in the previous step.

The terms constructed in the first step are called *minterms*. Each of them contains all variables, possibly inverted. The final formula obtained is also called the *canonical sum of minterms*. A shorthand representation of the formula can be obtained by using the summation symbol and the codes of individual lines as explained previously:

$$x(a,b,c) = \text{SUM}(2,3,6)$$

This formula means that the function x of variables a, b, c has value 1 on lines 2, 3, 6 of the truth table and is 0 otherwise. For more examples of the use of algorithm SP, see problems in the Workbook.

If the construction of the sum of products form is so simple, the construction of the *product of sums* form must be equally easy; after all the AND and OR and NOT functions are related by the dual relationships. In fact the algorithm is the dual of the SP algorithm. It is obtained by replacing zeros by ones and vice versa, and AND by OR (and vice versa):

ALGORITHM PS:

1. For each line with a 0 in the output column, construct a term which is the OR function of all input variables. Variable a is present as a if its value in this line is 0; it is present as a' if its value in this line is 1.
2. AND all the terms obtained in the previous step.

Compare algorithms SP and PS word by word to see how they are related.

The terms constructed in the first step of algorithm PS are called *maxterms*. The final formula obtained is called *the canonical product of maxterms*.

The justification of this algorithm is a dual of the justification of algorithm SP:

$x=1$ iff the combination of inputs is NOT as on line zero and line one and line four and line five and line seven. In other words iff the combination is other than on line zero and other than on line one, etc. The combination is other than on line zero iff $a=1$ OR $b=1$ OR $c=1$. But this describes function

$a+b+c$

The combination is other than that on line 1 iff $a=1$ OR $b=1$ or $c=0$ in other words $a=1$ OR $b=1$ OR $c'=1$. This describes

$a+b+c'$

etc. In summary

$$x=(a+b+c)(a+b+c')(a'+b+c)(a'+b+c')(a'+b'+c')$$

This is the same result as one that we would obtain by applying the PS algorithm.

Note that the SP and PS canonical formulas of the truth table of x have a different number of terms (three and five) although they describe the same truth table. This is usually the case. Can you give a general rule relating the number of terms in PS and SP? If the circuit is hidden inside a black box, we have no way of knowing which of the two implementations has been used. It could, in fact, be one of a number of other implementations of this function.

2.4.3   Derivation of Formula from Word Description

In many situations the formula may be derived directly from the word description of the (desired) behavior of the device. Note, however, that the resulting formula will usually not be in one of the canonical forms. This is not a problem if it implements the same function.

Consider the green light controller in the display controller. It goes ON if none of the engines are too cold AND none are overheated:

GREEN = (none too cold) AND (none overheated)

But according to our previous specification this is the same as

GREEN = BLUE'.RED'

If we already have the signals for BLUE and RED, we can use them to construct the signal for GREEN (Figure 2.10). Note that in the derivation of the formula, we have not even constructed the truth table.

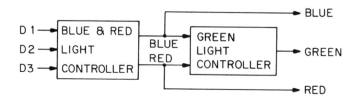

Figure 2.10   GREEN light controller can use BLUE and RED light signals.

Consider the following two examples in which word specification is again sufficient to derive a functional description of the desired circuit directly:

1. In a hypothetical car designed for safe driving the following conditions must be satisfied to allow the driver to start the car:
    a. The key must be inserted (denote this condition by K),
    b. Driver's seatbelt must be attached ($B1$),
    c. If there is a passenger (P), the seatbelt of his seat must be attached ($B2$),
    d. The driver must pass a safety test built into the controller, such as dialing a sequence of three 5-digit numbers (T),
    e. All doors of the car must be closed (D).

The translation of the above conditions into a logic formula is obvious except, perhaps, for the condition concerning the passenger. This condition can be restated as follows:
Either there is no passenger (P is not TRUE) OR the seatbelt is attached. This formulation can be expressed as

$P' + B2$

Now the whole controller can be described as follows:

$C = K.B1.(P' + B2).T.D$

since all conditions for starting must be satisfied simultaneously. Note that we have six input variables and the complete truth table has $2^{**}6 = 64$ lines (of which only four contain a 1). The direct translation from the word description thus greatly simplifies the construction of the formula. Note also that the resulting formula is not in canonic form: it has the product of sums' form, but the terms are not maxterms since they do not contain all variables.

2. Consider the design of a "keep them awake" design for a computer terminal room. It controls a fan which is turned ON iff it gets too hot or when there are many users and the supply of oxygen may be low. Specifically, the fan should be turned ON iff room temperature is over 23 degrees C (T0) OR at least 10 people have been in the room (P1) for at least 20 minutes (L) AND the temperature is over 21 (T1) OR there are at least 15 people in the room (P2) OR there are at least five users in the room (P3) and it is between 11 P.M. and 4 A.M. (N). From this description the controller can be immediately described by

$$C = T0 + P1.L.T1 + P2 + P3.N$$

Similar notes apply to this example as to the previous one. Note that there are seven inputs, and the truth table would have 128 lines!

For more examples see the Workbook.

These examples were intended to show that in some cases construction of the formula from the truth table is not the most efficient approach. It would be wrong to conclude that truth tables are useless: they are used to define basic functions, circuits with less trivial behavior than just described: they are used in testing and form the basis of several methods allowing the reduction of the number of components needed to build the circuit, etc. We will see examples of the use of truth tables in the following sections.

2.5 IMPLEMENTATION OF SIMPLE LOGIC FUNCTIONS

A brief history of digital technology was given in Chapter 1. It will be useful to be a little more specific about some of its aspects at this point.

The first implementation of logic functions in commercial products was by switches and relays. Although relays are no longer used in those applications in which we are interested, an understanding of relay circuits will contribute to our comprehension of logic functions in general.

A relay is an electromechanical device. It consists of a switch which mechanically opens or closes the path of current flow. The switch is activated by the passage of current through a control coil. When not activated, the contact (switch) stays in its "normal" position where it is held by a mechanical spring. The normal position may be closed or open, as required, and we can distinguish a normally open or normally closed contact (NO or NC). If we use the following notation:

c: current flows through the control coil
r: current can flow through the relay's contact

then the NO relay can be described by

$r=c$ (current can flow iff control coil is activated)

and the NC relay can be described by

$r=c'$ (current can flow iff control coil is deactivated)

Consider, for example, the NC relay. When current flows through the coil ($c=1$), the relay is activated and the contact moves from its passive (closed) position, in other words opens, and the current cannot flow through the relay ($r=0$). When current does not flow through the coil ($c=0$), the contact is in its passive (closed) position and current can flow through the coil ($r=1$). The truth table of the NC relay is thus as shown in Figure 2.11.

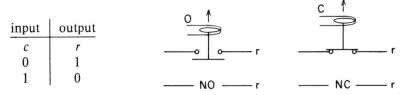

input	output
c	r
0	1
1	0

Figure 2.11   The truth table and schematic diagram of a normally closed (NC) relay.

The picture shows the symbol for a NC relay: the contact is always shown in its passive (normal) position.

The truth table is that of $r=c'$. Remember that the coil current (c) is the input variable and the contact opens or closes the current path through the relay (r) which is the controlled (output) variable. Similar reasoning shows that a NO relay implements function $r=c$.

Consider now the two circuits shown in Figure 2.12.

$$\begin{array}{c}\text{a}\\ \boxed{\begin{array}{c}\text{NO}\\ \text{NO}\end{array}}\text{ x}\\ \text{b}\end{array}\qquad\qquad \begin{array}{ccc}\text{a} & \text{b}\\ \text{NO} & \text{NO} & \text{x}\end{array}$$

Figure 2.12   Two relay circuits. The circuit on the left implements $x=a+b$, the circuit on the right implements $x=a.b$.

In the first circuit the current does not flow ($x=1$) iff both the a and the b paths are open, i.e., when a and b are deactivated ($a=b=0$). In other words, $x=0$ iff $a=0$ AND $b=0$. This is the definition of the OR function and so $x=a+b$. Similar reasoning shows that the second circuit implements $x=a.b$.

In general assume that we are given two relay-based switching circuits implementing functions f and g (Figure 2.13). Connecting the circuits in series generates the function $x=f.g$. Connecting the circuits in parallel generates the function $y=f+g$.

Figure 2.13   Series and parallel connection of relay circuits.

We have noted that relays are no longer used to build complex switching circuits. Today's circuits use IC (Integrated Circuit) components. Although their physical principle is quite different (they are purely electronic devices working on a microscopic level), the basic function is quite similar: they are based on opening and closing the path of electric current. In this sense they resemble relays.

Commercial IC components can be divided into several categories called *logic families* according to the technology they use. Each family is based on a different circuit or even a different physical principle. Each family consists of a number of device types which completely satisfy the needs of a certain category of applications. Some families are better suited for relatively less complex circuits; others are not suited for very fast circuits, etc. There are differences in speed, power consumption, density of integration, and thus the complexity of the component that can be produced on a single chip, etc. Some logic families are obsolete since better circuits were developed based on the same principles, but there are several families which are very popular and in a sense non-competitive since they address somewhat separate applications. There is a great advantage to using components belonging to the same family: they can be directly connected together as building blocks without any conversion (*interface*). All voltage levels and other physical parameters are compatible within one family and design is relatively simple. We will usually use the popular TTL family, whose most popular implementation is also called the 74 family, in our experiments and examples. We will see that building of moderately complex digital circuits does not require any knowledge of electronics. This is the consequence of the compatibility between components in one logic family.

Components belonging to different logic families can also work together. In fact, most practical circuits use components belonging to at least two different families. This is because certain functions are better implemented in one family and other functions in another family. The cooperating components must, however, be interfaced. The voltage levels at which they operate may have to be converted. This conversion is usually not very complicated, and special components are available for this purpose; but it adds another level of complexity, not required within one family.

Do not get apprehensive after reading the previous paragraphs; this text does not deal with electronics. One should, however, be aware of the basic realities.

We have seen that switching circuits with relays consist of paths with switches placed as obstacles—opening or closing paths. They act as *gates*. A gate is the name commonly used for components implementing basic switching functions. They act as gates in the logic paths established in the circuit. Note that the logic paths do not have to be electric paths; there are, for example, pneumatic equivalents of electronic gates which function on the principle of air flow. More generally fluidic components are available which control the flow of a gas or liquid to implement logic circuits. The common principle is transfer and processing of information via the control of a logic path. Basic gates have established symbols shown in Figure 2.14.

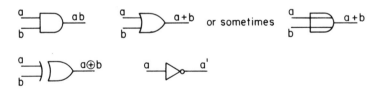

Figure 2.14 Common symbols of standard gates. Examples of gate symbols: AND, OR, XOR, NOT. The "bubble" on the output line of the NOT symbol represents negation and can be used with any line.

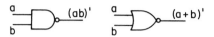

Figure 2.15   Representation of NAND and NOR gates.

Note that the most commonly used symbol for the very popular NAND and NOR gates uses this bubble notation (Figure 2.15).

In semiconductor gates input and output logic values are represented by voltage levels—HIGH and LOW (H and L). The specific values of these levels vary from one family to another. The notation H and L is quite common, and manufacturers describe their products in data sheets by a modified form of a truth table in which output and input values are not represented as 0 and 1 but as L and H. This is because it is up to the designers to decide whether they want to use H to represent Boolean 1 and L to represent 0 or vice versa. The first convention (0 for L, 1 for H) is called "positive logic"; the second is "negative logic." When a certain gate type is being described the full name consists of both specifications. As an example, "A 7400 IC is a positive two-input logic NAND gate." Since positive logic is almost the rule, the qualification "positive" is often left out and implied: 7400 is usually described as a NAND gate. In the H/L notation the example in Figure 2.16 is a description of a device based on its physical function. Its logic interpretation implied by the truth tables is AND gate for positive logic and OR gate for negative logic. This is important to realize—logic function depends both on the physical function and the kind of logic accepted.

a	b	x	a	b	x	a	b	x
L	L	L	0	0	0	1	1	1
L	H	L	0	1	0	1	0	1
H	L	L	1	0	0	0	1	1
H	H	H	1	1	1	0	0	0

Figure 2.16   Voltage level table (function table) of a device, its interpretation in positive logic (AND gate logic table), interpretation in negative logic (OR gate logic table).

As an example of the function of the component described by the above function table, consider the waveforms in Figure 2.17. For more examples on positive and negative logic see the Workbook.

A single gate is a circuit much too small to be economically placed on one chip. Several gates or other components of the same kind are thus normally placed on one chip. Standard ICs are then assigned a number and referred to by these type numbers. In the very popular TTL logic family some examples of common ICs are:

7400-quad 2-input NAND (4 independent, 2-input NAND gates)
7402-quad 2-input NOR
7404-hex inverter (6 independent inverters)
7408-quad 2-input AND
7410-triple 3-input NAND (3 independent 3-input NAND gates)
7411-triple 3-input AND
7420-dual 4-input NAND (2 independent 4-input NAND gates)
7432-quad 2-input OR
7486-quad XOR gate

As an indication of the cost of popular ICs, the cost of these components is typically between 10 and 40 cents.

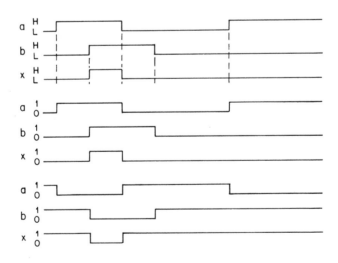

Figure 2.17   An example of the behavior of a device with functional table from Figure 2.16, its positive-logic interpretation, its negative-logic interpretation.

NAND gates are the basic type of TTL gates. More complicated components are produced by combining on one chip a number of basic gates. This gives rise to a classification of complexity of ICs based on the number of gates or circuits of equivalent complexity present on one chip. The following categories are distinguished:

SSI small scale integration up to 12 gates/chip MSI medium scale i. 12 to 100 gates LSI large scale i. 100 to 1000 gates VLSI very large scale i. over 1000 gates

At the beginning of the IC era the SSI scale was the only one possible with the available technology. The VLSI technology began to emerge around the end of the 1970's. This level of complexity is still very high even for the present "state of art."

It should be noted that the cost of an IC component is not too closely related to its complexity. To understand this paradox, one has to consider what determines the cost of a product. The basic components are the costs of development of the product, tools of production including testing, and costs directly associated with production, such as material, testing, etc. The cost of one product is

cost = (development)/N + production cost per item

(N is the number of items produced). The development costs are extremely high for complex products. They involve weeks or months of work by highly qualified engineers designing the product and also production and testing equipment. Included in this item is the set-up cost of production which is also very high. In contrast the material and costs per item are relatively small. This means that if a relatively large number of identical items (N) are produced, the very high starting cost can be practically ignored; and the cost of the finished product is close to the cost of material which is relatively low. As a result, popular components (such as 7400 chips) can cost 10 cents or less. In summary, the volume of production is the determining factor. In IC production of the more popular types of ICs, the volume is always in millions. It is then possible that two different IC types of comparable complexity can differ in price by almost an order of magnitude because of their larger or smaller popularity.

2.6 LOGIC DIAGRAMS

The most common engineering representation of a switching circuit is by a logic diagram. This is a diagram showing the components used (using the previously shown standard symbols) and their interconnections.

Let us construct a logic diagram of the function $f=ab+a(c+d)$. Since we want to use basic gates, we have to convert this formula into one that uses only basic functions. We can write

$f=g+h$ where
$g=ab$, $h=ak$ where
$k=c+d$

These expressions can all be built from elementary gates (Figure 2.18).

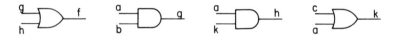

Figure 2.18   Circuits implementing subfunctions of $f=ab+a(c+d)$.

Combining these diagrams (connecting identically labeled lines), we obtain the diagram in Figure 2.19.

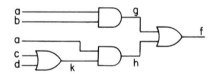

Figure 2.19   The complete logic diagram of $f=ab+a(c+d)$.

In practice we do not have to go through this lengthy sequence of steps and can produce the diagram directly from the formula. We construct the diagram from the left with the input symbols and construct the circuit to end up on the right with outputs (the desired function or functions). As an example consider the function $x=(a+b)'+(a\text{XOR}c)$. Its representation is shown in Figure 2.20. Figure 2.21 shows the same diagram in a more common form with intermediate labels deleted and a simplified representation of inputs.

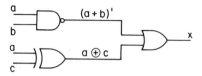

Figure 2.20   Logic diagram of $x=(a+b)'+(a\text{XOR}c)$ with labels for intermediate outputs. Intermediate labels are not usually shown.

Diagrams showing all physical components (gates, resistors, capacitors, etc.) present in the circuits are called *circuit diagrams*, as opposed to *logic diagrams* which show only the logic components.

Circuit diagrams are the basis of design, and they also provide the documentation from which the function of the product can be understood and the product maintained, tested, and repaired.

As an example of how the logic diagram can be used to determine expected outputs, let us examine the output of the last circuit for input combination $(a,b,c)=(1,0,1)$:

The output of NOR1 (from the definition of the NOR function) is $(1+0)'=0$. The output of XOR1 is $(0\text{XOR}1)=1$. Inputs to OR1 are $0,1$ and the output is $x=(0+1)=1$.

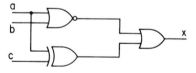

Figure 2.21   Logic diagram of $x=(a+b)'+(a\text{XOR}c)$ without intermediate labels. Input *a* for the second gate is derived from input *a* for the first gate. (A dot at the junction of two lines represents a connection while two crossing lines without a dot are not connected.)

We can thus obtain the output value for any given combination of inputs by tracing the logic paths in the diagram. We could construct the whole truth table or just check if the output of a circuit is what it should be for a certain combination of inputs according to the diagram. For maintenance we might also need to establish the desired values of certain intermediate signals. By paper and pencil tracing, we could also check whether the circuit is correct: whether the outputs are as prescribed by the desired use.

The opposite operation—finding the logic expression describing the circuit from the diagram—is equally simple. We proceed from left to right, adding labels to intermediate lines until we reach the output and the final formula. In the example shown in Figure 2.22 we proceed in the following sequence:

1. Output of OR1 is $a+b$ (enter expression into diagram).
2. Output of OR2 is $a'+b'$ (enter into diagram).
3. Output of AND1 is $f=(a+b)(a'+b')'$.

The last step is possible because we know the inputs of AND1 from steps 1 and 2. All that is required is the knowledge of standard symbols and the circuit diagram.

If we want to build the circuit from the diagram and if we want to use standard ICs, we may have to perform another step: in the previous diagram AND1 is an AND gate with one input negated. No such gate is commercially available. We thus have to translate the diagram into symbols representing commercially available components, or better still use only these symbols in the original diagram. Consider

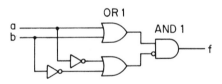

Figure 2.22   Derivation of function from a logic diagram. The function implemented by this circuit is $f=(a+b)(a'+b')'$.

$f=ab'+a'b$. This function can be rewritten as $f=(a(b)')+((a)'b)$ and can be implemented by commercially available chips as shown in Figure 2.23. It requires one-half of 7408 (two AND gates), one-third of 7404 (two inverters), and one-fourth (one OR gate) of 7432. We need three chips at a total cost of about 60 cents plus some interconnections.

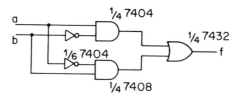

Figure 2.23   Implementation of $f = ab' + a'b$ with commercial ICs.

If we noticed that in fact $f = a\text{XOR}b$ we could use one-fourth of 7486 (one XOR gate). This may seem wasteful, but the 7486 costs only 35 cents and there are no connections between chips (which reduces cost and increases reliability). Note also that although a substantial number of the gates available on this chip are wasted at this point it may be used by another circuit in the same product since individual gates on one chip are quite independent. This sharing of ICs between different circuits of the same device is quite standard since circuits are generally much more complicated than our example. For more examples see the Workbook.

To produce a digital system ICs belonging to related circuits are placed on one board made of insulating material; and when more than a few pieces are being produced, the connections between chips are made by metallic strips produced by etching a "mask" of the circuit into a board covered with a layer of metal. Since the process is basically photographic, the connections are essentially printed on the board, and the final product is thus called a Printed Circuit Board, a PCB.

As an interesting point it should be noted that NAND and NOR gates have the important property that they can be used to implement any other basic function and therefore any logic function. As an example, the NAND gate can implement AND, OR, NOT functions as follows:

$a' = (aa)' = \text{NAND}(a,a)$
   or $a' = (a.1)' = \text{NAND}(a,1)$ inverter
$ab = ((ab)')' = (\text{NAND}(a,b))'$ AND gate
$a+b = ((a+b)')' = (a'.b')' = \text{NAND}(a',b')$ OR gate

The corresponding diagrams are shown in Figure 2.24.

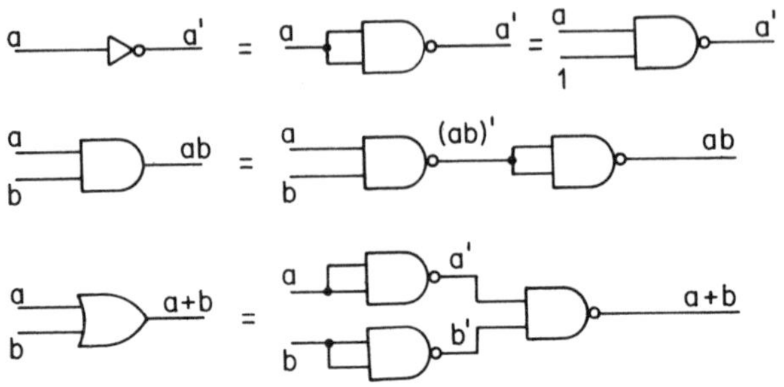

Figure 2.24   Use of NAND gates to implement AND, OR, NOT.

Formulas using NOR gates can be derived similarly.

Since all functions can be implemented as canonical sums of products, this means that any circuit can be built using only one type of chip throughout and partially explains the popularity of the NAND chip. The AND and OR gates do not have this property! For more examples see the Workbook.

We will now consider the problem of the efficient design of switching circuits to realize arbitrary truth

2.7   DESIGN OF SIMPLE SWITCHING CIRCUITS

Two methods of design of switching circuits were described in the previous section:

1. The SP and PS algorithms which make it possible to construct the formula and thus design the circuit for any truth table.
2. The derivation of the formula directly from a word description.

The disadvantage of both methods is that the final result is usually not optimal in the sense that the same function can often be implemented with fewer and simpler gates. As an example consider the truth table in Figure 2.25.

The use of algorithm SP leads to

$$x = a'b'c + a'bc + ab'c + abc$$

Closer inspection of the table shows that in fact $x=c$ and the rather complex circuit on the left of Figure 2.26 is fully equivalent to the "circuit" on the right with no gates. In other words, although the SP algorithm produces a formula which requires four inverters, four AND gates and one OR gate, examination of the function shows that it can be implemented without any gates.

a	b	c	x
0	0	0	0
0	0	1	1
0	1	0	0
0	1	1	1
1	0	0	0
1	0	1	1
1	1	0	0
1	1	1	1

Figure 2.25   A truth table.

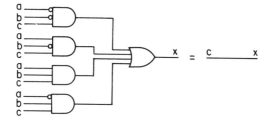

Figure 2.26   Two implementations of the truth table from Figure 2.25.

This example shows, of course, an extreme situation, but it is obvious that some method of minimization of the complexity of the formula is very desirable, particularly if gates and their interconnections constitute a substantial part of the total cost of the device. Several methods were developed which successfully solve this problem, under restricted assumptions.

The method described in this section is based on the following restriction: it is being assumed that the resulting formula should be in the SP form, but not necessarily canonical. The resulting circuit then is a two-stage or two-level AND-OR circuit, i.e., one level of AND gates corresponding to the individual product terms of the formula and one OR gate corresponding to the final Boolean summation. The inverters required, if any, are not counted.

This restriction on the structure of the circuit is not very severe: all switching circuits can be converted into this form; the SP algorithm produces an SP formula from any truth table, but not minimal. The method thus applies to all truth tables. The resulting circuit is, in general, very simple although if other types of gates were allowed, further simplification would sometimes be possible (recollect the $f=a'b+ab'=a\text{XOR}b$ formula). The method is thus relatively very efficient. The elimination of inverters from the count is often justified since many circuits are "double-rail" circuits in which both the original and inverted value of each variable are available and there is thus no need to invert input signals.

The approach described in the following paragraphs is very simple. A very similar (dual) procedure can easily be developed to produce two-stage OR-AND circuits (PS form). This will not be done here but it should be realized that the two algorithms do not usually produce circuits of the same complexity, just as the SP and PS algorithms. If true minimization is desired, both possibilities should be considered in each case.

The method is based on the fact that function

$$x=f+g.a+g.a'$$

where f and g are any Boolean functions, can be simplified:

$$x=f+g.a+g.a'=f+g(a+a')=f+g.1=f+g$$

and in this way two AND gates and one inverter can be saved. This process of simplification can be repeated as many times as possible; and if the order in which simplifications are performed is appropriate, it leads to a minimal AND-OR circuit.

For a demonstration of the application of this principle, consider the first example of this section and its simplification:

$$f = abc + ab'c + a'bc + a'b'c = a(b+b')c + a'(b+b')c =$$
$$= ac + a'c = (a+a')c = c$$

There are two ways in which this type of simplification can be achieved: manual (in which simplification is based on inspection of a modified representation of the truth table) and automatic (simplification of the truth table by a computer program). Automatic simplification is, of course, preferable whenever possible and justified by the complexity of the function. In many situations, particularly when the number of inputs is small, manual simplification is possible and preferable since it will be faster to perform. The manual method will be outlined and demonstrated.

Consider the truth table of $f = ab + ab' = a$ (Figure 2.27).

a	b	f	line number
0	0	0	0
0	1	0	1
1	0	1	2
1	1	1	3

Figure 2.27   A truth table with adjacencies.

The minimal SP representation of the function is, of course, related to the SP algorithm. It can, in fact, be obtained by adding an extra step to this algorithm. The SP algorithm is based upon the processing of lines with a 1 in the value column. We have to examine these lines. In our case the two relevant lines $(2,3)$ differ in the value of exactly one variable (b). It is clear from the original SP algorithm that two lines which differ in exactly one input value (logically *adjacent lines*) produce terms which differ in exactly one variable which is in the original form in one of them and inverted in the other. Two such terms can be combined. In our case $f = ab' + ab$ can be reduced to a single term by the previous formula: $f = a$. This is the basis of the method:

Look for pairs of logically adjacent lines with 1 in the function value, and when you find one, combine the corresponding terms into one. The merging of the two terms is performed simply by leaving out the variable in which the two lines differ. This follows immediately from the SP algorithm.

Note that logically adjacent lines do not have to be consecutive lines in the table and that consecutive lines are not always logically adjacent.

In some truth tables written in the standard form adjacencies are not easy to spot (Figure 2.28).

a	b	f	line number
0	0	1	0
0	1	0	1
1	0	1	2
1	1	0	3

Figure 2.28   A truth table with non-obvious adjacencies.

In this case the two relevant adjacent lines are lines number 0 and 2. These lines are logically but not visually adjacent, and this makes them harder to find. The situation gets more complicated with a larger number of variables. The basis of the manual method is a different representation of the truth table which makes almost all logically adjacent lines also visually adjacent. One variation of this representation is called the *Karnaugh map*. The basic diagram which is used in place of the standard truth table for two, three and four variables is shown in Figure 2.29.

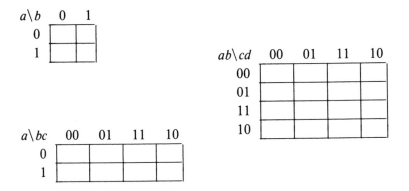

Figure 2.29   Karnaugh map patterns for two, three, and four input variables.

The empty cells are reserved for output values and are filled as needed. Their role is identical to that of the output column in the standard truth table. In the last example they will be filled as shown in Figure 2.30.

$a \backslash b$	0	1
0	1	0
1	1	0

Figure 2.30   Karnaugh map for the truth table from Figure 2.28.

Zeros are often left out and empty cells are implied to represent them (Figure 2.31). For more examples see the Workbook.

$a \backslash bc$	00	01	11	10
0		1	1	
1		1	1	

Figure 2.31   Karnaugh map with zeros represented by empty cells.

The important feature of the map is the *order* in which the values of input variables are listed: two geometrically adjacent columns are labeled by values which differ by exactly one value. The same is true for the first and the last column which are also adjacent. A similar rule is used for lines. As a consequence, two cells on the same line in adjacent columns—and this means either directly geometrically adjacent or cells in the first and the last column—are logically adjacent. Similarly, two cells in the same column on adjacent lines are logically adjacent. There are no other logically adjacent cells. Thus a Karnaugh map converts logical adjacency to visual adjacency, and this makes simplification easier.

If adjacent cells contain a 1 they can be merged and the corresponding terms combined. In the last example the second column is filled with ones and the two cells differ in the value of a. The term is thus obtained by using the SP rule and ignoring a. The result is $b'c$. Similarly, the third column can be represented by bc. Note that we could proceed horizontally instead of vertically. The middle of the first line can be represented by $a'c$, the middle of the third line by ac. This alternative is not surprising since we know that the same function can often be represented by several different formulas. The result of our simplification is

$$f = b'c + bc$$

As we know this function can be further simplified to

$$f = c$$

This can be seen from the Karnaugh map: the two pairs of cells representing these two terms are adjacent; their columns are represented by the following two pairs of values for b,c: $(0,1)$ and $(1,1)$. These two pairs are clearly adjacent when viewed as functions of b and c only, which is justified since it was determined that the corresponding function values do not depend on a. Their merging and the basic rule of the SP algorithm gives

$$f = c$$

which is the fully reduced representation for f. The previous example shows that there are many patterns of adjacency. Some are at first a little more difficult to discern but are easily learned. It must be remembered that they contain 2 or 4 or 8, etc. (a power of 2) cells and are obtained by combining the simpler adjacencies. Some examples are shown in Figure 2.32.

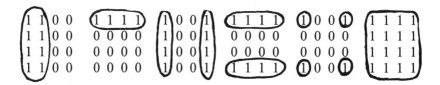

Figure 2.32   Some less obvious adjacency patterns.

It is left as an exercise to determine what are the simplified formulas corresponding to the individual patterns. Two hints are:

1. Each of the patterns represents one block of adjacent cells and thus one term.
2. Adjacency is not only directly geometrical but also along the sides. These adjacencies are easily recognized if we think of the

Karnaugh map as drawn on a closed surface with opposite sides of the table connected together.

The terms corresponding to blocks of adjacent cells which cannot be further enlarged are called *prime implicants* (PIs). They are terms which can appear in the final simplified formula for the function and cannot be further simplified through combination with other terms. The following is an algorithm describing how to obtain a PI using a Karnaugh map and starting with a cell (pattern) x containing a 1.

ALGORITHM PI:

While there is a pattern y adjacent to pattern x
    and
    geometrical form of y is the same as
    geometrical form of x
replace x by y combined with x.

Note that "adjacent" and "geometrically identical form" must be understood in the more general sense including adjacency of border columns and rows of Karnaugh maps. This algorithm formulates the construction of PIs as a process of progressive growth of a single-cell pattern.

In many situations there is more than one PI (Figure 2.33).

$a\backslash bc$	00	01	11	10
0	0	1	0	0
1	0	1	1	0

Figure 2.33   A Karnaugh map with two PIs.

In this example there are two PIs. The second column is $b'c$ and the middle of the second line is ac. Since the method of simplification is essentially a modification of the SP algorithm which is based on "covering" all ones in the truth table, we must also cover all the cells containing a 1 and OR the corresponding terms to obtain the full representation of the table. This gives

$$f = ac + b'c$$

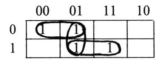

	00	01	11	10
0	1	1		
1		1	1	

Figure 2.34   A Karnaugh map with three PIs, two of which are essential.

In the example in Figure 2.34 there are three prime implicants. They are the beginning of the first line $(a'b')$, the second column $(b'c)$, and the middle of the second line (ac). The first and the last must be used to produce the formula—they are *essential* PIs: the first covers cell $a'b'c'$ which none of the other two PIs covers. The third covers cell abc which none of the other two PIs covers. But these two PIs combined cover all ones in the map, and there is no need to use the remaining one. The result is

$$f = a'b' + ac$$

In summary, only two of the three PIs are needed to represent the function. Consider now Figure 2.35.

ab\cd	00	01	11	10
00		1	1	1
01	1	1		
11				
10				

Figure 2.35   A Karnaugh map which can be described by two different minimal formulas.

In this example $a'bc'$ and $a'b'c$ are essential PIs and must be present in the final formula. $a'c'd$ and $a'b'd$ are not essential, but one of them must be present in the formula since the two essential PIs do not cover cell $a'b'c'd$. Only one of them is necessary, and the following two representations of f are equivalent and minimal:

$$f = a'bc' + a'b'c + a'c'd$$
$$= a'bc' + a'b'c + a'b'd$$

Note that both expressions contain the essential PIs (the first two terms).

The minimization process based on Karnaugh maps can be summarized as follows:

ALGORITHM KM
1. Find all PIs
2. Find and retain for the final formula all essential PIs
3. Find the smallest possible number of PIs to cover all the remaining ones in the map.

For more examples see the Workbook. The last step of the algorithm is simple for a few variables and the common use of Karnaugh maps is restricted to up to four variables although it can be extended to five and six at the cost of losing some of its simplicity of visual identification. For more variables the problem of finding the minimal coverage is more complicated. For a large number of variables it may require too much computer time even for very fast computers and may not be economically feasible. It should, however, be realized that minimization of the number of gate components has ceased to be a problem of essential importance in most problems of digital design. This is particularly true for very complicated functions which are nowadays often implemented by MSI, LSI, and VLSI components. Minimization still retains its importance in the design of circuits which are to be placed on one *chip* i.e., which are to become MSI or LSI chips. Design with MSI components (covered later in this chapter) is quite different—and, in fact, much simpler—and design with LSI components is again completely different. In summary, the Karnaugh map and related methods are difficult to use in more complex situations, but it is precisely in these situations that they lost some of their importance. This shift is due to developments in semiconductor technology.

2.8 DON'T CARE CONDITIONS

In many situations the values corresponding to some combinations of inputs are irrelevant. In other words we don't care what the circuit does in response to a certain combination of inputs. This is usually because such a combination of inputs never occurs in the environment in which the device operates.

Consider a machine processing student application forms at a university which does not admit females over 20 years old. The machine is supposed to print a red dot on forms submitted by students which are male and over 20 years or females and under 20 years. The machine operates by reading two entries on the form—sex and age. These are the input variables. What does the machine do when it reads an application from a female student over 20 years old? We don't care; presumably another machine screens out all such applications, and they never reach the machine which prints the dots.

On the other hand, we cannot design a machine from an incomplete truth table. All cells must contain a 0 or a 1. We have to fill in, eventually, even the cells which represent the don't care combinations. At the beginning we should fill the entries by a symbol indicating that this is a don't care cell. We use an X for this purpose. It is important to realize that X is not a third logical value in addition to 0 and 1, but just a symbol to be replaced by a suitably chosen logical value 0 or 1. The choice as to which value to fill in depends on minimization criteria. Consider the Karnaugh map in Figure 2.36.

$xy\backslash z$	0	1
00	1	
01	1	
11	1	
10	X	

Figure 2.36   A function with don't care entries.

One of the cells is a don't care. If we replace the X by a 0, we can simplify the function to

$$f=x'y'z'+yz'$$

If we replace X by 1 we can get

$$f=z'$$

which is a much simpler result. In this specific situation it is thus preferable to replace X by 1. For more examples see the Workbook.

The Karnaugh map procedure can be extended to solve the problem with don't cares.

2.9   NAND GATES IN TWO-LEVEL CIRCUITS

It is very interesting that two-stage AND-OR circuits can be mechanically replaced by circuits using only NAND gates. This fact is based on De Morgan's rules. Consider the function

$$f = ab + cd'$$

It can be modified by the following sequence of steps:

$$\begin{aligned} f \quad &= f'' = ((ab + cd'))' = ((ab)'(cd'))' \\ &= \text{NAND}(\text{NAND}(a,b), \text{NAND}(c,d')) \end{aligned}$$

The last expression can be implemented by three NAND gates. In fact if d' has to be obtained from d, the original circuit requires an inverter in addition to AND and OR gates but the NAND circuit does not since an inverter can be implemented by a NAND gate. Note that the structure of the NAND circuit is absolutely identical to the structure of the original AND-OR circuit. Thus the two circuits in Figure 2.37 implement the same function. This means, for example, that when we minimize a circuit by the Karnaugh map method, we can draw the NAND gate implementation directly from the resulting AND-OR formula without having to perform the conversion. The conversion was shown only to justify the procedure. As an example the formula

$$f = abc' + a'bc + ab'$$

can be directly converted into the circuit shown in Figure 2.38 by thinking in terms of AND and OR gates but drawing NAND gates instead. Note that the formula can be simplified, but the rule holds. The rule holds for any two-stage AND-OR circuit.

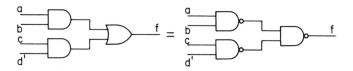

Figure 2.37   Structurally identical circuits implementing the same function with AND, OR gates and NAND gates only.

Note that the representation of $f = ab + c$ in Figure 2.39 is not a two-stage AND-OR circuit, and therefore the NAND-only circuit on the right obtained by mechanically replacing AND and OR gates by NAND gates is not equivalent and does not represent the same function (think of the correct replacement as an exercise). It is important to realize that the substitution applies strictly to two-stage AND-OR circuits and nothing else. For more examples see the Workbook.

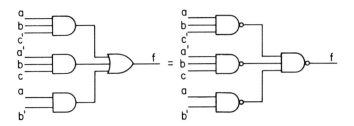

Figure 2.38   Circuit using only NAND gates to implement $f = abc' + a'bc + ab'$.

Figure 2.39   For direct conversion to a NAND gate circuit the original representation must be a two-level AND-OR circuit. The circuit shown on the left is not of this type and the circuit on the right is not its equivalent.

If AND-OR circuits can be replaced by NAND-only circuits in this straightforward manner, can OR-AND circuits be replaced by one type of gate as well? The answer is that OR-AND two-stage circuits can be replaced by NOR-only circuits. The justification is left as another exercise.

These interesting results add another reason to justify the popularity of the NAND gate. The above described property is particularly important for IC technology: as was mentioned, logic chips always contain more than one gate. Switching devices usually consist of a number of switching circuits. Each of them uses a certain number of gates and frequently does not use all gates on each chip. Because of their functional independence, individual gates on each chip can be used in different circuits. The possibility of implementing each individual circuit with the same type of gate such as NAND improves the utilization of individual chips: fewer chips remain unused. This not only slightly decreases the number of components and the corresponding cost, but also reduces the number of connections and the area required by the components and connections on the PC board. These are not negligible factors.

2.10 DESIGN OF MORE COMPLEX CIRCUITS

2.10.1 Introduction

When the function to be implemented requires roughly 10 gates or more, economic considerations require a different implementation from AND-OR or similar SSI-based circuits described in the previous sections. This is because with the growing number of IC packages and interconnections the cost increases and reliability decreases to a point where more complex ICs become more economical.

The first step in the redesign of a complex circuit is the exploration of the possibility of a different conceptual approach. The more complex a circuit, the more alternative implementations there are. As an example, one can examine various implementations of adders differing in circuit complexity and speed of operation. For more examples see the Workbook.

Let us assume that the conceptual approach has been determined. There exist a number of MSI and LSI components which make it possible to design and implement even very complex functions in a few packages. Three such approaches will be introduced in this section. They are based on *multiplexers*, Programmable Logic Arrays (PLA), and *Read-Only-Memories* (ROM). Other components which are used for similar applications will not be described since the intent is to present only a survey of the most important or representative concepts.

It should be mentioned that frequently needed functions, such as certain decoders, encoders, adders, etc. are also available as commercial ICs. For these applications no circuits need to be designed.

Approaches which will be introduced in this section can be classified by three criteria: complexity of the basic component, method of description of the desired function, and permanence of implementation. We will see that the relative merits of the individual approaches can be summarized as follows:

1. Complexity of the basic component: multiplexers are the simplest, PLAs are more complex, and ROMs are technologically the most advanced.

2. Description of function: design with multiplexers and ROMs is based on implementations of truth tables. PLAs use direct implementations of Boolean expressions. This classification is helpful in choosing the most suitable method in some situations. Although ROMs and PLAs can both be used to implement functions of a larger number of inputs (as can multiplexers, but less efficiently), ROMs are better suited for functions which are not easily described by a few Boolean terms. PLAs, on the other hand, can be used very economically to implement functions of a relatively large number of inputs if they can be described relatively simply. Note that formula minimization can be very useful in this method.

3. Multiplexers resemble gates in that they can be removed from a circuit and used to implement any other functions by simply making the correct connections. Connections in PLAs and ROMs, on the other hand, are custom-designed and manufactured for a specific function. Once finalized, they cannot be transferred to implement a different function. However, there are certain types of PLAs and ROMs which allow modification at a certain cost.

2.10.2 Multiplexers

Multiplexers, also called *data selectors*, are best described as electronically controlled switches: the output value of a multiplexer (a "mux") is, at any time, equal to the value of one of its inputs (selected by special control lines). To allow the selection of an input, each input line is assigned a number ("address") by which it can be selected for connection to the output. The diagram in Figure 2.40 shows the basic structure of an 8-to-1 multiplexer with arbitrarily chosen values connected to its input ("data") and control lines. For the values of data and controls shown in the diagram the output value is as indicated and the function of the device is schematically the same as that of the multi-input switch shown on the right.

This multiplexer has eight input lines and one output. The control lines are labeled a,b,c. The combination of control values determines which of the input lines is "connected" to the output: it is the line whose label (address) is identical to the combination present on the control lines. The values on the control lines can be changed at any time, and in this way the value on arbitrary input lines can be read from the output in any order. The response of the device is very fast;

the time between the change of address on control lines and the time when the output stabilizes to the value of the selected data line and can be reliably read is less than 50 nanoseconds.

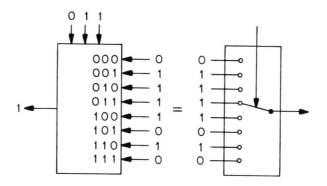

Figure 2.40   The function of an 8-to-1 multiplexer.

As an example of the function of the multiplexer consider the diagram in Figure 2.40. Assume that (a,b,c) changes from $(0,0,1)$ to $(0,1,0)$. About 50 nanoseconds after the change of values on control lines the output changes from 0 (the value present on input line 001) to 1 (the value present at input line 010). The value remains constant until either the value on line 010 changes and the output then changes to the same value, or the address on the control lines changes and the output then assumes the value present on the currently addressed data line, after at most a 50 nanosecond delay.

The multiplexer drawing in Figure 2.39 is intentionally presented in a somewhat non-standard form to suggest how the multiplexer can be used in digital circuits. The form shown is very similar to the form of a standard truth table with three independent variables (and eight lines). Given a truth table with N input lines, we can use a multiplexer with N control lines to implement it. The independent variables will be connected to the control lines, and the desired function values (corresponding to the value column of the truth table) to the input lines whose addresses match the input line combinations. Figure 2.42 shows an example of a 3-input truth table and its implementation with an 8-to-1 multiplexer. Note that the value connected to line 011 is the value required in the truth table for input 011, etc.

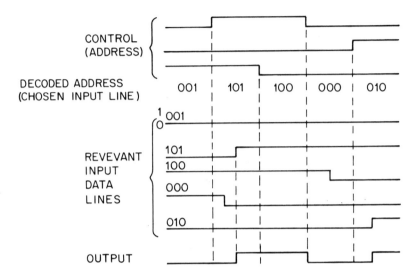

Figure 2.41 An example of the function of the multiplexer from Figure 2.40.

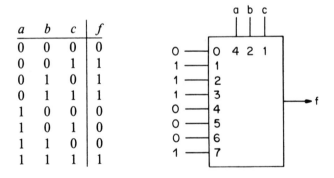

a	b	c	f
0	0	0	0
0	0	1	1
0	1	0	1
0	1	1	1
1	0	0	0
1	0	1	0
1	1	0	0
1	1	1	1

Figure 2.42 A truth table and its implementation with a multiplexer.

Design of a switching circuit from its truth table is a matter of seconds with the use of multiplexers. There seems to be a problem, however: typical multiplexers are 4-to-1, 8-to-1, and 16-to-1. With our design method this seems to limit the usefulness of multiplexers to functions of four variables at most. There are two ways to overcome this complexity limitation: folding (which allows us to double the length of the implementable truth table) and the use of multiplexer trees (which makes it possible to use multiplexers in the design of arbitrarily complex switching circuits).

1. *Folding*

Assume that we have a truth table with four inputs u,v,x,y and an 8-to-1 multiplexer with three control inputs. Let us connect u,v,x to control lines. (This choice is quite arbitrary.) For each combination of input variables u,v,x there are two distinct lines in the truth table: one corresponding to $y=0$ and the other to $y=1$. The function values corresponding to these two lines are zeros and ones in some combination. For each combination of u, v, x there are only four possible ways in which f can depend on y:

a. $f=0$ for both $y=0$ and $y=1$
b. $f=1$ for both $y=0$ and $y=1$
c. $f=0$ for $y=0$ and $f=1$ for $y=1$ (i.e. $f=y$)
d. $f=1$ for $y=0$ and $f=0$ for $y=1$ (i.e. $f=y'$)

We have connected u,v,x to control lines. What should be connected to data lines? That depends on the combination of function values: if for a given combination of u,v,x the corresponding value combination in the truth table is as in alternative a above, we connect a 0 to the line labeled u,v,x. If the combination is as in b, then we connect 1 to it. For combination c the value is y and so y is connected to the corresponding input line; for combination d the value is y'. This algorithm is very simple and can best be understood on an example (Figure 2.43).

a	b	c	f
0	0	0	0
0	0	1	0
0	1	0	1
0	1	1	1
1	0	0	0
1	0	1	1
1	1	0	1
1	1	1	0

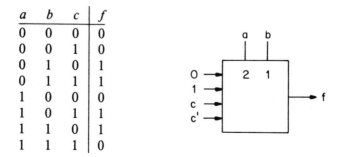

Figure 2.43   Implementation of a 3-input truth table using the folding method.

The example shows a 3-input logic function implemented by a 4-to-1 multiplexer with two control lines. Combination $(a,b) = (0,0)$ has output value 0 for $c=0$ and $c=1$. A 0 is thus connected to data line labeled 00. Combination $(a,b) = (0,1)$ has a 1 on lines corresponding to $c=0$ and $c=1$. A 1 is thus connected to line 01. Combination $(a,b) = (1,0)$ has 0 on the line corresponding to $c=0$, and 1 for $c=1$. In summary, $f=c$ for $(a,b) = (0,1)$, and c is connected to the data line labeled 10. Combination $(a,b) = (1,1)$ has value 1 for $c=0$ and 0 for $c=1$ and therefore has c' connected to line 11; our original method would require an 8-to-1 multiplexer and the current method requires only a 4-to-1 multiplexer. In practice this represents a saving of one-half of the components and a saving of space since the IC chip implementing the multiplexer contains two such circuits and the second half can be used to serve in another circuit. One restriction of the method is that it requires in general both the c and c' value in addition to 0 and 1. This, however, may not happen in all circuits, and besides both d and d' are usually available at the same time from memory elements as we will see in the next chapter. This disadvantage is therefore real only if c' is not available and has to be obtained by an inverter. The first method does not require c or c' since it only uses 0 and 1 inputs which are always available without special circuitry.

In summary, the folding method allows us to double the size of the truth table which can be implemented by a given multiplexer. For more examples see the Workbook.

2. *Multiplexer Trees*

Assume that we only have 4-to-1 (i.e., 2-address) multiplexers and want to build a function of four variables a,b,c,d. This is not possible by one multiplexer even if we use the folding method. It will now be shown how this can be done with more multiplexers. For simplicity let us use the original method, using the truth table directly rather than folding it. Connect c,d to the two control inputs of our multiplexers. There are four possible combinations of a,b, and we will dedicate one 4-to-1 multiplexer to each of these combinations. The output corresponding to the multiplexer dedicated to $(c,d) = (0,1)$ will have values corresponding to the appropriate quarter of the truth table, etc. Since there are four dedicated multiplexers, the output of one of them must be selected (for a given combination of a,b) to give the desired output. The selection will, of course, be performed by a multiplexer. The choice depends on the values of a,b since the first level of multiplexers is dedicated to all combinations of a,b, and these will be the control variables of the second level selector (multiplexer). Figure 2.44 shows an example. Consider, for example, the first level multiplexer which is dedicated to combination $(a,b) = (0,0)$. Its data inputs correspond to the output values given in the first four lines of the truth table which contains all the values for inputs with $(a,b) = (0,0)$. This multiplexer thus implements the first quarter of the truth table. The other three first level multiplexers would be considered similarly. To see how the circuit works, assume that the input combination is $(a,b,c,d) = (1,1,1,0)$. Inputs $(a,b) = (1,1)$ select the output of the fourth of the first level multiplexers. Values $(c,d) = (1,0)$ select its 10 data line. This line has a 0 connected to it, and the whole circuit thus produces a 0 on its output as prescribed in the truth table.

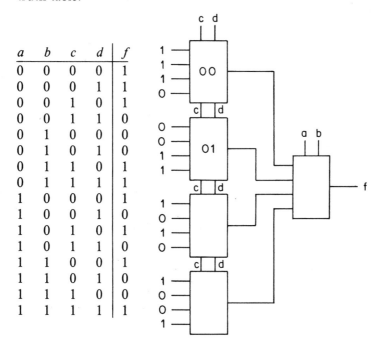

a	b	c	d	f
0	0	0	0	1
0	0	0	1	1
0	0	1	0	1
0	0	1	1	0
0	1	0	0	0
0	1	0	1	0
0	1	1	0	1
0	1	1	1	1
1	0	0	0	1
1	0	0	1	0
1	0	1	0	1
1	0	1	1	0
1	1	0	0	1
1	1	0	1	0
1	1	1	0	0
1	1	1	1	1

Figure 2.44   A truth table implemented by a multiplexer tree.

The method can, of course, be used with the folding method and any other multiplexer. The number of levels is (at least theoretically) also unlimited. In theory any number of inputs can therefore be accommodated. In practice the complexity of the circuit will determine whether it is economical or not and whether this or another method should be used for implementation. In some situations (when the truth table has a uniform structure), it may even be advantageous to use an AND-OR circuit.

For more examples see the Workbook.

   3. *Multiplexer Structure and MSI Chips*

What are multiplexers, i.e., what is their internal structure? They are MSI circuits built from gates (internally on the chip). They are essentially quite simple as the example of a 4-to-1 multiplexer in Figure 2.45 demonstrates.

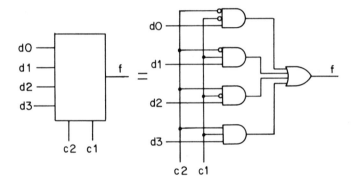

Figure 2.45   The internal structure of a 4-to-1 multiplexer.

To see how this circuit works, assume that $(c2,c1) = (1,0)$. All the AND gates with the exception of A2 have a combination of control inputs containing at least one zero. Outputs of these AND gates are, therefore, zeros, and they play no role in the final output which is generated by an OR gate. The control inputs a2 are both 1 and the output of A2 is equal to d2: if $d2=0$ the output is $1.1.0=0$, and if $d2=1$ the output is $1.1.1=1$. In summary, if $(c2,c1) = (1,0)$ the output of the multiplexer is equal to d2 which is exactly what is expected of a multiplexer with these inputs. Note that the function of control signals is to "gate," i.e., let through or block, the data signals.

For more examples see the Workbook.

Commercially available multiplexers have extra inputs to provide more flexibility. As an example the 74153 16-pin dual 4/1 multiplexer (which costs about 60 cents) has the following pin assignment ("pinout"):

function	ins
Enable #1, #2	1, 15
Address "1", "2"	14, 2
Inputs #1 (lines 0,1,2,3)	6, 5, 4, 3
Inputs #2 (lines 0,1,2,3)	10, 11, 12, 13
Output #1, #2	7, 9
Ground, +5V	8, 16

The chip contains two independent 4-to-1 multiplexers with common control lines, i.e., the same input lines, are addressed on both multiplexers at any time. In addition to the expected lines, there are two *enable* lines, one for each multiplexer. The enable pin provides overall control over the multiplexer. On this specific chip when enable=H all outputs of the multiplexer produce L, no matter what values are connected to the input data and control lines. When enable=L, the multiplexer behaves as described previously. By this definition the enable input is *active low*: the chip performs its standard function when enable=L (the chip is "active" when enable=L). For this reason the diagram of the chip is usually drawn as in Figure 2.46 to indicate the active behavior of individual pins: note that the enable line is drawn with a bubble (for active low, i.e., L on enable activates the multiplexer). Pin numbers are written next to the lines. This is standard in circuit diagrams to simplify the understanding of the function of the chip. The functions of the pins are indicated next to the lines inside the rectangle. This is not common on circuit diagrams but standard on data sheets produced by manufacturers of chips.

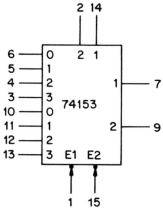

Figure 2.46   The 74153 multiplexer.

The name of the component—multiplexer—derives from its original use. *Multiplexing* is the transmission of several unrelated signals over one communication line in an "interleaved" way (one at a time in a sequence). Since this is a common process in communication even inside computers, it will be briefly described:

Assume that there are four signal lines at which signals may change every 0.01 sec. In other words, individual lines have signal frequency 100 Hz. The signal is to be transmitted from the source to a more or less distant destination. To save on transmission costs, each line is read ("sampled") 100 times a second (at regular intervals spaced 0.01 sec). The lines are sampled in sequence in a fixed order (e.g., lines 0, 1, 2, 3, 0, 1, ...). The value obtained is transmitted over one communication line. The communication line thus transmits four multiplexed signals at 400 Hz. The stream of signals is *demultiplexed* at the other end of the line: the signals read from one communication line are placed on four output lines at appropriate times in the same order in which they are sampled at the source. Observation of the four output lines thus gives the same result as if the four lines were each transmitted over individual lines. The signals at the other end then appear to be communicated over independent lines (Figure 2.47).

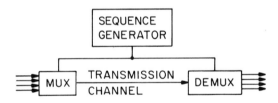

Figure 2.47   Multiplexed transmission of several signals over one communication line. Source signals are multiplexed and the output of the line demultiplexed.

This solution is easily implemented by a multiplexer/demultiplexer combination. The control lines of the multiplexer and of the demultiplexer must be fed the correct address sequence (in our case 0,1,2,3,0,...) and properly synchronized. The multiplexer places the value of line 0 on the communication line; after 0.01/4 sec this value is replaced by the value from line 1 (under the control of the control lines of the demultiplexer), etc. There is a certain delay between the instant the signal is placed on the line by the multiplexer and the instant it arrives at the demultiplexer at the other end. The signal travels at the speed of light which is about 30 cm/nanosecond. If the two stations are 300 m apart the transmission will take 1000 nsec = 1 microsecond. The control signals supplied to the demultiplexer at the other end of the line must be such that the signal is read when it arrives which is one microsecond later than when it was sent, or sampled by the multiplexer. The clock signals which control the multiplexer/demultiplexer pair must be mutually delayed by one microsecond as is indicated in the timing diagram in Figure 2.48. In this case the delay is probably insignificant in relation to the length of the data signal and can thus be neglected.

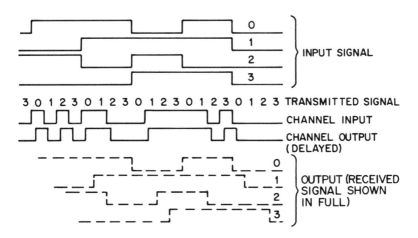

Figure 2.48   An example of the tranmission of a multiplexed signal.

2.11 PROGRAMMABLE LOGIC ARRAYS

We have seen that logic functions can often be conveniently described in the sum of products form. Even when the number of variables is quite large, the formula can have very few terms. Minimization methods help to reduce the number of terms even when the original description leads to a complex expression. AND-OR circuits were originally built with SSI components when this was the only technology available. When progress in fabrication methods advanced to the level where MSI and LSI devices became feasible, designers started thinking about more generally applicable devices that they could produce with the new technology. (Note that this seems to be a recurrent problem: designers of circuits based on the emerging VLSI technology generally agree that one of their main problems is not the technology but how to use it efficiently.) One obvious need was for a device which could be used to implement any AND-OR circuit of moderate complexity, i.e., with a moderate number of gates and variables. Such a device should have the form of an array of AND gates followed by an array of OR gates. The connections should not be permanently established for all manufactured chips in order to allow the use of the chip for different AND-OR circuits. There are two possible ways to establish non-permanent connections: allow extra inputs to select some and eliminate other gates as is done in the multiplexer or design the connections in such a way that they can be physically modified, in other words, generate the basic structure but allow certain flexibility with connections to be opened or closed.

The first of these two approaches has been the subject of some research. Circuits implementing logic functions in this way are called Universal Logic Modules—ULMs. A ULM capable of realizing any function of n inputs is called a ULM of order n or simply an n-ULM. The number of inputs required depends on whether only one value of input variables is available—"single-rail ULMs"—or both x and x' are available for all inputs—"double-rail ULMs." Double-rail ULMs require fewer inputs, but the number is still too large to allow economical implementation on a single chip. The ULM approach therefore has not achieved practical acceptance.

The second approach has been accepted and the resulting device is called a Programmable Logic Array (PLA). The word "programmable" refers to the fact that the specific connections can be established after the basic circuit structure has been defined. The connections are established either by the manufacturer by modifications to the basic production mask (PLAs) or "in the field" by the customer (Field Programmable Logic Arrays—FPLAs).

The diagram in Figure 2.49 shows a hypothetical PLA. We will see that commercially available PLAs are much larger. The basic structure, however, remains the same.

Note that the circuit consists of NOT, AND, and OR gates with final connections left unspecified. The customer has to define the connections by specifying the desired form of the function to be established. If the customer defines, for example, the functions $x=ab+a'b$ and $y=ab+a'b'$ they can be obtained by connecting the gates of the above non-programmed PLA as shown in Figure 2.50. For more examples see the Workbook.

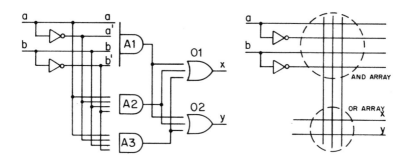

Figure 2.49   The structure of a hypothetical PLA (left) and its usual representation (right).

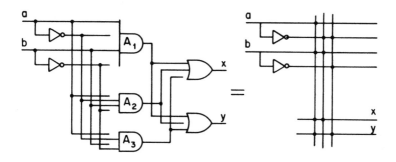

Figure 2.50   A PLA implementation of $x=ab+a'b$, $y=ab+a'b'$.

The number of terms, inputs and outputs in commercial PLAs is limited. This means that the overall minimization of the functions often determines whether the PLA approach is feasible or not. This problem of minimization is more complex than the one discussed in previous sections: in general the PLA implements several functions and at least some of the variable inputs are shared among them. The problem is thus one of minimizing the overall design rather than that of minimizing one function. This is usually achieved by allowing the functions to share some of the terms, such as ab in the example above. Individual functions are often not completely minimized when overall minimization is achieved. Note that the goal is not, in fact, minimization but simply the reduction of the complexity of the circuit to fit the parameters of the PLA chip.

Commercially available chips are more complex than the circuit in the example above. They are moderately priced and can cost around $10. Two examples of commercial PLAs are as follows:

1. DM7575 is manufactured by National Semiconductor. It has 14 data inputs and 8 outputs. This means that up to eight functions can be implemented on one chip. The total number of independent variables, most of which should be shared by several functions for efficient utilization, is 14. The total number of built-in AND terms is 96 and if many of them are shared the utilization of the chip will be high.
2. The SN54S330 is an FPLA produced by Texas Instruments. It has 12 inputs, 6 outputs, and 50 product terms.

Note that a circuit implemented on a PLA must be quite efficiently minimized: consider the DM7575 PLA. It has 14 data inputs. This means that the full truth table corresponding to implementable functions has 16384 lines (2**14). The chip allows only 96 product terms which is about 0.5 percent of the maximum number of terms possible. In addition, it is built to accommodate up to eight such functions. This fact gives an indication of the limitations and advantages of PLAs: only functions which can be very efficiently minimized can be implemented on PLAs. When a function can be implemented on a PLA, it can be obtained very efficiently since the chip is mass-produced and relatively simple.

2.12 READ ONLY MEMORIES

A Read Only Memory (ROM) functions like a multiplexer in which the data connections to H or L have been made internally and there is no external control over their values. In other words a ROM has no data inputs. If we regard the data inputs of a multiplexer as writing information into the multiplexer, the output line can be thought of as allowing information from the chip to be read. Since ROMs do not have data inputs they cannot be written but only read—hence *read only memories*. The information is stored in ROMs permanently, and the chip acts as a memory of the information written into it during manufacture.

The multiplexer needs many of its lines for data inputs. This limits its maximum size. A ROM does not have this limitation since there are no data lines. All that is needed is output lines for reading and address lines to select the value from the desired internal storage location. The number of internal locations accessible via address lines grows exponentially with the number of address lines, and the storage capacity can be enormous: only a few lines are needed to allow access to a vast array of memory locations. The limiting parameter is the maximum packing density achievable by the given technological process rather than the number of pins that can be reasonably accommodated on one chip. Towards the end of the 1970's the practicable ROM size was $2^{**}15=32786$ single bit locations. (In standard terminology this is referred to as 32k. The abbreviation $1k=2^{**}10=1024$.)

There are several basic types of ROMs, and the classification is similar to that of PLAs. A ROM in the proper sense is a read-only memory which must be programmed by the manufacturer according to a customer-supplied specification. A PROM (Programmable ROM) is one which can be programmed once and for all by the customer with a special purpose device called a PROM programmer. Some PROMs can be erased (usually by ultraviolet light) and reprogrammed in a PROM programmer. Still others (less common) can be repeatedly electrically modified directly in the circuit in which they work, but the process of writing is very slow compared to the process of reading— milliseconds compared to less than microseconds, i.e., about 1000 times slower. Writing new information into such chips (EAROMs—Electrically Alterable ROMs) is economical only if it is required very infrequently. This type of ROM is thus intended mostly for reading and infrequent writing. It is sometimes called a "read-mostly ROM." More information on various types of memory components is presented in Chapter 9.

There are differences in complexity and cost between the individual types of ROMs: in general, the complexity of the chip grows in the order in which the categories were named. All the categories are used for the same purpose, essentially storage of truth tables. They are, however, not used in the same circumstances.

ROMs are relatively cheap except for a large initial cost of modification of the mask. They cannot be modified once completed. This means that they can be economically used only for circuits produced in very large quantities (where the initial cost can be spread over a large number of products) which have been extensively tested and are known to perform well. In the direction towards electrically alterable

ROMs (EAROMs) the application changes: programmable and particularly reprogrammable ROMs cost more per chip but can be very cheaply programmed or reprogrammed by the user. They are advantageous for circuits produced in limited quantities or during the development stages of products intended for mass-production.

ROMs can be organized in a number of ways: the same total number of bits can represent a truth table of a certain length, or it can store two truth tables of half this length, etc. For example, a 16k ROM can store one truth table of one function of 14 variables. It will have one output to read the value and 14 address inputs to control the address of the location ("line number of the truth table"). It could also store two truth tables of functions of 13 variables, each of which requires 8k bits. This chip will have two output pins, one for each truth table, and 13 address pins (addressing of both truth tables will be common; output values corresponding to the same line will be read from both at the same time). And this can theoretically go on and on: four truth tables of 12 variables, etc.

The two tables in Figure 2.51 show the "address space" (the list of addressable locations) of a 13-address and a 12-address ROM. If both devices can hold 2**13 bits, then the first device consists of 2**13 1-bit cells; and therefore each access to it produces a single output. The second device has 2**12 2-bit cells, and each access to it produces two outputs corresponding to the contents of the 2-bit cell accessed.

$a\,b\,c\,d\,e\,f\,g\,h\,i\,j\,k\,l\,m$	$a\,b\,c$	.	.	$k\,l$
0 0 0 0 0 0 0 0 0 0 0 0 0	0 0 0	.	.	0 0
0 0 0 0 0 0 0 0 0 0 0 0 1	0 0 0	.	.	0 1
0 0 0 0 0 0 0 0 0 0 0 1 0	0 0 0	.	.	0
0 0 0 0 0 0 0 0 0 0 0 1 1	0 0 0	.	.	1 1
. . .		.	. .	
. . .		.	. .	
1 1 1 1 1 1 1 1 1 1 1 0 1	1 1 1	;	.	0 1
1 1 1 1 1 1 1 1 1 1 1 1 0	1 1 1	.	.	1 0
1 1 1 1 1 1 1 1 1 1 1 1 1	1 1 1	.	.	1 1

Figure 2.51   The address space of a 13-address ROM and a 12-address ROM. Address lines are labeled $abc\ldots klm$.

Differently structured chips are, obviously quite different even though they store the same number of bits. They have a different number of pins and their functions are different. In addition, the internal circuits which decode the address and allow access to the desired location will also be different. We have seen that ICs can only be manufactured at an attractive price if there is a large demand for them. This determines that not all of the possible configurations are commercially available. In fact, only a very limited number of configurations are manufactured, and for most needs commercially available chips have to be configured into arrays achieving the specific configuration needed in individual applications.

ROMs are used in switching circuits in those applications where PLAs fail because of their limited complexity, where the functions to be implemented have truth tables which cannot be simplified enough to allow PLA implementation. As an example of such an application, we will consider a character generator for display of encoded characters. The truth table of this application is quite non-uniform and consists of 35 independent functions. The chip which implements it (e.g., TMS 4100) is not sold as a ROM because it is manufactured for this special application and is described in the manufacturer's data books as a character generator rather than a ROM. This is not uncommon; a number of special purpose ROMs fall into this category.

The TM 4100 chip accepts a code of a character and converts it into a set of symbols which are used to drive a "5×7" display. This is one of the formats of the very popular "dot matrix display" used in CRT computer terminals, printers, programmable billboards and scoreboards, etc. In these displays symbols are represented by a combination of black and white dots arranged in a "matrix." In our case the matrix has five columns and seven rows. As an example Figure 2.52 shows the display of letters ETO:

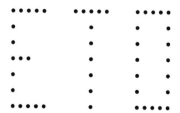

Figure 2.52   Examples of 5×7 displays.

The character generator under discussion outputs a set of zeros and ones which represent the pattern of a given symbol in a given column. The input of the chip consists of seven lines for the code of the symbol and five lines to identify the column to be displayed. In the example in Figure 2.55 if the code is that for letter T and the column code specifies column 1, the output would be 1000000. For the same letter code and column three the output will be 1111111.

As an example of the use of this chip, consider a simplified programmable scoreboard consisting of just one symbol represented by a 5×7 matrix of bulbs. The circuit could be basically connected as shown in Figure 2.53.

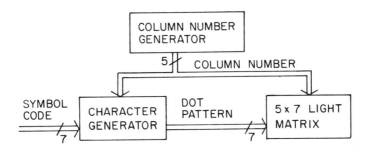

Figure 2.53   Use of a character generator in a display.

The column number generator turns ON signals to one of the five columns at a time. This signal is fed into the character generator and in conjunction with the symbol code determines the pattern fed from the character generator to the display. The signals are transmitted over a set of seven multiplexed lines. Only one of the columns is activated since it is controlled by the same signal from the column number generator (Figure 2.54).

Only those bulbs in the chosen column which are selected by the signal from the character generator are turned ON. All other bulbs (other bulbs in the same column and all bulbs in other columns) remain OFF. The column number generator could generate the column sequence 1,2,3,4,5,.1,2,.. repeatedly at a frequency of 60 Hz. The thermal inertia of bulbs and of the human eye would make the display appear steadily illuminated.

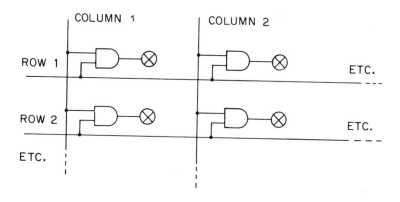

Figure 2.54   A simplified diagram of a dot display.

Note the complexity of the implemented function: each column represents seven functions (each dot is an independent function), and there are five columns. There are thus $5 \times 7 = 35$ functions altogether. Each of them is a function of the character code which is seven bits long. In other words, the character generator implements 35 functions of seven variables (128 lines in a truth table). Imagine how complex a switching circuit built from simple gates ("random logic") implementing these functions would have to be, how expensive and unreliable compared to a one-chip character generator. For more examples see the Workbook.

2.13 PHYSICAL BEHAVIOR OF ICS

Physical gates do not work quite so ideally as it might seem from the previous sections. The deviations from the ideal are, fortunately, quite small. They are, however, important, and their neglect can lead to problems. Also the understanding of certain more complicated components and design approaches is not possible without the knowledge of at least the basic facts. In this section two such factors, propagation delays and logic levels, will be briefly discussed.

Delays. All physical components exhibit inertia in their dynamic behavior. When forced to change state, they respond with a certain delay. The final state is reached some time after the initial stimulus has been given. Between the initiation of the change and the stabilization of the new value, the device produces an intermediate and meaningless signal which must be ignored. The inertia of mechanical components is large, and the delays are therefore so long that the response is much too slow for efficient processing of information in most applications. In semiconductor components delays are extremely short (on the human scale of time) since the moving bodies are electrons and the moving mass and distances are very small. Yet even here delays play an essential role for the following two reasons:

1. In a digital system a large number of semiconductor devices interact. These components have very similar but not identical parameters. Incompatibility between the specific values and their combinations can cause the whole system to work improperly.
2. Even though the delays in ICs are almost unimaginably short, they are the cause of the limits on the speed of the fastest systems, particularly computers. In other words, although the speeds are extremely high, they will never be high enough to satisfy all needs.

The delay in an information processing element can most easily be measured in terms of the *propagation delay*. It can be defined as the time that is required for the stimulus (input signal) to produce a stable response of the output (Figure 2.55). Propagation delays may depend on initial logical values; in the timing diagram in Figure 2.55 the two delays are not identical. In addition the delay depends on a number of physical parameters of the environment and the component. Our concept of propagation delay is based on the time in which the device is *guaranteed* to produce a *stable* non-ambiguous response to an input stimulus no matter what the initial conditions are. In other words, the propagation delay represents the "worst case" behavior, and the device is guaranteed to work at least as well.

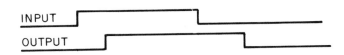

Figure 2.55   An idealized digital signal and its delayed form which could be observed, for example, on a signal line of non-negligible length.

In our analysis we ignore a number of important details: the stimulus has to be applied for at least a certain minimum duration of time in order for the device to respond (extremely short input pulses do not cause a transition): the signal is not an ideal square wave with exactly defined edges; and levels and the stable levels reached by the same component may vary within a certain range (Figure 2.56).

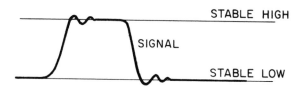

Figure 2.56   The actual shape of a digital signal.

In order for the device to respond properly, the waveform must satisfy certain minimal requirements. If, for example, the slope of the transition between two input values is too small (the transition is too slow), some devices may respond erratically ("jitter"), as shown in Figure 2.57. In this situation the waveform must be properly shaped by an intermediate component to guarantee the desired behavior. These and other details are essential for the digital designer. In our text they will be mostly neglected.

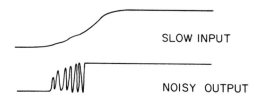

Figure 2.57   Erratic response of a gate to a change which is too slow.

The length of the propagation delay is one of the most important distinguishing factors among different logic families. A related measure is the speed which is essentially the number of transitions that a device can undergo per unit of time. In semiconductor devices the propagation time of different technologies covers a very wide range, roughly as follows: the fastest (at this stage only experimental) technology, the Josephson junction-based devices operate in pico-seconds (1 psec = $10^{**sup-12}$ sec). The fastest commercially available family, ECL, has propagation times close to one nanosecond. The most commonly used family, TTL, has propagation delays around 10 ns. Another very popular family, MOS has delays approaching 100 ns. Given the wide range of speeds, one could ask why some of the slower families are being used at all. The answer is that the suitability of a family is determined by a combination of considerations, speed, power consumption, packing density, noise immunity, cost, etc. Each of the named families has its advantages which make it the best choice in certain applications. This topic is dealt with in Chapter 9. For some examples see the Workbook.

Logic Levels. The H, L levels with which semiconductor logic devices work are not precisely defined values. They are ranges of voltages with standard interpretation. As an example, the level conventions for the TTL family are shown in Figure 2.58.

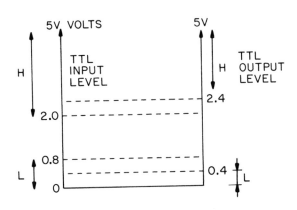

Figure 2.58   Standard voltage levels for the TTL family.

The interpretation of the diagram is as follows: the input recognizes level H if it is at least 2.0 Volts and level L if it is at most 0.8 V. The output produces at least 2.4 V for level H and at most 0.4 V for level L. The difference between input and output levels primarily serves the purpose of increasing the noise margin discussed below. These levels are guaranteed by manufacturers if the components are installed in proper environment (voltage levels, temperature, etc.). Note in this context that:

1. A given gate's output can only be connected to ("drive") a limited number of inputs of other gates. When this limit is exceeded, proper voltage levels cannot be guaranteed. The measure of the driving capability of a gate is the maximum number of "standard gates" ("unit loads") that can be connected to its output in order that the circuit can be guaranteed to work as specified. This number is called the fan-out of the gate. The standard gate is defined in terms of physical parameters or simply as a standard basic circuit of the given family, such as a NAND gate. The typical *fan-out* is 10 loads of the same family. A typical gate can thus have its output connected to the inputs of up to 10 standard gates of the same family.

    Some ICs represent more than one standard load. If this were not so, there would be no point in defining a unit. The number of unit loads that a given input represents is called the *fan-in* of the input. A typical gate can thus drive 10 standard inputs or five inputs with fan-in 2, etc.

2. *Noise* is any signal superimposed on the ideal waveform. It is generally due to various types of electrical interference and is always present to some extent. If the amplitude of the noise signal is too large, it can corrupt the true signal to such a degree that the gate will misinterpret its logical value. The resistance of a device to noise, its ability to interpret correctly the value of even a corrupted signal, is called *noise immunity*. Different logic families have different levels of noise immunity: what may be an acceptable amount of noise for one family may be too much for another family. The diagram in Figure 2.59 shows (left to right) an ideal signal, the same signal corrupted by noise, its interpretation by a noise sensitive inverter, and its interpretation by an immune inverter.

Figure 2.59   A pure digital signal, a noisy signal, the response of an ideal inverter, the response of a noise-sensitive inverter.

Noise immunity is largely a function of the width of the zone between the guaranteed input and output levels. In the previously given example of TTL levels, the minimum guaranteed output level for H is 2.4 V and the minimum input level which is guaranteed to be interpreted as H is 2.0 V. The *noise margin* is 0.4 V. If noise is superimposed on an H level signal, then if the amplitude of the noise is not more than 0.4 V, it is guaranteed to be interpreted correctly.

2.14 HAZARDS

Hazards are circuit malfunctions due to improperly balanced delays on converging logic paths. Consider the circuit in Figure 2.60 and the timing diagram derived with the consideration of gates with delays (delays are specified in parentheses in nanoseconds).

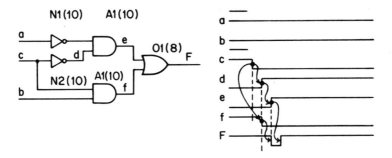

Figure 2.60   Response of a circuit in the presence of propagation delays. Arrows indicate causes of transitions. The circuit implements the function $F = a'c' + bc$.

The value of F is 1 for inputs 0,1,1 and 0,1,0. The outputs should remain unchanged during the transition 1 to 0 on c if $a=0$ and $b=1$. This does not happen for the delay magnitude shown: for a brief period of time the output goes to 0 (a "spike"). This malfunction is clearly due to the additional delay on the input path of A1 introduced by the two inverters N1, N2. Note the following:

1. No intermediate transition occurs during the opposite transition on c (0 to 1).
2. Hazards may or may not be critical: if the circuit in question controls a traffic light, then the brief spike is irrelevant; the light will theoretically be turned OFF for a few nanoseconds, a length

of time to which the light bulb cannot react. The hazard will thus be ignored by the complete system. If the circuit controls the pulsing signal to the counter in the buzzer controller from the beginning of this chapter, it will generate unwanted pulses which may cause the counter to produce incorrect counts; and the buzzer will not function as desired. It will be seen later that hazards are, in general, much more dangerous in sequential than in combinational circuits.

3. The circuit in Figure 2.61 is the implementation of the illustrated Karnaugh map and uses the two prime implicants denoted A and B:

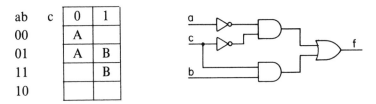

ab	c	0	1
00		A	
01		A	B
11			B
10			

Figure 2.61   Karnaugh map with essential PIs A, B and the corresponding circuit.

The transition which causes the hazard is between the two PIs as shown in the table. This suggests how the hazard could be removed by adding an extra AND gate "connecting" the two PIs: $a'b$. This addition does not change the truth table (the resulting circuit in Figure 2.62 implements the same truth table) but removes the hazard. This is because during the transition the $a'b$ gate remains ON and the output of the OR gate thus remains ON. On the other hand, this additional gate adds to the complexity and cost of the circuit.

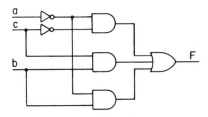

Figure 2.62   The same function with the hazard removed.

Another way of eliminating a hazard is by making sure that all delays are properly matched, possibly by adding artificial delays into certain logic paths. Still another solution is to prevent outputs of the device to respond to transient values by synchronizing outputs with properly timed clock signals. This generally converts the switching circuit into a sequential one.

A corollary of this discussion is that a hazard is not a property of a truth table but of its *implementation*. The truth table above can be implemented by a circuit with a hazard or a hazard-free circuit. Note also that the presence of the hazard is not a necessary consequence of minimization. If the PIs are not adjacent (loosely speaking), there will be no hazard in the minimized circuit. On the other hand, if they are and the number of gates is minimized, there may be a hazard.

4. Hazards of the type described above are called *static hazards*. They occur during transitions which should not cause a change in the value of output. *Dynamic* hazards occur when a change in the output is expected but instead of a single change there is a series of several transitions before the output settles down to the correct value. For more examples see the Workbook.

2.15 FAULTS AND THEIR DETECTION

Faults are physical causes of incorrect behavior of a digital system. The malfunction is either on the *logical* level (the logic function of the faulty circuit is not what it should be) or *parametric* (a physical parameter such as speed, power requirements, etc. are not as specified). A fault in the sense understood in this section is not due to designer's error although its nature is often such that it can be eliminated with a modification in design.

Another classification of faults is by their stability; faults are *permanent* if they are permanently present from the moment of their appearance and are *intermittent* if they appear or disappear depending on the physical environment, most often temperature.

Faults can be caused by a number of factors: improperly made connections, connections which become loose because of mechanical vibrations or temperature variations, effects of humidity or dirt, faulty IC components (this is generally the least likely cause of fault), etc.

Faults can appear at any time during manufacture, after delivery, or during operation. More important circuits must be tested frequently during operation, and most circuits are tested several times at various stages of production. Testing accounts for a growing proportion of the total cost of digital circuits and is becoming a critical task because of the growing complexity of systems. The most complicated circuits and even some components are designed with special circuits added just to allow or simplify testing. Theory of testing is an increasingly important part of the theory of digital systems.

The problems of faults and testing will be demonstrated for the case of a subclass of the general type of faults: "permanent logic faults of line-stuck-at logical value type in acyclic circuits (such as AND-OR circuits of the type discussed previously) with no redundancy." Some of these characterizations will be explained later.

Any line (connection) in a circuit can get stuck at a constant logic value and no variations of level on its input will be able to affect the value on its output end: an unwanted connection to the ground will cause the line in a TTL circuit to always behave as L. A loose connection or the absence of a connection to the rest of the circuit or an unwanted connection to power will cause the line to get stuck at H. Or the gate itself may be faulty. These are to some extent idealized situations. It is quite possible that a loose connection will instead become the source of noise and intermittent behavior or that an unwanted connection will destroy a part of the circuit. We are, however, going to ignore such physical possibilities (which are, unfortunately, in reality at least as common as our idealized faults) so that we can develop a systematic approach to the testing of a class of faults. This category of faults represents an idealized model of actual faults.

Example: Consider a two-input AND gate whose output is stuck-at-0 (s-a-0) (Figure 2.63).

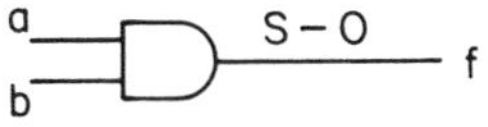

Figure 2.63 An AND gate whose output is stuck at zero.

We do not care what the reason of the fault is. We want to know if we can apply a certain combination of inputs and check, by examining the ouput of the circuit, whether the fault is present or not. In order to construct such a combination of inputs (if there is any), we can proceed as follows:

If the output is not stuck-at-0 we can make it 1 by $(a,b)=(1,1)$. If we apply this combination to a *faulty* gate stuck-at-0, the output will stay at 0. We will observe a discrepancy between the expected and the the real output. This reasoning indicates that when we want to demonstrate the presence of a certain fault, we have to find a combination of inputs which will cause the faulty circuit to produce the incorrect output.

Note that we are interested in finding the solution to the relatively simple problem of checking whether a fault is present or not. This is called *fault detection*. The problem of finding exactly which line is the cause of the problem (*fault identification*) is much more difficult and often impossible. Even fault detection is impossible in some types of circuits as will be seen later.

Assume now that our AND gate has an input line s-a-0. In other words the gate "perceives" the value of a to be always 0, no matter what is the value on the input end of this line. If we want to find the presence of this type of fault, we have to apply $a=1$. If $b=1$, then the output should be 1 (but will be 0 because of the fault). If $b=0$, the output should be 0 and so by applying $(a,b)=(1,0)$ we will get the correct output even if the fault is present. This means that input $(1,0)$ is useless for the determination of the presence of this specific fault. Only combination $(1,1)$ will allow us to detect that a is s-a-0. Note that the test pattern is exactly the same for b s-a-0. This means that we can detect the presence of a-0 or b-0 but when we detect the fault we cannot identify it; we cannot decide whether line a or line b (or both) is the cause of the malfunction.

We can now state our problem more accurately: we have a circuit on which only inputs and outputs are accessible. We want to find a set of test patterns (a test set) such that any possible fault in the circuit will be detected as a discrepancy between the expected and measured logical value, by at least one test pattern from the set.

For a more complicated circuit with more inputs, the test set could be very large. An obvious restriction that should thus be placed on the test set is that it should be minimal. It should contain as few test patterns as possible and yet allow the detection of all faults. It is possible that even then the test set will be too large and we will have to restrict our attention to a subset of all possible faults. We can then identify the more critical parts of the circuit and enumerate all faults of interest and then find the minimal test set for only these faults. In this case a satisfactory result of the test gives only a partial answer to the problem: the circuit may be faulty even if the results of the partial test show correct function of the subsystem.

There are a number of ways of finding test sets for a given circuit. The method used in the above example of the AND gate is called *path sensitization* because it is based on the finding of the logical path sensitive to the fault. The following example shows the use of this method in a more complicated situation and demonstrates that the problem of test set generation is quite similar to the problem of finding the minimal number of gates implementing a given logical function.

Example: Consider the function $f=ab+a$ (*fmc* implemented as in Figure 2.64.

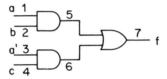

Figure 2.64   An implementation of $f=ab+a\,'c$.

Assume that line 5 is s-a-0. In order to detect this we have to apply inputs which should cause 5 to go to 1. Such a combination is $(a,b)=(1,1)$. Since we assume that we can only observe line 7, we have to "neutralize" line 6: if we allowed 6 to go to 1 the output of the circuit would be 1 no matter what is on line 5. We thus have to choose inputs so that the value on line 5 is 0. Since a must be 1 by our previous reasoning about line 5, $a\,'$ is 0 and so it does not matter what is on c. We thus have two patterns which will detect the 5-0 fault: $(1,1,0)$ and $(1,1,1)$. It may turn out that one of the two equivalent test patterns is more advantageous since it allows us to detect another fault.

Note that we are assuming that only one line is stuck at any time. This appears to be a reasonable assumption since the probability of two independent lines getting stuck at "the same time" is very small: the fault on one line can be repaired in a short time and so the probability of the two occurring together is essentially the product of the two probabilities—a very small number. Unfortunately the essential assumption in this reasoning is often wrong in practice: two physically close lines are often affected together since they may both be overheated or shorted, etc. Yet the method has some validity and provides a systematic approach to a simplified problem instead of a computationally unusable approach to the more general problem. The number of assumptions made suggests, however, that the problem is very complex.

The table in Figure 2.65 summarizes information on test detection patterns for the last circuit for various stuck-at faults which form a subset of the complete set of possible faults. We restrict our attention to lines 1, 2, 5. An X entry in the table indicates that the input combination which labels that row detects the fault which labels the column.

abc	1-0	1-1	2-0	2-1	5-0	5-1
000						
001						
010		X				X
011						
100				X		X
101				X		X
110	X		X		X	
111	X		X		X	

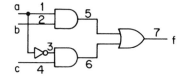

Figure 2.65   Test detection patterns for the circuit in Figure 2.64.

Note that certain test patterns are *essential*: there is only one pattern (0,1,0) which allows detection of 11. Essential patterns must be included in any test set. All the five combinations which can be used in detection (lines with an X) do not have to be included. Our objective is to cover each fault (column) by at least one test pattern (row) and not to try all possible detecting combinations. To minimize the cost, we want to minimize the size of the test set. In our case any of the following test sets will do, and they are all minimal: removing any one combination from a particular set will mean that we will not be able to detect at least one of the listed faults.

010, 100, 110   or
010, 101, 110   or
010, 100, 111   or
010, 101, 111

Note that the implementation of the same formula in Figure 2.66 (with an inverter) has a different fault table and in general a different test set. This shows that test sets are associated with circuits and not with functions.

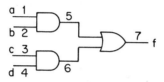

Figure 2.66   A different implementation of $f=ab+a'c$.

Consider now Figure 2.67.

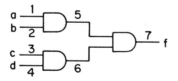

Figure 2.67   Implementation of $f=(ab)(cd)$.

To detect 5 s-a-0, we have to apply $(a,b,c,d)=(1,1,1,1)$. The same combination detects 6 s-a-0. This means that we cannot locate the fault as being caused by line 5 or 6 if we only have access to a,b,c,d and f. If it is important to be able to identify the fault, we have to make lines 5 and 6 accessible (Figure 2.68). This modification makes no difference to the logic but represents an additional requirement on circuit implementation which may be very difficult to accommodate.

The PC board is usually quite crowded, and the routing of connections very complex. After all, connections are made usually in one layer on each side of the board and must not cross one another. The addition of an extra component to a circuit can thus present a very undesirable modification.

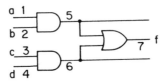

Figure 2.68   An implementation of $f=(ab)(cd)$ with accessible internal connections.

Consider the circuit in Figure 2.69 a which implements the function $f=ab+ab=ab$ and is logically equivalent to a single AND gate.

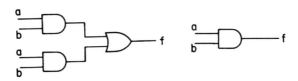

Figure 2.69   (a) a circuit with redundant path, (b) an equivalent circuit.

Since $A2$ duplicates $A1$, the circuit is *redundant*. If $A1$'s output gets stuck at 0 there is no way of even detecting it from the value of f since $A2$ takes over its function. In general redundant circuits contain fault possibilities which cannot be tested unless special precautions are taken, such as an extra access to certain parts of the circuit or an extra fault-detecting circuit. For more examples see the Workbook.

2.16   RELIABLE DESIGN

Reliability of a circuit can be increased in a number of ways which can generally be classified as either improving the reliability of the physical parameters of the circuit or improving reliability by a modification of the logical structure of the circuit. In the first category are possibilities such as better circuit layout, improved cooling to decrease temperatures, use of better materials and components, etc. Our concern in this section is with the second category of approaches: the modification of the structure of the circuit.

Consider the RED light part of the alarm system discussed previously. The fact that the RED light is OFF does not necessarily mean that there is no overheating. It could also mean that the bulb is burned out, that the controller is not working, that the sensors malfunction, that communication between sensors and controller is faulty, etc. The importance of the system is such that any reasonable precaution should be taken to guarantee that it works properly. The reliability of individual parts of the system would have to be evaluated, and those which do not seem to have sufficient safety margins redesigned. Assume that the RED light controller turns out to be the weak point of the system. One way of improving its reliability is by triplicating the basic simple controller and adding a "majority vote" circuit (Figure 2.70).

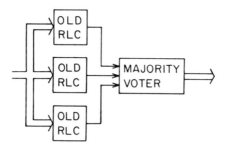

Figure 2.70   Reliability achieved by triplication and majority vote.

The majority vote circuit reads outputs of the three simple controllers and outputs the majority value: for the output combination $(0,1,1)$ the majority vote will be 1, for $(0,1,0)$ it will be 0, for $(1,1,1)$ it will be 1, etc. Note the following:

1. The implied assumption is that if there is a failure it occurs in only one simple controller. Or, more accurately, we assume that if a controller fails, it can be repaired before another one fails. This may require adding another circuit which, when a failure

occurs (and is recognized by a lack of consensus of outputs) identifies which output disagrees with the majority, etc.

2. A new potential source of failures has been added by the majority voter. If *this* circuit fails, the whole system fails even if the three simple controllers work correctly! To avoid this, the majority voter must be at least as reliable as the three simple controllers combined.

3. It is a surprising fact that although the reliability of a triplicated circuit is initially higher than that of a single circuit, it drops faster with time and aging of components and connections than the reliability of a single controller. The diagram in Figure 2.71 shows the probability of "survival" to time t for both the triplicated and non-redundant systems. For $t < T$ the reliability of a TMR (Triplicate Module Redundancy) system is better, for $t > T$ it is worse than the reliability of the simple system.

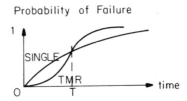

Probability of Failure

Figure 2.71   Probability of survival as a function of time. It is derived on the basis of the assumption that the probability of individual controller failure is $1-e^{**}(lambda*t)$ where lambda is the Mean Time Between Failures (MTBF). TMR—triplicated module.

In other words after a certain amount of time, a triplicated system becomes *less* reliable than a simple one. This is because after a certain period the probability of a failure of two out of three components becomes higher than the probability of a failure of a single component. This time limit can be easily calculated as a function of the reliability of individual modules, and steps can be taken to guarantee that the system is highly reliable as long as necessary.

4. Increased reliability generally requires more complicated circuits and more components, often at higher price. It also means increased space requirements which may be a critical consideration in satellites and airplanes.

5. The example of triplication of critical components shows one possible approach to the design of *fault-tolerant* systems. There are a number of variations on the basic requirements and solutions: circuits may be designed to identify and switch OFF the apparently faulty component. There may be a stand-by module to switch automatically in and replace a faulty one — *self-repairing* systems. The system may be designed so that when it fails, it produces the "conservative" outputs which will demand increased attention of the operator: the RED light controller could be designed to turn the RED light ON if it is "in doubt," rather than turn it OFF. Such a circuit is called *fail-safe*. If it fails, it produces the safer output.

REFERENCES

A large number of texts deal with the topics presented in this chapter. The same texts also deal with sequential circuits. The coverage is often more detailed than given here. Of the more recent ones, the books by Williams and Sandige give an excellent and very readable introduction for anybody who is interested in the practical aspects of design, how the various technologies work and compare, etc. The book does not require a profound knowledge of electronics. The book by Blakeslee is similarly oriented but does not go into so many implementation details. A large number of solved problems are collected in the books by Tokheim and Zissos. For a more theoretical point of view Kohavi is a popular textbook. The text by Friedman concisely covers the basics and treats in some detail more specialized topics such as hazards, physical design considerations, etc., from a theoretical point of view. The topic of faults and testing is covered in some detail in Breuer–Friedman. It is also investigated in the October 1979 issue of *Computer Magazine* dedicated to this subject.

There are a number of periodicals which regularly publish papers on subjects related to this chapter. The reader interested in the recent technological and theoretical advances should read: *IEEE Transactions on Computers, Computer* (IEEE), *Digital Design, Computer Design, Electronics*, EDN, to mention a few. Some of the regular conferences devoted at least partially to related topics are COMPCON, NCC (National Computer Conference), and the Annual International Symposium On Fault Tolerant Computing.

PROBLEMS

1. What is the decimal equivalent of
   a. 101, 1101, 1001, 11, 1111 in base 2 (binary)
   b. 12, 7, 17, 15, 77, 117 in base 8 (octal)

2. Prove the identities of Boolean algebra.

3. Determine whether the following are true identities. Write the dual rules.
   a. $ab+a=a$
   b. $abc+a'bc=bc$
   c. $(a+b)c+a=a+b$

4. Construct the truth tables for
   a. $ab+c$
   b. $ab'+ac$
   c. $(a+b')(a+c)$

5. Derive the product of sums (sum of products) forms for functions in Problem 4.

6. Derive the formula for the following functions:
   a. Output is 1 iff the input combination a,b,c is the binary equivalent of decimal 1 or 4.
   b. An octal 7-segment display uses LED (Light Emitting Diode) bars arranged as shown in Figure 2.72 to display octal digits 0–7.

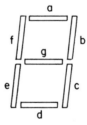

Figure 2.72   A 7-segment display element.

The device has three inputs u,v,x whose values represent binary equivalents of octal digits. Individual bars are driven by individual circuits with inputs u,v,x. Derive the formulas for the driving circuits.

7. Draw circuit diagrams for functions from previous problems.

8. Draw circuit diagrams for functions from previous problems using only the 74-series ICs listed in the text.

9. Derive the functions representing the following circuits:

a. Figure 2.73.

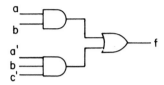

Figure 2.73   Problem 9a.

b. Figure 2.74.

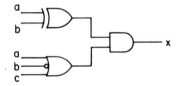

Figure 2.74   Problem 9b.

c. Figure 2.75.

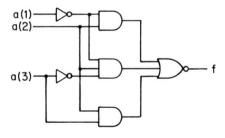

Figure 2.75   Problem 9c.

10. Draw circuits derived in Problem 5 using only NAND gates (NOR gates).

11. Draw Karnaugh maps for functions from previous problems. Simplify the functions using the maps.

12. Formulate the KM algorithm for the product of sums form. Compare minimized expressions from Problem 11 with those obtained using the modified algorithm.

13. The commercially available 7-segment display has four inputs u, v, x, y representing the codes of decimal digits 0-9 in binary. Four input variables can represent any number from 0 to 15 decimal. Assuming that only values up to 9 can appear on the input, use the don't care entries to redesign the decoders which drive individual segments. Draw the patterns displayed by your decoder for illegal inputs corresponding to inputs 10 to 15. Redesign the decoder if any two different inputs generate identical outputs.

14. Use both methods of design with multiplexers to implement the following functions:
  a. $f = ab \text{XOR} a'b'$
  b. $g = (abc' + a')b'$
  c. $k = f + g$ (f and g are as defined above)

15. Use the folding method and a tree to implement
  a. $f = (ab + c'd')(ac + ef)(a'd + bf')(bd' + af)$ using 1-of-4 and 1-of-16 multiplexers
  b. $f = (abcd + a'c')(a'c + bd')$ using 1-of-4 multiplexers

16. Implement the following functions using a PLA with three inputs, six terms and two outputs.
  a. $f = ab + cd, g = a'b + ac'$
  b. $f = abc + a'b' + ab'c + ac', g = abc' + a'b' + b'c'$
  c. $f = ab + abc' + bc + b'c', g = abc + b'c + bc'$

17. Assume that an 8×4-bit ROM has the following contents:

address	contents
0	0101
1	1101
2	0001
3	1111
4	0000
5	1000
6	0101
7	1100

Show the sequence of outputs corresponding to the following sequence of address codes: 011,100,000,010,111,101.

18. Simulate manually the response of the circuit in Figure 2.76 to the given input waveforms.

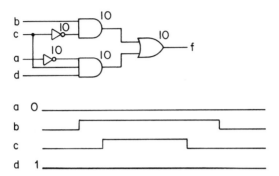

Figure 2.76 Problem 17.

19. Find which of the following functions could produce hazards when minimized. Identify the hazards and show how they can be eliminated.
a. $a'b'+bc'$
b. $b'c'+a'b$
c. $a'c'd+acd$
d. $a'b'+ab'c'$

20. Derive the fault table, find essential test patterns and minimal test sets for the following circuits:

a. Figure 2.77

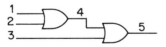

Figure 2.77 Problem 19a.

b. Figure 2.78

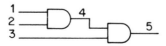

Figure 2.78 Problem 19b.

c. Figure 2.79

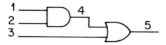

Figure 2.79   Problem 19c.

d. $f=ab+c'$ implemented with and without an inverter

21. Consider a TMR system. Design
    a. an implementation of the majority voter
    b. a circuit which outputs 1 iff the module's output does not agree with the majority output.

22. Design switching circuits necessary to allow a TMR circuit to logically/physically disconnect a faulty module and switch in a replacement.

Chapter 3

COMPUTER SIMULATION OF HARDWARE

3.1 INTRODUCTION

Every product has to be tested before its full-scale production can begin. The first phase of testing is functional testing: does the product perform according to specifications?

There are two ways in which functional testing can be performed:

1. Build and test a prototype, i.e., a more or less exact copy of the product with identical functions. In the case of digital systems the prototype would be built from electronic components connected by wires. It would not be packaged in a neat box with labels, etc., but would be mounted on a "breadboard"—a working area arranged for easy access to components, ease of connection and modification.

2. Design a model of the product and test it. This model would not use the same physical structure and components as the intended product but would *simulate* the product's functions in an indirect way, usually based on a physico-mathematical description. Typically it would be a computer program; in the past the model would often be implemented on an analog computer. In our case the model of a complex digital circuit will not be made from ICs but will instead be a structural representation of the circuit. The function of the simulator will be similar to that of a person given a circuit diagram and asked to follow its function with certain starting conditions, inputs, and gate parameters.

The first method, or prototype testing, must always be used in testing, sooner or later. It must eventually be verified that the physical components when assembled according to specifications actually perform as expected. It has to be realized, however, that this approach has certain limitations: building a prototype is time-consuming and expensive for all products of any complexity. In addition testing a prototype amounts to testing just one combination of components and environment out of a practically infinite number of possibilities: individual components have different parameters (e.g., the delays of all 7400 NAND gates are not identical), so do their interconnections, the rate of change of these parameters with aging and temperature is not identical, the circuits will not be all assembled under identical conditions, etc. The consequence of this is that the usual statistical fluctuations may cause a certain number of unpredictable variations in function in a larger or smaller proportion of seemingly identical copies of the prototype. The testing procedure will, of course, be designed to minimize these variations; a number of prototypes may be built and tested in all predictable environments and functional conditions, but this will further increase the cost of testing.

Given the drawbacks of prototype testing, as much of the testing process as possible should be implemented in a way which allows easy modification of the overall design, component parameters, and environment—both physical and functional—quickly and inexpensively. This is the role of *testing through simulation* which has the following positive and negative features:

1. Simulation is faster, cheaper and more flexible if suitable programming tools are available. It allows repetitive testing with various sets of "component" parameters and topologies, that is, different arrangement of circuit structure. Various combinations can thus be tested, as if several prototypes were built and tested.

2. Simulation is necessarily a simplification of reality since an absolutely accurate description of even a simple physical component is not possible and the more accurate the description gets, the more complicated it is and the more computer resources of memory and time it requires. The model must be realistic, giving reasonably accurate insights into the function of the device, but it cannot be accepted as fully representative. It should be pointed out that testing can be and usually is performed at several levels of detail: at the level of electrical components such

as transistors, resistors, etc., at the logic level of gates, etc., at the level of transfer of information between more complex components, and at the high level of mutually connected systems. Each of these levels is usually simulated with different tools designed specifically for that purpose.

Taking into account the advantages and disadvantages of both methods, one must conclude that the best approach from the point of view of speed of testing, its cost, and accuracy is to use simulation in the first phase, to verify the functional soundness of the design, remove deficiencies, polish the design to the degree where no further information can be gained from continued simulation, and then complete testing on a prototype.

The approach used in industry, particularly in digital design, is usually a further refinement of the process described above: the transition from simulation to prototype is not abrupt but continuous. The initial testing is on a pure model, usually a computer simulator. When the basic design approach is verified, the simulator begins to make a transition into a prototype: some parts of the model are replaced by physical components, subsystems of the prototype are built to replace subsystems of the program, testing and modifications continue until eventually the whole simulation model is replaced by a prototype. A number of "development systems" specifically designed for this approach to testing are commercially available. They are manufactured by producers of integrated circuits and are typically tailored for the ICs of the specific manufacturer to increase the attractiveness of their products. Their complexity and cost are comparable to those of more sophisticated microcomputer systems.

The above justification of simulation describes the "real world" uses for simulation of digital circuits. In addition to these there is a pedagogical justification of simulation: with computer simulation any systems, limited only by the capacity of the computer, can be "built" and observed in action. This is not possible in the laboratory because too many components of many types would be required, too much time would be needed to set up the circuits, and some of the functions internal to the components could not be observed. This last problem is quite critical since the more complex ICs have many of their basic functions hidden and inaccessible from the outside. To understand the function and to experiment with design in the educational environment, therefore, requires the availability of simulation. It is from this point of view that the rest of this chapter deals with simulation.

Computer simulation can be performed with more or less difficulty depending on the available programming language. We can distinguish three categories of languages:

1. General purpose programming languages such as Pascal, ALGOL, FORTRAN, etc. These languages make hardware simulation quite complicated. Trying to simulate each new circuit via a new program is very unattractive.
2. General purpose simulation languages. These are languages which simplify general purpose simulation. They include SIMULA—which is, however, a true general purpose language such as Pascal with extra features to simplify simulation, SIMSCRIPT, SIMONE, and others. Use of these languages makes simulation of hardware somewhat easier, but the process is still quite difficult and inefficient.
3. Special purpose simulation languages designed for the simulation of hardware such as DDL, CDL, AHPL, and others (for references see end of this chapter). Simulation with these languages is quite easy since the process consists of generation of a formal description of the simulated circuit rather than writing a program and its "execution," usually interactively from a computer terminal. The problems associated with most of these languages are their cost, limited availability, and sometimes relative obscurity, to a beginner since most of these languages are designed for specialists.

The rest of this chapter illustrates simulation via the use of a programming language HARD (HARDware description language) for the simulation of combinational circuits. This application of HARD shows only a small part of the capabilities of the language, and more examples are given later on at appropriate places in the text. The examples given below are intended to convey a general picture of simulation and do not necessarily reflect fully the exact rules of HARD. A complete specification of the language is given in the Reference Manual of the language available from the author.

3.2 SIMULATION OF COMBINATIONAL CIRCUITS

When we want to experiment with a circuit, first we have to draw the circuit diagram and build the circuit, and second we have to apply desired combinations of inputs and examine the resulting outputs.

The procedure is essentially the same for simulation. First we have to draw the diagram, produce a formal description of the circuit, and, finally, we have to present input values via a computer terminal and obtain the requested outputs.

The use of HARD is perhaps best understood through examples. The following examples concentrate on the description and simulation aspect and ignore the mechanics of the use of a specific computer system such as signing-on and off, etc. These other actions vary from one computer system to another.

3.2.1 Circuit Description Phase

Example 3.1: Consider the circuit in Figure 3.1.

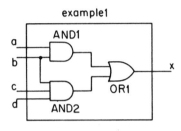

example1

Figure 3.1   Circuit example1.

Its HARD description is

    CIRCUIT: Example1
    PARTS: INPUT: a,b,c,d
                 OUTPUT: x
                 AND: and1(2), and2(3)
                 OR: or1(2)
    CONNECT: a TO: and1
                 b TO: and1, and2
                 c TO: and2
                 d TO: and2
                 and1 TO: or1
                 and2 TO: or1
                 or1 TO: x
    END.

The description is practically self-explanatory, particularly when accompanied by the circuit diagram. It can be seen that it consists of three basic parts. The whole description is terminated by END.

The CIRCUIT line assigns the circuit a name (example1). The user can choose any name. It will be seen later that the description in effect defines a type of module with the assigned name, of which any number of copies can be used as parts of another circuit if needed. In other words, the description does not create the equivalent of, for example, one 7402 chip but is instead the equivalent of, for example, the 7402 chip specification.

The PARTS section lists all the components of the circuit, including circuits' inputs and outputs, their names, and parameters:

AND: and1

specifies that and1 is the name of an AND gate. The name and1 was chosen arbitrarily.

OR: or1

similarly declares or1 to be the name of an OR gate.

Numbers in brackets following names of gates in the PARTS part specify the number of inputs of each gate: and1 has two inputs, and2 has three inputs, or1 has two inputs.

The CONNECT part specifies which outputs are connected to which components. For example,

a TO: and1

means "connect the output of a to the input of and1."

Example 3.2: Consider the more complicated circuit in Figure 3.2.

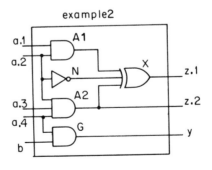

Figure 3.2   Circuit example2.

Its description is

        CIRCUIT: example2 !note that no blank spaces
                   are allowed inside
                   the "identifier" example2!
        PARTS: INPUT: $a(4),b$
                   OUTPUT: $z(2),y$
                   AND: $a1(2),a2(3)$
                   NAND: $g(2)$
                   NOT: n
                   XOR: $x(3)$
        CONNECT: $a.1$ TO: $a1$
                   $a.2$ TO: $a1,n,a2$
                   $a.3$ TO: $a2$
                   $a.4$ TO: $a2,g$
                   b TO: g
                   $a1$ TO: x
                   $a2$ TO: $x,z.2$
                   n TO: x
                   x TO: $z.1$
                   g TO: y
        END.

A few comments on this description follow:

1. Although names are arbitrary, they must be unique; two different components in the circuit must not have the same name. A name must begin with a letter, but the rest may include digits: and1 is legal but 1and is not.
2. All components must be listed in the PARTS section.
3. All connections must be specified. Connection of one output to several inputs may be specified on one line. For example

$$a2 \text{ TO: } x.3,z.2$$

The same holds for outputs.
4. All text enclosed between exclamation marks (!) is treated as a documenting comment and has no effect on the circuit description.
5. a(4) means that there are four input lines. They are referred to as $a.1$, $a.2$, $a.3$, $a.4$. This notation is called the "dot notation."

Example 3.3: Circuit in Figure 3.3.

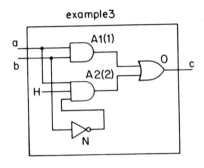

Figure 3.3   Circuit example3.

The description is

CIRCUIT:	example3
PARTS:	INPUT: a,b
	OUTPUT: c
	AND: $a1(2),a2(3)$
	OR: $o(2)$
	NOT: n
DELAY:	$a1(1),a2(2)$
CONNECT:	a TO: $a1,a2$
	b TO: $a1$,n
	H TO: $a2$
	$a1$ TO: o
	$a2$ TO: o
	n TO: $a2$
	o TO: c
END.	

Several comments are in place:

1. DELAY: $a1(1),a2(2)$ means that gate a1 has a delay of one time unit and $a2$ a delay of two time units. This delay is constant, but a variable delay can also be prescribed.
2. Delay 0 is the default; it is assumed when not specified otherwise.
3. H is high and L is low—a constant value connected to the wire. This makes it possible for the user to use levels rather than Boolean values and allows experimentation with positive and negative logic; basic gates are all assumed to be based on positive logic.

The three examples above illustrate how to describe a combinational circuit given its circuit diagram. The description is entered into a file via a terminal and constitutes the source of the simulation. A special program which constitutes the first part of the simulator translates ("compiles") the source file into an internal representation of the circuit which contains only the information essential for the simulation proper.

The second part of the simulator is the simulator proper. This program takes the internal representation generated from the source file by the compiler part and performs the simulation under the interactive control of the user from a terminal. An example of this process is given in the following section.

3.2.2 Simulation Run

To run a simulation of a circuit whose description is stored in a file the user specifies the file and then identifies the requirements concerning the input and output. The simulation then takes place as described below in an example.

Consider again circuit example3 described in the previous section. The communication between the simulator and the user might look like this:

```
ENTER FILE NAME: example3.id
ENTER NAMES OF LINES TO BE DISPLAYED: c,n
ENTER DESIRED LENGTH OF SIMULATION: 10
ENTER INPUT VALUES a,b AND INPUT TIME:
l,h,0
h,h,4
end
VALUES ARE (UNSPECIFIED INITIAL
VALUES ASSUMED 0):
```

TIME	C
0	L
1	L
2	H
3	H
4	H
5	H
6	H
7	H
8	H
9	H
10	H

DO YOU WANT ANOTHER RUN (YES, NO): no

3.2.3 Modularity of Simulation

The following example shows how complicated circuits of a tree-like structure can be built from circuits described previously:

Example 3.4 (Figure 3.4): Consider a system using subsystems from example 3.1 (Figure 3.1)

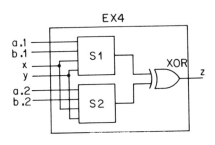

Figure 3.4   Circuit EX4.

Its description is

CIRCUIT:	ex4
PARTS:	INPUT: $a(2),b(2),x,y$
	OUTPUT: z
	XOR: xor(2)
	EXAMPLE1: $s1,s2$
CIRCUIT:	$s1.x$ TO: xor
	$s2.x$ TO: xor
	xor TO: z
	$a.1$ TO: $s1.a.1$!s1's a's first input!
	$a.2$ TO: $s2.a.1$
	$b.1$ TO: $s1.a.2$
	$b.2$ TO: $s2.a.2$
	x TO: $s1.a.3,s2.a.3$
	y TO: $s1.a.4,s2.a.4$
END.	

The structure of the circuit described above can be described by a two-level tree (Figure 3.5). Trees can be built to any level within the constraints of the computer. Note that there must always be an overall description such as ex4 above which establishes the connections at the highest level, the root of the tree.

Figure 3.5   A hierarchical description of the structure of circuit EX4.

During simulation the user has to give names of all the files necessary to reconstruct the whole circuit.

3.3 CONCLUDING REMARKS

This chapter presented an overview of simulation illustrated by a
brief description of the hardware simulation language HARD and its
uses. The description level demonstrated was the "gate level." We
will see later that other levels of description are possible.

The language is quite simple to use and can best be learned by its
use. The problems listed at the end of this chapter show the types of
situations in which simulation of combinational circuits may be useful.
The problems are intended to provide only this indication. Other problems can be invented by the reader or taken from problems given for
manual solution in the previous chapters.

REFERENCES

There are a number of publications on simulation in general and simulation
of digital systems in particular. In this second category the recommended
references are Breuer(1975) which is an introduction to the simulation of
digital systems and the more recent tutorial edited by vanCleemput (1979).
Current material is available in proceedings of specialized meetings, such as
the Design Automation Conference and the International Symposium on
Computer Hardware Description Languages and their Applications.

PROBLEMS

Use HARD to simulate the following circuits:

1. Zero delay
   a. $x=ab+ac$
   b. $x=((ab)'(ac)')'$
   c. $y=ab'+a'b$
   d. $y=((a+b)'+(a+b)')'$
   e. $z(1)=a(1)a(2)+a(3)$
      $z(2)=a(1)a(2)'$

2. Circuits from Problem 1 with
   a. constant non-zero delay
   b. constant non-zero delay variable from run to run
   c. variable random delay

   See the Reference Manual for description of specification of needed parameters. If you do not have access to HARD, you could invent a way of describing these parameters.

3. Consider circuits with hazards from Chapter 2. Use variable random delay to show the unreliable and inconsistent behavior of these circuits.

4. Consider circuits with stuck lines from Chapter 2. Check testing methods from Chapter 2 to design tests, and try your test sets.

5. Consider circuits designed for reliability from Chapter 2. Check under which conditions they perform reliably and when they fail.

6. Using external descriptions simulate
   a. $y = f1(x,y) + f2(x+y,x)$
      where $f1$ and $f2$ are copies of
      $f(a,b) = (a+b)(a'+b')$
   b. $z = (f(x,y) + g(xy,x))h(y,x)$
      where f is as above and
      $g(a,b) = (a\,\mathrm{XOR}\,b)$
      $h(a,b) = (a+b)'.a'$

7. Simulate circuits described by the following diagrams:

   a. Figure 3.6

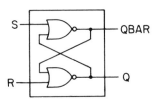

Figure 3.6   Problem 7a.

This and the following circuits have *feedbacks*, or lines joining inputs and outputs. Circuits of this type will be studied in detail in Chapter 4. Note the presence of delays.

b. Figure 3.7

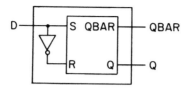

Figure 3.7   Problem 7b.

The box represents the circuit from part a.

Chapter 4

SEQUENTIAL CIRCUITS

4.1 DESCRIPTION OF SEQUENTIAL CIRCUITS

Consider the following black box which "recognizes" the input sequence 011: the device has one input and one output. They are both binary, values 0 and 1. The input is checked at the beginning of each second. When the last three inputs of the sequence of inputs form the series 011, the device outputs a 1; otherwise, the output is 0. It is assumed that when the device is initially turned ON, its initial state is ready to recognize the sequence 011. The following is an example of a possible input sequence and the corresponding outputs that would be produced:

$$1110101110010110110\ldots$$
$$0000000100000010010\ldots$$

Let us attempt to give a formal description of the observed function of the device: the response to a 0 is always 0. The response to a 1 is 1 iff (if and only if) it was preceded by 01. This behavior cannot be represented by a truth table since a truth table would have to have either 0 or 1 in its input=1 row and our circuit sometimes produces a 0 and sometimes a 1 output in response to a 1 input. We have to devise a new method of description. The best starting point is to try to explain the behavior of the device.

The explanation of the "ambiguity" of the response of the recognizer to a 1 input can be formulated as follows:

If the device observed input sequence ..01 it is in a different *state* from after reading, for example, ...0. The device thus has at least two *internal* states and makes transitions between them in response to the observed input sequence. If we know the *present state* of the black box and if we know its present input, we can immediately *predict* its output: if the present state corresponds to previous input sequence ...01 and the present input is 1, the output will be 1. If the box is in another state, then its output will be 0, whatever is the present input, etc. (Figure 4.1).

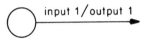

Figure 4.1   A partial description of the behavior of a 011 recognizer corresponding to previous input ...01.

If we know the present state and input, we can also predict what will be the *next state* of the circuit: if the present state corresponds to having previously read ...0 and the present input is 1, the next state of the black box will be that of having read ...01: the device will be ready to recognize 011 (Figure 4.2).

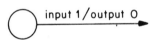

Figure 4.2   Another part of a description of the 011 recognizer. It corresponds to previous input ...0.

It is now clear that in order to describe fully a sequential device, we need only the following information:

1. The list of all possible internal states
2. The initial state
3. The response of the device to a given input, i.e.:
   a. next state when current state is given
   b. output

This information is complete in the sense that it allows us to predict correctly the behavior of the device if we know the inputs. (We will see later how this information can be used to construct the circuit which implements the function.)

The description of the behavior can have a number of forms. It could be described in words as follows:

1. If the circuit is in the initial state (call it, for example, A) and receives a 0, it goes to a new state (call it B). In state B it will remember having seen 0, the possible beginning of a 011 sequence. On input 1 the device remains unchanged, still awaiting the beginning of "its" sequence. The situation is thus the same as at the beginning; the device remains in the initial state ("makes transition" to state A).

2. State A has now been fully specified, but we have a new state that has to be described, state B. State B corresponds to having received ... 0. If the circuit is in state B and received a 1 input, it has just seen the beginning of sequence 011: it previously encountered a 0 input (since it is in state B) and now has received 1. It must go into a new state corresponding to having seen 01. Call it state C.

   On input 0 the circuit stays in state B; it remembers having just seen a 0, the possible beginning of 011. (The previous 0 loses any significance.)

3. We have fully described states A and B and have state C to describe. In state C the circuit remembers having seen ... 01.

   On input 0 the sequence becomes 010 which is not the desired sequence. On the other hand, the last 0 could be the beginning of 011. The device thus makes transition to state B which represents this information. On input 1 the circuit recognizes having just seen its input sequence 011. It outputs a 1 (all the previously listed combinations result in output 0) and goes into the initial state, awaiting a 0, the beginning of a new sequence.

At this point there are no states left undescribed and the *description* of the function of the box is complete. Note that this description is quite independent of the implementation of the device. It must be stressed that a sequential machine does not in general remember the previous input sequence bit by bit. It only "knows" in which state it is and that the previously encountered input sequence was such that it made it go into this state.

The device could be implemented, for example, by three men, each representing an internal state of the device. They could be hidden in the black box, and at any point in time exactly one of them would be receiving the input and controlling the output. The "state A" man would be the first in charge when the box is turned ON. When the man in control of the box receives an input, he will

1. Produce the output corresponding to the input and the state he represents
2. Tell the appropriate state-man to replace him in his position of control.

All actions will be performed in agreement with the above description.

A word description of the type given above is needed at the first stage of the design of a sequential circuit. It will be later transformed into one of the following more compact forms: the (next-) *state diagram* or the (next-) *state table.*

The state diagram is particularly useful for the understanding of the function of the device since it is graphic. The state table is well suited for design and for systematic recording because of its tabular nature. Note that all three methods are completely equivalent in that they all fully describe the function of the black box and one can be derived from the other. They only differ in their suitability for a particular use in the design process.

The *state diagram*, also called the *state graph*, is a graphic representation of the word description. States are represented by circles ("nodes") labeled by state names. They are connected by "edges" indicating transitions. Edges are "directed," an arrow indicating the direction of the transition, and labeled by input values which cause the transition and the corresponding output value. Inputs and outputs are separated by a slash (/). The state diagram of our device obtained from the previously given word description is given in Figure 4.3.

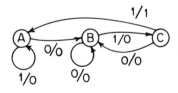

Figure 4.3   A complete state diagram of a 011 recognizer.

As an example of the interpretation of the diagram consider state B: on input 1 the circuit goes into state C and produces a 0; this is illustrated by the transition from node B labeled 1/0. On input 0 the circuit goes into state B and outputs a 0, indicated by the transition from node B labeled 0/0.

The *state table* is a systematic tabular representation of the state graph. Note that any graph, such as a road map, can be described in a similar way. Its rows are labeled by the names of present states, its columns by input combinations. Entries are next state symbols and outputs separated by a slash. In our case the state table is as in Figure 4.4.

present state\input	0	1
A	B/0	A/0
B	B/0	C/0
C	B/0	A/1

Figure 4.4   A state table for a 011 recognizer.

As an example of the interpretation of the state table consider the transition from the present state B and input 0: according to the word description and state graph, this condition should produce output 0 and transition to state B; the corresponding entry in the table is B/0 for next state/output. This information is given at the intersection of line B, present state, and column 0, present input, of the table. Note that transitions may be controlled by a timing signal and allowed to occur only at predetermined times rather than as an immediate response to input signals. The circuit may be defined and designed so that the response of its output to input signals is either immediate or delayed until the change of state. This somewhat fine but important distinction will be mostly ignored in the rest of this chapter since it will become clear that with a few restrictions all methods presented here apply to both situations.

There is a certain amount of non-uniformity of terminology concerning the representation of state diagrams. A state table such as in Figure 4.4 is sometimes called a *state map* since its form is similar to that of a Karnaugh map. The term "state table" is then used to represent a table similar to a truth table in which the left part of each row represents the present state and the right part, the next state. A table showing both next states and present outputs such as Figure 4.4

is sometimes called the state/output table or map. In this text the term state table will be used in the sense defined above and illustrated in Figure 4.4.

Example 4.1: Consider a *serial decimal adder*. This is a two-input, one-output device. Inputs and outputs are decimal digits 0 to 9. Inputs are digit by digit representations of the two operands (least significant digit first); output is the digit by digit representation of their sum. As an example the following addition:

$$272+686=958$$

is entered into the serial adder and the result output as follows; rightmost digits enter/leave first.

Input 1	2	7	2
Input 2	6	8	6
Output	9	5	8

The device described above is sequential: the output produced by the leftmost digits 2, 6, is 9 because of the carry from the addition of 7, 8 while the same rightmost digits (2 and 6 produce 8 because there is no carry at this point).

This device is called a serial adder because the two operands are entered digit by digit, individual digits in series.

The decimal serial adder has two states since the output depends on whether there is a carry from the previous addition or not. One state, denoted A, is the "no-carry" state; the other, denoted B, is the "carry" state, Figure 4.5.

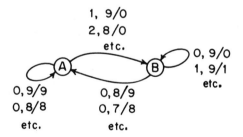

Figure 4.5 The state diagram of a serial decimal adder. Only a few of the many possible input/output combinations are indicated.

Example 4.2: Consider the *binary* serial adder. Its principle is the same as that of the decimal adder, only the base of the number system is different. The arithmetic rules will therefore have a different form. They can be summarized as shown in Figure 4.6.

op1	op2	sum	carry
0	0	0	0
0	1	1	0
1	0	1	0
1	1	0	1

Figure 4.6   Binary addition table.

The rule concerning the carry appears in the last line of the truth table. The implementation is basically the same as that of the decimal adder; there are two states, one for carry and one for no-carry. The only difference is in the combination of inputs and outputs (Figure 4.7).

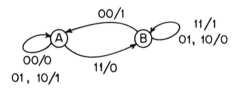

Figure 4.7   The state diagram of a binary serial adder.

The corresponding state table is shown in Figure 4.8.

state\op1 op2	00	01	11	10
A	A/0	A/1	B/0	A/1
B	A/1	B/0	B/1	B/0

Figure 4.8   A state table for the diagram in Figure 4.7.

Example 4.3: In a course on introductory programming students get frequent programming assignments. Each student must be up to date, and this requirement is supported by reminders sent to students who are behind with their hand-ins. A student who submitted two out of the last three programs is sent a reminder (R). A mild warning (M) is sent to those who submitted one out the the last three and a severe warning (S) to those who have not submitted any of the last three programs.

This task could be performed by a sequential machine, possibly "implemented" as a professor, or a computer program which reads a sequence of binary inputs in which 0 represents no program handed in and 1 represents a program handed in on time.

One way of describing this "machine" is by considering it as three independent machines producing the M, R, S notices and listing the critical sequences to be recognized. Consider, for example, the S machine which sends a severe warning when none of the last three programs was handed in on time. Its critical sequence is 000. This leads to the state graph for S shown in Figure 4.9.

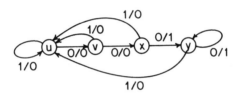

Figure 4.9   State diagram of the warning notice generator.

Output 1 means "send severe warning" output 0 means "no action." The corresponding state table is shown in Figure 4.10.

state	input	0	1
A		2/0	1/0
B		3/0	1/0
C		4/1	1/0
D		4/1	1/0

Figure 4.10   State table for Figure 4.9.

Note that the machine in Figure 4.11 performs the same function and is simpler, that is, has fewer internal states.

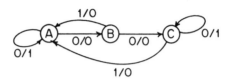

Figure 4.11   A simplified warning notice generator performing the same
function.

This simpler graph is equivalent to the previous one in that for the
same input sequence it will produce the same output sequence. In other words, the machine based on the first graph will be functionally indistinguishable from the one based on the second graph. The second
graph could be obtained directly by a more careful analysis of the
problem. Fortunately, there is no need to worry about obtaining the
most economical description the first time since there are simple ways
to minimize the number of internal states of a machine. The best approach is to formulate the description as naturally as possible and then
use the algorithm to obtain the minimal final machine. For a given
problem the final machine is minimal in the sense that there is no
machine with fewer internal states which performs the same function.

An internal state is, in fact, a state of the memory of the machine.
Our first machine could be implemented by one person instead of
three which remembers in which of the three states it currently is.
Sequential circuits, therefore, have an internal memory to remember
the present internal state or its code. In binary circuits memory elements are binary, and each of them stores a 0 or a 1. These elementary memory elements are called *flip-flops* and will be described in the
next section. At this point we need only to realize that states have to
be coded in binary so that they can be remembered; internal state
codes must be assigned to state symbols. Our choice of symbols was
completely arbitrary, and in this sense any *state assignment* will do. In
the last example four different states require four different codes and
therefore at least two binary elements. We could assign

$$A-00 \quad B-01 \quad C-10 \quad D-11$$
or
$$A-11 \quad B-00 \quad C-01 \quad D-10$$

etc.

Substituting assigned codes for state symbols transforms the state table into a *transition table*. The difference between the two types of tables is that a state table uses arbitrary symbols to designate states while the transition table uses assigned codes and therefore implies something about the implementation. In our case, the transition table for the first state assignment is shown in Figure 4.12.

state\ input	0	1
00	01/0	00/0
01	10/0	00/0
10	11/1	00/0
11	11/1	00/0

Figure 4.12   The transition table of the circuit from Figure 4.10.

We will see later that the state assignment may be critical for the complexity and even the proper function of the circuit in certain situations.

Finally, note that the total number of different binary codewords using n variables is 2**n. This means that with n flip-flops (each of which stores one binary value) we can implement a circuit whose state table has at most 2**n internal states. To reduce the complexity of the circuit, we must minimize the total number of internal states. For more examples of state diagrams see the Workbook.

4.2 FLIP-FLOPS

A flip-flop is a digital component capable of storing a single bit. In this sense it is the simplest sequential device. In order to be able to store one bit, it must have two states in which it can stay as long as needed; they must be stable. For these reasons flip-flops are also called bi-stables.

It was indicated in the previous section that flip-flops are used to store the present code of the internal state of a sequential circuit, each flip-flop storing a single bit of the code. The internal state undergoes transitions, and so the state of each flip-flop must be modifiable by the circuit. There must be an input or inputs which allow the circuit to change the value stored in the flip-flop. If access to the internal state of a flip-flop is classified as reading, then modification of the internal state should be called writing. Flip-flops are thus elementary read-write memory components. Contrast this with ROMs introduced in Chapter 2.

Flip-flops implemented as semiconductor devices can hold their information only while the power supply provides appropriate power level. When the voltage of the power supply begins to fluctuate or the power supply fails, the flip-flop loses the stored information, and its future contents will be unpredictable. Semiconductor writable memories are *volatile*.

A number of types of flip-flops have been developed and are available as commercial ICs. They can all be classified by the following two criteria:

1. The state table—in other words what are the rules of the dependence of transitions and outputs on inputs and the present state.
2. The nature of the dependence of the timing of the transition on the timing of input.

It is important to realize that these two criteria are completely independent. Any category as defined by criterion 1 can be implemented with any characteristic defined by criterion 2. Not all such combinations are commercially available since some of them do not have practical applications and others can be obtained by suitably connecting inputs and outputs of other types of flip-flops.

4.2.1 Categories By State Tables

R-S FLIP-FLOP. This flip-flop has two inputs: R (reset) and S (set). It has one output traditionally called Q, which represents the internal state of the flip-flop. Internal states of flip-flops must be accessible since they "remember" the state of the rest of the circuit which must be able to access the state of each flip-flop in order to function properly. In other words, internal states of flip-flops are also their outputs. The inverse Q' is always available as another output of the chip. This is due to the internal construction of the flip-flop in which both Q and Q' are automatically present, as will be seen in an example at the end of this section. This fact is very useful since it simplifies circuits by allowing the elimination of many inverters. The transition table of the $R-S$ flip-flop is shown in Figure 4.13.

q	RS	00	01	11	10
0		0	1	-	0
1		1	1	-	0

Figure 4.13   The transition table of an $R-S$ flip-flop showing the dependence of Q on q, R, S.

Notes:

1. The table uses q for the present state of the circuit and leaves Q to denote the next state of the same line. This use of lower and upper case symbols for current and next values is a common practice in sequential circuits. Remember, however, that q and Q represent the same variable observed at different times: Q is the state that will be reached from the present state q.
2. Input combination $RS=11$ is "forbidden," and the corresponding column is left unspecified. This is due to the internal arrangement of the circuit.
3. The state table can be easily remembered if we realize the following: input 00 has no effect on the output; that is, it does not change the internal state. Input S sets the output to 1 independent of the value of q. Input R resets the output to 0. The words "set" and "reset" or "clear" are normally used with this meaning for logic values in sequential circuits.
4. If we interpret the state table as a truth table or Karnaugh map specifying the dependence of Q on q, R, S we obtain the following *characteristic equation* of the $R-S$ flip-flop: $Q = S+R'q$. It must be remembered that this equation relates the future state Q to the present state and inputs and is not a Boolean expression in the same sense as in the previous chapters. Also RS combination 11 must be avoided, and the equation does not hold for these input values.

J-K FLIP-FLOP. This is essentially an improved $R-S$ flip-flop in which the restriction on RS is removed. Input combination 11 is allowed, and it "toggles" (inverts) the output (internal state). Otherwise, the function of J is the same as the function of S, and similarly K and R are analogous (Figure 4.14). The characteristic equation is easily obtained by interpreting the state table as a Karnaugh map: $Q = qK'+q'J$.

q	JK	00	01	11	10
0		0	0	1	1
1		1	0	0	1

Figure 4.14   The transition table of a $J-K$ flip-flop.

The D FLIP-FLOP—"data" or "delay" flip-flop—has only one input *D*. The output value follows the input value (Figure 4.15).

q	D	0	1
0		0	1
1		0	1

Figure 4.15   The transition table of a *D* flip-flop. its characteristic equation is: $Q = D$.

The T FLIP-FLOP—"toggle"—has one input. Its high level inverts—toggles—the output value (Figure 4.16).

q	T	0	1
0		0	1
1		1	0

Figure 4.16   The transition table of a *T* flip-flop. Its characteristic equation is: $Q = T$ XOR q.

4.2.2 Categories By Input Signal Sensitivity

It is often desirable or even necessary to limit the possible interference of the input and output values of flip-flops. Consider, for example, the *T* flip-flop and assume that there is no timing restriction on its function.

Assume that initially $Q = 0$. When $T = 1$, the output toggles to 1. If *T* remains at 1, *Q* will toggle again (to 0), etc. (The output will begin to *oscillate* between 0 and 1.) The frequency of oscillation would depend on the internal parameters of the flip-flop, and these vary from one type to another and even for flip-flops of the same type from one product to another. The behavior of the chip would thus be unpredictable. If we want to have control over the flip-flop we can do one of the following:

1. Make the T signal sufficiently short so that the flip-flop can toggle only once. When doing this, it must be realized that there is a lower limit on the duration of the input; flip-flops just as all other devices need a certain minimum time, the "set-up time," to react to the input. In addition the travelling pulse undergoes a number of distortions as it travels from its source to its destination: noise, transmission delay, and distortion of shape. Signal shaping may thus become a very delicate problem and this approach should thus be avoided if possible.

2. The flip-flop could be made sensitive to the *change* of the input signal rather than its *level*: the T flip-flop could be made to respond for example to a "positive-going" signal (a low-to-high transition) rather than to value 1. In practice instead of making the flip-flop sensitive directly to its input, another auxiliary signal is added which controls the sensitivity; the *clock* input of a positive-edge sensitive T flip-flop makes it respond to its T input only when the clock input is going positive. At all other times the normal input is ignored (Figure 4.17).

Commercially available edge-sensitive devices require a sufficiently fast rising edge. Slowly rising edges can be conditioned by a gate with "Schmitt action" (Figure 4.18).

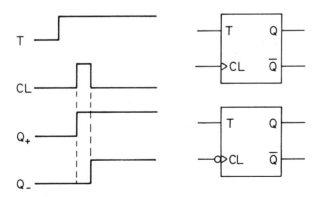

Figure 4.17 The behavior of a positive-edge triggered T flip-flop and a negative-edge triggered T flip-flop, symbols of positive and negative-edge triggered flip-flops.

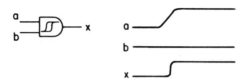

Figure 4.18   A pulse-shaping AND gate with Schmitt action.

3. Another possibility is to "isolate" the input from the output: the $J-K$ flip-flop, for example, is commonly made with two stages in series (placed on one chip). The first or input stage—the "master"—responds on the positive going edge of the clock input. The second or output stage—the "slave"—responds on the negative going edge of the same pulse. The slave output is internal and inaccessible from the outside (Figure 4.19).

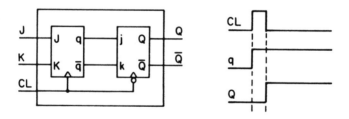

Figure 4.19   The principle of a master-slave $J-K$ flip-flop. Signal q is internal, thus unobservable; Q is the observable output of the device.

In a circuit where certain inputs and outputs are connected together such as in the common internal arrangement of the T flip-flop, the outputs would thus be allowed to change after all flip-flops have settled internally to the new states, and in this way they would be prevented from immediately influencing the circuit. Their influence would appear only with the arrival of the next clock pulse. In terms of transition tables this *master-slave* principle can be interpreted as holding the present states unchanged on the outputs of the slave stage and allowing the next states to establish themselves inside flip-flops on the internal outputs of the master stage. The transition then takes place when the input stage of the whole circuit is disabled by the completion of the clock pulse. In this sense the present and next state coexist for a brief period of time and are isolated.

In summary, we distinguish:

1. *level-sensitive* flip-flops whose behavior is not controlled by a clock signal. These flip-flops respond "immediately." Note that flip-flops in this category usually have a control input (the "enable" signal) which enables the input to affect the flip-flop. The enable input is usually a level signal (e.g., H enables and L disables flip-flop input).

2. *edge-sensitive* flip-flops controlled by a clock signal. They can be

   a. positive-edge sensitive
   b. negative-edge sensitive

3. *master-slave* flip-flops controlled by a clock signal. These flip-flops respond to the input value present on one edge of the clock signal and output the new state on the following edge of the clock signal.

Some examples of commercially available flip-flops from the 74-series are the following:

7474—dual edge-triggered D flip-flop with CLEAR and RESET inputs. This IC has two independent flip-flops on one chip. Note in the diagram in Figure 4.20 the symbol for edge sensitivity on the CLock input (the small triangle). The flip-flop is sensitive to the positive-going edge; flip-flops sensitive to the negative-going edge have a bubble on the triangle. The flip-flop responds to the value of the D input on the positive-going edge of the clock pulse. The SET and CLEAR inputs override all other inputs including the clock: i.e., they cause a transition to 1 for SET and 0 for CLEAR even in the absence of the clock pulse. They are both active low, as indicated by the bubble; they cause a transition when low and are inactive when high. The diagram on the left shows the standard symbol of the D flip-flop, and the timing diagram on the right is an example of its function.

7473—dual JK master-slave flip-flop. The response is again controlled by a CLock input which is ACTIVE LOW and level-sensitive. The operation of the master-slave arrangement is as explained previously. The master stage responds (the flip-flop "triggers") to the *J*, *K* inputs when the CLock goes up and the slave responds on the down-going edge of the clock pulse. The response therefore appears at the end of the negative clock pulse and is caused by the input values present on *J, K* at the beginning of this pulse (Figure 4.21).

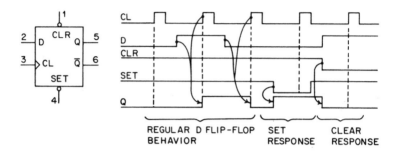

REGULAR D FLIP-FLOP   SET   CLEAR
BEHAVIOR   RESPONSE   RESPONSE

Figure 4.20   The function and partial pin assignment of a 7474 dual, edge-triggered *D* flip-flop.

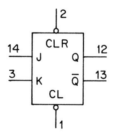

Figure 4.21   Partial pin assignment of a 7473 dual master-slave *J = K* flip-flop.

7475—4-bit bistable latch. This IC consists of four level-sensitive *D* flip-flops without clock control. Each flip-flop has its own *D* input pin. In addition there are two G pins shared by two latches each. Their function is to enable the latch for normal operation or disable the *D* input. In the disabled mode, *G* low, the latch does not respond to the *D* signal; the state is latched. The assignment of pins and an example of the behavior of this IC are shown in Figure 4.22.

The term *latch* is often used for flip-flops to suggest their ability to capture and hold the value of a binary signal. In a more restrictive sense the term latch is used for bistable memory elements without clock inputs.

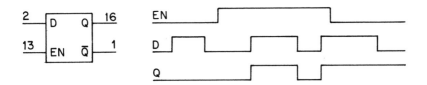

Figure 4.22   Partial pin assignment of a 7475 4-bit latch and an example of its idealized behavior.

Latch circuits can be made from standard gates. The principle which makes this possible is the existence of feedback paths between the outputs and inputs of the circuit. As an example consider the implementation of a D latch shown in Figure 4.23.

The circuit works as follows: assume that $D=0$ (see timing diagram). One of the inputs of $N1$ is 1, and the output of $N1$ is $Q=0$. Inputs of $N2$ are 00, and its output is $Q'=1$. This is consistent with the value of Q and the definition of the D flip-flop. When D changes to 1, the input to $N2$ changes to 01 and its output becomes $Q'=0$. For a short while $Q=Q'=0$ because of the delay through the inverter, etc. Inputs of $N1$ change to 00, and its output changes to $Q=1$, as expected of a D flip-flop. In summary, the circuit has two stable states, and its behavior agrees with the description of a D flip-flop.

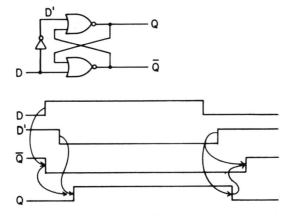

Figure 4.23   The D latch can be made from NOR gates. An example of its behavior is on the right. Note that delays sometimes cause Q and Q to be inconsistent ($Q=Q'$). Causes of transitions are indicated by arrows.

Notes:

1. The presence of feedback in the above circuit is a typical property of sequential circuits. This fact is the reason for the need for correct timing and a possible source of problems if timing conditions are not guaranteed. This was indicated in the example of the T flip-flop and will be investigated in more detail in a subsequent section. The easiest solution to this problem is the use of edge-sensitive flip-flops and a synchronizing clock. This solution is possible only if the function of the circuit allows the use of a synchronizing clock. More on this will appear in the following sections.

2. The circuit above can be changed into an $R-S$ latch by disconnecting the inverter and connecting the R, S inputs to lines labeled R, S. Examine the behavior of this circuit, in particular its response to the input combination $R = S = 1$.

For more examples on flip-flops see the Workbook.

4.3 SYNCHRONOUS AND ASYNCHRONOUS CIRCUITS

It was indicated in the previous section that timing is a critical parameter in sequential circuits and that a number of problems can be prevented by controlling state transitions by clock pulses.

Circuits in which transitions are controlled by a train of regularly spaced pulses of uniform shape are called *synchronous*. In synchronous circuits logic values cause transitions only at accurately defined instants such as the positive-going edge of the clock pulse. For this reason there is no undesirable interference between input and output values; the design is easier and operation safer. Synchronous circuits are therefore used whenever possible.

There are situations in which it is undesirable or impossible to use fully synchronous circuits. They can be divided into two categories:

1. Applications in which certain input signals arrive at random times, not synchronous with a clock. This situation arises, for example, in the case of two cooperating synchronous systems which do not have a common clock.

2. Applications in which the required speed is not attainable by synchronous design. In order to see why an *asynchronous* circuit running without the control of regularly spaced clock pulses can

be faster, consider what determines the frequency of the clock in a synchronous circuit: the frequency must be such that any process which can possibly occur in the circuit has time to run to its full completion and stabilize. This includes delays of signals along transmission lines, operation of all stages of switching circuits, etc. The choice of timing must be very conservative to allow even the combination resulting in the slowest process to execute in the worst imaginable conditions. It is quite likely that this critical process will, in fact, proceed faster; the design is, after all, the worst-case design and will occur only relatively infrequently, for example once every 100 pulses. This means that the full duration of the pulse will be needed only 1/100 of the time and in the remaining situations the circuit will be wasting some of its time just waiting for the conservatively designed pulse to arrive. An asynchronous circuit in which a step begins as soon as the previous step is completed may thus be faster. It is, however, possible that this advantage of the asynchronous process will be eliminated by other factors which must be considered in the design of asynchronous circuits in order to ensure their reliable operation.

Digital systems, particularly the more complex ones such as computers, are usually built from synchronous modules with asynchronous interfaces.

4.4 ANALYSIS OF SEQUENTIAL CIRCUITS

Consider the circuit in Figure 4.24. To describe or analyze the function of the circuit means to construct its state table or an equivalent description. This means that we have to

1. describe the dependence of outputs on present states and inputs—the *output function*, and
2. describe the transitions.

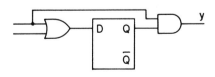

Figure 4.24   A simple sequential circuit.

130   **Sequential Circuits**

Deriving the output function is simple: it is implemented by a combinational circuit whose inputs are present states, outputs of flip-flops or equivalent devices, and circuit inputs. In our case $y = a.q$. Note that when the output circuit has direct connections to input signals, any change in input may immediately change the output even when the internal state does not change immediately. This will occur when flip-flops storing internal state codes are controlled by a clock signal and input signals are allowed to change asynchronously. To construct transitions, we need to describe the dependence of flip-flop inputs on their present states and circuit inputs. This dependence is called the *excitation function*. Its tabular representation is an *excitation table*. Excitation tables and flip-flop state tables then determine transitions. In our case the excitation function is $D = a + b$. There is no feedback in this example and therefore no dependence on present states, outputs of flip-flop D. The corresponding excitation table is shown in Figure 4.25.

a	b	D
0	0	0
0	1	1
1	0	1
1	1	1

Figure 4.25   Excitation table of the circuit from Figure 4.24. $D = a + b$.

The transition table of the circuit is shown in Figure 4.26; the state table of the D flip-flop is on the right to help in the derivation. The representation of the transition table and related tables in the rest of this chapter is based on the representation of Karnaugh maps. This is because these tables can be interpreted as generalized truth tables and their representation as Karnaugh maps leads to simplified formulas and circuits. The readers who skipped the section dealing with Karnaugh maps will be able to understand all the material if they replace tables organized as Karnaugh maps by tables organized as truth tables and derive all formulas as the canonical sum of products' expressions. Their results will be more complicated but valid.

q \ ab	00	01	11	10		q\D	0	1
0	0	1	1	1		0	0	1
1	0	1	1	1		1	0	1

Figure 4.26   Transition table of the circuit in Figure 4.24 (left) and the state table of a D flip-flop used in its derivation.

To see how the transition table was derived, consider the combination $q,a,b=1,1,0$. For this combination the value of input D is $D=a+b=1+0=1$. From the state table of the D flip-flop we see that $Q=1$ is the next state. This value is given in the transition table. For $q,a,b=0,0,0$ the D input is $D=a+b=0+0=0$, and so the next state of the flip-flop is $Q=0$. This is shown in the table. Other transitions are derived similarly.

Combining the transition table and the output equation, we obtain the transition/output table in Figure 4.27.

q	ab	00	01	11	10
0		0/0	1/0	1/0	1/0
1		0/0	1/0	1/1	1/1

Figure 4.27 Transition/output table of the circuit in Figure 4.24.

A systematic description of the analysis of a sequential circuit from its circuit diagram is as follows:

Algorithm A (Analysis of a flip-flop-based sequential circuit):

1. Obtain output functions: dependence of outputs on inputs and states.
2. Obtain excitation equations and tables: dependence of flip-flop inputs on circuit inputs and flip-flop outputs.
3. Derive next states for each combination of present states and inputs from excitation tables and flip-flop state tables. This step generates the transition table.
4. Complete the table by filling in output values derived from output functions.

Example 4.3: (Figure 4.28)

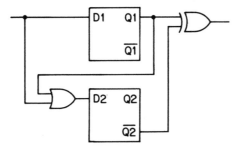

Figure 4.28 A sequential circuit.

1. $y = q1 \,\text{XOR}\, q2'$
2. $D1 = a$, $D2 = a + q1$. Excitation table is in Figure 4.29.

$q1,q2$	a	0	1
00		0	1
01		0	1
11		0	1
10		0	1

$q1,q2$	a	0	1
00		0	1
01		0	1
11		1	1
10		1	1

Figure 4.29   Excitation tables for $D1$ and $D2$

3. Next-state tables for both flip-flops are in Figure 4.30.

$q1,q2$	a	0	1
00		0	1
01		0	1
11		0	1
10		0	1

$q1,q2$	a	0	1
00		0	1
01		0	1
11		1	1
10		1	1

q	D	0	
0		0	1
1		0	1

Figure 4.30   Transition tables for both flip-flops. The rightmost table is the transition table of a D flip-flop.

To see how the $D1$ and $D2$ tables were derived, consider, for example, combination $q1,q2,a = 1,1,0$. Flip-flop $D1$ has excitation signal $D1 = a = 0$ (according to step 2) and according to the D transition table this means that the next state $Q1$ is $Q1 = 0$. Flip-flop $D2$ has excitation input $D2 = a + q1' = 0 + 0 = 0$ and so its next state is $Q2 = 0$. The results derived are entered in the appropriate cells in the table above.

4. Combining the two transition tables and outputs (obtained from the output equation in step 1. we finally get the table in Figure 4.31.

$q1,q2$	a	0	1
00		01/1	11/1
01		01/0	11/0
11		00/1	11/1
10		00/0	11/0

Figure 4.31   Transition/output table for the circuit in Figure 4.28. Entries in the table are $Q1,Q2$/output.

Example 4.4: Other flip-flops are handled in the same way but may have more complicated transition tables (Figure 4.32).

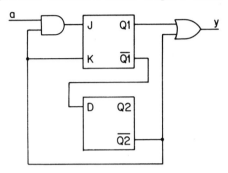

Figure 4.32 A sequential circuit with $J-K$ and D flip-flops.

1. $y = a + q1 + q2'$
2. $J = a.q2'$, $K = q2'$, $D = q1'$ (Figure 4.33).

$q1,q2$	a	0	1	0	1	0	1
00		0	1	1	1	1	1
01		0	0	0	0	1	1
11		0	0	0	0	0	0
10		0	1	1	1	0	0

Figure 4.33 Excitation tables of J, K, D.

3. Transition tables are in Figure 4.34.

$q1,q2$	0	1	0	1
00	0	1	1	1
01	0	0	1	1
11	1	1	0	0
10	0	0	0	0

q	JK	00	01	11	10
0		0	0	1	1
1		1	0	0	1

q	D	0	1
		0	1
		0	1

Figure 4.34 Transition tables of the circuit in Figure 4.32: $q1$, $q2$.

As an example consider $q1,q2,a = 0,0,0$:
$J = a.q2' = 0.1 = 0$
$K = q2' = 1$
$D = q1' = 1$
and so $Q1 = 0$ (from the JK transition table) and $D = 1$ (from the D transition table).
For $q1,q2,a = 0,0,1$ we have
$J = a.q2' = 1.1 = 1$
$K = q2' = 1$
$D = q1' = 1$
and thus $Q1 = 1$, $Q2 = 1$.
4. Combining transition tables and output we obtain the table of Figure 4.35.

$q1,q2$ a	0	1
00	01/1	11/1
01	01/0	01/1
11	10/1	10/1
10	00/1	00/1

Figure 4.35   Combined transition/output table for the circuit in Figure 4.32 and its corresponding diagram.

Example 4.5: We have seen in the example of an *RS* latch that sequential circuits can be implemented *without* flip-flops if we take advantage of inherent delays of gates and transmission paths. The analysis of such circuits is simple if we modify the diagram by adding delay elements, formally behaving as D flip-flops, into feedback paths (Figure 4.36). Note that delay elements are not actually present in the circuit although delays are inherent in the function of all physical components.

For more examples of analysis see the Workbook.

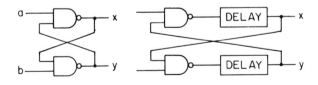

Figure 4.36   A circuit with feedbacks but no flip-flops (left) can be analyzed by treating gate delays as level-sensitive D flip-flops.

4.5   SYNTHESIS OF SEQUENTIAL CIRCUITS

Synthesis (design) of sequential circuits is the inverse of analysis, and the corresponding algorithm can be derived from algorithm *A* with a few minor modifications:

Algorithm S (synthesis of sequential circuits):

1. Construct the state table from a word description of the problem.
2. Minimize the number of states.
3. Choose flip-flop types.
4. Assign states and convert state table to transition table.
5. Obtain excitation equations.
6. Obtain output equations.

Example 4.6: Consider the state table and graph in Figure 4.37 presumably obtained from a word description by steps 1 and 2 above:

present\input	0	1
A	C/1	A/0
B	B/0	C/0
C	C/0	B/1

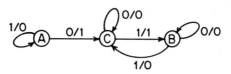

Figure 4.37   Device description as a basis for synthesis.

Since there are three internal states, we need two flip-flops (2**2=4). Let us use *JK* flip-flops. Assume that the circuit is synchronous and so state assignment is arbitrary. Note, however, that different state assignment and different flip-flop types will result in different circuits, some more complex than others. Let us assign

A 00

B 01

C 11

The transition table obtained from the state table by substituting codes for state symbols and the JK state table are in Figure 4.38.

$q1,q2$ a	0	1		q JK	00	01	11	10
00	11/1	00/0		0	0	0	1	1
01	1/0	11/0		1	1	0	0	1
11	1/0	01/1						
10	XX/X	XX/X						

Figure 4.38   Transition table (left) obtained from Figure 4.36 assuming the use of $J-K$ flip-flops and given state assignment.

Note that the combination of states $q1,q2=1,0$ never occurs and consequently the last row in the transition table is filled with don't cares. The next step is to obtain *excitation tables* from the Karnaugh maps of the flip-flop inputs $J1$, $K1$, $J2$, $K2$ (Figure 4.39).

	$J1,$	$K1$	$J2,$	$K2$
$q1,q2$ a	0	1	0	1
00	1X	0X	1X	0X
01	0X	1X	X0	X0
11	X0	X1	X0	X0
10	XX	XX	XX	XX

Figure 4.39   Excitation tables implied by the transition table in Figure 4.37.

As an example of the derivation of the excitation table, consider combination $q1,q2,a=0,0,0$. The present state of $q1$ is 0 and the desired next state is $Q1=1$. The $J-K$ flip-flop goes from 0 to 1 on $J=K=1$ or $J=1$, $K=0$. In other words, $J=1$ and $K=X-a$ don't care will allow us to simplify the circuit. For $q1,q2,a=0,1,0$ we want transition $q1=0$ to $Q1=0$. This can be achieved by $J=K=0$ or $J=0$, $K=1$, so that J must be 0 and $K=X$.

In the derivation of the excitation table from a transition table for this circuit, we need to know which values of $J1$, $K1$ will generate the desired transition from $q1$ to $Q1$. It is advantageous to rearrange the transition table of the flip-flop to make this information immediately available (Figure 4.40).

present state	desired next state	required inputs $J\ K$
0	0	0
0	1	1
1	0	X
1	1	X

Figure 4.40   Values of $J-K$ needed to produce the desired transitions.

Now the completion of the rest of the circuit's excitation table becomes simple. Consider $q1,q2,a = 1,1,0$. On flip-flop $JK1$ we want a transition from $q1 = 1$ to $Q1 = 1$. The last line of our modified $J-K$ table shows that this is accomplished by $J1 = X$, $K = 0$. To make the derivation of functions easier let us now separate the combined tables into one table for $J1$, one for $K1$, one for $J2$ and one for $K2$ (Figure 4.41).

		$J1$		$K1$		$J2$		$K2$	
$q1,q2$	a	0	1	0	1	0	1	0	1
00		1	0	X	X	1	0	X	X
01		0	1	X	X	X	X	0	0
11		X	X	0	1	X	X	0	0
10		X	X	X	X	X	X	X	X

Figure 4.41   Excitation tables for $J1$, $K1$, $J2$, $K2$.

These tables show that the excitation functions are

$$J1 = q2'.a' + q2.a \quad K1 = a \quad J2 = a' \quad K2 = 0$$

Output equations can be obtained from the output table extracted from the transition/output table in Figure 4.37. The output table is given in Figure 4.42.

$q1,q2$	a	0	1
00		1	0
01		0	0
11		0	1
10		X	X

Figure 4.42   The output table for the circuit from Figure 4.37. The output function is $y = q2'.a' + q1.a$.

The resulting circuit is shown in Figure 4.43.

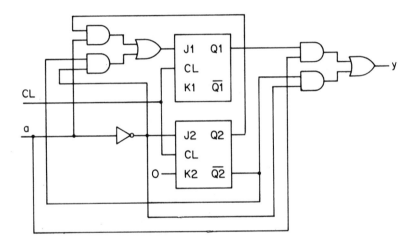

Figure 4.43   A sequential circuit implementing the function described in Figure 4.37.

For more examples of sequential circuit design see the Workbook.

4.6   IRREGULAR BEHAVIOR

There are several categories of malfunctions of sequential circuits particularly relevant to the behavior of asynchronous circuits. Some of these problems are outlined in this section.

4.6.1 Hazards

Consider the asynchronous circuit in Figure 4.44, which realizes the transition table in Figure 4.45.

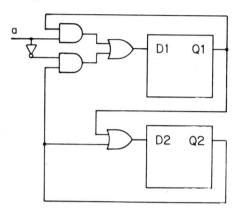

Figure 4.44   A sequential circuit with a hazard in the $D1$ excitation circuit.

$q1,q2$	a	0	1
00		00	00
01		01	01
11		11	11
10		10	01

Figure 4.45   The transition table of the circuit from Figure 4.44.

Assume that the present state is $(1,1)$ and input a changes from 1 to 0. Theoretically, there should be no difference in excitation values, and the circuit should remain in state $(1,1)$. In reality the hazard in input $D1$ causes a brief transition of $D1$ from 1 to 0. If the transition is long enough, depending on the delay in the inverter path, etc., and the flip-flop responds fast enough, then the circuit will go into state $(0,1)$. This state is stable, and the circuit will remain there. The next state will thus be $(0,1)$ rather than the desired $(1,1)$. The successive behavior of the circuit will, of course, be incorrect.

The category of sequential hazards is more general than the previous example indicates. In particular, some sequential hazards can be removed by redesigning the excitation circuit. Other sequential hazards are essential; they are caused by the form of the transition table and can only be removed by making sure that output and input values cannot interact during the critical transitions. This can be achieved by inserting artificial time delays into the critical feedback paths.

In conclusion, it should be stressed that hazards are due to undesirable intermediate values of signals. The categories of irregularities described below are of a different nature.

4.6.2   Differences In The Behavior Of Synchronous And Asynchronous Circuits

Consider the state table of a *synchronous* circuit in Figure 4.46.

present	input	0	1
A		B	A
B		C	A
C		C	A

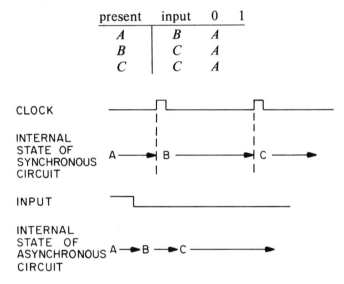

Figure 4.46   A demonstration of the different behavior of synchronous and asynchronous circuits.

Assume that the circuit starts in state *A* and the input changes from 1 to 0. According to the table the circuit will make a "transition" to state *A*, i.e., stay in state *A*, and wait for the next clock pulse.,

An *asynchronous* circuit with the same state table starting in *A* with input 1 will behave differently: when the input changes to 0 the first transition will be to state *B* (second line of the same column) as required by the table. If input 0 is still present, the circuit will make another transition in the same column—input is unchanged—and go to state *C*. This is because there is no controlling pulse to prevent an asynchronous circuit from responding when a response is called for by the table. In state C the circuit will stabilize since here the required transition is to the same state; no change is called for. State C is a *stable* state for input 0. States A and B are *unstable* for input 0.

Stable states of asynchronous circuits are easy to recognize. They correspond to those cells in the table which are labeled by the same state symbol as the line symbol of the cell. In our case state A is stable with input 1, column labeled 1; state C is stable with input 0, column labeled 0.

In asynchronous circuits a single input change can thus cause the state to flow through a series of intermediate states. A table which shows only symbols of final states is called a *flow table*.

As a consequence of the lack of synchronization, asynchronous circuits are quite vulnerable to undesired signals such as those caused by hazards. Synchronous circuits are much better protected from them.

The behavior of asynchronous circuits would become quite unpredictable if inputs were allowed to change before the circuit reaches a stable state. The exact result of a change of input during transitions could depend on the exact timing. The physical parameters of circuit components and timing differences of the order of nanoseconds could cause completely different transitions in different implementations of the same circuit. Timing would become extremely critical. Asynchronous circuits are thus usually required to work in the *fundamental mode* in which input changes are allowed only after the circuit has had enough time to settle down in a stable state.

One immediate consequence of the loose transient behavior of asynchronous circuits is the possibility of *cycles*.

4.6.3 Cycles

Consider the partial flow table of an asynchronous circuit in Figure 4.47.

present state\input	0	1
A	A	B
B	C	A
C	.	.

Figure 4.47   A transition table demonstrating the possible consequences of a cycle.

Assume that the circuit is in state A with input 0. When the input changes to 1, the flow table requires the circuit to go to state B. In state B with input still at 1, the required next state is again A, etc. The

circuit begins to oscillate between states A and B: A, B, A, B, A, ...
Oscillations can be interrupted only by the change of the input back
to 0. Exactly what this change of input to 0 will cause depends on the
exact timing. If the circuit is in state A at the moment of the change,
it will remain in this state, transition to the first column on the same
line. If the circuit is in state B, it will go to state C, etc. Cycles can
thus lead to unpredictable behavior and must be eliminated.

4.6.4 Races

Another potential malfunction is due to races. Consider the flow
table in Figure 4.48.

present	input	0	1
A		A	B
B		A	B
C		A	B
D		A	D

Figure 4.48   A table which can lead to a race.

Assume that the circuit is in stable state A with input 0 and the input
changes to 1. The circuit should make a transition to the stable state
B. Assume now that the circuit is implemented with the following
state assignment:

$$A\ 00,\ B\ 11,\ C\ 10,\ D\ 01$$

The corresponding transition table is shown in Figure 4.49.

$q1,q2$	a	0	1
00 (A)		00	11
01 (D)		00	01
10 (C)		00	11
11 (B)		00	11

Figure 4.49   The transition table corresponding to Figure 4.48.

The transaction A to B requires the simultanous change in both
state variables: $(0,0)$ to $(1,1)$. As we know, an exactly

simultaneous change of two values is physically impossible. One of the two states will change first. The alternatives are:

1. (0,0) to (0,1) occurs first. This represents transition *A* to *D*. But state *D* is stable with input 1 and the circuit may remain in *D* if the difference in timing is sufficiently long, making an incorrect transition. The race between the changing values is, in this case, critical since it causes the circuit to behave differently from its specification.
2. (0,0) to (1,0) occurs first. This means transition to *C*. For input 1 state *C* is unstable, and another transition is made to *B* which is the desired final state.

The above example of a race on the change of input from 0 to 1 in state *A* demonstrates a *critical race*, one which may lead to an incorrect transition.

Assume now that the same circuit is in state *B* with input 1 and the input changes to 0. Transition *B* to *A* (i.e., (1,1) to (0,0)) is required, and a race occurs. In this case no matter which signal changes first the final state will be *A*, the desired final state. The race is *non-critical.*

Races can often be removed by proper state assignment. In our case

$$A\ 00,\ B\ 01,\ C\ 11,\ D\ 10$$

is a *race-free assignment* in which no input changes can lead to races; i.e., there is no requirement for simultaneous changes in more than one state variable. This can be easily verified by examining the transition table corresponding to the original flow table and the new state assignment.

Race-free assignments cannot always be obtained by reassigning the outputs of the chosen flip-flops. In many situations it is necessary to add auxiliary flip-flops to generate auxiliary intermediate states. The transition between states is then through a chain of race-free transitions which guarantee that the circuit behaves as required. The cost of this approach is increased complexity of the circuit and extra transitions which slow down the circuit (remember that transitions must be allowed to reach the stable state).

In summary, races are due to the physical impossibility of two or more signals changing exactly simultaneously. They are critical if they can cause the circuit to fail to reach the desired stable state. Races are a property of the implementation rather than the flow table and can always be eliminated, usually by increasing the complexity of the circuit and decreasing its speed.

4.6.5   Testing Of Sequential Circuits

Testing of sequential circuits is a much more complicated problem than testing of combinational circuits. This can be seen from the fact that whereas design of test sets for switching circuits consists of the specification of suitable test vectors applied independently, test sets for sequential circuits consist of *sequences* of input vectors. The subject of sequential testing is beyond the scope of this text. The interested reader is referred to the text by Breuer and Friedman.

4.7   COUNTERS AND REGISTERS

Flip-flops are elementary SSI components which can be combined with combinational elements to construct sequential circuits. Just as MSI combinational components such as multiplexers simplify the design of combinational circuits, MSI sequential components simplify the design of sequential circuits. Counters and registers are examples of such MSI components, which are among the essential building blocks of computers.

4.7.1   Counters

In a restricted sense counters are components which receive and count input pulses and display the count in a coded form. A given counter counts to a certain fixed maximum value and then starts again from 0. The total number of different states that a counter can enter is called the *modulus* of the counter.

A binary modulo-5 counter produces the following counting sequence: 000 001 010 011 100 000 001 010 etc. A modulo-8 counter produces the following output sequence: 000 001 010 011 100 101 110 111 000 001 etc. Note that a modulo-N counter counts from 0 to $N-1$; it has N different states: a decimal counter counts from 0 to 9, a modulo-16 counter counts from 0 to 15, etc.

In a more general sense counters are components which, in response to input signals, produce a repetitive sequence of outputs, such as 010 011 000 111 010 011 000 111, etc. or 1110 1001 0000 0010 1110 1001 0000, etc. Since counters are commonly used components, a large number of types have been designed, and several of them are available as semiconductor MSI components. They differ in speed, complexity, and flexibility. From the point of view of *complexity* and *speed* the two main categories are *synchronous* and *asynchronous*, which are better known as *ripple* counters. From the point of view of flexibility counters differ in the ease of access of individual flip-flops which constitute their internal storage elements.

Ripple counters are simple and slow. The circuit in Figure 4.50 shows a modulo-8 ripple counter built from negative-edge sensitive T flip-flops. The counter can, of course, be built from any other type of clocked flip-flops, but representation with T flip-flops is the most natural since toggling is the principle of the function of counters. Note that T flip-flops are connected so that they always toggle when enabled by a negative-going clock input. The clock is connected only to the first flip-flop. The remaining flip-flops have their clock inputs connected to the data output of the previous flip-flop. A sample timing diagram of a modulo-8 ripple counter is given in Figure 4.51.

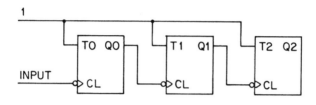

Figure 4.50   A modulo-8 ripple counter.

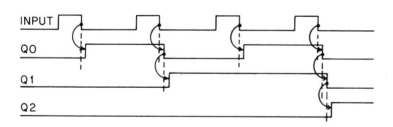

Figure 4.51   A sample of input and output signals of a single modulo-8 counter.

Note the following:

1. If the input signal is a train of clock pulses with frequency f the output of flip-flop Qi is a train of pulses with frequency $f/2^{**}i$.

The successive stages thus divide frequency by two. For this reason counters are also called *frequency dividers* and are commonly used to derive a fractional frequency from very accurate standard frequencies produced by components such as quartz oscillators. Our modulo-8 counter could also be called a divide-by-8 counter.

2. The input, usually a clock signal, enters only the first flip-flop. The pulse then ripples through the series of flip-flops with an increasing delay with respect to the original clock signal. This fact is indicated in the timing diagram above. This asynchronous behavior is the consequence of the simplicity of the circuit but also the cause of its limited speed.

3. If it takes time *T* for a signal to propagate through one flip-flop, then an *N* stage counter will require time *NT* to respond to the input on those of its transitions which require the propagation of the signal through all stages. Such a transition is one from the maximal count 111..1 to the initial state 000..0. The maximum frequency of the input signals is thus approximately 1/*NT*. In other words, we have to wait *NT* after the active edge of the pulse to be sure that all flip-flops are stable and show the correct outputs. At any time before *NT* some flip-flops may still be in a transient state.

Synchronous counters are more complex because all flip-flops respond synchronously at the time of the arrival of the clock pulse and therefore must at this moment be "aware" of the state of all other flip-flops in the counter. Asynchronous counters in effect propagate this information through individual stages. Since synchronous counters operate synchronously, transmission delay is eliminated, and operation is faster. A modulo-8 synchronous counter can be implemented as in Figure 4.52. Its timing diagram is shown in Figure 4.53.

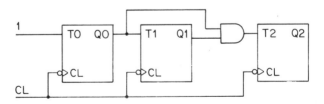

Figure 4.52   An implementation of a modulo-8 synchronous counter.

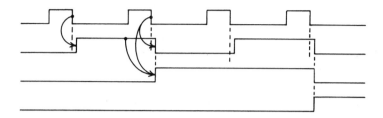

Figure 4.53   The timing diagram of a synchronous modulo-8 counter. Note that the causes of transitions are different from those in a ripple counter.

Note that:

1. Disregarding delays in combinational components, the delay of the counter with respect to the input is approximately the same as that of a single flip-flop, independent of the number of stages of the counter.
2. The circuit must be more complex than that of a similar ripple counter since all flip-flops must have all information about the states of all other relevant flip-flops. For example flip-flop Q2 will toggle on the next clock signal iff $Q0 = Q1 = 1$.
3. The cause of the indicated change of $Q1$ is the EDGE of the *clock* and the *level* value of $Q0$ previous to the change.

The basic circuits discussed above count in the natural binary modulus; for N flip-flops they count from 0 to $2^{**}N$-1. They are modulo-$2^{**}N$ counters. To obtain other counts, for example modulo-6, etc., we can proceed in one of the following ways and there are other alternatives:

1. Design the desired counter as a sequential circuit using algorithm S. There are, in fact, simpler algorithms based on certain common properties of all counters.
2. Use a modulo-M counter with $M = 2^{**}N$ if we want to count to $K < = M$. A feedback and the use of CLEAR inputs of individual flip-flops allow us to interrupt the natural count when K is reached and reiinitialize the counter to 0. For example, a modulo-6 counter could be made by sensing the combination

110=6 and clearing all flip-flops on the arrival of the next input pulse as shown in Figure 4.54. Note that the connection of $Q2'$ to the AND gate can be deleted since the counting sequence is 000, 001, 010, 011, 100, 101, 110, and the condition $Q1 = Q2 = 1$ is thus satisfied at the same time as condition $Q1 = Q2 = 1$, $Q0 = 0$.

3. Use a commercially available IC counter based on the same strategy of clearing all its flip-flops at an appropriate time. This will be demonstrated later.

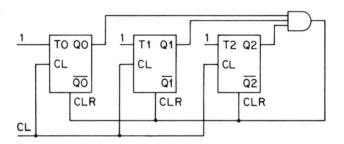

Figure 4.54   A modulo-6 counter built from a modulo-8 counter with a feedback. The AND gate clears all flip-flops to 0 when it detects combination 110.

Commerical MSI counters differ in the following aspects:

1. Principle—ripple or synchronous
2. Modulus—standard values are 2, 5, 8, 10, 12, 16.
3. Flexibility

   a. counting only up, only down, up/down as desired
   b. cascadability (explained below)
   c. edge sensitivity (positive, negative)
   d. presettability (explained below).

Cascadability. Counting to a large number can be accomplished by counting groups of smaller counts: 256 counts is 16 counts of groups of 16 each. Such cascaded counting can be achieved by arranging several counters in series (Figure 4.55). The second counter increments its count by 1 when the first counter makes the transition from

1111 to 0000. In terms of addition, the transition from 1111 to 0000 corresponds to generating a carry. Some counters, the cascadable ones, provide a signal—the "carry out"—which produces a 1 when the count goes from 1111 to 0000. This makes it possible to cascade the components directly without any need for intermediate logic to sense the transition of all bits as shown in Figure 4.56. Note that "non-cascadable" counters can also be cascaded if special interface between the counters is provided. This is shown in our first circuit in Figure 5.55.

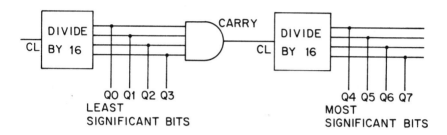

Figure 4.55   Two cascaded modulo-16 counters implement a modulo-256 counter.

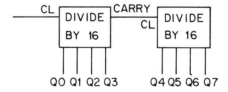

Figure 4.56   Connecting cascadable counters to obtain a modulo-256 counter. Note the absence of the AND gate.

Presettable counters. Some MSI counters have a set of inputs which make it possible to set all flip-flops to any combination of Boolean values at any time. The combination is loaded at the end of the next clock pulse under the control of a LOAD control input. The loaded combination becomes the next state of the counter. The counter can thus make transitions out of its built-in counting sequence. We will see shortly how this function can be used in the design of sequential circuits. Some common counters of the 74 series are:

7490. A modulo-10 (decade) ripple counter. Not cascadable. Negative-edge triggered. Not presettable. Counts only up. Maximum frequency is 18 MHz. Chip has 14 pins of which two are not used, i.e., not internally connected. This counter is "programmable": it may also be connected to behave as modulo-2 or modulo-5 counter.

74160. Another modulo-10 counter but synchronous. Maximum frequency 32 MHz. Presettable and cascadable. Positive-edge triggered. 16 pins.

74191. Modulo 16, up/down. Positive-edge triggered. Synchronous. Maximum frequency 25 MHz. Presettable.

4.7.2 Design With Presettable Counters

When a counter is left to respond naturally, it automatically proceeds in the ordinary counting sequence (0, 1, 2, ..). With a presettable counter the sequence can be interrupted in any state and the next state loaded into the counter via the LOAD inputs. Since the outputs of the circuit play the role of flip-flop outputs in standard sequential circuits, that is they form a code of the internal state, this property can be used to implement sequential circuits with counters.

Assume that we want to implement the sequential function of Figure 4.57 with a hypothetical modulo-4 presettable counter:

present	input	0	1
00		01/0	00/1
01		00/0	10/0
10		01/0	00/1

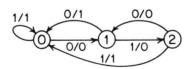

Figure 4.57   A transition/output function to be implemented with a presettable counter.

Examine state 00. For input 0 the counter should proceed from state 00 to state 01. In other words, for this combination of present state and input, the function is ordinary counting from 0 to 1. For state 0 and input 1 the next state is 00. This "transition" (00 to 00) does not represent counting. It is forced and can be achieved by loading the desired next state (00). In summary for state 0:

On input 0 the counter counts and LOAD is passive.
On input 1 the counter makes a forced transition to 00.
LOAD must be active and load inputs must represent values of the next state—00. Similar reasoning can be applied to other states and the whole circuit can be designed with the general structure shown in Figure 4.58.

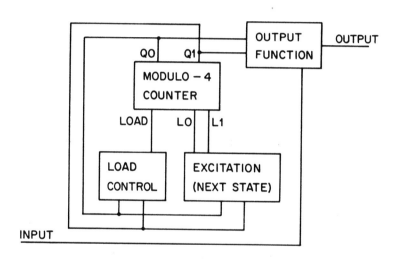

Figure 4.58   The general structure of a sequential circuit implemented with a presettable counter.

The Karnaugh map of LOAD control and inputs L0, L1 is shown in Figure 4.59. Note the following:

1. State 11 should never occur and corresponding entries in LOAD, L0, and L1 tables are don't cares. In practice we may wish to formulate this line of the table in such a way that a corrective transition will be made if this state is reached by an incorrect transition caused by a malfunction.

2. Combinations which require ordinary counting do not load counter's flip-flops. In terms of our Karnaugh maps this means that when $L=0$ (LOAD inactive) $L0=L1=X$ (don't care). The value on $L0$, $L1$ is irrelevant for non-loading combinations since it will not be loaded for this combination anyway. As we know, don't cares tend to simplify the circuit and should be used whenever possible.

$q0,q1$	a	0	1	0	1	0	1
00		0	1	X	0	X	0
01		1	0	0	X	0	X
11		X	X	X	X	X	X
10		1	1	1	0	0	0
		L		$L0$		$L1$	

Figure 4.59   Excitation tables for the LOAD, $L0$ and $L1$ inputs of the counter.

Excitation functions derived from the above Karnaugh maps are

$$L=q0+a.q1'+a'.q1$$
$$L0=a'.q0$$
$$L1=0$$

and the excitation circuit is shown in Figure 4.61. The output circuit is a standard combinational function of a, $q0$, $q1$ derived from the Karnaugh map as in ordinary sequential circuits with flip-flops, and is shown in Figure 4.60. The whole circuit is shown in Figure 4.61.

$q0,q1$	a	0	1
00		0	1
01		0	0
11		X	X
10		0	X
	$z=a(q0+q1')$		

Figure 4.60   The output function of the circuit from Figure 4.57.

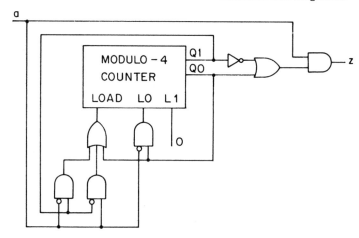

Figure 4.61   The details of implementation of the device from Figure 4.57.

As we can see, sequential circuit design with counters is much easier than design with flip-flops and can theoretically be used for circuits of any complexity since counters can be cascaded. It is clear, however, that for a large number of states, the excitation functions can become very complex and that another method should be considered. We will see that the most advanced digital components—microcomputers—can be used in these situations. Their advantage is simplification of design and implementation. Their disadvantage is limited speed. This set of trade-offs is similar to what was seen for various approaches to switching design: use of the most complex components tends to make design and circuits simpler but sometimes limits the speed of the device. For more complicated circuits working at speeds slower than the microsecond range, circuits built with microcomputers tend to be cheaper, more flexible, and more easily serviced. For another example of design with counters see the Workbook.

Analysis of sequential circuits with counters follows the same rules as analysis of circuits with flip-flops. Examples are given in the Workbook.

4.7.3 Registers

In many applications, particularly in computers, a certain group of several related bits forming a codeword may always be accessed—read or written—together. It is then advantageous to store them together in a single multibit memory device. The use of read-write memories for this purpose is not suitable in many applications because the number of needed memory locations is often very small and also because read-write memory chips are slower than individual flip-flops because of the necessity of address decoding and several phases in the transfer of the desired information. In addition, it is often necessary to perform some elementary logic operation on the codeword at high speed, and elimination of an unnecessary data transfer can speed up the operation considerably.

Registers are groups of flip-flops connected together in such a way that they can be accessed together. A very common variety of registers is the *shift register* which is a register with the additional capability of performing a left or right shift, a transfer of the stored pattern one position to the left or right. Shift registers are available as commercial MSI ICs. They can be used in the design of sequential circuits in a way similar to counters. Registers can also be used as an interface from serial input to parallel output (SIPO) or from parallel input to serial output (PISO) devices. Large shift registers up to thousands of bits are sometimes used as semiconductor memories, and some of the latest types of computer memories—magnetic bubble memories—are basically shift registers with sizes up to one million bits.

Access to individual flip-flops in registers can be *serial* or *parallel.* In *serial input* registers the arrival of a new clock pulse shifts the value present on the input line into the input position. In a shift-right register this will be the leftmost value. The old values are at the same time shifted one position to the right, and the outmost, in our case rightmost, bit is lost. For a shift-left register the directions will be reversed. The following is an example of a sequence of states of a 4-bit shift-right serial-input register starting from an arbitrary initial value and corresponding to input sequence 11011 . . .

> register 0010 1001 1100 0110 1011 . . .
> input 1 1 0 1 1 .

The same input sequence acting on a shift-left register produces

> register 0010 0101 1011 0110 1101 . . .
> input 1 1 0 1 1 .

In *serial output* registers only one flip-flop, storing the "oldest" bit, is accessible. Shift registers with serial input and serial output function as queues—the first bit in is the first bit out.

In many applications all bits must be input together—in *parallel.* An example of the response of a parallel INPUT register to a series of input codewords is shown below. In computers this use of registers is standard and the most common function of the register is temporary storage of an intermediate value.

register 0110 1110 0000 0101 ...
input 1110 0000 0101 1101 ...

If parallel access and serial access are to be implemented as alternatives on the same component, additional combinational elements must be present on the chip. They add negligibly to the complexity of the circuit. An additional requirement is that there must be extra input lines, one for each flip-flop. This requires no additional gates but extra input pins. Production and assembly considerations place a relatively low limit on the maximum number of pins that a standard IC can have; this upper limit is typically 40 pins. In general the number of pins should be as small as possible and this is one of the reasons why commercial shift-register ICs have a limited number of stages, or internal flip-flops and limited control and access functions. A large number of input/output access alternatives are also unnecessary in most applications.

From the access point of view commercial IC chips are classified as

SISO—Serial In/Serial Out
SIPO—Serial In/ Parallel Out
PIPO—Parallel In/ Parallel Out
PISO—Parallel In/Serial Out

PIPO registers with controllable left/right shifting are also called universal shift registers. The diagram in Figure 4.62 shows an implementation of a SISO register, made from D flip-flops, shifting right on the arrival of a clock pulse.

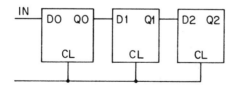

Figure 4.62   An implementation of a 3-bit SISO shift-right register.

A similar register with controllable left/right shifting can be implemented as in Figure 4.63. Clock inputs are left out, and only inputs of D1 are shown in full.

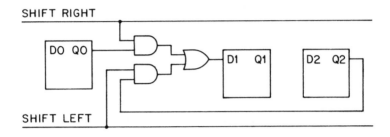

Figure 4.63   A partial diagram of a shift-left/right register.

To see the function of the circuit consider flip-flop D1.

When signal shift-left=1 (and therefore shift-right=0)
$D1 = q0$.shift-right $+ q2$.shift-left$= q2$
(which stipulates input from the flip-flop on the right).

When shift-left=0 (and therefore shift-right=1)
$D1 = q0$.shift-right $+ q2$.shift-left$= q0$
(which stipulates input from the flip-flop on the left).

4.8 COMPUTER SIMULATION OF SEQUENTIAL CIRCUITS

Simulation of sequential circuits with flip-flops using HARD is a simple extension of simulation of combinational circuits:

1. A description of the circuit is created and stored in a file. It consists of the same basic parts as the description of a combinational circuit plus flip-flops.
2. The description is compiled into a file.
3. The compiled description is executed.

New types of elements are allowed in the declaration part. They are connected according to certain rules. In the following examples only descriptions will be demonstrated and explained since steps 2 and 3 of the simulation process are the same as for combinational circuits.

Example 4.7: Consider the circuit of Figure 4.64.

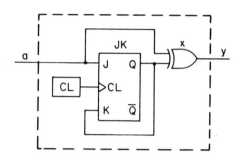

Figure 4.64   Circuit ex1.

Its description is as follows:

CIRCUIT:	ex1;
PARTS:	INPUT: *a*;
	OUTPUT: *b*;
	XOR: *x*, CLOCK: CL;
	JK: *jk* (*L*); ! L denotes a level sensitive flip-flop!
CONNECT:	*a* TO: *jk.j*, *x*,
	jk.q TO: *jk.k*, *x*,
	x TO: *y*,
END.	

Note the following:

1. The dot notation is used for flip-flops with standard names of flip-flop lines: *jk.j*, (*jk 'sj*),*jk.q*, etc.
2. Although all standard lines for flip-flops are available they do not have to be specified if not used in the circuit.

Example 4.8: The description of circuit ex2 of Figure 4.65 is as follows:

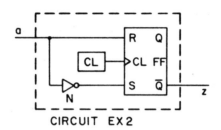

CIRCUIT EX2

Figure 4.65   Circuit ex2.

CIRCUIT: ex2;
PARTS: INPUT: a;
              OUTPUT: z;
              NOT: n;
              RS: $ff(P)$; ! P means positive-edge sensitive!
              CLOCK: $cl(3, 1)$; !period 3, pulse width 1!
CONNECT: a TO: $ff.r$, n;
              cl TO: $ff.cl$;
              n TO: $ff.s$;
              $ff.q'$ TO: z;
END.

4.9   DATA TRANSFER BETWEEN REGISTERS

It is quite common for several registers to communicate groups of bits. The path of data transfer is controlled by control signals generated by the *control unit* of the circuit.

Example 4.9: A, B, C are 2-bit registers. Communication paths are to be designed in such a way as to make it possible for the contents of register A or register C to be transferred into any other register or a pair of registers by a transfer-control signal. In other words, we want to be able to transfer

$$A \text{ to } B \text{ or } C \text{ or } (B,C)$$
$$C \text{ to } A \text{ or } B \text{ or } (A,B)$$

This function could be implemented as shown in Figure 4.66. The path of transfer is controlled at "control points" by a control unit using special control signals such as A to B, C to (A,B), etc. Each of these signals enables the transfer from the specified source to the specified destination—one or two registers. At any time at most one transfer can take place to avoid interference with other logic values. In other words, the data path can transmit only one set of logic values at a time. The circuit switching between alternative paths could also be implemented by multiplexers.

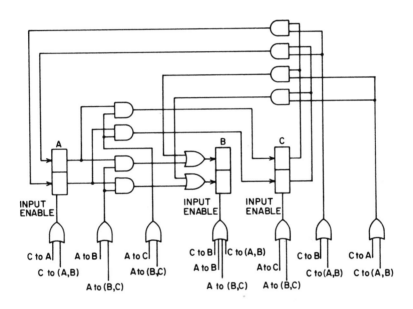

Figure 4.66   A possible implementation of a multiple communication path. *A* to *B*, *A* to *C*, etc. using control signals which enable or disable the passage of information.

The arrangement shown above can be simplified. Two ways of doing this are common. They are based on the use of special semiconductor components:

    1. *Open-collector* gates. Open-collector gates are semiconductor ICs with a part of the output stage left out to be "wired" at the PC

board level. Several open-collector gates can have their outputs connected directly together (all these outputs connected to the power supply via a resistor) creating the equivalent of a multi-input gate. Such an arrangement is called "wired OR." If the output of any of the connected open-collector gates goes to 0, the output of the whole group becomes 0. This behavior is identical to that of an OR gate in negative logic and is the origin of the term "wired OR." Note that in positive logic the function is in reality the NOR of the connected gates. Several types of gates are available in this arrangement. An example of the simplified connection with its Boolean equivalent and standard representation is shown in Figure 4.67.

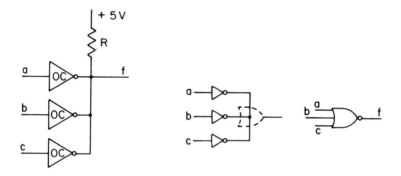

Figure 4.67   The "wired OR," symbol and logical equivalent in positive logic. The equivalent function of this circuit in positive logic is $f = (a+b+c)'$.

Note that this direct connection of outputs of several gates together is NOT possible with ordinary gates. Direct connection of outputs of ordinary gates would result in their destruction or at least an improperly defined voltage level. Besides such a connection does not make sense from the logical point of view. Open-collector circuits are outdated because of their limited speed, difficult maintenance, and other disadvantages. The following approach is now standard.

2. *Tri-State* devices. These devices, when observed from the output, behave in one of two ways:

   a. As standard logic gates connected to the circuit

b. As a line *disconnected* from the circuit (invisible to the circuit).

In addition to the ordinary gate inputs a tri-state component has a tri-state enable/disable input (Figure 4.68) which puts it into state *a* (enabled) or *b* (the *high-impedance* or *floating* state) above. The enable/disable input thus acts as a control signal of a switch; the control is, however, at the electronic level and there is no moving part.

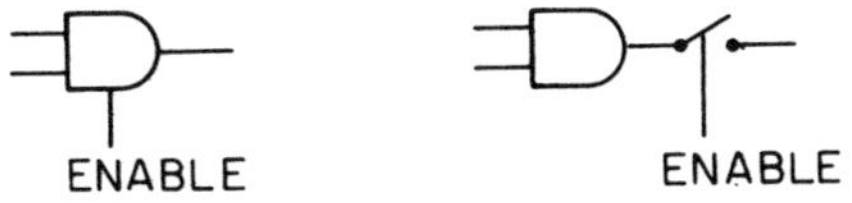

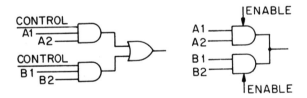

ENABLE   ENABLE

Figure 4.68   A tri-state AND gate (left) and its functional equivalent.

With tri-state elements the circuits in Figure 4.69 are functionally almost equivalent. The only difference is that with both tri-state devices disabled the output of the second circuit is electrically disconnected, "floated." The first circuit always has a 0 or 1 output. Note that control must be designed in such a way that at most one tri-state device is enabled at any time and other tri-states connected to the same line are floated. Enabling two or more connecting tri-states has the same consequences as directly connecting outputs of standard gates—an undefined signal or the destruction of a component.

Figure 4.69   Purely logical control of a data path (left) and control with tri-state devices.

Many IC components with a tri-state function are available. They considerably simplify circuit design. As an example, consider tri-state memory chips: any number of such ICs may be connected to the same set of lines without the need for a complex AND-OR interface which is replaced by the tri-state control. These outputs have to be properly controlled as described previously.

Because the use of tri-state devices, and in the past the use of open-collector gates, is standard, their symbols are often left out of diagrams, since they would only obscure the basic idea. In block diagrams showing only register transfer level components, individual lines are also left out and replaced by a common vector line since the number of lines is often large and the connections identical. Our original diagram could be redrawn showing only registers, bus and control points as in Figure 4.70.

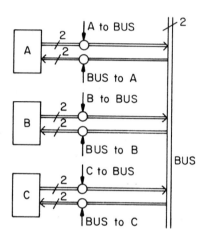

Figure 4.70   A simplified diagram showing only individual data paths and register but not all digital components involved.

Note the following:

1. The set of wires providing the common communication link between registers is called a *bus*. Its "width," or number of wires, is indicated by a slash (/) with the number of lines written across it. A bus is an essential component of all circuits in which several alternatives of transfer between a set of registers are possible. In particular, this is the case for internal communication between individual components of digital computers. An important property of a bus is that it can carry only one set of signals at a time. This implies that only one source of data can be electrically connected *to* the bus, but several destinations can be connected *from* the bus at one time.
2. Note that the role of a bus is essentially passive. It provides only a controllable communication channel, possibly amplifying the

electrical signal. Amplification of the signal is usually necessary to increase the fan-out since a number of output components are typically connected to each line of the bus. A convenient way of visualizing a bus is as a pipe with a number of devices attached to it with the connections controlled by valves. Valves play the role of tri-state devices.

3. The control and transfer are not register to register as it might seem from the above diagram but rather from register to bus and from bus to registers: Control signals are not literally

$$A \text{ to } (B,C)$$

but rather

$$A \text{ to BUS, BUS to } B, \text{ BUS to } C$$

4. Most register transfers are synchronous: they take place at regular times under the control of a clock signal. This implies that the control signal has an additional component, the clock pulse, which is not shown in our diagram.

An even more common way of drawing the circuit is by leaving out all components except the registers and data processing modules, the bus and connections between registers, processing modules, and the bus. Our diagram could thus be drawn as in Figure 4.71.

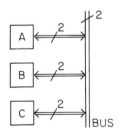

Figure 4.71   A block diagram showing only registers and data paths in a generalized representation.

All connections in the diagram in Figure 4.71 are *bi-directional*: data transfer is possible from the bus to registers and from registers to the bus. This, of course, implies one set of elements and control for each direction, communication lines may be shared. In many situations certain transfers are allowed in only one direction: from a specific register only to another register or a bus. Such one-way connections are called *uni-directional.*

The register-transfer level (RTL) perspective which ignores gate-level details is very common for the investigation of more complex systems, particularly the internal structure of computers. This is partially because including all details of combinational and sequential logic would obscure the basic concepts in already complex systems, and partially because these details are standard and repeated for every communication path in the system. The RTL perspective will be used almost exclusively in the chapter on computer organization.

4.10   RTL DESCRIPTIONS IN HARD

The RTL alternative of HARD will again be illustrated by several examples showing only some of the facilities available. Consider the following description:

RTL:	ex1;
PARTS :	INPUT: $a(8)$;
	OUTPUT: $z(8)$;
	REGISTER: $r1(8)$, $r2(8)$, $r3(8)$;
	BUS: bus(8);
SEQUENCE:	1: a TO: bus;
	bus TO: $r1$, $r2$;
	2: $r2$ TO: bus;
	bus TO: $r3$, z;
	GO TO 1;
END.	

Note the following:

1. Although the general structure of an RTL description is similar to that of a *circuit* description (name, list of parts, body), there are certain differences: name is RTL rather than *circuit*, the *connect* part is replaced by a SEQUENCE part which follows its own special rules.

2. In the SEQUENCE part all transfers which take place *simultaneously* (on one clock signal) are listed together with a common

sequence number. Steps normally occur in the order of numbers. In our case the first clock pulse enables all transfers listed under 1, the next clock pulse all transfers listed under 2, etc.

3. The GO TO 1 statement is a control statement which specifies that upon completion of all actions specified in this step, control passes to step 1 — the next clock pulse enables transfers in step 1. From there control progresses to 2, etc. Control may be implemented on the basis of a counter with the state diagram from Figure 4.72. The control unit could be implemented as in Figure 4.73.

Figure 4.72   The state diagram of control implied by RTL description ex1.

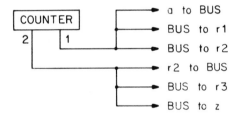

Figure 4.73   Implied control unit for ex1.

The function is as follows: when the counter is in state 1 a signal is generated to enable transfer of a to bus, bus to $r1$, and bus to $r2$. When the counter is in state 2 a signal is generated to enable transfer of $r2$ to bus, bus to $r3$, and bus to z.

4. Note that although detailed connections are not specified, they are implied by the SEQUENCE part of the description. In our case a detailed diagram implied by the description is as shown in Figure 4.74.

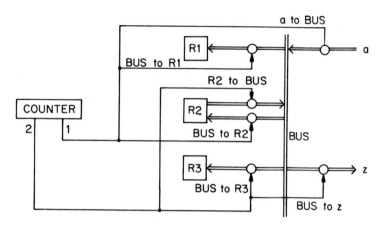

Figure 4.74   Circuit connections implied by RTL description ex1.

Example 4.10:

     RTL: ex2;
     PARTS: INPUT: $a(4)$;
                     OUTPUT: z;
                     REGISTER: $r(4)$, $s(4)$, $t(4)$;
                     BUS: $b(4)$;
     CONDITION: C: $a(1)=1$;
     SEQUENCE: 1: a TO: r;
                     C: GO TO 3;
                     END C;
                     2: r TO: b;
                     b TO: s, t;
                     3: $s(3)$ TO: z;
                     s TO: t;
                     GO TO 1;
     END.

Note the following:

1. Part CONDITION defines logical conditions. In our example the condition labeled C has the value of the logical function (input line) $a(1)$.
2. Step 1 is followed by step 3 if C is TRUE (i.e., C=1 for $a(1)=1$). It is followed by step 2 otherwise. The state diagram of the counter is thus as in Figure 4.75.

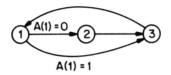

Figure 4.75   Implied state diagram for ex2.

3. The implied circuit is as in Figure 4.76.

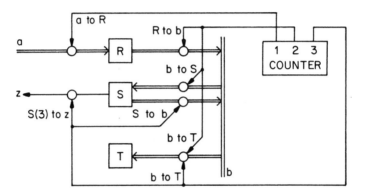

Figure 4.76   The implied circuit implementing ex2.

4. The description and the diagram show that all register transfers do not have to be made via an explicitly specified bus.

REFERENCES

References listed in Chapter 2 deal with combinational and sequential circuits and should be studied as extensions to the current chapter. The reader interested in more solved problems should read the text by Zissos which deals mainly with sequential circuits.

PROBLEMS

1. Construct a state diagram and table for the following circuits:
   a. Recognizer of sequence 0101: Whenever this sequence appears on the input the machine outputs a 1.

b. A one-time recognizer of sequence 0101: A 1 is produced when sequence 0101 occurs for the first time.

c. A modulo-6 counter: a device which outputs the count of 1s on the input coded in binary positional notation. It counts from 0 to 5. The output sequence should be 000 001 010 011 101 000 001, etc.

d. A divide-by-6 device: it outputs a 1 for every six 1s on the input and a 0 otherwise:

input 1111111111111111 ...
output 000001000001000 ...

e. Serial ternary (base 3) adder.

2. Convert the state tables from problem 1 to transition tables by assigning binary codes to the state symbols.

3. Analyze the following sequential circuits:

a. Figure 4.77.

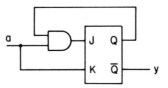

Figure 4.77   Problem 3a.

b. Figure 4.78.

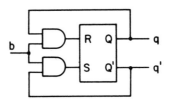

Figure 4.78   Problem 3b.

c. Figure 4.79.

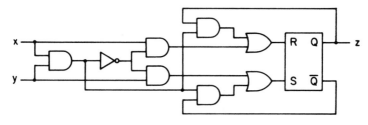

Figure 4.79   Problem 3c.

d. Figure 4.80.

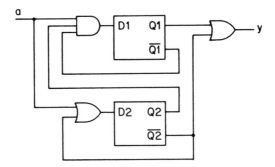

Figure 4.80   Problem 3d.

e. same as in d but using T flip-flops.
f. Figure 4.81.

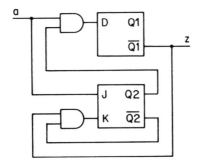

Figure 4.81   Problem 3f.

g. Draw the response of the circuit in Figure 4.81 assuming that both flip-flops are positive-edge triggered, negative-edge triggered, master-slave, level. Choose your own clock and input signals.
h. Repeat Problem 3g but assume that one flip-flop is positive-edge triggered and the other negative-edge triggered.

4. Design the following synchronous circuits:
   a. A $J-K$ flip-flop using D flip-flops.
   b. Circuits for devices described in problem 1. Repeat with different types of flip-flops.
5. Examine the following transition tables of asynchronous circuits and find stable states, cycles, critical and non-critical races.

a. Figure 4.82.

PS\Input	00	01	11	10
00	00	01	11	01
01	11	11	01	10
11	11	10	11	01
10	00	10	11	01

PS — Present State

Figure 4.82   Problem 3a.

b. Figure 4.83

PS\Input	00	01	11	10
00	01	11	00	11
01	11	11	10	11
11	10	11	00	11
10	00	11	10	00

Figure 4.83   Problem 5b.

6. Design modulo-3 synchronous and ripple counters using flip-flops and sketch their timing diagrams.

7. Design the following sequential circuits using standard MSI counters:
   a. a modulo-9 counter (use a decade counter)
   b. a modulo-23 counter (use cascaded decade counters)
   c. a device which repetitively produces the sequence 010 110 000 111
   d. a device with the state graph of Figure 4.84.

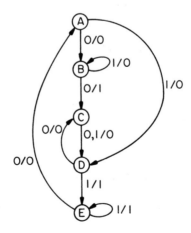

Figure 4.84   Problem 7d.

8.
    a. Draw the state graph and table of a 3-bit shift-left register.
    b. Repeat for a shift-right register.
    c. Repeat for a shift left/right register.
    d. Explain why shifting can be classified as a Boolean operation.

9. Simulate the circuits from the previous problem.

10. Draw a block diagram and then the complete circuit diagram of a circuit consisting of 3-bit registers A, B, C and a bus. Include clock lines. Use tri-state devices. The following register transfers are desired under the control of externally generated signals. It is guaranteed that the bus will not be connected to more than one source register at a time.

    A to B
    A to C
    C to A
    C to B

11. Repeat for a system consisting of registers A, B, C, D, and a bus with the following desired transfers:

    A to B, C, D
    A to B
    B to A
    B to C, D
    C to D
    D to C
    D to A, B
    D to A

    Which connections are uni-directional and which are bi-directional?

12. Simulate circuits from problems 10, 11 at the RTL level.

13. Simulate the bus system from Figure 4.85 at the CIRCUIT level.

    The desired control sequence is:

    1: A TO: B,C;
    2: C TO: B;
    GO TO 1;

14. Simulate the circuit from Problem 13 at the RTL level and draw its block diagram.

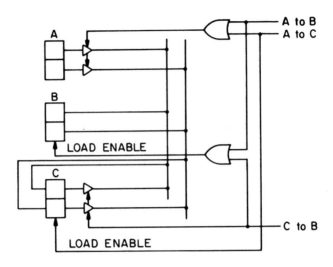

Figure 4.85   Problems 13 and 14.

Chapter 5

CODING

5.1 INTRODUCTION

Digital systems process three types of encoded information:

1. numerical values
2. symbols
3. internal control messages.

All processed information is internally coded, typically in binary. Over the years several coding schemes were developed for the coding of all three categories of information. Some of the most common ones will be described in this chapter.

Numbers in the context of this chapter are codewords* representing numerical values. The codes in common use are most often designed to optimize some of the following criteria:

1. Minimize complexity of arithmetic operations as judged by the complexity of their execution in the given number system. This criterion to a large extent determines also the speed of arithmetic operations.
2. Facilitate conversion to and from the standard decimal notation, or any other notation required for input and output.
3. Facilitate detection and correction of errors.
4. Maximize efficiency of storage utilization.

---

* We use "code" and "codeword" interchangeably although their meaning is not strictly equivalent—"code" is the system, "codeword" is the representation of a specific symbol in the given code.

Encoding of numbers is not the main subject of this chapter, but is dealt with in more detail in the next chapter in the context of arithmetic.

Symbols (also called *characters*) include letters, digits and special symbols (both printable control codes such as ,$%—and non-printable control codes such as printer line feed, carriage return, etc. Control codes are used, for example, in communication between input/output devices and a computer). Letters and digits are often designated by the common name "alphanumeric" or "alphameric" symbols. Note that in our interpretation symbols are abstractions rather than specific realizations, such as fonts, etc.

Internal control messages transmit information between various parts of digital systems and determine their behavior. They are completely design-dependent, and there are no standards governing their coding. This category is not studied in this chapter, but is dealt with in the chapter on digital computers. The major examples of this category of information are instructions executed by computers.

5.2   CODING OF SYMBOLS

The choice of a code for a set of symbols is to some extent an arbitrary decision. There are few reasons why the code of A should be 1000001 rather than 1000000. There are, however, certain criteria which should be considered when a code is being designed. The criteria leave much room for choice, and they are sometimes in conflict. The importance of individual considerations depends on the application: criteria essential in some applications may be irrelevant in other applications.

The following are some considerations applicable to codes representing characters:

1. Codewords of two alphabetically adjacent letters should be adjacent in the following sense: if the code for A is 1000001 then the code for B should be 1000010. This property will considerably simplify processing of strings of letters or text since it will make it possible to handle letter codes as numbers, alphabetical relationships are replaced by numerical relationships, and arithmetic circuits can do the work of a special logic circuit for the processing of symbols. For example, relation A precedes B can be replaced by relation $code(A) < code(B)$; the value of the code

of A is smaller than the value of the code of B. Note that this
basic requirement is not satisfied for the EBCDIC code defined
later in this chapter.

2. Codes of digits 0 to 9 should be related to their binary positional
representation to simplify arithmetic conversion between the
symbol code and the value. It must be remembered that digits
can be used both as symbols and as representations of value:
digit 2 represents a symbol and not a value in the string R2D2.
It represents a value in the message "Mary is 2 years old." The
code of a digit does not have to be identical to the positional
binary representation of its value but should be closely related.
As an example, the ASCII code of digits is 011X where X is a
four-bit representation of the value of the digit: 0110000 is the
code of 0, 0111001 is the code of 9. The conversion of these
codes to values is straightforward and consists of deleting the
three most significant (leftmost) binary digits 011. Note that this
requirement implies that codes of successive digit codes should
have adjacent codes.

3. Codes of symbols of standard arithmetic operators and relational
symbols should be adjacent to simplify their recognition. This is
very useful, for example, in the design of translators for programming languages. In ASCII this requirement is not satisfied
since the codes for ()*+ are adjacent but separated from codes
for < = >.

4. The code of all symbols should have the same number of bits.
This simplifies their storage and interpretation.

5. The code should be sufficiently rich to include all desirable symbols from the chosen character set and preferably leave some
unassigned codes for future expansion.

6. The code should be modular in the sense that, in addition to the
full code including all desired symbols, a subset should be clearly
defined which covers all the most essential symbols and has a
simpler representation. As an example the ASCII 7-bit code
represents all standard symbols. When some of them are not
essential, such as lower case letters, a subset is defined which
uses only six bits. This makes it possible to save on storage,
transmission, etc. in those applications which do not require the
full character set.

7. Where the cost of transmission is an important consideration,
the efficiency of the code may be critical; the cost and length of
transmission are proportional to the number of bits relayed. The

symbols which appear most often should have the shortest codes, and those that are used only rarely should have the longest codes. The combinations should be such as to minimize the cost and length of the average transmitted message. An example of a code designed for efficient transmission of English messages is the Morse code. Note that codes designed according to this criterion in general have codes of varying length and violate requirement number four. This criterion is usually not considered in codes designed for internal representation of symbols in computers.

8. Codes should be such that errors created by transmission or system faults can be detected (*error-detecting codes*). In some situations it may even be necessary to be able to correct a code, i.e., recognize where in the code an error occurred and what the correct code should be. Such codes are called *error-correcting codes.*

9. Codes should be designed to allow simple implementation of decoding and encoding. This is partially implied by the previous requirements. As an example of this consideration ASCII codes of letters are designed for similarity of upper-case and lower-case letters—they have the same last four bits. The code of A is 1000001, the code of a is 1100001, etc.

The requirements listed above restrict our freedom in the choice of a code but do not give a clear-cut answer to a number of questions: should digits precede letters, capital letters, lower-case letters, arithmetic operators? What should be the order of symbols of arithmetic operators? Some of these decisions have been made rather arbitrarily for the codes which are now in standard use. Some of the above criteria were not considered at all. The existing codes are thus not fully satisfactory but will likely remain in use because of their widespread acceptance and the cost of a possible conversion to a new standard.

The following are only the most common or interesting codes in use in information processing and will be described briefly below: ASCII, BCD, BCDIC, EBCDIC, Baudot, Excess-3, Hollerith.

ASCII (American Standard Code for Information Interchange), also called ISO, is the most common code today. It usually uses seven bits, (7-bit ASCII) to represent $2**7=128$ different symbols including upper-case and lower-case letters, digits and special symbols, printable and non-printable. A 6-bit subset which does not include lower-case letters and other symbols is often used. An 8-bit extension uses the eighth bit to add error-detecting capability (parity check) in a way that will be explained later. The table of 7-bit ASCII codes is shown in Figure 5.1.

Bits Shown in Transmission	Bits Shown in Transmission Sequence: 8^a,7,6,5							
Sequence: 4,3,2,1	0000	0001	0010	0011	0100	0101	0110	0111
0000	NUL	DLE	SP	0	@	P		p
0001	SOH	DC1	!	1	A	Q	a	q
0010	STX	DC2	"	2	B	R	b	r
0011	ETX	DC3	#	3	C	S	c	s
0100	EOT	DC4	S	4	D	T	d	t
0101	ENQ	NAK	%	5	E	U	e	u
0110	ACK	SYN	&	6	F	V	f	v
0111	BEL	ETB	'	7	G	W	g	w
1000	BS	CAN	(	8	H	X	h	x
1001	HT	EM	)	9	I	Y	i	y
1010	LF	SUB	*	:	J	Z	j	z
1011	VT	ESC	+	;	K	[	k	{
1100	FF	FS	,	<	L	\	l	:
1101	CR	GS	-	═══	M	]	m	}
1110	SO	RS	.	>	N	¬	n	~
1111	SI	US	/	?	O	—	o	DEL

[a] Bit 8 is used as a parity. Can be 1 or 0 depending on whether odd or even parity is used.

Figure 5.1 The 7-bit ASCII code.

BCD (Binary Coded Decimal) is a 4-bit code for the representation of decimal digits 0.... It is, therefore, a numeric code. All digits are represented by four bits which form the positional representation of the corresponding binary value: 0000 for 0 to 1001 for 9. The decimal value 21 is represented by a pair of codes 0010 0001. This value could be represented in binary as 10101. Similarly, 139 is represented in BCD as 0001 0011 1001, etc. Representation of numerical values in BCD is quite inefficient from the point of view of storage utilization. For example, a number with two decimal digits always requires eight bits in BCD representation but at most five bits in binary positional

representation. (For a general comparison see the Workbook.) We will
see later that BCD arithmetic is quite complex compared with positional binary arithmetic. BCD representation is thus used only when
most processing consists of handling of numbers input and output in
decimal with relatively little intermediate arithmetic. The term BCD
code is also sometimes used for a 6-bit character code developed by
IBM in 1962. The correct name of this code is BCDIC (BCD Interchange Code). Since the numeric BCD code is one of the most important representations of numbers it will be discussed again in Chapter
6.

EBCDIC (Extended BCDIC code) is in many respects similar to
ASCII. It is an 8-bit IBM code and as such widely used, although
currently not as popular as ASCII. The code is shown in Figure 5.2.

The BAUDOT code is an old communication code. Its interesting
properties are:

1. It uses five bits and yet has codes for all upper-case letters, digits
   and certain special symbols. This is interesting since $2**5 = 32$
   and the code is defined for 62 symbols.
2. Each code with two exceptions can represent one of two different symbols, and yet there is no confusion (at least in
   theory).

These properties are achieved by two special "shift" symbols:
"letters" (code 11111) and "figures" (code 11011) whose function is
similar to the function of the "shift" key on ordinary typewriters. All
characters following one of these codes are interpreted as belonging
into one set of characters until the occurrence of the other special
code. As an example the sequence 11011, 01101, 01110, 01111 is interpreted as "figures," !, :, (while the same sequence with "figures"
replaced by "letters" 11111, 01101, 01110, 01111 is interpreted as
"letters," F, C, K. The Baudot code does not satisfy most of the criteria listed previously and is used mostly by outdated communication
equipment. It is included in our overview only because it still can be
encountered and because of its interesting principle.

EXCESS-3 (XS-3) is a numerical code based on BCD. It can be obtained from BCD by adding 3 to the BCD value. Its truth table is
symmetrical around the middle: the code of 4 is the complement of
the code of 5, etc. In general the code of digit i is the complement of
the code of digit 9-i. (Figure 5.3).

Character	Binary code	Character	Binary Code	Character	Binary code
Blank	01000000	d	10000100	H	11001000
¢	01001010	e	10000101	I	11001001
.	01001011	f	10000110	J	11010001
<	01001100	g	10000111	K	11010010
(	01001101	h	10001000	L	11010011
+	01001110	i	10001001	M	11010100
	01001111	j	10010001	N	11010101
&	01010000	k	10010010	O	11010110
!	01011010	l	10010011	P	11010111
$	01011011	m	10010100	Q	11011000
*	01011100	n	10010101	R	11011001
)	01011101	o	10010110	S	11100010
;	01011110	p	10010111	T	11100011
¬	01011111	q	10011000	U	11100100
-	01100000	r	10011001	V	11100101
/	01100001	s	10100010	W	11100110
,	01101011	t	10100011	X	11100111
%	01101100	u	10100100	Y	11101000
—	01101101	v	10100101	Z	11101001
>	01101110	w	10100110		
?	01101111	x	10100111	0	11110000
:	01111010	y	10101000	1	11110001
#	01111011	z	10101001	2	11110010
@	01111100			3	11110011
´	01111101	A	11000001	4	11110100
=	01111110	B	11000010	5	11110101
"	01111111	C	11000011	6	11110110
		D	11000100	7	11110111
a	10000001	E	11000101	8	11111000
b	10000010	F	11000110	9	11111001
c	10000011	G	11000111		

Figure 5.2   The EBCDIC code.

XS-3 is basically a BCD code and is used as such. Its advantage compared to the standard BCD is in simpler implementation of arithmetic operations requiring 9's complementation. There will be more on this in Chapter 6.

The HOLLERITH code is used to represent symbols by configurations of holes punched into paper cards. The character set includes upper case letters, digits, punctuation marks and a few special symbols used in business data processing. It was originally designed for the

80-column cards with 12 rows in which each character is represented in a single column.

There are many other coding schemes, particularly for the representation of numbers. Some codes have very interesting arithmetic properties. The most common number representations will be studied in the following chapter.

decimal	XS-3
0	0011
1	0100
2	0101
3	0110
4	0111
5	1000
6	1001
7	1010
8	1011
9	1100

Figure 5.3   The XS-3 code.

5.3 ERROR DETECTION

Information can be corrupted by noise at any stage during its lifetime—storage, processing, transmission. The rate of appearance of errors is generally very small since modern devices work very reliably and are quite noise-resistant. On the other hand, information is processed at very high speeds (up to 10**9 bits/second) and so errors may occur. In many applications all errors must be prevented. This can be done by using suitable codes and corresponding encoding and decoding devices. Codes can be error-correcting and the decoder can reconstruct the original code when it recognizes an erroneous one. Or codes can be just error-detecting and the system can ask for retransmission of a code recognized as incorrect.

Error detection and correction are the subject of coding theory and will not be studied in depth in this text. Some unpleasant facts which apply to all error handling techniques are as follows:

1. Error detection and correction require the addition of extra bits. In other words, if the minimum size of the code for a certain application is seven bits, the size of a corresponding error-detecting code may be eight or more bits, etc.

2. Special circuits must be added to generate and decode the codes and perform error checking or correction. The length of messages increases and so does the cost of storage and transmission while speed of transmission drops. In this sense error-correcting codes are always more expensive than error-detecting codes designed for the same conditions. (See the Workbook.) For economic reasons, only the simplest error-detecting codes are common, and error-correcting codes are used relatively infrequently. The most common error-detecting code is based on *parity checking* and is explained in the following paragraph. Another simple coding scheme is dealt with in the Workbook.

Consider the 7-bit ASCII code. Many computers use the group of eight bits—one BYTE—as the basic unit of storage. This means that when we are using ASCII we have an extra bit which can be used without extra cost; otherwise, the eighth bit is wasted. Since $2**8 = 256$ is too much to use to encode the commonly required symbols and $2**7 = 128$ is just enough, the eighth bit can be used to convey information about the intended value of the first seven bits. The simplest way to do this is to assign the value of this bit so that the total number of bits with value 1 is even. This *even parity* code has a single-error detecting quality: if at most one of the eight bits is corrupted (inverted), this fact can be recognized since instead of an even number of ones (and an even number of zeros) the resulting code will have an odd number of ones (and an odd number of zeros). It will have odd instead of even parity. Note that this approach has two limitations:

1. It allows only detection but not correction. When odd parity is recognized, one of the bits is known to be inverted, but it cannot be determined which one it is. It may, in fact, be the parity bit.
2. If two or any even number of bits are corrupted, even parity will be preserved and we cannot detect that errors are present. The scheme allows single-error detection. This is not a serious restriction since the occurrence of more than one error in an 8-bit code is theoretically very unlikely. If the probability of one error is $1/10**9$, then the probability of two errors is $1/10**18$ if they are independent. The following are some examples of even parity and odd parity codes:

00010100 01001110 11111111 00000000

is a sequence of even parity codes, presumably no errors, while

10010100 00001110 11110111 00001000

is a sequence of odd parity codes, presumably a single bit error
in each word of the sequence. There is no reason why detection
should be based on even parity; we can design the code so that
odd parity is correct and even parity is an indication of error.
Odd parity interpretation of the above two sequences is just the
opposite of their even parity interpretation: the first sequence is
one of erroneous codes; the second is correct. Both odd and
even parity codes are used, and most devices which work with
codes are designed so that they can be switched from odd to
even parity and vice versa according to the situation.

Augmenting a code by a parity bit allows only single error detection and no error correction. One category of more sophisticated
codes which allows multiple error detection and correction is the
group of Hamming codes. The additional power of these codes is
obtained at the cost of increased storage requirements: the more
error handling, the more extra bits are needed (see the Workbook).

5.4 ENCODERS AND DECODERS

Encoders and decoders are devices which convert signals representing symbols from one system into another. Encoders convert signals
into a code, decoders convert codes into signals more directly
representing the symbols in the given application. Some conversions
are very common, and commercially available ICs are available which
implement them. Other conversions are less frequent, and suitable encoders and decoders may have to be designed for particular applications. Some examples are as follows:

Common conversions: BCD code to 7-segment display, BCD to 1-
of-10 (a four-bit code into a signal on one of ten lines), etc. Note
that multiplexers and demultiplexers also belong to this category.
Less frequent conversions: Baudot to ASCII and vice versa, etc.

A Few examples of Commercially Available ICs:

7447—BCD to 7-segment decoder/driver. Decodes a 4-line BCD input
into a combination of signals driving the seven independent segments
of a 7-segment LED display of the type used in many pocket calculators. This IC actually implements seven functions of four variables and
in addition generates appropriate power for the display. A sketch and a

sample function of one segment are shown in Figure 5.4. A 1
turns a segment ON and a 0 turns it OFF. The rest of the truth
table should consist of don't care entries since BCD codes are
allowed only up to combination 1001. In practice standard symbols are displayed for the remaining codes, and these symbols
determine the rest of the table.

input number	binary	input\segment g
0	0000	0
1	0001	0
2	0010	1
3	0011	1
4	0100	1
5	0101	1
6	0110	1
7	0111	0
8	1000	1
9	1001	1

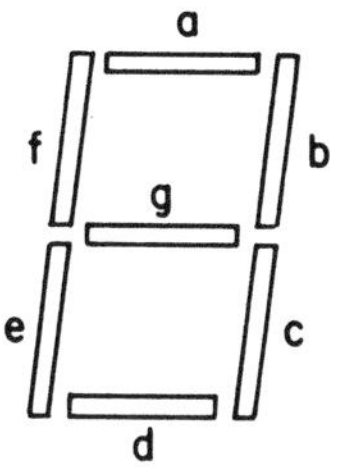

Figure 5.4   The 7-segment display and the function of the BCD-to-7 segment decoder.

7442—BCD to 1-of-10. In response to a BCD code the IC produces a 1
on exactly one of its ten output lines: 0100 turns line four ON, 0110
turns line six ON, etc.

2376—keyboard encoder. This IC is connected to the output lines of a
standard 88 key keyboard and produces an ASCII code corresponding
to the depressed key. The IC also performs other functions such as
"debouncing," elimination of stray signals generated by the bounce of
the mechanical contact associated with the key when the key is
depressed, etc. For a design example, see the Workbook.

REFERENCES

A recent text on the history and development of coded character sets is the
book by MacKenzie. Coding from a theoretical point of view is the subject of
a number of books on information theory such as Abramson. Coding in its
relation to hardware is dealt with in Wakerly. Interesting practical considerations and examples of some commercial ICs are presented in Lancaster.

PROBLEMS

1. Derive the 7-bit ASCII codes of E, e, f, 7, G, z, 5 if the following are given:

   $$code(A) = 1000001, \; code(a) = 1100001, \; code(0) = 0110000.$$

2. What are the codes of 17, 27, 132, 256 in
   a. binary (positional notation)
   b. BCD
   c. XS-3
   d. octal (positional base eight notation)
   e. hexadecimal (positional base 16 notation). Compare the efficiency of these codes; that is, how many bits of storage they require.

3. Add a parity bit to the ASCII codes obtained in Problem 1 assuming
   a. even parity
   b. odd parity

4. Design the following encoders using elementary gates:
   a. octal to BCO (Binary Coded Octal)—eight input lines input lines, 256 output lines,
   b. decimal to BCD (ten input lines, four output lines)
   c. 1-of-10 multiplexer (one input line, four BCD address lines, ten outputs)

5. Design the following decoders using elementary gates:
   a. BCO to octal (three lines to eight lines)
   b. BCD to decimal (four lines to ten lines)
   c. ten-to-1 demultiplexer (ten input lines, four BCD control lines, one output line)
   d. 8-to-256 decoder (8 input lines, 256 output lines, exactly one of them carrying a 1 at any time)

6. Design a circuit to check a 4-bit code for odd (even) parity: The circuit outputs 1 for correct parity and 0 when it detects an error. Design the circuit as
   a. combinational (all 4 bits supplied at the same time, in parallel)
   b. sequential (input is serial, one bit at a time)

7. Modify your circuit from Problem 6 to allow the control of odd/even parity by an external input "parity." When parity = 1 the circuit checks for odd parity, when parity = 0 it checks for even parity.

8. Design a circuit to generate the fourth bit to a given 3-bit codeword to produce an odd (even) parity code. Design the circuit as
   a. combinational
   b. sequential

9. Modify the circuit from Problem 8 to allow external control of parity (as in Problem 7).

Chapter 6

NUMBER REPRESENTATION AND ARITHMETIC

6.1 INTRODUCTION

An introduction to the representation of numerical values in binary was presented in Chapter 2. It was shown how the concept of positional notation used in standard decimal representation carries over into representations based on a different *radix* (base), in particular the radix 2 — binary — system.

The notational system introduced in Chapter 2 has a number of very serious limitations which make it quite unsuitable for ordinary calculations without an extension: the system can represent only non-negative integer numbers (with no fractional part) 0, 1, 2, ... whose amplitude is severely limited by the number of available bits—the largest number representable by n bits i $2^{**}n-1$. This means that

1. We cannot represent fractional numbers;
2. We cannot represent negative numbers;
3. Even with relatively large words, the maximum magnitude is too small for many uses. A common word length is 16 bits. The maximum number representable by 16 bits is $1111111111111111 = 2^{**}16-1 = 65535$, which is quite small.

Most of this chapter is devoted to the description of extensions and/or modifications which remove these restrictions and the study of basic arithmetic operations in these extended systems. It is shown that obvious modifications lead to rather inefficient arithmetic and that further modification is required to simplify the implementation of arithmetic circuits and make them faster. The chapter concludes with a discussion of BCD arithmetic.

It should be stressed that number representation, arithmetic, and the design of more efficient arithmetic units have traditionally been areas of intensive research and that a large number of ingenious and conceptually complicated methods have been devised to speed up arithmetic operations. There are several texts dealing with the subject in considerable detail, and our presentation is only a survey of the basic results.

6.2 REPRESENTATION OF FRACTIONAL NUMBERS

The possibility of representing fractional numbers is built into the positional system: weights associated with individual positions are growing powers of the base going from right to left. The fundamental position is the position with weight $(radix)^{**} = 1$. Marking this position in the code and continuing from this position to the right give positions with weights $radix^{**}(-1)$, $radix^{**}(-2)$, etc. Thus, for example, in decimal (base 10), $1.15 = 1*10^{**}0 + 1*10^{**}(-1) + 5*10^{**}(-2)$. The marker of the fundamental position is the dot, the decimal point.

Similarly, in binary, $1.01 = 1*2^{**}0 + 0*2^{**}(-1) + 1*2^{**}(-2) = 1.25$ decimal. If we want to STORE number 1.01 in binary we could attempt to mark the position of the radix point, "point" for short, inside the code. With binary symbols the point can be represented only by a combination of zeros and ones, and such a combination would be indistinguishable from the numeric part of the code since the point can appear anywhere in the code and its position is unpredictable. This means that we cannot store fractional numbers in this form unless we stipulate *externally* that the point is *implied* in a certain position. We can represent 1.01 as 101 and stipulate that the point is between the first and second bit from left. Or we can represent it as 00101 and stipulate the point's position between the third and fourth bit, etc. As a consequence the same code can represent different values depending on the implied position of the point. Thus, 01101 can be interpreted as 0.1101 or 01.101 or 011.01, etc. It can even be interpreted as 0.0001101 (leading 0s deleted in the stored code or 011010000.0 (trailing 0s deleted), etc. The correct interpretation depends on the accepted convention which is in turn dictated by the requirements of the situation.

In a specific context it is clearly desirable to fix the position of the point; otherwise, every code would have to be accompanied by the specification of the location of the point. With small numbers the point will be towards the left end of the code; with large numbers the point will be towards the right end. In any case the position will be fixed but not physically represented when the code is physically stored, for example in a register. The name *fixed-point representation* is derived from this property. Because the sign is not represented, it is also called *pure binary fixed-point representation* as opposed to the sign-magnitude fixed-point representation covered in a following section.

The implications of fixing the point in a certain position are given by the fact that the position determines the maximum representable magnitude and the accuracy of representation. Assume that four bits are available to store individual numbers. In other words, all registers and memory words of the system consist of 4-bit words. This is unrealistically low for most systems but will make it easier to illustrate the concept. The maximum number representable corresponds to code 1111, and the smallest distance, or difference between two numbers represented in the system is 0001. This number determines the precision with which a value can be represented in the given system.

1. Assume that the point is placed to the right of the rightmost bit, INTEGER representation: *xxxx*. The maximum value is 1111. = 15 decimal, and the minimum distance is 0001. = 1 decimal.
2. Assume that the point is located to the left of the leftmost bit, FRACTIONAL representation: *.xxxx*; the maximum value is .1111 = 1/2+1/4+1/8+1/16 = 15/16, and the minimum distance is .0001 = 1/16.

In summary, moving the point to the left decreases the value of the maximum representable number but increases the accuracy of representation and vice versa. The position of the radix point must be chosen to satisfy these two conflicting parameters, and the requirements of the application within the bounds imposed by storage limitations. For more examples, see the Workbook.

What happens to *arithmetic operations* when positional notation is extended to fractional numbers? Since the rules are essentially the same for all bases, let us explore the consequences in the decimal system below:

$$
\begin{array}{rrr}
157 & 15.7 & 0.157 \\
218 & 21.8 & 0.218 \\
\hline
375 & 37.5 & 0.375
\end{array}
$$

Note that the position of the radix point is irrelevant to the process of addition. Shifting the decimal point of both operands by the same number of positions is reflected by the same shift of the result: $15.7+21.8=37.5$ is obtained from $157+218=375$ by shifting the decimal point of both operands and the result by one position to the left, i.e., by division by $10**1=10$. The same rules apply to subtraction. Division and multiplication obey similar rules. Extension of positional notation to include fractional numbers, therefore, does not require any change in the mechanics of basic arithmetic operations, and circuits implementing them are identical. The difference is only in the interpretation of codes.

6.3   IMPLEMENTATION OF PURE BINARY ADDITION

We have seen that addition is basically the same in all positional systems working only with non-negative numbers. Since fractional numbers are treated identically, we can restrict our attention to integer numbers. Consider the following addition in the decimal system:

operand 1	18
operand 2	23
carry-in	10
result	41

Addition of two multidigit operands consists of repeated addition of three digits: one from each operand and one from the carry generated by addition in the previous position. The process can be systematically described by the following algorithm:

Algorithm ADD.
  Carry := 0
  Position := 0 (start with rightmost digit)
  Repeat
    Add carry and digits of operands for the
      current position to obtain digits $s(2)$, $s(1)$
    Current digit of result := $s(1)$
    Carry := $s(2)$
    Position := position + 1

until $s(2) = s(1) = 0$ and all digits of operands to the left of the current position are 0.

The only step of the algorithm which depends on the base of the system is addition of the three digits of operands and carry. In order to be able to execute the algorithm or implement it in hardware, we have to know how to add three digits in a given system. This is trivial and for the binary system the Karnaugh map of Figure 6.1 describes the rules.

carry	op1 op2			
in	00	01	11	10
0	00	01	10	01
1	01	10	11	10

Figure 6.1   Sum digits $s(2)s(1)$ in binary addition of three operands.

Breaking the table down into a carry $(s(2))$ and a sum $(s(1))$ table allows us to construct the Boolean expressions for the maps Figure 6.2. The corresponding equations relating carries, sum, and operand digits are:

carry out: cout $= cin(op1 + op2) + op1.op2$
sum: sum $= cin(op1 \text{ XOR } op2)' + cin'(op1 \text{ XOR } op2)$
                $= cinXORop1XORop2$

carry	op1 op2					00	01	11	10
in	00	01	11	10		0	1	0	
0	0	1	0	1		0	1	1	1
1	1	0	1	0					

SUM   CARRY-OUT

Figure 6.2   The sum and carry tables for binary addition.

These equations describe the *full adder* which calculates the carry and the sum digits as a function of the carry-in and operand digits. A *half adder* is a similar device with only two inputs — the two operands. The *full adder* circuit can be implemented as in Figure 6.3. According to algorithm ADD, N full adders can be connected in series to obtain an

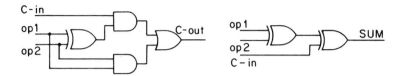

Figure 6.3   A full adder implementing addition for a single position.

N-bit adder (Figure 6.4). The *N*-bit adder of Figure 6.4 is called a *ripple carry adder* since the carry must ripple through all *N* stages before outputs stabilize to the correct values; see the timing diagram in Figure 6.5.

Because of this fact, the ripple carry adder is relatively slow; note that its asynchronous principle is similar to that of ripple counters. A number of more efficient designs have been developed which remove or restrict this limitation and work faster. These faster adders are more complex and expensive.

The ripple carry adder is a parallel adder in the sense that all operands are presented to it in parallel (at the same time). It consists of a series of full adders and is in this sense a serial circuit. The name "serial adder" is, however, reserved for circuits which accept individual bits of operands one pair at a time. Serial adders are, of course, slower but simpler than parallel adders.

With our notation which does not allow negative numbers, *subtraction* is of limited use. The general principles of subtraction remain the same, and the rules can be derived from our knowledge of the

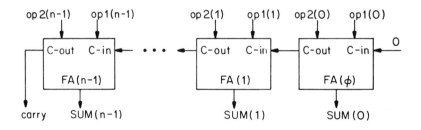

Figure 6.4   A sequence of full adders implementing multidigit binary addition (the ripple carry adder).

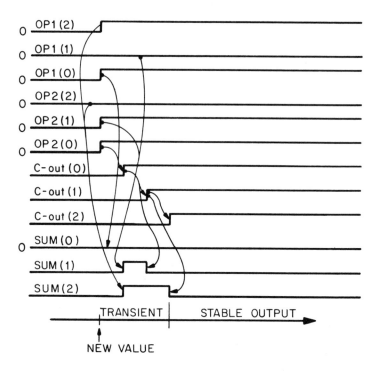

Figure 6.5   A sample timing diagram showing how the carry propagates through the adder: $n=3$, $op1=101$, $op2=011$.

corresponding operation in decimal. The truth table is different from that of binary addition, and the concept of a carry is replaced by the concept of a borrow. Subtraction will not be investigated in any detail since the complement notation discussed in a later section makes it possible to perform subtraction using a standard adder and eliminates the need for a subtracter.

6.4 CONVERSION BETWEEN DIFFERENT BASES

6.4.1 Integer Numbers

Assume that we want to represent an *integer* number x in binary. A rule for the calculation of individual bits in the positional representation $x=b(N)b(N-1)...b(0)$ can be obtained from the following formulas:

$$x = b(0)*2^{**}0 + b(1)*2^{**}1 + \cdots + b(N)*2^{**}N =$$
$$= b(0) + 2* [b(1) + 2*(b(2) + .. + 2*(b(N-1) + b(N)))..]$$
$$= b(0) + 2*q(0)$$

Dividing the value of x by 2 gives quotient $q(0)$ and remainder $b(0)$. Similarly, division of $q(0)$ by 2 gives quotient $q(1)$ and remainder $b(1)$, etc. The same rule applies to any base if we replace 2 by the new radix. We can describe the process as follows:

Algorithm CB (Conversion to Binary). To convert number x to binary $b(N)b(N-1)...b(0)$:
$q:=x,i:=0$
Repeat
    Divide q by 2 to obtain new quotient q and remainder r,
    $b(i):=r;i:=i+1$
until $q=0$

Algorithm CB is a special form of the more general Horner's rule. As an example of the use of this algorithm, let us convert decimal value 13 to binary.

13/2	$= 6$ (new value of q) and remainder $r=1$	$(=b(0))$
6/2	$= 3$ (new value of q) and remainder $r=0$	$(=b(1))$
3/2	$= 1$ (new value of q) and remainder $r=1$	$(=b(2))$
1/2	$= 0$ (new value of q) and remainder $r=1$	$(=b(2))$

The result is 1101, the binary equivalent of decimal 13. The algorithm used to obtain this code differs from algorithm CB only in that 2 in algorithm CB is replaced by 8 for the octal system. The same number converted to octal (base 8) follows:

$$13/8 = 1, r=5$$
$$1/8 = 0, r=1 \text{ end of algorithm.}$$

The result is 15, the octal equivalent of decimal 13.

Conversion from binary to decimal is most obviously made by simple addition of weighted bits: $1101 = 1*1 + 0*2 + 1*4 + 1*8 = 13$ decimal. A more efficient method is obtained by using the same formula as above, this time from inside: multiply $b(N)$ by 2 and add $b(N-1)$; multiply the result by 2 and add $b(N-2)$, ... add $b(0)$;

$$1101 = 1+2*(0+2*(1+2*1)) = 1+2*(0+2*(3)) = 1+2*6 = 13$$

Note that the "obvious" method of addition of weighted digits can start from left, the most significant bit—MSB— or right, the least significant bit—LSB. The more efficient method based on the bracketed formula must start from the MSB, corresponding to the inside of the formula.

6.4.2   Other Useful Bases

The digital systems of interest in this text work with binary representations. In this sense binary notation is all that really matters since our systems store all information in binary. This is a consequence of the currently most efficient and economical technology and may not be necessarily true in the future. Manual handling of binary codes may be quite confusing and may create unnecessary problems and cause costly mistakes: digital computers often have word sizes such as 32 or even 68 bits. A long list of codes, each consisting of 32 or 68 bits, is very hard to process manually if it is necessary. Fortunately this does not happen often and is the lot of a relatively small group of computer programmers. To alleviate this problem of perception and memorization, we need to devise a shorthand notation which will reduce the length of codes and be easy to convert to/from binary.

The conversion between a code based on radix r and one based on radix $r1$ is easy when $r1 = r^{**}j$ where j is an integer. This is because in this case a single symbol in code $r1$ represents a group of j symbols of code r and vice versa and the individual groups are completely independent. Conversion from code r to code $r1$ then consists of replacing groups of j symbols in code r by a single symbol of code $r1$ starting from the fractional point. For conversion from $r1$ to r, individual symbols are replaced by groups of j symbols. In binary the most natural related bases are thus *octal* (base $8 = 2^{**}3$) and *hexadecimal* (base $16 = 2^{**}4$). One problem with base 16 notation is that it requires 16 different symbols to represent digits; binary requires 2, octal 8, hexadecimal 16. The solution is to use digits 0 to 9 with their standard meaning and letters A, B, C, D, E, F to represent decimal values 10 to 15. This rather awkward and unnatural representation indicates why larger base systems are not used: the next suitable base is 32. It would be very economical since it would reduce the length of binary codes by a factor of 5—5 bits would be replaced by just one symbol, etc. It would, however, require a very long and artificial set of symbols such as all digits and almost all letters of the alphabet. Its use would be very inefficient since it would have to be used with a table. This disadvantage would outweigh the advantage.

Example 6:1: Convert 110101. binary to octal ($8 = 2**3$ and so $j=3$): The rightmost group 101 represents 5 and will be represented by digit 5. The leftmost group 110 represents 6 and is represented by this digit. The result is that binary 110101 is equivalent to octal 65. (Check the correctness of this result by converting both to decimal.) Now convert the same binary code to hexadecimal: the rightmost group of four digits ($16 = 2**4$) is represented by 5 ($0101 = 5$) and the group of four bits to the left of this group represents 3 (0011 obtained by adding insignificant leading zeros). In summary hexadecimal 35 is equivalent to binary 110101 and octal 65.

Example 6.2: Convert A6.F from hexadecimal to binary:

1. F is 1111
2. 6 is 0110
3. A is 1010 A6.F hexadecimal is 10100110.1111 binary. Since the groups are independent conversion can be performed in the opposite order as well: 3, 2, 1.

It has already been stated that hexadecimal and octal notation are used only as shorthand notations for binary. It must be remembered that the physical storage of information in all systems considered in this text is in binary form.

6.4.3 Conversion of Pure Fractions

Conversion of *pure fractions* of the form $0.xx....x$ can be derived from the following formula:

$$x = b(-1)*2**(--) + ... + b(-N)*2**(-N) =$$
$$2 = 1/2*(b(-1) + 1/2*(B(-2) + 1/2*(...+ 1/2*b(-N))..)$$
$$2 = 1/2*(b(-1) + f(-1))$$

The process of conversion to binary consists of repeated multiplication by 2. The integer part of the first result is $b(-1)$ and the fractional part is $f(-1)$. The fractional part is multiplied again, etc. The essential difference between integer and fraction conversion is that, while the representation of an integer always consists of a finite number of digits, the representation of a fraction may have an infinite number of digits. This is well known from decimal arithmetic: $1/3 = 0.33333...$ in decimal. A notable fact is that even when decimal representation of a given value is finite the full binary representation of the same value may require an infinite number of bits.

Example 6.3: Convert decimal $x=0.7$ to binary:

2∗0.7	=	1.4	and so	$b(-1)$	=	1, $r(-1)$	=	0.4
2∗0.4	=	0.8		$b(-2)$	=	0, $r(-2)$	=	0.8
2∗0.8	=	1.6		$b(-3)$	=	1, $r(-3)$	=	0.6
2∗0.6	=	1.2		$b(-4)$	=	1, $r(-4)$	=	0.2
2∗0.2	=	0.4		$b(-5)$	=	0, $r(-5)$	=	0.4

Now we are in the same situation as in the second step: $r(-5)$ = $r(-1)$. Since the value of r determines the next step, $r(-6)$ will be the same as $r(-2)$, etc., and $b(-6) = b(-2)$, etc. The rest of the code will thus be repetitive and infinite: 0.7 decimal is 0.10110 110 110 110 ... binary. The consequence of this result and the fact that only a fixed and finite number of storage locations is available to store the value is that in many situations numbers have to be stored in an approximated form: *truncated*—with all the less significant bits exceeding the available space deleted, or *rounded*—with the representation adjusted so that the value stored is the closest possible approximation to the true value. In decimal, 1/3 is truncated and rounded to 0.333 if three decimal digits can be stored, 2/3 is truncated to 0.666 but rounded to 0.667.

This implication of physical limitations can cause significant numerical inaccuracies. As an example, 3000∗2/3 = 2000, but 3000∗0.666 = 1998, and numerical errors of this type can accumulate to lead to completely incorrect results. Note that truncation after k bits leads to a maximum error less than $2^{**}(-k)$.

6.5   REPRESENTATION OF NEGATIVE NUMBERS

Our notation must allow for the representation of positive and negative numbers. This requires a representation for the + and −signs. Since there are only two signs, binary representation is easy. The common convention is to represent + by 0 and−by 1. We will see later that this assignment is necessary if we want to be consistent with the more popular "complement" representation.

It was argued in the previous section that there is no sensible way of representing the binary point. The reason for this was that the point is a position marker. Its place is given by the needs of a specific application and is thus generally unpredictable. This makes any binary combination that could represent it positionally unrecognizable, indistinguishable from a value. This is not so with the sign. The sign represents a certain property of the number, and we can place it in a certain fixed position identical for all numbers. Consistently with the usual decimal convention, the symbol is commonly placed to the left of the first digit.

Fixed point signed numbers can thus be represented in the following form:

$$\text{sign} \qquad \text{magnitude}$$
$$b(N-1) \quad 0\,b(N-2)...b(0)$$

This N-bit representation is called the *sign-magnitude* or signed-magnitude representation.

The general form given above indicates that with the same number of bits the magnitude of a number expressed in the sign-magnitude form is restricted with respect to pure magnitude representation since one bit is "wasted" to represent the sign. Assume, for example, that four bits are available to represent a number and that the point is placed to the right of the last bit (integer representation). 1111 represents 15 in pure magnitude representation and -7 in the sign-magnitude representation. 0111 is 7 in both representations. A similar relationship holds for any position of the point.

It could seem that we are losing some of the power of number representation. The size of the set of representable numbers seems to have been halved. This is not so, and we can represent *almost* the same number of different numbers in both representations:

In pure magnitude notation pure binary representation integers 0 to 15, 16 different numbers altogether, are represented as 0000 to 1111. In sign-magnitude representation 0000 to 0111 represent 0 to 7 and 1000 to 1111 represent -0 to -7, 15 different numbers altogether, 0 and -0 represent the same values.

Arithmetic with sign-magnitude representation is the same as arithmetic in decimal since decimal notation is, in fact, sign-magnitude representation using a special symbol for the sign. Standard arithmetic rules are well known and quite straightforward. We will see that their implementation is not trivial and that a simplification is possible.

Let us develop the algorithm for *addition* of numbers in the sign-magnitude form. We will make the standard assumptions that we know how to add two non-negative numbers as explained in the previous section, how to subtract $x-y$ when $x \geqslant y \geqslant 0$, and how to compare magnitudes. Abbreviations ADD(x,y) and SUBTRACT(x,y) will be used to represent these operations. With these assumptions the algorithm for addition of numbers a,b—any sign—is as follows ($abs(a)$ is the absolute value—magnitude—of a).

Algorithm SMA (sign-magnitude addition):

If $a,b \geq 0$ then $a+b = \text{ADD}(a,b)$
If $a,b < 0$ then $a+b = -\text{ADD}(-a,-b)$
If $a \geq 0$, $b < 0$ then
   If $a \geq \text{abs}(b)$ then $a+b = \text{SUBTRACT}(a,-b)$
   else $a+b = -\text{SUBTRACT}(-a,b)$
If $a < 0$, $b \geq 0$ then
   If $b \geq \text{abs}(a)$ then $a+b = \text{SUBTRACT}(b,-a)$
   else $a+b = -\text{SUBTRACT}(-b,a)$

The following examples illustrate the use of the algorithm.

$$
\begin{array}{lll}
3 + 4 & = 7 & \\
(-3) + (-4) & = -((-(-3))+(-(-4))) & = -7 \\
4 + (-3) & = (4-(-(-3)))) & = 1 \\
3 + (-4) & = -((-(-4))-3) & = -1 \\
(-3) + 4 & = (4-(-(-3)))) & = 1 \\
(-4) + 3 & = -((-(-4))-3) & = -1
\end{array}
$$

Note that we can implement the general adder directly from the algorithm as shown in Figure 6.6. In this very primitive partial implementation[*] derived directly from the algorithm, the rectangles

---

[*] The example of the design of the general adder, which is a somewhat more complicated circuit than the circuits dealt with previously, shows a systematic approach to the design of complex circuits. It is called "top-down design" since it proceeds from major problems to smaller subproblems and easier-to-design subcomponents. The result is a modular product which consists of a number of interconnected modules with well defined functions, which implement solutions to rather general subproblems such as addition of positive numbers, etc. The top-down approach can be described by the following algorithm:

Algorithm TDD (Top-down design):
1. Describe the solution in a modular form by breaking it down into natural subproblems and specifying their dependencies.
2. Draw the block diagram of the circuit assuming that devices performing the specified subfunctions are available.
3. If devices for the required subfunctions are not commercially available, use algorithm TDD to design them.

This is an algorithm only in a rather loose sense of the word since in several places it does not specify exactly what to do. As a consequence, several different designers using this approach could obtain different and valid solutions to the same design problem; this could not happen with a true deterministic algorithm.

The top-down approach has a number of important advantages: it is systematic and will lead to faster design, and the resulting device will be better organized and as such easier to maintain and modify. Note that this algorithm can be easily modified to apply to the design of a computer program and, in fact, to the systematic solution of any problem.

represent modules whose function is explained by the legend. If we assume that the operand is of the form

$$a = a(N)a(N-1)...a(1)a(0)$$

where $a(N)$ is the sign and the other digits represent the magnitude, then some of the "modules" are as shown in Figure 6.7.

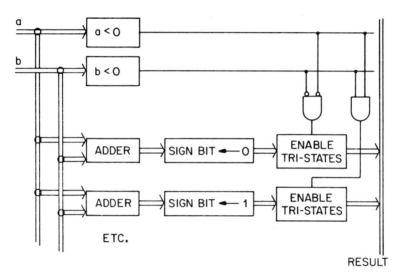

Figure 6.6   A block diagram of a sign-magnitude adder showing some of the major components of the device.

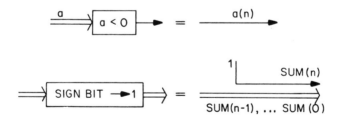

Figure 6.7   A detailed diagram of some modules from Figure 6.6.

The adder may be a complex device, and the subtracter is of similar complexity.

The point of this exercise in design was to show that although a general adder can be designed it is not very simple. It uses a number of components of different types. A general subtracter could be designed similarly. It can be seen that the reason for the complexity of the device is that the sign and the relative magnitude of the two operands determine which of the six possible alternative operations to perform.

There is, fortunately, another representation which completely eliminates the problem of multiple alternatives. In the *radix-complement* representation all operands are handled identically whatever are their signs and relative magnitudes. The radix complement, in our case 2's complement, representation seems more complicated than positional representation. This is partially because we are not familiar with it. It is, however, very advantageous from the point of view of the simplicity of basic arithmetic operations, and is the most commonly used representation of numbers in digital computers. It will be described in the next section. A related *radix−1 complement* (in our case 1's *complement*) notation is based on a similar principle and has similar properties. It is used less frequently since arithmetic in this system is slightly less efficient. It will not be studied in this text but is presented in the Workbook.

6.6   RADIX-COMPLEMENT REPRESENTATION

Radix-complement representation is another form of fixed-point representation which allows representation of negative numbers and simplifies basic arithmetic operations For illustration of the principle we will assume that our system is decimal rather than binary, works with integers, and uses four decimal digits for storage of numbers.

The radix-complement (in this example 10's complement) representation uses the same codes for non-negative numbers as the sign-magnitude system. The leading digit of a positive number must be 0 and the remaining three digits, assuming that there are four digits altogether, represent the magnitude:

$$13 \quad \text{is stored} \quad \text{as } 0013$$
$$172 \qquad\qquad \text{as } 0172$$

Positive number 1973 cannot be represented in our system since it requires four digits for the magnitude and one for the sign: it *overflows* the storage size.

Negative numbers are represented by the 10's complements of their magnitudes:

$$-13 \text{ is stored as } (1)0000-13 \qquad = 9987$$
$$-172 \text{ is stored as } (1)0000-172 \qquad = 9828$$
$$-1973 \text{ overflows because its magnitude is too large.}$$

Digit 1 in the fifth position is written in brackets to indicate that it cannot actually be stored since only four digits are available for storage. It is only used in the process of complementation. Note that the 4-digit representation of our numbers could be obtained also by subtracting from 100000 or 1000000, etc., any power of 10 with at least four 0s:

(-13)	converts	to $(10)0000-13$	$= (9)9987$
(-13)		to $(100)0000-172$	$= (99)9828$
-172		to $(10)0000-172$	$= (9)9828$
-172		to $(100)0000-172$	$= (99)9828,$

and the complements are STORED identically in the available 4-digit storage. The extra leading nines are dropped since there is no room to store them.

Note that digit 9 plays the role of the $-$ sign. The rest of the code of a negative number is *not the magnitude* of the number. The magnitude of a negative number can be obtained by complementing the number to obtain the "original" positive equivalent:

$$\text{magnitude}(9987) \qquad = \text{magnitude}(-13)$$
i.e.
$$\text{magnitude}(9987) \qquad = \text{magnitude}[(1)0000-9987]$$
$$= \text{magnitude}(0013) = 13$$

It will now be shown that, in 10's complement representation, addition is governed by the same rule for all combinations of signs and magnitudes of operands. This common rule of addition is simply standard decimal addition in which all the digits *including the "sign digit"* are added together as in the addition of two positive numbers:

problem	representation	result
$13+182$	$0013+0182$	0195
$183+(-17)$	$0183+(10000-0017)$	
	$0183+9983$	$(1)0166$

(The leading 1 is automatically dropped since only four digits are stored.)

$$(-15)+6 \quad 9985+0006 \quad 9991$$

The last result begins with a 9 and therefore represents a negative number whose magnitude is $10000-9991=9$. The result thus represents -9.

$$(-8)+(-11) \quad 9992+9989 \quad (1)9981$$

which represents -19 since the sign is negative (leading digit is 9) and the magnitude is $10000-9981=19$.

It is clear that when we add two sufficiently large numbers the result may cause an overflow. Let us investigate the general conditions in which this situation can arise:

1. When we add two numbers with *different signs*, there *cannot* be an overflow: if a number is represented by a 4-digit 10's complement code, then its magnitude is representable by three digits. This is obvious for a positive number. For a negative number, complementation leads to a legal 10's complement code of a positive number representing the magnitude, and the statement is again correct. Assume that a is non−negative and b is negative. Since $x = a+(-b) = a-abs(b) = abs(a)-abs(b)$, the magnitude of the result is $abs(x) = abs(abs(a)-abs(b)) \leqslant max(abs(a), abs(b))$. Since a and b both have magnitudes representable by three digits the same must be true for x. This confirms that adding two numbers with different "sign digits" cannot cause an overflow.

2. When two numbers of the *same sign* and sufficiently large magnitudes are added, the result *may* cause an overflow. Let us see how the overflow will manifest itself in the result:

500 + 600	= 0500 + 0600	= 1100
(−500) + (−600)	= 9500 + 9400	= (1)8900

   In both cases when an overflow occurs the sum is represented by a code which is not a legal code for the expected result. In other words the "sign digit" does not have the same value as the sign digits of the two operands as should be the case, since both operands have the same sign.

An examination of the above arguments shows that the general properties of 10's complement notation for integers and four digits of storage apply to *any* radix-complement notation with minor differences. In particular these properties apply to radix 2, any number of storage bits, and any location of the binary point.

Let us consider the rules for *subtraction* using the same "environment" as previously (4-digit decimal integers). The rules are very simple when we realize that

1. $a-b=a+(-b)$
2. $-b$ is represented as the complement of b

Subtraction is thus performed by first complementing b and then adding the complement to a:

$$17-3 = 17 + (-3) = 0017 + 9997 = (1)0014$$
(leading 1 is dropped)
$$3-17 = 3 + (-17) = 0003 + 9983 = 9986$$
(represents -14)
$$(-4)-(-5) = 9996 + 0005 = (1)0001$$
$$(-5)-(-4) = 9995 + 0004 = 9999 \text{ (corresponds to } -1)$$

The only problem with radix-complement representation seems to be the need for complementation. Complementation is needed to

1. Allow the change of the sign of numbers and in particular to generate codes for negative numbers when their magnitude is given and
2. Implement subtraction.

Decimal complementation is not a trivial operation as we have seen. Fortunately, *binary* complementation is extremely simple and is given by the following algorithm.

Algorithm BC (binary 2's complementation):
To complement a binary number
1. invert all bits in its code
2. add 1 to the least significant bit

Step 1 is called "bitwise" complement or 1's complement. A justification of this algorithm is given in the Workbook. Note that the same result is obtained by using the following alternative algorithm: complement all bits of the original number which are to the left of the least significant (rightmost) bit of value 1.

Example 6.4: Assume four bits of storage. Convert

1. 0010
   a. invert: 1101
   b. add 1: $1101+1=1110$

For a check let us convert the same code using the original definition of 2's complement:

$$
\begin{array}{r}
(1)0000 \\
-\quad 0010 \\
\hline
(0)1110
\end{array}
$$

Using the alternative algorithm, 0010 converts immediately to 1110 (the last two bits remain unchanged since the rightmost 1 is the second bit from the right).

2. 1110 (Converting this code should give the starting value in the previous example.)

    a. invert: 0001

    b. add 1: $0001 + 1 = 0010$

It can now be seen that 2's complement representation of numbers leads to extremely simple general purpose addition and subtraction in fixed point representation. Figure 6.8 shows the table of 4-bit codes and their corresponding decimal values.

0000	0	1111	−1
0001	1	1110	−2
0010	2	1101	−3
0011	3	1100	−4
0100	4	1011	−5
0101	5	1010	−6
0110	6	1001	−7
0111	7	1000	−8

Figure 6.8   4-bit 2's complement codes and their decimal equivalents.

Note that in the radix-complement representation there is no duplication of 0 as in the sign-magnitude representation. There is thus no waste, in our case the 4-bit system represents 16 different numbers : seven positive numbers, 0, eight negative numbers, or eight non-negative and eight negative. The number of positive numbers and the number of negative numbers are *not* the same.

The code of number −8 is worth a closer look: the leading 1 indicates that the number is negative. Its magnitude should be obtained by complementing the code. But 2's complement of 1000 is again

1000, a negative rather than a positive number. How do we know that 1000 represents −8? There are several ways to confirm this:

1. The value must be consistent with other codes and arithmetic rules.

   Example:
   $1000+0001=1001$
   corresponds to $x+1 = -7$
   Assigning 1000 to −8 is thus consistent.

2. What would the code represent if we extended the system to a 5-bit code? First, we have to find out how to extend a 4-bit code to a 5-bit code and preserve the value of the represented number. For positive numbers we simply add a leading 0 which does not change the represented value. Thus, 0101 represents +5 as does 00101 and 000101, etc. It can be easily deduced from the definition of the complement that adding a leading 1 to the code of a negative number does not change the represented value. It can also be seen from the fact that a positive number can be prefixed by 0s and from the alternative of Algorithm BC. Thus, 1011 represents −5 as does 11011 and 111011, etc. Returning to code 1000 we see that 1000 represents the same value as 11000 and the complement of 11000 is 01000 = 8 decimal.

In *summary*, 2's complement representation has the following properties:

1. Positive numbers are represented exactly as in the sign-magnitude representation; the leading bit is 0, and it is followed by the magnitude expressed in binary positional representation. Negative numbers have codes starting with a 1, and their magnitude can be obtained by complementing the code (algorithm BC). This leads to the code of the magnitude of the number represented as a positive number. The only exception to this rule is code 100...00. This code represents $-2^{**}(N-1)$ for an N−bit code.

2. Addition of numbers in 2's complement representation follows exactly the same rules as addition of numbers in positional representation. The mechanics of the operation does not depend on the signs of the operands. The sign bit is *included* in addition, which is *not* the case in sign-magnitude representation.

3. Overflow can occur only with two operands of the same sign. It

is recognized from the fact that the sign bit of the "result" is the inverse of the sign bit of the two operands.

4. To calculate $a-b$ complement b and add the result to a.
5. The value of the represented number is not changed by prefixing the code with any number of sign bits which are not stored. In other words, leading zeros are insignificant for positive numbers, and leading ones are insignificant for negative numbers.

1's complement addition is similar but slightly more complicated. This makes 1's complement representation somewhat less popular, even though the formation of 1's complement is simpler than the formation of 2's complement since it consists of pure logic negation. For more examples related to 1's and 2's complement representation, see the Workbook.

6.7 MULTIPLICATION AND DIVISION

Let us first assume that the operands are non-negative integers expressed in positional notation with no sign digit.

Multiplication is essentially repeated addition. The most obvious strategy is to follow this definition blindly and calculate

$$23*17 = 17+17+17+....+17 = 391$$

This approach is extremely inefficient, and a much more efficient approach is standard in positional notation. It is based on breaking down multidigit multiplication into a sequence of single digit multiplications, shifting, and addition.

$$23*17 = 3*17 + 2*10*17 \qquad \text{or} \qquad \begin{array}{lr} 3*17 & 51 \\ 10*2*17 & 340 \\ \hline & 391 \end{array}$$

The method of repeated single digit multiplication followed by shifting and addition is much faster but requires the knowledge of the multiplication table of the chosen system. The multiplication table for the decimal system is quite large, but the binary multiplication table is extremely simple, for any binary code x,

$$1*x = x$$
$$0*x = 0$$

The resulting process is very easy: $101101*101$ can be calculated in these steps:

```
        101101
        000000
        101101
       _____
       11100001
```

Multiplication by 0 can be ignored if we do not forget to shift:

```
101101*101      101101    (weight 1*2**0)
                101101    (weight 1*2**2)
               _____
               11100001
```

Note that this method does *not* work with numbers expressed in 2's complement form. In the above example 101101*101 is a product of two negative numbers (when we interpret the codes as 2's complement codes), and the result should be the same as the product of the corresponding positive magnitudes: 010011*011. But

```
010011*011    is      010011
                      010011
                     _____
                     00111001
```

This result is different from the result obtained above. Multiplication of numbers in 2's complement notation is slightly more complicated.

In general, multiplication is a more complicated process than addition and subtraction and requires more time, and the circuits are more complicated. Small and inexpensive computers often do not include multiplication hardware.

Division is even more complicated than multiplication. It is basically a trial-and-error process of repeated subtraction. It will not be studied in this text, but an example is given in the Workbook.

6.8 FLOATING-POINT REPRESENTATION

It was shown that very large numbers can be represented in fixed-point notation by moving the point to the right. Very small magnitudes can be represented by moving the point to the left. The problem is that once the position of the point is fixed, the scope of representable numbers and the accuracy of their representation is also fixed. If the point is placed on the left end of the code, only small numbers can be represented; if it is placed at the right end; only large numbers can be represented, if it is placed in the middle, only medium-sized numbers can be represented.

In many situations, particularly in scientific and engineering numerical calculations, we need to be able to represent values of very large and very small magnitudes in the solution of the same problem. This cannot be achieved in simple positional notation of any of the kinds discussed previously. The solution is a combined positional representation using a pair of numbers to represent the value. One number is the value scaled to a standard form with the point located in a certain fixed position, the *normalized mantissa* in fixed-point notation. The other is a scaling factor which in effect moves the point from the implied normal position to wherever it belongs for the given number—hence the name *floating-point* representation. The notation is based on standard *scientific notation*, also used in engineering.

Example 6.5:

$$
\begin{aligned}
373 &= 0.373*10**3 \\
-2539.1 &= -0.25391*10**4 \\
0.0013 &= 0.13*10**(-2)
\end{aligned}
$$

Note the normalized form of the mantissa—the decimal point precedes the first non-zero digit of the mantissa (i.e., fractional representation). The value of the base of the multiplication factor is usually fixed: 10 in scientific notation, a power of 2 in the binary system as will be seen later.

There is no need to store the base if it is constant. A number can thus be represented in floating point notation by its mantissa and exponent, both of which are signed numbers. The mantissa is usually but not always fractional and the exponent an integer. Normalization of the mantissa is usually defined by requiring that its magnitude be at least 0.1 and less than 1.0.

The following are examples of normalized floating-point decimal representation:

$$
\begin{aligned}
373 &= (0.373,3) \\
-2539 &= (-0.2539,4) \\
-0.001 &= (0.1,-2)
\end{aligned}
$$

Consider now floating-point binary representation. In any given digital system there is a fixed number of bits reserved for the mantissa and a fixed number of bits reserved for the exponent. Let us assume that eight bits are reserved for the mantissa and four for the exponent.

The *mantissa* is usually represented in the sign-magnitude form consisting of the sign bit and magnitude with the point fixed after the sign bit (i.e., fractional representation).

Examples:

$$11111111 \text{ corresponds to } -0.1111111$$
$$01111111 \text{ corresponds to } +0.1111111$$

The range of representable magnitudes is symmetrical with respect to 0.

The *exponent* should be represented so that the magnitude of the scaling factor is symmetrical around 1 since 1 is for multiplication the equivalent of 0 for addition. The available magnitudes could be, for example, -3, -2, -1, 0, 1, 2, 3. Since the exponent is an integer, we could use the sign-magnitude representation with the point placed at the right end—integer representation of the exponent. 2's complement would also be useful, since multiplication requires addition of exponents which can be positive or negative, and division requires subtraction of exponents. In practice it is more natural to use a different ("biased") representation of the exponent for the following reasons:

Since 0 is a number whose magnitude is smaller than the magnitude of any other number, it would be consistent for 0 to have the smallest exponent. Assuming, for example, sign-magnitude representation in our example the smallest exponent is 1111 (corresponding, for example, to -7) and 0 could be represented by

$$00000000 \ 1111 \text{ or } 10000000 \ 1111$$

On the other hand it is natural to represent 0 by all zeros:

$$0 = 00000000 \ 0000$$

Both requirements can be satisfied by using a *biased exponent*, i.e., expressing the exponent as an integer in the excess$-2^{**}(N-1)$ form. N is the number of bits representing the exponent. The exponent expressed in this form is called the *characteristic*, and its use is common in computers. In our example ($N=4$) the characteristic 0000 corresponds to exponent -8, characteristic 1111 corresponds to exponent $+7$, etc. As a consequence of biasing the exponent, the range of the exponent is slightly increased. In our example from $(-7,7)$ corresponding to pure sign-magnitude representation, to $(-8,7)$ for biased representation. For more examples see the Workbook.

The choice of the value of the *base* is largely independent of the choice of representation of the mantissa and exponent. The base could be 10, 2, 8, etc. In general, any integer or rational number would do. An arbitrary choice of the value of the base could create computational problems; we will see that addition and subtraction require alignment of operands. In floating-point representation this operation is most easily implemented by adjusting the exponent and shifting the mantissa. This is possible only if base b of the system and base B of the scaling factor satisfy the relationship

$$B = b^{**}j \text{ where } j \text{ is a positive integer.}$$

In this case, alignment of two floating-point numbers is achieved by adding the difference of their exponents to the smaller exponent and shifting the corresponding mantissa by a number of places equal to $j*(\text{exp1-exp2})$ assuming $\text{exp1} > = \text{exp2}$. This rule can be verified on the following binary examples:

$$0.1011*2^{**}(-3) = 1.011*2^{**}(-4) = 0.01011*2^{**}(-2)$$
$$0.1011*8^{**}2 = 101.1*8^{**}1 = 0.0001011*8^{**}3$$

The consequence of this restriction on the choice of the value of the base is the following generalization of the concept of a *normalized mantissa*: a normalized binary mantissa must have at least one 1 among the first j value-bits if $B = 2^{**}j$. The only exception is the code for 0 which consists of all zeros.

In our previous example the choice $B = 2$ means that the range of representable magnitudes example is from $2^{**}(-8)$ to $2^{**}(+7)$. If the value of the exponent is k, the minimum distance of two in this range — the accuracy of representation — is $0.0000001*2^{**}k$. The choice $B = 16$ implies that the range of magnitudes is from $16^{**}(-8)$ to $16^{**}(+7)$ and the minimum distance in the $16^{**}k$ range is $0.0000001*16^{**}k$ (binary).

In summary, the larger the value of B the larger the range of representable magnitudes but the smaller the accuracy; the same result as when we move the point in fixed-point notation to the left.

Arithmetic in floating point notation is conceptually simple but the process longer and the circuits more complicated.

Addition and *subtraction* can be performed by adding (subtracting) properly aligned mantissas:

$$0.13*10**4 + 0.25*10**3 \text{ corresponds to } \begin{array}{r} 1300 \\ +250 \\ \hline 1550 \end{array}$$

Numbers are properly aligned if their scaling factors are identical. Since bases of both scaling factors are identical, alignment is achieved by equalizing the exponents. Alignment of exponents causes shifting of mantissas (assuming $B=b**j$). A normalized mantissa cannot be greater than 1, and so shifting must be to the right. The larger of the two exponents is left unchanged and the smaller exponent adjusted:

$$0.13*10**4 + 0.25*10**3 = 0.13*10**4 + 0.025*10**4$$
$$= 0.155*10**4$$

Note that shifting can temporarily destroy the normalized form of the mantissa. It can, at the same time, reduce its precision because of the limited number of available storage digits. If, in the last example, only two decimal digits of storage were available for the mantissa, the operation would be

$$0.13*10**4 + 0.25*10**3 => 0.13*10**4 + 0.02*10**4$$
$$= 0.15*10**4$$

and one digit is lost. This is an unavoidable consequence of storage space limitations. In some situations the result must be renormalized after the completion of the operation:

$$0.13*10**4 + (-0.12*10**4) = 0.01*10**4 = 0.1*10**3$$

In summary the process of floating-point addition can be described by the following algorithm:

Algorithm FPA (Floating Point Addition):
Assume that $op1=(m1,exp1)$, $op2=(m2,exp2)$, $exp1>=exp2$, $B=2**j$. Addition consists of the following steps:

1. Align the two operands if necessary: shift $m2$ by $j*(exp2-exp1)$ positions to the right
2. Add mantissas
3. Normalize the mantissa of the result and adjust the exponent correspondingly.

The algorithm for subtraction is similar.

Note the following:

1. Addition and subtraction may cause an *overflow*.

   Consider again the binary system from the previous example and operands

   $$m1 = m2 = 01111111 \text{ (positive numbers)} \quad \exp1 = \exp2 = 0111$$

   The sum of these two numbers has magnitude larger than the maximum magnitude representable in the system. The result is too large to be stored. Note that

   $$m1 = m2 = 11111111 \text{ (negative mantissa)} \quad \exp1 = \exp2 = 0111$$

   also causes an overflow. An overflow occurs when the *magnitude* of a number is too large for the chosen representation.

2. Addition and subtraction can also cause an *underflow*.

   Consider

   $$m1 = 01111111 \quad m2 = 01111110 \quad \exp1 = \exp2 = 0000$$

   The magnitude of the difference of these two numbers is too small to be represented in the chosen system with the mantissa in normalized form. An underflow results when the *magnitude* of a number is too *small* for the chosen representation.

For more examples on floating-point arithmetic see the Workbook.
For *multiplication* and *division* consider the following examples:

$$(0.25*10**4)*(0.30*10**3) = 0.075*10**7 = 0.75*10**6$$
$$(0.96*10**-2)/(0.32*10**2) = 0.30*10**-4$$

Note that floating point multiplication and division involve multiplication or division of the mantissas and addition or subtraction of the exponents, possibly followed by normalization. These operations can be performed by following the algorithm below.

Algorithm FPMD (Floating-Point Multiplication/Division).
Multiply (Divide) m1 by m2 as fixed-point numbers;
Add (Subtract) exponents;
Normalize the result.

Note that problems with the loss of precision, overflow, and underflow are even more pronounced for multiplication and division:

1. Loss of accuracy is more significant since for two numbers with d significant digits, the number of significant digits of the product is $2*d$. If the result is representable with only d digits, there is always a loss of accuracy, no matter what is the relative magnitude of the two operands.
2. Multiplication involves addition of exponents, and overflow or underflow can happen very easily. Addition requires no operation on exponents other than normalization. Multiplication requires addition of exponents. To allow floating-point representation to provide more accurate representation, digital computers typically use two or three times more bits to represent floating-point numbers. In addition they usually have two different formats of floating-point codes: single precision and double precision, which usually requires twice as much storage to improve the accuracy of the mantissa while leaving the range of the exponent unchanged.

In summary, floating-point number operations have the following properties:

1. Floating-point representation uses a normalized mantissa, an exponent, usually biased and an implied base $B, B = 2**j$ in binary systems, to allow representation of a wide range of values in scaled form.
2. Floating-point representation has the advantage of a wide range of number representation but has significant negative implications:
   a. Increased complexity of operations which causes longer execution and more complex and expensive circuits.
   b. In order to improve the accuracy of representation digital systems represent floating-point numbers by more bits than fixed-point numbers. The use of floating-point representation where fixed-point representation would be sufficient may thus result in a significant waste of storage.
3. Arithmetic operations involve the possibility of overflow and underflow, particularly for multiplication and division.
4. As a consequence of the slower execution and inefficient storage associated with floating-point representation, fixed-point representation should be used whenever possible and floating-point arithmetic avoided.
5. Computers in the range up to around $100,000 typically provide floating-point arithmetic only as an option. This is because

floating-point arithmetic is expensive and in some applications unnecessary. If floating-point hardware is not available, floating-point arithmetic can be implemented as a programmed function based on fixed-point operations. This is obvious from the above presentation.

6.9 BCD AND XS-3 ARITHMETIC

The BCD CODE is not positional. This makes BCD arithmetic more complicated since the carry and borrow do not propagate in the same way in all positions. This section presents a brief outline of BCD addition and a few notes on subtraction.

To see the problems of BCD addition consider the following examples:

```
1.   13  BCD equivalent   0001 0011
     22                   0010 0010
     ──                   ─────────
     35                   0011 0101
```

In this case there is no propagation of carry between the decimal digits, and so addition of the combined BCD codes as binary numbers gives the correct results. This is not so in the following example:

```
2.   13                   0001 0011
     18                   0001 1000
     ──                   ─────────
     31 binary addition   0001 1011
```

The correct BCD code of the result is 0011 0001. Note that the result obtained by pure binary addition is deficient in two ways: the last four bits do not constitute a valid BCD code, and the first four bits do not reflect the carry in the corresponding decimal addition. The algorithm for BCD addition is obtained by modifications of the algorithm for binary addition. The modifications must guarantee that:

1. Each part of the result represents the correct BCD code;
2. The carry is allowed to propagate between individual BCD groups.

The modification can be derived from the table in Figure 6.9 which shows from left to right: the carry and sum generated by unmodified binary addition, its decimal equivalent, the desired BCD code and carry into the next BCD group.

carry	sum	decimal	desired code	desired carry
0	0000	0	0000	0
0	0001	1	0001	0
.	....	.	....	.
0	1001	9	1001	0
0	1010	1	0000	1
0	1011	11	0001	1
.	....	..	....	.
0	1111	15	0101	1
1	0000	16	0110	1
1	0001	17	0111	1
1	0010	18	1000	1

Figure 6.9   Carry and sum corresponding to pure binary addition with the decimal equivalent (three leftmost columns). The corresponding desired BCD code and carry (right).

The table shows that all codes and carry up to decimal 9 generated by unmodified binary addition are as desired. Codes above decimal 9 differ from the desired BCD code by decimal 6. The desired behavior can thus be achieved by

1. Leaving the result of binary addition unchanged and generating no carry for sums smaller than 01010 (decimal 10),
2. Adding 0110 (decimal 6) and generating a carry for sums greater than 01001 (decimal 9). A BCD adder can be implemented similarly to a binary adder. An N-bit ripple carry BCD adder is shown in Figure 6.10.

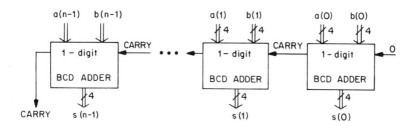

Figure 6.10   The block diagram of an N-bit BCD ripple carry adder.

The 1-decimal-digit BCD adder can be designed by using four ordinary full adders with a special adjustment for the irregular propagation of the carry: the adder behaves normally for sums up to 01001, but a carry is generated and 0110 added when

1. The binary sum is accompanied by a carry (result 16 and greater), or
2. The binary sum has form 1x1x (result 10 and greater), or
3. The binary sum has form 11xx (result 12 and greater).

This specification results in the circuit for the 1-digit BCD adder shown in Figure 6.11.

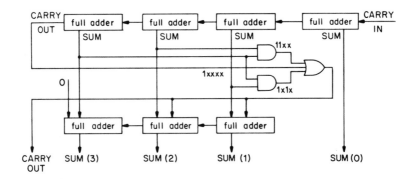

Figure 6.11   A BCD full adder processing one decimal digit of two operands and a carry.

BCD subtraction can be implemented using nines complements. This further complicates the arithmetic unit.

In summary: BCD arithmetic is more complicated and therefore slower and more expensive. It should be used only when it is economically justified. This is the case in those situations in which data are input or output in a form related to the BCD code, such as standard decimal input/output, and where relatively little arithmetic is performed. In these situations the saving achieved by avoiding the translation from BCD into binary for arithmetic and from binary results to

BCD for output may be greater than the loss associated with slower BCD arithmetic. Most of even the smallest computers implement some BCD arithmetic. For more information on BCD representation see the Workbook.

EXCESS-3 (often denoted as XS-3) codes are modified BCD codes, and very similar rules and remarks apply to both. The two major differences are:

1. An XS-3 code is obtained by adding 3 to the corresponding BCD code. Adding two XS-3 codes thus produces a code which differs from the corresponding BCD code by 6. This applies only to valid BCD results. In general, addition of XS-3 codes produces results as summarized in the table in Figure 6.11 which shows left to right: the carry and sum obtained by ordinary binary addition of two XS-3 codes, the decimal equivalent of the sum (not of the code), the desired XS-3 code and the desired carry.

carry	sum	decimal	desired code	carry
0	0110	0	0011	0
0	0111	1	0100	0
.	....	.	....	.
0	1111	9	1100	0
1	0000	10	0011	1
1	0001	11	0100	1
etc.				

Figure 6.12   The equivalent of Figure 6.8 for XS-3 representation.

The table shows that for results up to decimal 9 the correct code is obtained by subtracting 3 (or adding −3). For sums greater than 9 the correct code is obtained by adding 3. The carry is always correct.

2. Complementation of excess-3 codes is simple since the code is self-complementing: its 1's complement is the same as its 9's complement. This is a major advantage in comparison with the BCD code.

REFERENCES

The book by Flores is a classic text on computer arithmetic. A more recent book by Hwang has been published by Wiley and Sons. Advanced articles on computer arithmetic are collected in the book edited by Swartzlander. Shorter treatment of the subject is given in all recent texts on computer organization such as Hayes and Hamacher and in most books on digital design such as Williams, Roth, and Mowle.

PROBLEMS

1. Design a serial adder.

2. Convert
   a. 0.15, 13.75, −9.3 to binary
   b. 0.11, 11.01, −1.011 to decimal

3. What is 10011, 11001 binary in decimal assuming that the binary point is
   a. before the first bit
   b. three positions behind the last bit
   c. between the third and fourth bit

4. Add 1001+101, 111+10111, 100+11110 in binary and check your result in decimal.

5. Subtract the following sign-magnitude binary numbers: 01011−1001, 011−01110, 111−010, 011110−010001.

6. Convert the following magnitudes:
   a. 11.011 binary to decimal, octal, hexadecimal.
   b. 15.61 octal to binary, decimal, hexadecimal.
   c. 13.91, 118.7 decimal to binary, octal, hexadecimal.
   d. 10.F1, 3B.0C hexadecimal to binary, octal, decimal.

7. Add the following pairs of sign-magnitude numbers: 0111.01+0010.11
   0100.01+1001.11
   1010.00+1101.10
   00010.01+1101.11
   Which pairs cause an overflow?

8. Formulate an algorithm for subtraction of sign-magnitude numbers.

9. Construct a subtracter corresponding to your subtraction algorithm.

10. Find the 2's complement of 01101, 11.101, 101.11, 011.0

11. Find the magnitude of the following 2's complement numbers (the leading bit is the sign-bit): 1101, 101.11, 011.1, 11.01, 01101, 1.0111

12. Perform the following operations:
    a. Convert the following decimal pairs to 2's complement and add: $13+8$, $14+(-8)$, $(-15)+3$, $(-14)+(-17)$
    b. Repeat with 1's complement representation.

13. What are the decimal equivalents of the following 2's complement codes (the first bit is the sign-bit): 11.1, 011, 101.01, 011.1, 1011

14. 14. Convert the following decimal numbers to sign-magnitude binary form and multiply: $13*8$, $(-4)*19$, $(-13)*5$, $(-8)*(-7)$

15. Design a sign-magnitude multiplier.

16. Formulate an algorithm for the division of sign-magnitude numbers.

17. Assume eight bits for sign-magnitude fractional representation of normalized mantissa and four bits for the characteristic. Convert the following floating-point numbers to decimal, fixed-point representation:
    100101100111, 011011011011,
    010010011110, 100100011111,
    101101000001, 011001011101.
    Express these codes in octal, hexadecimal and compare their readability.

18. Add, subtract, multiply, and divide the pairs of floating-point numbers from the previous problem. Assume base
    a. 2
    b. 16
    Does an overflow or an underflow occur? Does it depend on the base of the scaling factor?
    Repeat assuming *integer* rather than *fractional* representation of mantissa.

19. Under the same assumptions as in Problem 18 determine which of the following numbers are normalized and normalize the remaining codes:
    001011010010, 100011010101, 110101111000, 010010110010,
    111111000100, 000010011001.

20. Convert the following decimal additions to BCD and execute in BCD:
    $13+17$, $18.1+13.4$, $14.53+9.2$

21. What is the effect of BCD representation on the accuracy of BCD arithmetic? How accurate is the result of $0.2+0.7$ in
    a. fixed-point arithmetic?
    b. BCD?

22. Formulate an algorithm for subtraction in
    a. BCD
    b. Excess-3

Chapter 7

INTRODUCTION TO COMPUTER ORGANIZATION AND ARCHITECTURE

7.1 DEFINITION OF ORGANIZATION AND ARCHITECTURE

Computer organization and computer architecture are terms which have been defined as follows:

> The *architecture* of a computer is the set of resources seen by the computer programmer. It includes general purpose registers, the status word, the instruction set, the address space, etc.

> The *organization* of a computer refers to the logical structure of the system, including the CPU, control unit, input/output, memory, etc.

The two definitions overlap to some extent, but it can be said that the organization of a computer is the digital designer's perspective of the system while the architecture is the programmer's perspective. These statements will become much clearer after the study of this chapter.

7.2 INTRODUCTION

It has been stated in previous chapters that computers are just one category of digital systems. No generally accepted definition of a digital computer exists, but it will be useful to formulate one since it will help to establish which parts a computer should have and what they should do. Within the framework of this definition, it will then be possible to study computers as a well-defined category of digital systems and use all the concepts and methods presented in the previous chapters. The definition will be derived from our intuitive understanding of what computers do or should be capable of doing.

We know that computers accept coded input information, process it, and output the requested results in coded form. Anybody who ever wrote a computer program knows that requested is not always the same as desired.

Our first description of what a computer does is too vague and we have to expand some of the statements.

1. There are two types of input information typically required:
    a. The *data* to be processed. In a payroll application, for example, this will be all information about employees that is needed to prepare the payroll. It is identical to the information that the payroll department would require for manual preparation of a payroll.
    b. A sequence of *instructions* called a *program* which specifies how the data should be processed. In our example the program plays the same role as a set of guidelines used by the payroll department to prepare the payroll.

    Both types of information, data and instructions, are entered into the computer in a coded form; a standard code may be binary but more commonly information is coded in a standard character set such as ASCII.
2. The standard processing capabilities expected of a computer consist of:
    a. Capacity to input and temporarily store programs and data.
    b. Capacity to process codes, including arithmetic operations on coded numbers and similar Boolean operations.
    c. Capacity to output requested intermediate and final results.
    d. Capacity to follow the code of the sequence in which operations are to take place. In other words the capacity to follow the desired flow of instructions in a program.

This summary of the characteristic properties of digital computers allows us to define the subject of this chapter as follows.

Definition of a digital computer. A digital computer is a digital system capable of receiving coded raw data and instructions which specify the desired sequence of processing. The processing capability must allow control over the order of operations desired, and these operations must include control over input and output and arithmetic and other Boolean operations on codes. The system is capable of output of processed data.

Note that this definition implies both certain physical components such as input and output devices and certain processing capabilities such as the ability to perform arithmetic. The design of a computer consists of the design of components which implement these capabilities.

The definition implies that a system with the specified properties can be built and that its design can be carried out on the basis of the concepts and techniques surveyed in the previous chapters. We will demonstrate this by proceeding as if we were digital designers requested to design a digital system according to the given specification. Our design will, of course, be a gross simplification of a real computer design. It will, however, be complete enough to demonstrate that there is essentially no conceptual problem in designing a computer with the knowledge of concepts presented previously. A simple working computer can, in fact, be built on this basis supplemented with a few rather elementary concepts from electricity such as an understanding of the power requirements of the integrated circuits involved, etc.

7.3   BASIC PARTS OF A COMPUTER

Assume that we are to design a digital system according to the specification and definition given above. It is obvious that the system must have the following components:

1. Input and output devices. These two categories of devices are usually grouped into one since a number of them perform both input and output functions such as the typewriter-like terminals. They are commonly referred to as peripheral devices or I/O.
2. The general processor with the desired processing capabilities.
3. Communication channels for transfer of information between I/O and the general processor.

At this point our model of a computer is as in Figure 7.1.

The *general processor*, an artificial term which is not normally used in computer science, must be capable of processing and storage of data — both raw and processed — and instructions. It must have a *memory*.

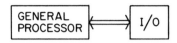

Figure 7.1 A first model of a computer.

The memory used to store data may be the same as the memory to store instructions. This is normally the case. The two memories may be physically separated, and there are a few computers which use this approach with good reason in special applications. This is the first example which shows that there are alternative approaches at every stage of design. In the following we will ignore these alternatives and proceed in the most natural way. Some different approaches will be described in the following chapters.

The general processor must also have a processing module which implements the required processing capabilities. It is commonly referred to as the *central processing unit* or the CPU. The term *mainframe* is often used to mean the CPU of a large computer.

All modules in our model including the communication channels are controlled by the CPU which executes instructions in the specified order. Our updated model is shown in Figure 7.2.

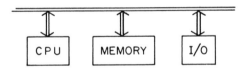

Figure 7.2 The standard block diagram of a computer. In this block diagram only the data and instruction communication paths are shown; the control by the CPU is implied.

7.3.1 The CPU

The CPU is the most interesting of the modules at this stage, and it must be studied first in order to get an understanding of what a computer does and how.

We have seen that the CPU performs two functions: it controls the whole system according to the externally supplied sequence of instructions, and it processes codes. These two functions are of very different natures, and the CPU can be divided into two submodules with very different functions which can be considered and designed independently:

1. The *control unit* which implements the control functions.
2. The data processing unit which is characterized by its capability to perform arithmetic and logic funtions and is thus called the *arithmetic-logic unit* or ALU for short.

The control unit, the ALU, and the communication channels are sufficient for the implementation of the CPU. This set of modules would, however, make the CPU rather inefficient and awkward to program. The reason for this is that both the control unit and the ALU permanently require certain very limited storage capabilities for certain special purposes.

Consider the ALU: the operation of the ALU produces a result which must be temporarily stored before it can be processed by the following instructions. This result is often used in the following operation as an operand. Storing it temporarily in the memory and fetching it immediately back would be unnecessary, would slow down the operation, and make programming more difficult. It is more convenient to provide a special register in the CPU dedicated specifically to this purpose.

The control unit must be capable of fetching instructions for execution in the proper sequence. It must keep track of the address of the memory location containing the instruction to be executed next. This address could be stored in the main memory, but the location used for this purpose could not be used for anything else, and its access would be relatively slow. It is thus more convenient to provide a special register in the CPU for this purpose.

We will see that there are a number of similar special purpose registers required by the CPU and that they are most logically included in the CPU itself. We will thus extend our model of the CPU to also include a number of registers, unspecified at this point. As a matter of fact, the number and functions of these registers are not unique, and different computers have a different number of registers with different functions. The choice is largely a subjective decision of the designers. There are, however, certain conventional solutions which are almost standard, and we will follow them in the following sections. Our present model of the CPU is thus as in Figure 7.3.

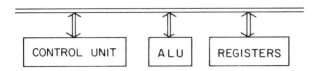

Figure 7.3   The block diagram of a possible organization of a CPU.

7.3.2 The Memory Module

A memory consists of a set of memory cells — basically registers. If we want to be able to store and retrieve information from them, they must be addressable; there must also be a way of specifying a memory cell and storing or retrieving information from it. The unit of information transferred between the CPU and the memory as an entity is usually called a *word* but there are other interpretations of the term as well. There are alternative ways of implementing the addressing capability, but the most natural is to view the memory as a set of boxes in a post office, each of them capable of storing a certain fixed amount of information, measured in bits, and assigned a fixed address. Addresses must be unique since addressing would become ambiguous if several memory locations shared the same address. Addresses can most naturally be a sequence of consecutive numbers, and the memory can be represented as a linear array for example as follows:

address	0	1	2	3	...
contents	0010	0100	1110	0000	...

In our example every location contains four bits. The typical word size is much larger. Addresses are not stored in the memory but are a means of identification just as numbers on post office boxes. In our example the contents of location 1 is 0100, and reading from this location results in obtaining this code. Access is made possible by a combinational circuit which decodes the supplied address and allows access to the specified location. The address decoder is of the same type as discussed in previous chapters. The physical arrangement of cells on the chip is, of course, two-dimensional, but the conceptual one-dimensional addressing model is valid and useful.

Memories of the type just described are usually referred to as *random access memories* or RAMs. More accurately they should be called *read/write* RAMs. The name is intended to convey the following properties:

1. Any addressable location can be accessed in about the same time.
2. Any location can be read from or written into.

It was mentioned in Section 2.12 that there are also "read-only" and "read-mostly" memories with random access. These memories are increasingly used in computers in combination with RAMs.

7.4 THE CPU

Our current CPU model consists of the control unit, the ALU, registers, and communication channels. The design of the control unit is possible only if we know exactly what instructions are to be implemented. The design of the ALU is partially determined by the required arithmetic and Boolean operations.

7.4.1 The Control Unit

The control unit is responsible for fetching the code of the instruction to be executed from the memory and then decoding the instruction code and generating control signals which will cause the instruction to be executed. This basic function is illustrated by the state diagram in Figure 7.4.

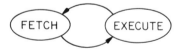

Figure 7.4   A basic state diagram description of the function of the control unit.

This breakdown is usually formulated as follows: the *instruction cycle* consists of the *fetch phase* and the *execute phase*. We will see that decoding is not a localized one-time operation but usually takes place in several steps of the execute phase. The fetch phase is identical for all instructions. The execute phase is different for different instructions.

7.4.1.1 The Fetch Phase. Fetching the instruction requires both the availability of the address of the next instruction and a means of exchange of information with the memory.

The address of the next instruction will be assumed to be stored in a dedicated register, usually called the *Program Counter* (PC). We will, of course, have to design the control unit in such a way that the PC contains the correct information when it is required.

The CPU and the memory will be connected by two buses. The *address bus* will be used by the CPU to deliver the address of the location to be accessed. The *data bus* will be used to communicate data — in a more general sense, including instruction codes — between the memory and the CPU. In addition there must be a set of control lines. Communication of data over a bus means that the source register is connected to the bus for a length of time sufficient for the data to be accepted and processed by the target component. In order to guarantee that the CPU has enough time to process the data and to provide a source register for transmission from CPU to memory, there will be a *Memory Data Register* (MDR) on the CPU side of the bus. Its function will be to hold data items communicated between the memory and the CPU in either direction. The source register for the communication of the address to the memory will be called the *Memory Address Register* (MAR) and will also be a part of the CPU. The communication of the address is unidirectional from the CPU to the memory. The communication of data is bidirectional to allow for both retrieval of data from memory and storage of results in memory. A control line from the CPU to memory must be available to indicate the desired direction of the transfer since the knowledge of the address is not sufficient to determine whether reading or writing is required. Our present model of the CPU is thus as in Figure 7.5.

In this model fetching the next instruction requires the transfer of the address from the PC to MAR, generation of the READ control signal, and waiting for the memory to place the data on the data bus from which it is copied into MDR. Note that all communication between the CPU and the memory is via MDR and MAR. The fetch sequence can be described informally as follows:

1. PC TO: MAR; READ
2. Wait for memory to place instruction code on the bus and into MDR.

This basic sequence can also be depicted by the state diagram in Figure 7.6.

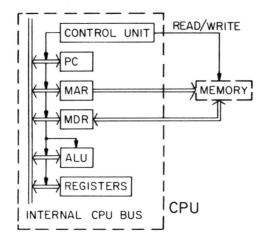

Figure 7.5   An expanded block diagram of the CPU.

Figure 7.6   A preliminary state diagram of the fetch phase.

We must now ensure that the PC contains the correct address. The most natural approach is to assume that instructions are stored in the same sequence in which they are to be executed and in consecutive memory locations. In other words if the current instruction is stored at location K the next instruction will be stored at location $K+1$, etc. With this assumption we can guarantee that the PC contains the correct address if we

1. Initially load PC with the address of the first instruction;
2. Increment the address in PC by 1 when the current address is no longer required by the control unit.

The addition $(PC+1)$ can, of course, be performed by the ALU since the ALU is not required to do anything else at this time. Assume that the ALU takes one operand from an auxiliary register A and the other directly from the internal bus and places the result of the operation into an auxiliary result register R. (The names A and R and the assumed arrangement are not standard. The names PC, MAR, and MDR are quite common.) The ALU communication with the rest of the CPU can now be schematically illustrated as in Figure 7.7.

Let us assume that the ALU is capable of incrementing the contents of register A in response to control signal INC. The operation

PC+1 TO: PC (increment PC)

can thus be performed by

1. PC TO A; INC !control signal to ALU!
2. R TO: PC

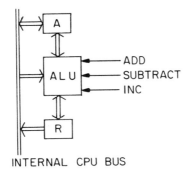

INTERNAL CPU BUS

Figure 7.7   Communication between the ALU and the CPU bus.

Note the following:

1. The operation must be broken down into two steps corresponding to two consecutive cycles because they both use the same internal bus. A bus can carry only one code at a time.
2. Our specification of the control sequence assumes that the speed of the ALU is such that the R register contains the correct data at the beginning of step b. This means that the duration of one cycle, the speed of the clock, must be sufficient to allow the data transferred from PC to A to stabilize on the bus and then the output of the ALU to stabilize (recall that the adder in general produces a number of intermediate results) and then the contents of register R to stabilize. Considerations of this type determine the frequency of the clock and, eventually, the speed of the whole computer. Usually the most restrictive parameter of

this type is the speed of memory and its value determines the choice of the cycle length of the clock. A more detailed analysis of timing is presented in the Workbook.

If we assume that the memory is fast enough to allow access and provide the result in the interval of one step in the control sequence, the "wait" in step 2 can be eliminated. The whole sequence required to implement the fetch phase can thus be described as follows:

1. PC TO: MAR, A; READ; INC !We are taking advantage of the fact that data from the same source — in our case the contents of PC — can be transferred to several targets at the same time!
2. R TO: PC
3. MDR now presumably contains the instruction code and PC the address of the next instruction.

Note that our assumption concerning the speed of the memory places a requirement on the choice of the memory. The chosen memory must be fast enough to be able to keep up with the speed of the clock. The implied structure of the existing part of the control unit is as shown in Figure 7.8.

To complete the fetch phase, it remains to store the instruction code temporarily for further processing. The register used for this purpose is usually called the *instruction register* (IR). The complete fetch phase is

1. PC TO: MAR, A; READ; INC;
2. R TO: PC
3. MDR TO: IR

This sequence is also depicted in Figure 7.9.

Any instruction has to be fetched before it can be executed and the fetch phase is identical for all instructions. The rest of the sequence (i.e., the execute phase) depends on the nature of the instruction, and we cannot proceed before specifying the *instruction set* of our computer.

7.4.1.2 The Execute Phase. Which instructions should our computer have? To start with we have to have instructions which can

1. Move data from memory to CPU for processing: LOAD instructions,
2. Move results from the CPU to memory: STORE instructions,
3. Perform basic arithmetic and logic operations.

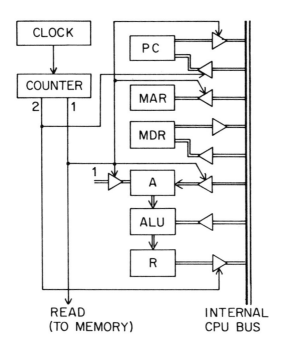

Figure 7.8   A partial structure of the control unit as implied by the preliminary control sequence of the fetch phase.

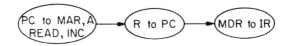

Figure 7.9   A more complete description of the fetch phase.

Each instruction will be assigned a binary code, called the *machine code*, consisting of two parts:

1. The specification of the operation to be performed by the instruction, such as add, load, etc. This part is called the *operation code* part of the instruction or the OPCODE. It is stored in the *opcode field* — in our case bits in certain fixed positions of the word — of the instruction code.
2. The *address part* which specifies the source or the destination of the operand. It is stored in the *address field* of the instruction

code. Note that while every operation must have the opcode part, the address part is not always needed. Consider, for example, an instruction which halts the computer. Such an operation does not have an operand and therefore does not need the address part.

It was already pointed out that it would be somewhat inconvenient to have instructions of varying lengths since this would complicate their storage in the memory which is made up of cells of identical size. If it is unavoidable to have instructions of different lengths — and this is common on commercially available computers — the longer instructions should occupy several words in memory. In our case this situation will not arise.

It is very common to add a special register to the existing set of CPU registers to simplify processing of arithmetic instructions. This register is used to store or accumulate intermediate results from the ALU and also as the implied source of one of the operands in arithmetic operations. It is called the *accumulator* (AC). Its exact function will become clear shortly.

We can now give a more detailed description of our basic instruction set. We will not yet assign binary machine codes to instructions but only specify their functions and abbreviations (*mnemonic names*).

instruction part		operation performed
mnemonic	symbolic address	
ST	x	store contents of AC in memory location x
LD	x	load AC from location x
AD	x	add contents of AC and location x and store result in AC
SU	x	subtract contents of x from AC and store in AC

Our present specifications are based on the structure of the CPU shown in Figure 7.10.

It may seem that we have not made provision for the access of I/O devices which is one of the basic functions of a computer. In fact, this is not so if we treat I/O devices as if they were cells in the memory with certain fixed addresses. If an input device is, for example, assigned address 1 then instruction

   LD 1

can be interpreted as requesting the transfer of the data stored in the input device or its data register, the *data buffer*, into AC. The CPU will not differentiate between a load from memory and a load from an input device. The device must, of course, be connected to the CPU in such a way that the device recognizes its address and properly responds. This decoding is one of the functions of this device's *interface*.

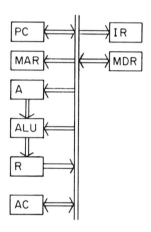

Figure 7.10   The assumed preliminary structure of the CPU.

If address 1 is assigned to an input device, the same address cannot be assigned to another I/O device or a memory location. This method of handling I/O, which is just one of a number of alternatives, is called *memory mapped* I/O and is quite common. It will be assumed in our example computer. More information about I/O is given later in this chapter.

Given the specifications of the functions of individual instructions, we can now proceed to the specification of the corresponding control sequences: first draw the state diagram (Figure 7.11) and then use it to design the control sequence.

4. address part of IR TO: MAR
      If opcode part of IR is ST then go to: 8
                                 else READ;
      If opcode is LD then go to: 9
            ! All our instructions fetch an operand (read)
            from the memory. The only exception is STORE
            which writes into memory!

5. AC TO: A !Gets operand for instructions AD or SU!
6. MDR TO: ALU
   If opcode is AD then ADD
   If opcode is SU then SUBTRACT
7. R TO: AC; go to: 1
8. AC TO: MDR; WRITE; ! Completes ST! go to: 1
9. MDR TO: AC; go to: 1

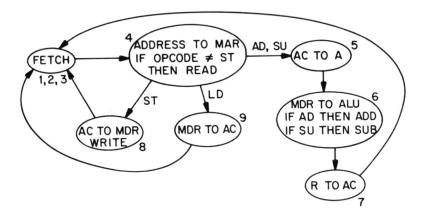

Figure 7.11   A state diagram of the existing control sequence with states labeled by the numbers of corresponding control steps.

The sequences of control steps executed for individual instructions are as follows:

    ST: 1, 2, 3, 4, 8
    LD: 1, 2, 3, 4, 9
    AD: 1, 2, 3, 4, 5, 6, 7
    SU: 1, 2, 3, 4, 5, 6, 7

Note that all instructions include the fetch part (steps 1, 2, 3) which is not shown in the above listing. Another point worth noting is that sometimes the same step does not perform the same operations for different instructions. For example, step 6 leads to different microoperations for the ADD and SUBTRACT instructions.

As an illustration of *programming* of our computer consider the following problem.

Example 7.1: We wish to have the computer read two numbers from input device address 1, add them together and output the result via output device address 2. The symbolic program to solve the problem is shown below. Recall that the program will have to be translated into binary machine code since the computer cannot directly process symbolic instruction codes which are only used to simplify programmer's notation.

mnemonic form of instruction	comment
LD 1	reads first number and stores it in the accumulator
AD 1	adds the contents of AC to the number read from location 1 (input)
ST 2	stores the contents of AC at location 2 (output device)

Note that the program assumes that the second operand is present in the buffer of the input device when the first load operation has been completed. Since the CPU works very rapidly (the load instruction will usually take about 1 microsecond) and most input devices work relatively very slowly in comparison, this assumption is not automatically satisfied. This potential problem will be ignored for the time being.

We now show in the next example that our present instruction set has certain basic gaps and must be extended.

Example 7.2: We wish to write a program to perform the following operations:

Read a number from input device 1.
If the number is negative then output 1
                    else output -1 at output device 2.
Output 0 at address device 2.

Assume that the address of the input is 1, the output address is 2, and location 3 contains number 1. Location 4 contains -1, and location 5 contains 0. We will ignore the problem of how these numbers came to be stored in these locations since this is essentially a programming problem and we deal with programming only to the extent to which it affects or justifies the architecture of the computer. Let us also assume that instructions are to be stored starting at location 10 (in the rest of this chapter we will use only octal or binary addresses) and that the PC contains 10 when we want to execute the program. How this is achieved is again mainly a programming problem and will be ignored here. The symbolic program solving our problem has the following form:

instruction part

address	instruction	comment
10	LD 1	
11	if AC<0	then continue with instruction located at 15
		else proceed to next instruction
12	LD 4	AC gets number -1
13	ST 2	outputs AC, i.e. -1
14	continue from	location 17
15	LD 3	AC gets 1
16	ST 2	outputs AC, i.e. 1
17	LD 5	AC gets 0
20	ST 2	outputs AC, i.e. 0

Note that instructions are mostly stored in the order in which they are executed and in consecutive locations. This is dictated by our design which augments PC by 1 after fetching an instruction and therefore expects the next instruction at the next address.

It can be seen from the program that our instruction set is insufficient since it allows only sequential execution of instructions implicit in the design, and our rather trivial problem requires a branching flow of control as shown in Figure 7.12.

Figure 7.12   The flow of control in a branching algorithm.

The operation described at address 11 is a *conditional branch* or conditional jump in the flow of execution. The jump is executed only if a certain condition such as the sign of the number in AC is satisfied. The operation described at address 14 is an *unconditional branch*, or unconditional jump — the change of sequential flow is interrupted and the jump performed whenever an instruction of this type is encountered. Instructions implementing both types of jumps should be available on all computers since a change of flow of control is an essential property of most algorithms.

The flow of control is determined completely by the contents of PC which stores the address of the instruction to be executed next. The two instructions required by the previous problem, therefore, involve conditional or unconditional manipulation of the contents of the PC. They can be implemented for example by the following expansion of the original control sequence obtained from the expanded state diagram in Figure 7.13:

4. If opcode is JN (Jump on Negative AC) then if AC<0 then address TO: PC;
   go to 1
   If opcode is JM (unconditional jump) then
   address TO: PC; go to 1

We now have a basic instruction set which, while not really sufficient to allow reasonable programming, does illustrate the basic principles of the design of the control unit. Our instructions are STORE, LOAD, ADD, SUBTRACT, JUMP, JUMP IF AC<0. Let us now make our design quite specific by making the remaining decisions concerning the word size, assignment of binary codes, etc.

Opcodes. So far we have six instructions. Six opcodes can be encoded by using three bits. This would, however, leave very little room for expansion since only two combinations would be unassigned. Most computers have at least fifty instructions, and many have several hundred. As a compromise we will use the first four bits of the word as the opcode and use the following arbitrary assignment:

opcode	instruction	mnemonic
0001	store	ST
0010	load	LD
0011	add	AD
0100	subtract	SU
0101	jump	JM
0110	jump if AC<0	JN

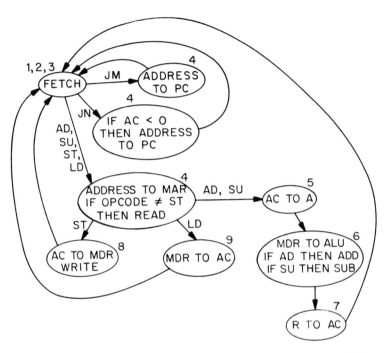

Figure 7.13   A state diagram of the updated control sequence. Note that several nodes are labeled 4. Since edges out of state 3 are labeled differently there is no ambiguity.

The remaining part of the instruction word is the address part. How long should it be? Its length will determine the *addressable space*, the range of memory addresses which can be accessed by instructions. If the address part has N bits we can address 2**N locations since possible addresses range from 00..0 to 11..1. The more bits we allow the larger will be the addressable space available for programs and data and the larger the range of problems which can be solved on the computer. A larger address part, however, in general requires larger words or multiword instruction, and this makes the computer more expensive. One reason for the increased cost is that the addressable space is large and words larger and, therefore, the memory requires more bits of storage. We do not, however, install the maximum size of memory if we restrict our programs to a memory subspace. Another reason for the increased cost is that the CPU will have to be designed to handle larger words. Buses will have to be wider to allow parallel transmission of more bits at a time. Registers will have to be bigger. The ALU will have to be larger; and if we desire to retain high speed, it will have to be more complicated since the speed of the ALU decreases with growing word size unless a more complex circuit is employed.

As a compromise we will accept 12 bits as the word size. This leaves 8 bits for addressing and thus allows direct access only to 256 memory locations with addresses 00000000 to 11111111. This is much less than almost any commercial computer provides but sufficient for illustration. The typical number of address bits is 12 to 24 and the word size from 12 to 60 bits.

Note that the choice of the instruction set, word size, and opcode assignment is one of the phases in design where there is the greatest freedom of choice. There are certain considerations which must be weighed when making the choice, but they are rather loose and conflicting and leave much room for a subjective decision.

As an example of what our decisions imply the following diagram shows the listing of the program and data in the previous programming problem. Two's complement representation is assumed.

octal address	octal contents	comment
0003	0001	number 1
0004	7777	number -1 (2's complement)
0005	0000	number 0
....	....	unused
0010	1001	load [1] (contents of loc. 1)
0011	3015	conditional jump to 15
0012	1004	load [4]
0013	0102	store AC in 2 (output)
0014	4217	jump to 17
0015	1003	load [3]
0016	0102	store in 2
0017	1005	load [5]
0020	0102	store in 2

Note that in our design there is no way of distinguishing between a data word and an instruction word. The code stored in location 10 can be interpreted as octal 1001 or a load instruction and the real meaning depends on the immediate context: if the code is fetched during the fetch phase, it will be stored in IR and interpreted as an instruction. If it is fetched during the execute phase, it will be interpreted as an address or the value of an operand, depending on the exact place in the control sequence in which it is fetched. This ambiguity of interpretation is the rule for most computers.

Let us now restate the control sequence incorporating the latest decisions. Note that we number bit location from left to right and 0 to 11. Some manufacturers number bits from right to left. The abbreviation OPCODE is used for IR[0:3], ADDRESS is used for IR[4:11].

1. PC TO: MAR, A; READ; INC;
2. R TO: PC
3. MDR TO: IR
4. If OPCODE=0110 then
   if [AC]<0 THEN ADDRESS TO: PC; go to: 1
   If OPCODE=0101 then ADDRESS TO: PC; go to: 1
   ADDRESS TO: MAR;
   If OPCODE=0001 then go to: 8
   else READ;
   If OPCODE=0010 then go to: 9
5. AC TO: A
6. MDR TO: ALU
   If OPCODE=0011 then ADD
   If OPCODE=0100 then SUBTRACT
7. R TO: AC go to: 1
8. AC TO: MDR; WRITE; go to:1
9. MDR TO: AC; go to: 1

As an example of possible implementation, the diagram in Figure 7.14 shows the part of the control circuit relevant to the STORE instruction. It is derived directly from the control sequence above.

Sequence flow is controlled by a switching circuit controlling the path of the propagation of the clock signal, in our case a single AND gate. This will be explained below.

Implementation of steps 1, 2, 3 is straightforward. The relevant part of step 4 is

4. ADDRESS TO: MAR;
   If OPCODE=0001 then go to: 8

Let us denote the combined conditions "STORE is in IR" and "step is 4" by S4. Step 4 can be reformulated as

4. S4: ADDRESS TO MAR; reset counter to 8, etc.

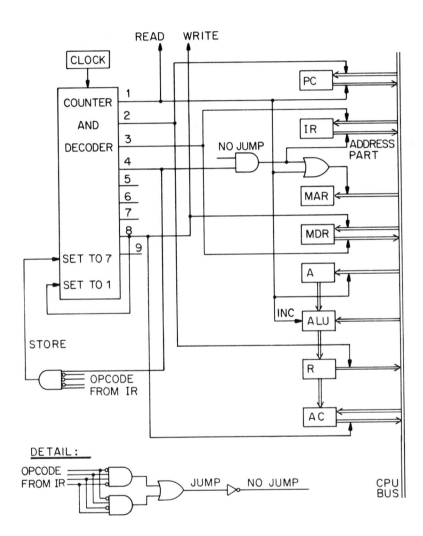

Figure 7.14   A possible implementation of the part of the control unit which generates control signals for the STORE instruction.

The condition for signal S4 can be described by

$S =$ (state is 4).(OPCODE=0001) $=$ (state is 4).$S =$

$=$

(state=4).(OPCODE.0)'.(OPCODE.1)'.(OPCODE.2)'.(OPCODE.3)

This function is implemented by the 5-input AND gate in the circuit in Figure 7.14.

Step 6 is implemented in a similar way.

7.4.2   An Introduction To Microprogrammed Control Units

The implementation of the control section outlined in the previous section is called *hardwired.* It can be manufactured from individual ICs in the same way as any digital system. Since the beginning of the 1970's, simpler CPUs are produced on single chips and are called microprocessors. The implementation of a hardwired CPU is permanent, intended to be unchangeable. Changes are possible only by modifying the structure of the circuit, physically changing connections, and replacing parts. Hardwired design is not the only way to approach the problem as can be recognized by an analysis of the function of the control unit.

Let us examine again what the control unit does by investigating the control sequence and the block diagram of the CPU. From the point of view of control the CPU can be viewed as in Figure 7.15.

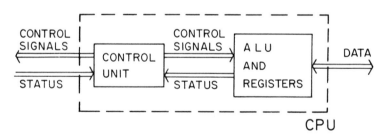

Figure 7.15   The function of the control unit.

The control unit can be considered as a black box which produces control signals in response to status information.

Status information consists of all signals which are necessary to choose the correct sequence of control signals dictated by the desired function of the control unit. It includes information about the contents of the instruction register, the sign of the contents of the accumulator, and in general a number of other signals, some of which will be introduced in the following sections.

Control signals initiate data transfers and operations of other modules. They include the READ, STORE signals to the memory, ADD, SUBTRACT signals to ALU, open data paths from PC to bus, from bus to MAR, etc.

It is irrelevant how the control unit black box is designed as long as it performs the required functions. The hardwired implementation presented in the previous section is an obvious possibility. This approach has advantages and disadvantages.

The main disadvantage of a *hardwired* control unit is its permanent character. The consequence of this is that once the control unit is designed, it can be changed only with significant expense and time. This implies the following:

1. If there were a design error, its correction is very expensive and time consuming.
2. Expansion of the function of the control unit is expensive and time consuming.
3. The control unit can perform only the functions for which it was designed. The full meaning of this statement will become apparent later.

Is there an alternative to a hardwired control unit? Let us consider the general process of the design of a control unit and formulate the ideal approach:

1. Identify all control and status signals which must be provided to satisfy the specification.
2. Design a flexible control unit which allows complete control over these signals and has access to all status information. The most flexible design is one in which the operation is controlled by a modifiable sequence of instructions specifying the desired operations and their order. In other words, a control unit whose control sequence can be programmed.
3. Program the control unit to implement the specification.

The outlined approach not only is esthetically more appealing but also removes all the problems of a hardwired unit listed above. The structure of the resulting *microprogrammed* control unit is quite simple, and its design postpones to some extent the main problem of physical implementation of the control sequence, which is most likely to produce errors. The consequences are:

1. If there is a design error, it is probably in the control sequence, and its correction requires only a modification of the control program and no hardware changes or circuit modification.
2. Expansion of the control unit is simple if it has available all control and status signals. It again requires only reprogramming of the control program and no hardware changes.
3. There is no limit to the number of different control programs that can be written for a given configuration of a microprogrammed control unit. In particular the same system may be microprogrammed to behave like any related computer and its behavior changed by simply changing its control program. The process of using a given CPU to behave like another computer is called *emulation*.

It would seem that microprogrammed control units are better than hardwired ones in all respects. This is not quite so. To see the reason for this and the implications, we must assume a more general perspective.

Our latest model represents the CPU as consisting of two cooperating digital systems. We have just indicated the advantages of implementing the control module by a computer-like unit. A microprogrammed control unit satisfies most of the requirements of our definition of a digital computer as we will see shortly. We can generalize this idea and conclude that *any* digital system can have its control unit implemented by a digital computer or be yardwired. Since a digital computer is capable of performing Boolean operations, any digital system, including elementary gates, can be implemented by a computer. This conclusion can be interpreted to a degree as implying *equivalence of hardware and software* since the distinguishing property of the computer implementation is the program (software).

The hardware-software equivalence is complete in a logical sense. Any truth table or transition table can be implemented in hardware or software. A software implementation uses a specifically programmed computer and I/O interfaces. Similarly, any computer program performs only Boolean and memory operations and can thus be replaced by hardware. The difference between the two implementations is that if we use the same technologies, the maximum *speed* attainable by a software-based system is of necessity *less* than the speed attainable by a hardware implementation. To see why this must be so, consider what a computer must do when it is made to produce a set of signals in response to certain status information. The computer is a machine which executes instructions. To generate a signal, the computer must fetch an instruction which specifies the desired action, decode it, fetch operands, possibly check certain conditions (the status), and produce a signal. There are thus a number of steps, each of which requires a certain minimum time to perform. The basic time unit is the time required by several stages of elementary gates and flip-flops to respond. The hardware system, on the other hand, requires only the time equivalent to the propagation of the signal through a logical path typically consisting of only a few gates. The hardwired implementation thus requires less time to generate the desired signal than the programmed implementation.

As a specific example of a hardwired-programmed comparison consider the last step in the execution of the STORE instruction. In our hardware implementation the control signal is generated by two AND gates (Figure 7.16). The whole step 4 in the control sequence is implemented by a one-stage circuit of AND gates (Figure 7.17).

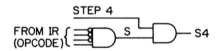

Figure 7.16   A hardwired implementation of the generation of the control signal in control step 4 of the STORE instruction.

Implementing control steps 4 and 8 in software requires a sequence of *microinstructions* (a *microprogram*) which could be described as follows:

symbolic microaddress	function of control instruction
AJ	if OPCODE=0110 then go to J
..	....
AS	if OPCODE=0001 then go to S
..	....
J	produce signals ADDRESS TO BUS TO
...	....
S	produce signals ADDRESS TO produce signals AC TO 1 TO go to 1

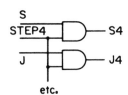

Figure 7.17   A hardwired implementation of the generation of control signals in step 4 of the control sequence. Here S is the control signal corresponding to the STORE instruction, J corresponds to the JUMP instruction, etc.

These instructions would be stored in the memory of the control unit, the *control store*, which acts as an independent computer.

Assume that the control unit is processing the STORE instruction and that it reached the software equivalent of control step 4. In order to produce all signals corresponding to S, the microprogrammed control unit has to perform the following steps:

1. Fetch the first microinstruction from address AJ.
2. Decode and execute the first microinstruction. This microinstruction does not produce any signals or jump since the condition is not satisfied.
3. Fetch the next microinstruction from location AJ+1.
4. Execute this microinstruction, etc., until address AS is reached.
5. Fetch microinstruction from location AS.
6. Decode and execute this microinstruction. This results in a jump to address S in the control store since the opcode is as required for STORE.
7. Fetch microinstruction from address S.
8. Decode and execute this microinstruction. This produces the required control signals.
9. Fetch the next microinstruction.
10. Decode and execute this microinstruction. This results in the equivalent of resetting the counter.

A hardwired control unit will require only the amount of time needed by the signal to propagate through two AND gates to achieve the same result. The difference in speed is obvious.

The following should be pointed out:

1. The above control program can be written in a more efficient form and thus produce a shorter sequence of executed instructions. The fact that a number of instructions will have to be fetched, decoded, and executed remains, however, unchanged.
2. The control unit can be made faster than a standard computer. It can use the fastest technology because it is much smaller than a real computer, and the cost of using the fastest components will be much smaller than if this type of component were used in a full-sized computer. This concerns memory technology in particular. Again the basic comparison remains valid if we compare similar technologies. The difference in speed between a hardwired and microprogrammed control unit is, however, getting smaller with advances in technology.

For most computers the advantages of microprogramming have more and more weight than the disadvantages, particularly with improving technology. More and more computers are thus built with microprogrammed control units. The trend towards microprogramming started in the late 1960's although the concept of microprogramming was presented in 1951.

The idea of microprogramming can be carried even further. The programmability of the control unit can also be made available to the user of the computer and not just to its designer. Computers which allow the user to write control programs into the control store, which must then be at least partially a writable memory and not a ROM, are called *microprogrammable* and are relatively rare. Most microprogrammed computers are not microprogrammable. Their control stores are ROMs, sometimes called "microms." Microprogramming can be used to simplify the design of a whole series of different computers on the same basic design. Individual computers in the series, a "family," can differ substantially in the complexity of their control programs and consequently in their instruction sets, in the technology used, etc. The most primitive would be relatively inexpensive and microprogrammed; the most sophisticated models very expensive and hardwired if very high speed is essential. The concept of a family of computers is very attractive to users since a user of a certain computer can buy a more advanced model of computer from the same manufacturer and use programs running on the old computer on the new computer. This makes different computers in the same family "software compatible" which is a very important economic consideration. The negative consequence of keeping a given architecture relatively unchanged over a lengthy period of time is that it seriously limits the possibility of progress in architecture, while allowing technological and structural advances.

Microprogrammability, i.e., the facility to allow the user to write microprograms, has not been found very attractive in practice since most users do not have the interest, need, and expertise to write new control programs to emulate other computers. This feature is thus not likely to become widespread among standard commercial computers. Microprogrammability of the control unit may, however, be very useful when certain special sequences of operations are required relatively frequently and can be implemented more efficiently as user-designed microprogrammed instructions. These special operations may be of an arithmetic or I/O character. There is thus a limited interest, and a few microprogrammable computers of smaller size are commercially available.

7.4.3   An Example Of A Microprogrammed Control Unit

It has been stated that a microprogrammed control unit is basically a computer. Its inputs are status information signals; its outputs are control signals which control the data transfers and operations of the main CPU. The design of a microprogrammed control unit thus follows the same pattern as the design of a computer although there are certain special considerations dictated by the necessity to speed up the operation and reduce the size of the control store so that it can be built economically with expensive technology.

The first step in the design of a computer is the specification of its function in terms of its instruction set. We have seen that the microprogram is essentially just an encoded control sequence and the required actions are the following:

1. To generate a set of control signals.
2. To allow conditional jumps out of the linear control sequence when the status information satisfies certain conditions.
3. To allow unconditional jumps.

The above listing of required capabilities does not include any arithmetic operations and only limited logic in the form of conditional jumps. In this sense, the system does not fully satisfy our definition of a computer, and it is a simplification to refer to it as a computer.

The most obvious and easiest method of generating control signals is to define a class of microinstructions whose function it is to define directly the desired control signals as follows: each control bit of a control generating microinstruction specifies whether a certain control signal is to be generated or not. Individual control bits of the *microinstruction register* (MIR) can then be connected to the corresponding control lines (Figure 7.18). The connection is controlled by the microdecoder and is enabled only if the micro-opcode defines a control signal generating microinstruction. In the case of such a microinstruction a 0 or a 1 is then placed on each control line in agreement with the contents of MIR. We will now outline the design of a microprogrammed control unit for our computer.

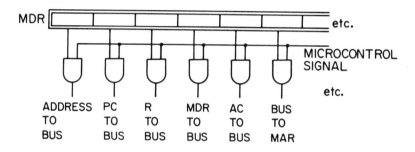

Figure 7.18 A possible approach to the generation of control signals by a microinstruction.

First we have to identify the required control signals. Inspection of the control sequence shows that we have to be able to generate the following signals:

IR(address) to bus, PC to bus, R to bus, MDR to bus, AC to bus, bus to MAR, bus to ALU, bus to PC, bus to IR, bus to AC, bus to A, bus to MDR, READ, WRITE, ADD, INC, SUBTRACT.

We need 17 different control signals altogether. If we want to reserve one bit of each control microinstruction for a control signal, then the MIR must have 18 bits for control signals plus a few bits for micro-opcode to distinguish between the three types of microinstructions: control, conditional jump, jump. One bit is left unassigned. The connection between MIR and control lines is schematic as in Figure 7.18.

Since we have three types of microinstructions (those that generate control signals, those that cause conditional jumps, and those that cause unconditional jumps), we will add two bits to specify the opcode and arbitrarily specify the value of these two bits as follows:

microinstruction	bit 18	bit 19
control signal	0	0
unconditional jump	0	1
conditional jump	1	0
unassigned	1	1

Assume that control bits and control signals are assigned in the order given in Figure 7.19. As an example of interpretation of a control microinstruction the following code:

$$01000 \ 11000 \ 00100 \ 10000$$

corresponds to

1. PC TO: MAR, ALU; READ; INC;

A 1 activates a control line; a 0 leaves it passive. (The required control signals are PC to bus, bus to MAR, bus to ALU, READ, INC.)

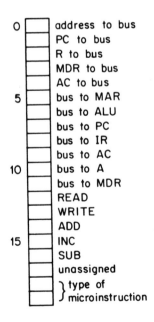

Figure 7.19   Assignment of control signals and control bits.

Jumps can most naturally, but very inefficiently, be handled much as they are by computer jump instructions. There could be a micro-opcode for each type of conditional jump.

Inspection of the control sequence of our computer shows that conditions which need to be checked are as shown in Figure 7.20.

condition		micro-code
instruction=JN	opcode=0110	000
AC>=0		001
instruction=JM	opcode=0101	010
instruction=ST	opcode=0001	011
instruction=LD	opcode=0010	100
instruction=AD	opcode=0011	101
instruction=SU	opcode=0100	110

Figure 7.20   Conditions and their microcodes.

A conditional jump microinstruction performs a jump to a specified microaddress when a specified condition is satisfied. It must contain the code of the condition to be checked and, in our present approach, the destination microaddress. We have seven conditions, and so three bits are sufficient to encode all conditions. We will assign condition codes arbitrarily as in Figure 7.20. As an example of interpretation, the code 0011111000001111110 means: conditional microinstruction (last two bits are the micro-opcode of a conditional jump) which causes jump to microaddress 111110000011111 if AC>=0 (condition code, the first three bits, is 001).

The complete microprogram can now be derived from the control sequence. It is shown in Figure 7.21.

Another look at the control sequence and our previous example indicates that there are many places where a conditional jump is required, and the standard computer approach just outlined results in a microprogram consisting mainly of jump instructions. Jump microinstructions do not generate any control signals; they only consume time and slow down the control unit. This was illustrated in the comparison of hardwired and software-based control units.

Inspection of the control sequence shows that most conditional jumps are lumped together: they correspond to places in the control

octal address	microcode	comment
0	01000100001010010000	control step 1
1	00100001000000000000	control step 2
2	00010000100000000000	control step 3
3	00000000000001010110	if opcode=JN go to 25 octal
4	01000000000001011010	if opcode=JM go to 26
5	10000100000000000000	address to MAR
6	01100000000001000110	if opcode=ST go to 21
7	00000000000010000000	READ
10	10000000000001001110	if opcode=LD go to 23
11	00001000001000000000	AC to A (step 5)
12	00010010000000000000	MDR to ALU
13	11000000000000111010	if opcode=SU go to 16
14	00000000000000100000	ADD
15	00000000000000111101	go to 17
16	00000000000000001000	SUB
17	00100000010000000000	R to AC
20	00000000000000000001	go to 0 (step 1)
21	00001000000101000000	AC to MDR; WRITE (step 8)
22	00000000000000000001	go to 0 (end step 8)
23	00010000010000000000	MDR to AC (step 9)
24	00000000000000000001	go to 0
25	00100000000000000010	if AC>=0 go to 0 (JN)
26	10000001000000000000	address to PC
27	00000000000000000001	go to 0

Figure 7.21   A microprogram to implement the full control sequence developed in the section on the control unit. Microaddresses in the left column are octal. Comments in the rightmost column explain the function of each microinstruction and its location in the control sequence where desirable. The "go to" comments give the octal form of the destination microaddress and not the number of the corresponding control step.

sequence where the next action depends on the opcode of the currently executed instruction. This suggests a solution to the problem of long sequences of unproductive conditional jump microinstructions which is described in the Workbook. It is based on the use of a hardwired module which generates correct microaddresses in response to the current state of the control unit. An example in the Workbook is concerned with timing and a comparison of speed of the hardwired and microprogrammed control units. A simplified diagram of the microprogrammed control unit is shown in Figure 7.22.

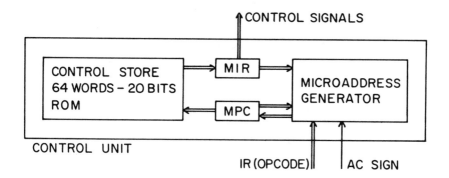

Figure 7.22   The structure of the microprogrammed control unit.

The following should be noted:

1. Register names are prefixed by M for micro-.
2. Microinstruction words are 20 bits long while computer words are 12 bits long; there is no relationship between the two.
3. Since the control memory is in a ROM, the microdata bus is unidirectional.
4. The incrementer adds 1 to the value in MPC. The control unit's control unit can be designed as hardwired or microprogrammed just as the control unit itself. A hardwired implementation will result in a faster control unit; a microprogrammed implementation results in a more flexible control unit in which not only instructions but even microinstructions can be programmed, via "nanoinstructions." The first approach is much more common since the extra flexibility is not generally needed. Note that at the lowest level the innermost control unit must be hardwired.

This concludes our design of a microprogrammed control unit.

7.4.4   General Remarks About Microprogramming

It has been noted that microprogramming is gaining in popularity. A number of monographs devoted to microprogramming have been published, and the topic is the subject of considerable research interest. The presentation in the previous section was intended to demonstrate a natural approach and justification. The end result was a rather naively designed inefficient control unit. Approaches are known which speed up the operation of the control unit and reduce the size of the microprogram.

The approach used in the previous section results in microcode called *horizontal*. Its extreme implementation is characterized by the fact that every control signal is assigned its own control bit. The advantage of this approach is that it allows the designer a complete access to all control signals and simplifies expansion and modification because even transfers not originally anticipated can be programmed if the necessary control signals are assigned bits in the microcode. The disadvantage of the horizontal microcode is its storage inefficiency since for most needs the absolutely unrestricted access to control signals is not needed and one bit per control signal assignment is unnecessary. The redundancy of encoding can be seen on the resulting microprogram which consists of microinstructions making very inefficient use of the control signal facility: all microinstructions are mostly zeros. This redundancy can be very significantly reduced if we realize that certain control signals are always generated in combination with other signals. In our case limiting ourselves just to the required transfers allows us to produce the following table of requested combinations of signals:

control signals	possible new microcode
PC TO: MAR, ALU	000000
R TO: PC	000001
MDR TO: IR	000010
ADDRESS TO: PC	000011
ADDRESS TO: MAR	000100
MDR TO: MAR	000101
MDR TO: AC	000110
MDR TO: ALU	000111
AC TO: A	001000
R TO: AC	001001
AC TO: MDR	001010
1 TO: READ	001011
1 TO: STORE	001100
1 TO: ADD	001101
1 TO: SUB	001110
NUMBER 1 TO: A	001111

The size of the table could be further reduced by one of the algorithms available for this purpose. In our case this is not necessary since we need six bits to specify the microaddress in unconditional jumps, and the encoding just presented requires only four bits. Two bits are thus already wasted. The highly encoded approach to the representation of control signals is called *vertical microprogramming*. Its advantage is the possibility of a substantial reduction in the size of the control store. In our case coding allows us to use 8-bit control words instead of 21-bit codewords, an almost two-thirds saving in control store. The disadvantage of highly vertical microcodes is that they severely restrict access to control signals and can make modifications of the control unit virtually impossible. As an example, assume that it has been decided to implement transfer AC to PC. In the original horizontal microcode this is achieved simply by the microinstruction 000010010000000000000. The control signals needed for this transfer cannot be generated with the vertical microcode given above, the solution would have to be an indirect transfer using an intermediate register or a redesign of the control unit.

Horizontal microprogramming results in a simpler control unit since there is no need for decoding as is the case for vertical microprograms (Figure 7.23). As a result of the relative advantages and disadvantages of horizontal and vertical microcodes, commercial computers use a compromise solution involving a certain amount of encoding but allowing free access to important groups of control signals.

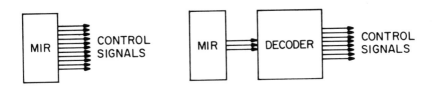

Figure 7.23 Control signal generation in a horizontal and vertical design.

The above examples show that microprogramming is essentially a mechanical process of conversion from an accurate statement of the control sequence to a binary microcode. The process is tedious and lengthy since most microcodes involve long codes with many bits. As a result, there is a danger of coding errors which is very critical for a program as important as the microprogram. To reduce this danger and to make the process more natural, a number of *high-level micropro-gramming languages* have been developed. Microprograms can be written in these natural-looking symbolic languages and translated into the final binary form by a computer program, a translator, much like programs in standard programming languages.

7.5 THE ALU

In our block diagram of the CPU the ALU is represented as a box with two 12-bit data inputs, one 12-bit data output, and control signals for choosing between ADD and SUBTRACT (Figure 7.24).

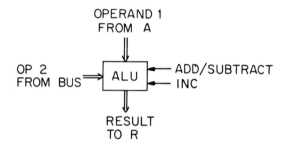

Figure 7.24   The ALU.

The ALU specification requires the capability of performing 2's complement fixed-point addition and subtraction as follows:

$$op1+op2 \quad op1-op2.$$

This is a minimal specification which does not even provide for certain basic signals such as operation overflow.

Our knowledge of basic arithmetic operations allows us to redefine subtraction as follows:

$$op1-op2 = op1 + 2\text{'s complement}(op2)$$
where
$$2\text{'s complement}(op2) = (op2)' + 1$$
and so
$$op1-op2 = op1 + (op2)' + 1$$

The last formulation shows that subtraction requires only an adder and an inverter (Figure 7.25).

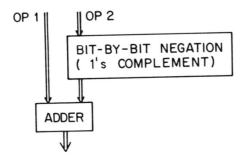

Figure 7.25   Block diagram of 2's complement subtraction.

Since only incrementation, addition, and subtraction are required in 2's complement fixed-point arithmetic, the whole ALU can be implemented as in Figure 7.26. The boxes denoted ADD, AND, and OR have the structure shown in Figure 7.27. Circuit SUB differs from circuit ADD only by having the ADD signal replaced by a SUBTRACT signal.

The following points should be noted:

1. It is assumed that control signals ADD and SUBTRACT are complementary:
   ADD = (SUBTRACT)'
   so that at any time the ALU is performing exactly one of these two operations.

2. The ALU consists of a set of basic arithmetic circuits and control. These two components are more or less independent and can be studied and designed independently. We have studied basic arithmetic circuits in previous chapters and control in the previous sections of this chapter.

3. The ALU operates continuously, not just when it receives a control signal. Its output is, however, ignored at all times except when the executed instruction is ADD or SUBTRACT.

4. Addition of further arithmetic operations such as multiplication, division, and floating-point arithmetic or Boolean operations does not alter the basic conceptual simplicity of the ALU which can always be seen as a set of arithmetic and Boolean units with control lines and communication channels. Increasing the

number of implemented operations does, however, add significantly to the complexity and cost of the physical implementation of the ALU. Most inexpensive CPUs (and ALU chips), therefore, provide only basic fixed-point arithmetic and elementary Boolean functions to keep the cost down. Some of them offer expansions as more or less expensive options.

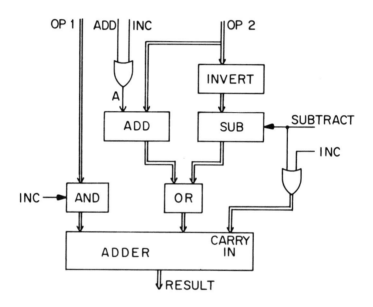

Figure 7.26   A block diagram of an ALU with 2's complement addition and subtraction.

7.6   MEMORY AND PERIPHERAL DEVICES

We have defined memory as an array of randomly addressable locations each of which can store the same number of bits. We have also assumed that the CPU has instructions which allow it to access any of these locations. Memory with these properties is usually called the main memory, in the past also *core memory* or simply the *core*.

Another name sometimes used for main memory is the *system memory*. The main memory or its major part is a read/write memory, a RAM. A small fraction of the main memory is often a ROM which stores certain basic programs intended to be an integral and indestructible part of the system. Such programs are often called the *firmware* to indicate that they form an intermediate category between software and hardware. They are in fact "hardwired software." Their function in standard computer systems is to make certain basic operations easier to program and to automate initialization of the computer for start-up. In computer systems used in control applications such as in control units of sophisticated home appliances, industrial machine tools, etc., most of the memory is ROM and only a small amount of RAM is allocated for data processed by the CPU. Both RAM and ROM usually share the same address space.

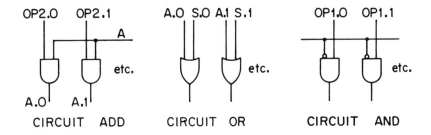

Figure 7.27   Details of modules ADD, OR, and AND from Figure 7.25.

Until the early 1970's most RAMs were manufactured from tiny magnetic cores organized in planes with control wires passing through the cores. These core memories were so standard that the main memory is still often called the core memory although the core technology is quickly disappearing from new designs and is being replaced by semiconductor memories.

The *core technology* will be described very briefly since it is becoming obsolete in most applications and is described in considerable detail in most classic textbooks on computers and computer organization. The principle of core memories is that ferromagnetic materials can be magnetized in one of two directions and retain their magnetization indefinitely unless subjected to a sufficiently strong magnetic field. The information stored in them can be interpreted as binary by associating one direction with a 0 and the other with 1. The stored information is not affected even when the power source is removed. This very important property of core memories is called *non-volatility* and is the main advantage of core memories over semiconductors which are volatile, meaning that they lose information when power falls below the minimal level. The direction of magnetization can be changed by a strong magnetic field which can be generated by a sufficiently strong electric current passing through the core. The direction of magnetization can be sensed by attempting to rewrite the information stored in the core and sensing whether voltage was induced in another wire passing through the core. In this way information can be read. Reading thus results in the modification of the original stored information: it is *destructive*. The original information must be restored, or rewritten, and this adds to the delay which is required for the same location to be reaccessed. This lengthens the minimal interval in which two successive accesses to the memory can be made (the *memory cycle time*). Note the difference between the memory cycle time and the *memory access time* which is the time from the initiation of a memory access to the appearance of stable data on the output. Since the access time of core memories is limited by the magnetic properties of the material and the size of the core, there is an insurmountable limit on the speed of core memories. This and the relative complexity of their mechanical production are the main disadvantages of core memories which make them less and less attractive in comparison with semiconductor memories which still have not reached their full potential and have already surpassed cores in most parameters.

Semiconductor memories are based on the same technologies as ROM memories introduced in Chapter 2. They are, in fact, arrays of flip-flops with decoders. Developments in semiconductor technology in the past decade made them economically competitive with core memories. They have the additional advantages of higher speed, higher storage density, and lower power consumption. The main disadvantage of semiconductor RAMs is their volatility. Once power is removed or allowed to fluctuate, semiconductor memory is affected in an unpredictable way and information is lost. This may be unacceptable in some applications, and core memories then become serious candidates to replace semiconductors. There are two other alternatives to eliminate the volatility problem: to provide a back-up power source or to develop non-volatile or partially non-volatile semiconductor memories. The first solution requires a highly controlled battery system. The cost of this solution makes such a system quite expensive. Non-volatile semiconductor memories or memories which can hold information for a limited but reasonable amount of time have been the subject of considerable research. The known solutions—electrically alterable ROMs—EAROMs—have the disadvantage that non-volatility is achieved at the cost of speed of access, and this affects the main advantage of semiconductors.

Semiconductor memories, just as all other semiconductor components, are produced in essentially two technologies:

1. *Bipolar* technologies which result in very fast components but are not so dense, have considerable power consumption, and are expensive. They are only used when speed is the primary consideration, for example, for relatively small auxiliary memories which act as high speed buffers between the main memory and the CPU, the *cache memory* of larger computer systems which will be briefly discussed in Chapter 8.

2. MOS technologies which are slower, denser, and cheaper and have smaller power requirements. They are currently the standard semiconductor memories. From the functional and structural point of view there are two subcategories of MOS memories:

   a. *Static* memories which maintain information without external intervention as long as power is available.

   b. *Dynamic* memories which can hold information only for a very limited length of time, in the order of milliseconds. They must be periodically reread and the information *refreshed* by special circuitry. The refresh can be timed to occur when the CPU is not accessing the chip and can thus be made *transparent* to the CPU; the CPU need not "be aware" of the fact that its main memory is dynamic. The main advantage of dynamic memories is their very high density which is the consequence of the extreme simplicity of the basic circuit. This simplicity is also the reason why these memories cannot hold information permanently. The highest density semiconductor RAMs are dynamic MOS memories. The densest commercially available *monolithic* (i.e., produced on one chip) RAMs were 64k bits in 1979. The maximum available density tends to grow very fast, approximately doubling every two years, and is expected to continue growing in the foreseeable future. Note that at the time of 64k dynamic RAMs there were packages containing 64k of static RAM.

These packages were, however, not monolithic, they contained several chips packaged together. They were more expensive than corresponding dynamic RAMs.

All types of RAM ICs consist basically of two modules: the storage module which is simply an array of flip-flops and the addressing part, which is a decoder. Both modules are implemented on a single chip. It has already been stated that a given storage capacity can be organized in a number of different ways, depending essentially on the design of the decoder and the internal communication channels. As an example a RAM with 64k storage locations could be accessed as

64k 1-bit cells
32k 2-bit cells
16k 4-bit cells
etc.

Economic and design considerations determine which of these configurations are commercially produced since the decoder is a part of the chip. It is clear that memory systems could be built more easily from chips with word sizes tailored to the required word length. The diversity of applications and the resulting wide range of required word lengths, on the other hand, make this impossible and require a very flexible word size. From this perspective 1-bit words are clearly most attractive since they can be used to build memories of any size and structure. Another useful size is one byte (eight bits) which forms the basis of the word size of many computers, particularly the 8- and 16-bit microprocessors. RAM chips are thus commonly available as arrays of 1-bit or 8-bit cells with other sizes not quite so popular and therefore more expensive.

Almost all memory systems require more than the basic amount of memory available on one chip. A complete memory system must therefore be built from a number of identical RAM chips. ICs are grouped to form sufficiently large cells, and groups are combined as necessary to build the required memory address space. This will be demonstrated shortly. The implication of this approach is that when a certain location is being accessed only one group of chips should be made accessible and the other groups disabled for this particular access since the other groups represent a different portion of the address space. This means that RAM chips must have a control INPUT to ENABLE/DISABLE access to them. The ENABLE control *signal* is generated by an *off-chip decoder* (a separate IC) which is a part of the memory system.

Example 7.3: Assume that it is desired to build a 1k×8 memory (1k words with eight static bits each) and that 256×8 static RAM chips are available. Each of them has the following inputs and outputs:

Address lines — a total of eight must be present to allow addressing of 256 locations present on the chip.

Data lines — eight lines to allow parallel transfer of all eight bits in a word in any direction.

Chip enable — controls the tri-state function of the chip by placing its inputs and outputs into high impedance mode (disconnected electrically from the rest of the circuit) when disabled.

Read/write — determines the type of access.

Power lines.

Since a 1k memory is desired, four such chips are needed. 1k addressable locations require 10 address lines. Of these, eight will be connected identically to chip address lines and will be decoded on (i.e., inside) the chip; the remaining two will be decoded by an off-chip decoder whose output will be used to enable only that IC whose address space corresponds to the two off-chip decoded lines. The circuit is connected as in Figure 7.28. The following should be noted:

1. All memory chips are connected directly and identically to the data bus. This is possible because the tri-state character of the output allows at most one of the chips to have its outputs electrically tied to the bus at any time.

2. The circuit is connected in such a way that the leftmost two bits select a RAM chip. The remaining eight lines are connected identically to all four chips and decoded on the chip. The enable signal turns exactly one of the chips into the active state for any specific value on the two off-chip decoded lines: address 0010001001 enables chip 0 (determined by the leftmost 00 pair of bits of the address) which then accesses its location 10001001 (the rightmost eight bits of the address). Address 1000111010 enables only chip 10 which accesses its location 00111010, etc. In general the address range 0000000000 to 0011111111 is implemented on chip 0, 0100000000 to 0111111111 on chip 1, etc. In other words the address space of chip 0 is 00xxxxxxxx, the address space of chip 1 is 01xxxxxxxx, etc. Note that the decision to decode the most significant two bits off-chip and the remaining eight on-chip is not the only possible solution. We could design the circuit to decode the most significant eight bits

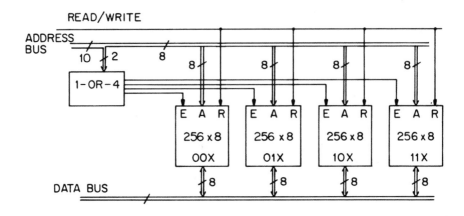

Figure 7.28   A 1k×8 memory configured from four 256×8 memory chips.

(the leftmost eight bits) on-chip and the remaining two off-chip, etc. Convention and specific conditions determine the preferable solution.

3. Note that if there is no need to have all four RAM chips installed because the programs in a specific application may be very short and require little memory, they can be disconnected or not installed. The rest of the memory will work properly, but care must be taken not to use addresses assigned to the missing chips. The use of "incompletely populated" memory boards or otherwise incomplete memory space is quite common for economic reasons.

Assume now that the same memory space is to be implemented with 1k×4 bit RAM chips. The memory can be configured as in Figure 7.29. Note that in this case all 10 address lines are directly and identically connected to both chips since they all have 10 address lines for their 1k 4-bit cells. There is thus no need for off-chip decoding. The data lines, on the other hand, are not connected in the same way. This is because a single 1k×4 chip does not provide sufficient word size for our needs: the required word size is eight bits and the chips provide only 4-bit words. Two chips must thus be combined. They are

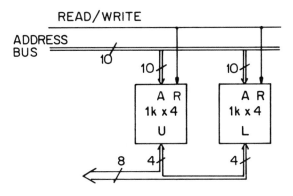

Figure 7.29   A 1k×8 memory configured from 1k×4 chips.

addressed identically, but one stores the upper half and the other the lower half of each word as shown below:

address	chip U		chip L
0			
1			
...			
1k-1			

This concludes the coverage of hardware aspects of main memory devices. The next section describes how different types of memories can be efficiently combined to make the best use of all advantages of various categories of memories.

7.6.1 Memory Hierarchies

Users and designers of computer systems face the following dilemma: they need large and fast memory to allow efficient processing and storage of large programs with large amounts of data, but fast memory is very expensive. Cheaper storage media are available, but they are so slow that their access times are incompatible with CPU speeds. Fortunately, most of the information that users want to store consists of independent programs and data sets which are not needed simultaneously. Most information can thus be stored in a slower but cheaper memory, which the CPU does not treat as memory, but an

I/O device, and retrieved and placed into main memory when needed for processing. The CPU does not see much difference between communication with these *secondary*, *auxiliary*, or *external* storage devices and communication with I/O. By their basic function all these devices belong together with memories and will be briefly described together in this section.

The justification of the need for secondary storage can be extended to apply to the processing of long programs using large data sets, too large to fit into the main memory available on a specific system. Such programs can be executed in segments with only the currently executing segment of the program or currently accessed segment of the data file residing in the main memory and the rest in auxiliary memory awaiting its turn. Segments of program and data are "swapped" between the two levels of storage as needed. To simplify programming, the software and/or hardware of the system can be designed in such a way as to make the secondary storage *appear* as an addressable extension of the main memory. This is the basis of the more advanced concept of *virtual memory* which will not be discussed here.

The reasoning which applies to large programs can be extended to a sequence of independent programs which the CPU can treat as a continuous stream of instructions. This type of processing is known as *multiprogramming*. In this mode the CPU is controlled by a master program, the *operating system*, which makes the CPU switch from one program to another. The switch from one program to another occurs when the presently executing program requires an I/O operation which cannot be performed immediately or when it exhausts its allocated amount of time.

In other arrangements the system can directly communicate with a certain number of terminals. This mode of operation is called *timesharing* since the users of terminals share their access to the computer in time. Both timesharing and multiprogramming are common on large modern systems because they increase the efficiency of usage of the powerful CPU. Their efficient implementation clearly requires a large memory.

The above arguments provide a justification of viewing memory as consisting of a hierarchy of categories. Only the top level, the main memory, is memory in our original sense since it is only this level which the CPU can directly address. The lower categories are treated essentially as I/O. Typical computer systems thus have two levels of memory, the main memory and one or more types of auxiliary memory. By extending our perspective we could include CPU registers in our hierarchy as the highest, fastest, and most directly addressable level.

We can summarize the distinguishing characteristics of various levels of memories as follows:

1. *Speed.* The auxiliary memory is the slowest; registers are the fastest.
2. *Cost per bit* of storage is highest for CPU registers and lowest for auxiliary storage.
3. Mechanics of *access*. CPU registers are accessed most directly, and data transfers with them take place on buses internal to the CPU. Main memory is accessed randomly by address, and data transfer is over a memory-CPU bus. Auxiliary devices are treated as I/O devices, with communication often via a special computer-like controller, usually called a "channel controller." To make data transfer more efficient, it is usually performed in *blocks* of data rather than by individual words as is the case for higher level memories. Access is sequential or semisequential rather than random. (Communication with I/O devices will be outlined later.)
4. Physical *organization* and *technology*. Registers are accessible essentially as independent memory cells. Main memory is accessible as an array. Auxiliary memory is accessible as a set of addressable or nonaddressable blocks. Access is at least partially sequential which allows simpler organization and thus lower cost but also implies lower speed since access to any storage cell in equal time is impossible.

The most important types of auxiliary storage devices are briefly described below; see also the Workbook. Some of the less efficient ones are so slow that they are not usually classified as auxiliary storage. This is particularly true for paper tape and paper card and to some extent for magnetic tape devices. Modern systems typically include only magnetic disks or recently their semiconductor equivalents in the category of secondary storage. The slower media described below have been included in this section because their basic function is related, and in the past they often played a role similar to modern secondary storage devices.

7.6.1.1 Magnetic Disks. These are currently the most important auxiliary storage devices. A disk storage unit consists of a *disk drive* and one or more storage *disks*. The disk drive consists of mechanical parts which cause the rotation of the disk, one or more reading/writing *heads* which can be moveable and whose purpose is to transfer the data and electronic parts which process the signal and control the whole device — the *controller*. Disks rotate on a common spindle at a high speed such as 3600 rpm. Information is stored on their magnetizable surface. Coding is binary, the density is very high, and the mechanism is extremely accurate and sensitive to environment. Because of the rotational motion and the planar surface, information is stored in concentric *tracks*.

There are several types of disk storage which differ essentially in their mechanical sophistication and therefore their speeds and costs:

1. Systems with *rigid* (also called *hard* as opposed to flexible) disks. This type is standard on all but small computers. It is more expensive than disk systems with flexible disks described below but allows higher density of storage and higher access speeds essentially because the rigidity of the disk provides higher precision and rotational speed. One disk drive usually accomodates a set or "pack" of several disks mounted on the same spindle. The disk pack is often removable, and this extends storage capacity to as many disk packs as the installation needs. Disk storage is nonvolatile, and disk removal does not affect information stored on it. The change of disks is, however, a manual process and relatively very slow. Disk drives with nonremovable disks have the advantage that their construction can be more rigid and their storage parameters higher, at the cost of fixing the amount of storage.

   Some disk drives have a set of heads for each track on the disk and their positions are fixed, *fixed-head* drives. Others have fewer heads which can move across tracks, *movable-head* drives. This reduces the number of heads and the cost of the disk drive but also the speed of access since the head must mechanically move to access the correct track before it can start reading the required information.

   Cells on tracks are numbered, and the track number, the cell number plus the disk number, if applicable, constitute their full address. Cells are rewritable surfaces whose location is identified by a permanently stored (engraved) "timing track" which is continuously monitored by the controller to allow the identification of the cell currently under the head. A schematic diagram of a disk drive is shown in Figure 7.30.

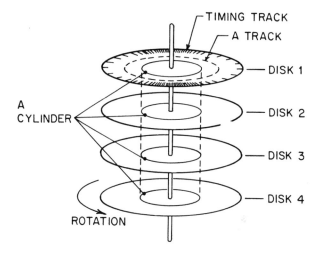

Figure 7.30   A schematic diagram of a disk drive.

Access (read or write) to a specific address on a disk drive with movable heads consists of two phases each of which contributes to the total delay of access: the head must first be moved over the required track — the *seek delay* — and then wait until the appropriate location appears underneath — the *latency delay*. These delays are in the order of milliseconds, i.e., three or more magnitudes slower than RAM access times. In order to make access more efficient and to free the CPU from being tied to the device, transfer of data is usually in blocks: if data is stored sequentially on the same track and on identically numbered tracks on several disks in the pack — the same *cylinder*, i.e., cylindrical section of the disk pack — the transfer of a block can be very fast once the starting location is reached. The data transfer rate from the present location is not limited by seek or latency delay and is fully determined by the speed of rotation and density of storage. Modern disk drives achieve transfer rates in the order of Mbytes/sec, i.e., comparable to RAM access times or faster. It must be remembered, however, that these can be obtained only after the relatively long initial access delay.

2. Disk systems with *flexible*, or *floppy*, disks. These smaller and slower systems are used in small and relatively inexpensive systems for which the cost of a rigid disk system could surpass the

cost of the rest of the system by several orders of magnitude. Their principle is identical, but the disks are made of flexible plastic. Heads are movable for smaller cost. The disk drive is mechanically much simpler and cheaper.

The cost of even a small disk system contains a large fixed part associated with the drive mechanism and the controller. Disk systems are thus economical only for relatively large amounts of storage in which the total cost is spread over a large storage capacity. The basic total cost of the disk system is to some degree independent of its size, and therefore large disk systems tend to have relatively low cost per bit of storage while small disk systems would be too expensive.

Disk drives will continue to be very important secondary storage devices in the foreseeable future although their position is threatened by new *semiconductor technologies* such as *magnetic bubble* devices and CCD devices. The greatest advantage of semiconductor technologies is that they are purely electronic and have no moving mechanical parts. This means higher reliability and, eventually, speed. These devices also provide higher storage density, lower power consumption, and in the future probably lower price. Semiconductor secondary storage of this type is not organized as RAM but as a group of shift registers. The cost of these memories is "incremental": larger systems consist of a number of relatively small and inexpensive modules, and the cost of the system is the sum of the costs of individual modules. This is an advantage over disk systems which have a relatively large initial cost. More detail is given in Chapter 9.

7.6.1.2 Magnetic Drums. Magnetic drums work on a very similar principle as magnetic disks, but information is stored on the surface of a rigid cylinder, or drum, rather than on a disk. They are much less common than disks although they were popular in the 1950's.

Disk and drum storage devices are often classified as *direct access* (DA) storage. The meaning of this term is that blocks of data can be accessed without much search, almost directly in comparison with purely sequential devices. In addition, storage access is possible at any time; the storage medium typically does not have to be mounted manually as is mostly the case with magnetic tapes, etc.

The following types of storage are often not considered secondary storage devices but rather I/O devices. The classification is disputable, and they are covered in this section because they are used for storage.

7.6.1.3 Magnetic Tape Storage. Magnetic tape storage is based on principles similar to audio tape recording. Information is stored by magnetizing a thin magnetizable layer on a flexible plastic tape. Large systems store information on reels which are processed on special, very high speed tape drives. Information is stored at very high density in the order of 1000 bits per inch of length (bpi). It is stored in digital representation, i.e., basically one direction of magnetization for 0 and the other for 1. There are, however, a number of variations on the coding of zeros and ones into magnetized and demagnetized zones. Information is stored in parallel tracks, usually seven or nine across the tape. This number has been chosen to allow simple storage of ASCII characters with parity checking. For faster access, data items are grouped into blocks for storage. In order to access the next block from the stopped condition of tape, the tape must get up to the proper speed which requires a certain amount of time and a certain length of tape. Similarly, stopping the tape after a given block requires a certain length of tape on which no information can be stored. Blocks are thus separated by *gaps* which take up space and reduce the efficiency of storage. In addition to useful information, blocks store extra parity information: the extra parity bit of each codeword stored in parallel with the character is called the *parallel* parity bit. Each track contains a *longitudinal* parity check code at the end of the block which contains information on the parity of the track. The information stored on a 7-track tape thus has the following form:

	001011.....01		011101.....11		0...
	101110.....00		110100.....10		1...
	010101.....00		101010.....00	1...	= = = = =>
GAP	111010.....11	GAP	100001.....11	GAP 1...	tape motion
	000001.....11		100100.....00		0...
	111101.....01		010101.....11		1...
	000011.....10		100001.....00		0...

Small systems use arrangement, media, and devices similar to or identical with ordinary audio tape systems. Information is stored purely sequentially rather than semisequentially as on large systems where all bits of one character are stored in parallel on several tracks. Encoding is by representing 0 by one frequency and 1 by another frequency rather than by magnetized individual domains (Figure 7.31). These small systems are very inexpensive but much slower and less reliable.

Figure 7.31   Digital information can be modulated and stored in analog form. Here 0 and 1 are represented by waveforms of different frequencies.

In all magnetic tape systems access to information is purely sequential with the small reservation concerning storage of tracks in parallel. If it is desired to read a block stored in the middle of the tape, all blocks preceding it must first be fully read. The main reason for this is that sufficiently accurate access to tape is irreproducible in the sense that recording the same information twice on the same tape does not store the data in exactly the same regions on the tape. Access by length of tape is thus impossible. Even if it were possible, it would still be sequential in that the tape would have to be moved to the position with the heads over the beginning of the desired block. The purely sequential access on magnetic tapes must be contrasted to the semisequential access on disks where a certain amount of overhead is involved in finding the location of the beginning of the block and the random access of RAMs. Magnetic tapes are therefore slower than disks. Their speed must be measured in terms of the maximum data transfer rate once the beginning of the block has been located. The smaller complexity of tape systems and the low cost of storage medium result in a very low cost of storage. Since the number of tapes used with one tape system is unlimited, the cost can be measured by the cost of a tape and the number of bits that it can store.

7.6.1.4 Punched Paper Tape Storage. Punched paper tape storage systems store information in the form of coded patterns of holes punched into the tape. Recording is in parallel as on large magnetic tapes. This method of storage was very popular in early computer systems. It is very slow, unreliable, permanent (write-only), and rather difficult to modify which has led to a substantial decline in its use.

7.6.1.5 Punched Paper Cards. Punched paper cards store information very much like paper tapes. The differences are the number of tracks which are called rows on cards; the material, wide and tough cards; and the fixed size of paper cards in comparison to potentially infinite paper tapes. Paper cards typically have 80 columns, each of which stores one character, usually represented in the *hollerith* code. Holes are punched by a *card punch*, which can be driven from a typewriter-like keyboard or by a computer as an output device. Cards are read by a *card reader* which senses the holes in the cards. Punched cards provide a relatively very slow input and an even slower output and are very unreliable compared to other storage media. They are being replaced by other devices but not as quickly as could be expected, partially because of their traditional popularity and a certain conservatism.

There are other means of storage, both traditional in the category of I/O devices and modern in the development stages in the category of true high speed secondary storage systems. They will not be covered at this point because they are not commonly used.

7.7 CPU COMMUNICATION WITH INPUT AND OUTPUT DEVICES

Most I/O devices have data transfer rates much inferior to the speed of the CPU. Even the very fast disk systems with high transfer rates require a relatively long time to access the beginning of a block before being able to transfer data at high speed. This presents a problem for the efficient utilization of the CPU which must be synchronized with the I/O device, i.e., transfer data when it is needed and when the I/O device is ready for it. Conceptually there are four solutions to this problem. One of them is a purely hardware solution; the others are software solutions in that they require a more or less complicated program to handle the transfer. The software solutions also involve a more or less complicated hardware interface between the I/O device and the buses of the system.

The hardware solution uses a WAIT input available on many CPUs which allows the suspension of the function of the CPU, usually for a brief period of time, to allow it to get synchronized with an I/O device. The software solutions include programmed I/O which makes the CPU take the full control of the transfer at the cost of its complete involvement in the operation. Direct memory access (DMA) requires very little attention of the CPU but a more sophisticated interface. The intermediate solution is data transfer initiated by the I/O device which signals the CPU its need for attention and requests it to interrupt its current activity. This is the interrupt-driven I/O which is more efficient than programmed I/O from the point of view of CPU utilization but more complicated. All four methods are used, often several of them in the same system. Typical uses are as follows:

Wait is used in systems with RAM speed inadequately matching the speed of the CPU. RAM access (the read and store operations) timing is then under the control of the memory module which drives the CPU via the WAIT input. This instance of communication is on the boundary between the standard memory access and true I/O.

Programmed I/O is used in situations in which the CPU is dedicated to the control of a certain I/O device and cannot proceed until it performs the required access. Note that since programmed I/O transfers data via the CPU it is relatively slow and cannot be used to service very fast I/O devices. Interrupt driven I/O is common for servicing of devices which may require attention at random times. It is more efficient than programmed I/O since it limits CPU involvement only to the servicing sequence and involves no unproductive instruction loops. Since the transfer is again via the CPU, it is just as slow as programmed I/O from the point of view of the I/O device.

DMA is the fastest method which requires very little CPU intervention, although it may require suspension of its activity for the time of the transfer. It also requires the most sophisticated interface since the data transfer is directly between the I/O device and the memory and is completely controlled by a DMA controller. This implies that it is also the fastest method of I/O with speeds limited only by the speed of the memory, the device, and its interface. It is thus used for communication with the fastest I/O devices.

We will see in Chapter 8 that large computer systems do not use any of these methods directly. They delegate execution of I/O to specialized "I/O processors" to maximize the utilization of their very powerful main CPU. The I/O methods discussed below are thus used by small computers and I/O processors of large systems.

7.7.1 WAIT

Most CPUs, particularly the simpler ones, have an input which allows an external device to interrupt the execution of an I/O instruction while it is attempting to complete a data transfer. At the appropriate time the CPU can then resume its operation with the preserved original values. The CPU maintains the current values in its internal registers and waits for the external device to communicate its readiness to complete the transfer. In many cases the WAIT signal is allowed to suspend CPU operation only for a very limited length of time of the order of microseconds since the primary application of this facility is communication with relatively slow RAM, and the times involved are very short. The physical reason for the limitation is the limited capability of some internal registers to hold information for a longer period of time without refresh.

7.7.2 Programmed I/O

When an algorithm requires access to an I/O device, the most natural strategy is to start checking whether the device is ready for the access. Checking continues until it is found that the device is ready at which time the access is performed and the next step of the algorithm can be executed. The transfer thus in general involves the execution of a waiting loop under the full control of the CPU. During this time the CPU cannot do anything else (Figure 7.32).

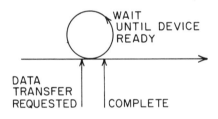

Figure 7.32   Programmed I/O.

In our computer with memory-mapped I/O this could be implemented as follows: assume that the device in question is an input device. The device must be able to communicate two independent types of information: the data and an indication of its readiness to communicate. The interface thus must include two registers, one to store temporarily the transferred data − the data buffer register − and one to store the status of the device − the status word register. Assume that the data is accessed as memory location 1 while the status word register is assigned address 2. The status word can contain other information in addition to the READY bit. Such information may be useful in interrupt driven I/O. Let us assume that the most significant bit

(MSB) of the status word is the READY bit which is cleared to 0 by the device when it wants to inform the CPU that it is ready and set to 1 when it is not. The programmed input sequence can now proceed as follows:

load status from address 2 into AC
if MSB (most significant bit) of status word is "not ready"
then return to previous instruction
read data from address 1

The first two instructions execute the waiting loop. The above algorithm is incomplete. Consider a situation in which this algorithm is to be used to read more than one word from the same input device. The CPU first waits for the device to clear its status bit to indicate its readiness for transfer. When this happens the CPU reads data and repeats the algorithm to get the second word. The way the process was described, the input device does not know that the CPU has read the first word and that it should supply the second. As a consequence, the status word is unchanged and so is the data register. The CPU will find the READY bit cleared and assume that the next data word has been placed into the data register while the register in fact contains the old information. The solution to this problem is simple: the CPU knows when it completed the transfer, and it should set the status bit to NOT READY. The input device can respond to this by getting the next data word, etc. The complete algorithm could be formulated as follows:

symbolic address	instruction
	....
Start	load AC from address 2
	if AC<0 then go to Start
	load AC from location 1
	process data as desired
	load -1 into AC
	store AC in location 1 (the status word)
	....

The above sequence is simpler than most real I/O sequences. In reality the exchange of status information between the CPU and the I/O device is more sophisticated and often involves requests for transfer, checks, and counterchecks. This communication overhead is usually called *handshaking* and can be partially implemented in hardware. In a number of situations the handshaking sequence must conform to a standard which is called a *protocol*. Handshaking is not restricted to programmed I/O. It is used wherever safe communication between two devices is needed, in particular in interrupt driven and DMA I/O (see the Workbook).

It has already been indicated that the major problem of programmed I/O is its inefficiency. The CPU cannot do anything else while waiting for the I/O device to get ready for the transfer. The transfer itself is inefficient; in most cases the desired operation is transfer of data between an I/O device and memory and the above sequence shows that transferred data must pass through the CPU, and this adds unnecessary delays. Programmed I/O may thus be acceptable in small systems in which the CPU is dedicated to a problem which cannot proceed without the requested data. It will be unacceptable in those systems which can work on other tasks while one task is awaiting an I/O operation. This situation is typical of most computer systems. An obvious solution to the problem is to have the CPU request an I/O operation from an I/O device, switch to another task, and have the I/O device itself interrupt the CPU when it is ready for the transfer. This is the function of interrupt-driven I/O.

7.7.3 Interrupt-driven I/O

In this mode the data transfer is initiated by an I/O device. It cannot be planned because it occurs at a random time and therefore cannot be programmed. A natural way to implement it is as follows:

When the CPU is finished executing the current instruction and before it fetches the next instruction for execution, the control unit checks if an interrupt is requested. If an interrupt is requested and is of sufficient urgency (*PRIORITY*) then the CPU stores all status information which is necessary to allow the CPU to resume execution of the current sequence of instructions at a later time, "services" the interrupt (the necessary action depends on the nature of the interrupt), restores status information when interrupt processing is completed and resumes execution of the interrupted program. Otherwise, the CPU fetches and executes the next instruction.

Note that the response to an urgent interrupt consists of the execution of a sequence of instructions which may constitute a long and complicated program. The process of servicing an interrupt may be graphically depicted as in Figure 7.33.

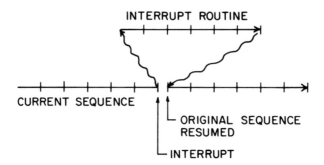

Figure 7.33   Interrupt-driven I/O: CPU receives an interrupt request while processing a sequence of instructions. It completes the execution of the current instruction, saves status information and jumps to an interrupt service routine. When service routine is completed, execution returns to the original sequence.

Very often there are several I/O devices and a hierarchy of interrupt urgencies. Individual interrupts can be assigned one of several levels of priority and interrupts of higher priority can be allowed to interrupt servicing of interrupts of lower priority (Figure 7.34). As an example, consider a system including a terminal and a tape drive which is executing a program. Assume that the terminal just interrupted the executing program and while its interrupt is being processed, the tape drive signals that it just reached the beginning of the next block. The tape drive runs quite fast, and data from it must be retrieved; otherwise, some will get lost. The CPU must abandon the terminal servicing program and jump to the higher priority tape drive program. When it is finished servicing the tape drive, it will return to the terminal interrupt; and when it is finished servicing that, the original program can resume execution.

How can interrupt processing be implemented? According to the above reasoning, the CPU should periodically check the status of interrupt requests. Since they can be generated at any time, randomly

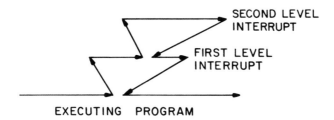

Figure 7.34   Nested interrupts. Only a higher level interrupt is accepted by the CPU servicing a given interrupt. Other interrupts must wait.

with respect to the regular operation of the CPU, there must be a set of interrupt flip-flops or registers in each interface capable of an interrupt and an interrupt line or set of lines connecting these interrupt flip-flops with the CPU. The interrupt line can be connected to all devices allowed to interrupt and any of these devices can "assert" this line (set the "interrupt requested" line to TRUE).

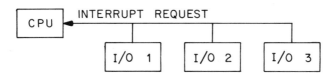

Figure 7.35   A system in which several devices can issue an interrupt request.

The way in which the CPU determines which device is requesting the interrupt and, in the case that several devices are requesting, decides which is the highest priority interrupt and should therefore be serviced first depends on the situation. One possibility is that this decision will be made by the interrupt routine itself and will thus be implemented in software. Another possibility is that the solution is fully implemented in hardware which is, of course, faster but more expensive and less flexible. There are a number of different approaches, but their discussion is beyond the scope of this text. A simple example will be given instead.

Consider the simplest situation in which all the devices have the same priority and there is no need to arbitrate between priorities of several interrupt requests. Assume also that it is not possible to interrupt an interrupt. This is natural in our situation since all interrupts are assumed to have the same priority. The sequence of events that should occur when the CPU senses an interrupt is as follows:

1. Check if interrupt servicing is allowed, enabled. It could be that the CPU is currently processing another interrupt and the new interrupt must wait for its completion. If interrupt is enabled, then proceed with the following sequence or else continue processing.
2. Disable further interrupts to prevent other interrupts from breaking into the servicing routine. Save all information necessary to resume processing of the current sequence.
3. Determine which device is requesting the interrupt.
4. Execute the appropriate interrupt routine.
5. Restore the status information of the original program and resume its processing.

In our CPU the above steps can be further expanded as follows:

1. The easiest way to introduce control over interrupts is to reserve a modifiable "interrupt enabled" IE bit in a CPU *status word register*. The status register can also store other useful information such as "AC overflow" bit, "zero AC" bit, "negative AC" bit, etc. (The individual status bits are often called *flag* bits.) This concentration of status information will make checking of frequently encountered conditions relatively easy. Setting and clearing of the interrupt bit can be under software or hardware control. Note that most CPUs distinguish two types of interrupts: *maskable* interrupts which can be disabled by the IE bit and *nonmaskable* interrupts which cannot be disabled. Nonmaskable interrupts are assigned to critical signals which when ignored could have catastrophic consequences. An example of such a signal is the condition of the power line: when the power level is moving towards an unacceptable value which could cause the system to break down and lose all information about its current state, this line can cause the system to suspend execution of the current program and save all essential information. This is possible because a power failure proceeds relatively slowly compared to the speed of the CPU, and the time between its reaching a

suspicious level, and the time it reaches an unacceptable level is in the order of milliseconds and therefore sufficient for the CPU to take the necessary steps.

2. Consider the CPU registers of our CPU. The PC contains the address of the next instruction and must be saved. The IR contains the previously executed instruction and its contents are thus irrelevant. The AC possibly contains intermediate data and must be saved. The status register may contain essential information and must be saved. Other registers are auxiliary and need not be saved. The process of saving this information may be built into the CPU which may automatically save all essential information in response to an enabled interrupt. It may also be left to the programmer of the interrupt routine to decide which information he or she wants to save by explicit STORE instructions. This may be the case, for example, when there are a large number of general purpose CPU registers rather than just a single accumulator. The service routine must save and then restore only those registers that it will use.

3. One of the ways in which the interrupting device can be identified is *polling*, individual checking of I/O devices until the one which initiated the request is found. Each device must then have a status register which includes an interrupt bit. The device sets the bit when it issues an interrupt request, and the CPU may clear it when it begins servicing the interrupt. This approach to the identification of the interrupting device has all the advantages and disadvantages of a software solution of a logic problem. The other extreme solution is to implement device identification completely in hardware. Note that since the status bit of the interface contains a number of bits with different functions, we need to be able to isolate the status bit currently needed. One way to do this is to introduce an instruction to extract a specific bit from the AC. Another possibility is to use standard Boolean operations and a *mask* word. As an example, assume that we want to extract the eighth bit from the AC. This can be achieved by ANDing AC with mask 000000001000 since AC AND 000000001000 = AC.8 Note that we also need to introduce instructions to enable and disable the interrupt bit of the CPU status word.

4. The appropriate servicing routine depends on the device and the nature of the interrupt since the same device may be able to issue several different types of interrupt requests. As an

example, a card reader may request an interrupt to process the data read from a card or to have the operator attend to a card jammed in the reading station, etc. Therefore, even for the same device the required service routine may have to be determined from the device's status word.

5. Both initiation and termination of an interrupt handling routine include a number of operations which are identical for all devices and can be advantageously handled by a special interrupt processing instruction or hardware.

In summary, it is clear that interrupt-driven I/O requires much less CPU time than programmed I/O. This is not because the CPU is not involved in the transfer since it is, in fact, involved more than in programmed I/O. It is, however, less tied to the I/O operation because it does not have to devote its attention to *waiting* for the device to get ready for the transfer. It is *requested* by the device to pay attention when it is ready. Interrupt-driven I/O must therefore be considered whenever the CPU can work on other tasks while waiting for I/O. This is almost always the case even in the smallest systems. On the other hand, it is clear that even interrupt-driven I/O has serious restrictions. It is relatively slow since all data transfer is performed by the CPU once the interrupt is acknowledged, and data transfer takes place through the CPU adding unnecessary delays when the desired communication is mostly between a device and the main memory. This becomes particularly serious when it is desired to transfer blocks of data. If the transfer is to take place at high speed, this method may be too slow.

The problem with interrupt-driven I/O is that since the data must pass through the CPU the original sequence must be interrupted and status information stored. An obvious solution is to block temporarily the control of the CPU over the communication channels between the memory and the device and allow another controller to take over for the duration of the transfer. The status can be frozen in the CPU, no saving is required, and, moreover, the CPU is eliminated as an intermediate stage in communication. The disadvantage is that the controller which temporarily assumes control over the communication must be more sophisticated than the interface for an interrupt-driven or programmed I/O. This mode of I/O is called Direct Memory Access.

7.7.4   Direct Memory Access (DMA)

DMA is used for high speed data transfer between a device and memory. A device capable of DMA must cooperate with a DMA controller whose functions are essentially equivalent to the data transfer capabilities of the CPU. The operation usually involves a whole block of data, and the information needed to perform it includes the knowledge of the memory address space involved in the transfer and the amount of data to be transferred. The communication takes place directly between the two communicating devices, and the operation of the CPU is usually temporarily suspended to prevent the two communication controllers — the CPU and the DMA controller — to access the same area in the memory and modify it without the mutual knowledge of the process. Note that the information could be written into an area which the CPU is currently processing, etc. In this mode of I/O the I/O device is stealing CPU's time, and the method is thus known as *cycle stealing DMA*.

Another possibility is to allow the DMA process to be multiplexed with the CPU operation: the CPU is not using memory access channels at all times. There are cycles during which the CPU is processing information internally on its own internal bus. During this time memory access channels are idle and could be controlled by a DMA controller. The DMA controller and the CPU can then take turns in accessing the memory, and there is no slowdown of CPU's operation. This *simultaneous DMA* requires a more complicated controller and is thus more expensive but faster.

Note the following:

1. A DMA transfer, although almost independent of the CPU, is still basically controlled by the CPU which must authorize it in response to a DMA request from the controller and generally supply the DMA parameters such as the starting address and the size of the block of data to be transferred. The CPU can also interfere with the DMA if necessary: it could, for example, interrupt it in response to an impending power failure.

2. When the DMA is in progress, the DMA controller must perform the same functions as the CPU when it communicates with the memory. The memory, in fact, is not aware that it is under DMA control and not the CPU's control. The DMA controller must generate read/write signals and provide the address on the address bus. It must act synchronously with the memory, keep track of how much data has already been transferred, and keep

the current memory address up to date. It might be required to inform the CPU when the transfer is complete.

7.8   SOME STANDARD I/O DEVICES

7.8.1   Computer Terminals

We will include in this category devices which allow input via a typewriter-like keyboard and which display output in standard ASCII characters or possibly another set of symbols. This definition is somewhat restrictive but generally conforms to the common usage in the computer environment. With our definition we can distinguish two types of computer terminals: hardcopy terminals and display terminals.

7.8.1.1 Hardcopy Terminals. These terminals function like typewriters connected to a computer system. Some, but very few, of these terminals are actually electric typewriters modified for communication with a computer. The output is printed on paper, providing a permanent record of the communication between the user and the computer. This is the main advantage of hardcopy terminals. The printed output records both user's input to the computer and computer's output to the user. The disadvantages of hardcopy terminals are their low speed and lower reliability since they always involve moving mechanical parts. They are also relatively noisy.

In the past most hardcopy terminals were teletypes. Teletypes continue to be used since they are relatively inexpensive and robust. Most of them are equipped with a paper-tape reader and punch which can be used to generate permanent computer-readable records of programs and data. Their disadvantages are noise, poor quality of print, and limited speed.

More and more hardcopy terminals are being used which are designed specifically for communication with computers. They are faster, quieter, and produce better quality print although there is always a trade-off between these parameters, particularly speed and print quality, for the same price range. These terminals are generally more expensive than traditional teletypes. Some of the modern hardcopy terminals have "graphics" capability and can produce graphs, etc.

Hardcopy terminals can be classified by the way in which they produce the printed symbol as *impact* terminals and *non-impact* terminals. Impact terminals generate the symbol in a way similar to typewriters. Their advantage is that they can make multiple copies. Non-impact terminals usually produce the symbol by the effect of localized heat on a temperature-sensitive paper. Many hardcopy and display terminals produce characters which are composed of dots. Dots are arranged in rectangular patterns, such as a 10x7 array of dots. Terminals working on this principle are called *dot-matrix* terminals. One of their advantages is the greater flexibility of produced character sets. The more sophisticated ones can even be programmed to produce user-defined symbols.

Note that hardcopy terminals consist of two largely independent modules: the keyboard and the printer. All that has been said about their printing capabilities and categories applies also to purely output-oriented printers which will be discussed in more detail later.

7.8.1.2 Display Terminals. These terminals use a TV-like screen to display symbols. They are commonly called VDU (Video Display Unit) terminals. Some display terminals are equipped with more sophisticated display capabilities which allow the display of individual dots or even continuous lines and therefore graphs and pictures. These *graphics terminals* are sometimes equipped with hardware to make frequently needed graphics functions such as rotation of display, enlargement of the picture, etc., easy and fast. Some of them are equipped with color displays. Graphics terminals are generally an order of magnitude more expensive than ordinary alphanumeric terminals.

CRT (cathode ray tube) terminals are the most common type of display terminals. They use a video tube of the same kind as that used on ordinary TV sets. Other display technologies are still mostly in development stages. The main advantages of display terminals are their speed, reliability, and quiet operation. Speed is limited essentially by speed of the computer — this limitation is sometimes painfully obvious in graphics applications which often require large numbers of calculations — and the limitations of human perception since in text displays the human user cannot match the possible speeds of display. Another advantage of display terminals is the ease of generation of graphics, including even dynamic, i.e. moving display. A disadvantage of display terminals is the lack of a permanent record. For this reason graphics terminals are often equipped with a hardcopy unit which can produce a copy of the screen when desired.

In the last few years more terminals have been produced with more or less powerful processing capabilities. They are called *intelligent terminals*, and standard non-processing terminals are consequently called *dumb*. Their processing power may be quite limited or so sophisticated that the terminal is in fact capable of stand-alone computing and is in fact a computer with built-in capability to communicate with a computer system.

Terminals and other I/O devices usually contain some buffer memory capable of storing at least one line of text for communication. This makes communication more efficient since data can then be transferred in larger blocks and locally edited before transmission. CRT terminals also contain memory to store the contents of the whole screen which must be periodically refreshed.

7.8.1.3 Communication Between Distant Terminals and the CPU.

Most terminals communicate with the central system over a communication line sometimes considerably long (*telecommunication*). The communication process is usually *asynchronous* since the terminal generates or receives data at random and relatively distant points in time and in random quantities. The speed of communication is measured in bits transmitted per second (bps) or the related "baud rates." Typical baud rates are 110 and 300 bps for standard hardcopy terminals and several thousand for CRT and graphics terminals. The process by which the communicating device requests the attention of the destination, waiting and receiving an acknowledgement, responding, sending data, and exchanging signals to conclude communication may be quite complicated; and several very rigidly defined standard sequences (*protocols*) have been worked out for their implementation. Asynchronous communication becomes very inefficient when large amounts of data are transferred at high rates. This is because the overhead consumes a significant amount of transmitted signals. It is then replaced by *synchronous* communication in which large blocks of data can be quickly transferred between two synchronized devices.

Telecommunication signals are usually carried over an ordinary telephone line. In this implementation transfer rates are limited by the physical parameters of the lines designed for communication of the audio frequencies and are not suitable for very high transfer rates. High transfer rates require especially conditioned lines. In any case digital information is not sent in digital form which would be highly distorted. It is first modulated into an analog signal which is transmitted and demodulated into the original digital signal. The *modem* (MODulator-DEModulator) is a device capable of both functions.

7.8.1.4 Printers.
Printers are output devices producing a hardcopy output record. They can be classified as impact or non-impact,

dot-matrix or fully-formed-character, serial or line devices. Most of these categories overlap and can be combined. Some printer technologies have been described in the section on terminals. Some other important and interesting types of printers in general use are described below.

Line printers print a whole line of text "at one time" rather than sequentially character by character as do serial printers. This is achieved, for example, by rotating a cylinder, which has one or more complete sets of symbols on its surface, along the printing paper. When a symbol desired at a certain position appears at the proper location, a hammer strikes the paper and the letter is imprinted on the paper. Each printing position has a hammer corresponding to it. This type of printer is called a *drum printer*. Another category of line printers uses a moving chain with character sets on it which moves along the line. Characters are printed by impacting hammers (*chain printer*).

Ink jet printers are very high speed, non-impact printers which paint symbols by a controlled stream of ink droplets.

Xerographic printers produce an image by a stream of light, for example *laser,* impacting a photosensitive paper.

Printers and terminals are the subject of considerable interest and development because the existing designs lead to relatively expensive devices which work at speeds considerably lower than the speed of CPUs. Significant progress is needed in this category of computer peripherals to obtain devices matching the performance of the electronic modules of computer systems and their low cost.

7.9 COMMON ADDRESSING MODES AND INSTRUCTION TYPES

Our example of a control unit was simplified beyond even the most trivial real situations for the sake of clarity and tutorial exposition. All commercial computers have much richer instruction sets, and the standard types of instructions and their variations will be the main subject of this section.

To see how our instruction set can be significantly improved consider the following two examples:

Example 7.4: Assume that it is desired to add values stored in locations 27 to 2576 and store the result in location 10. This problem is conceptually simple and the following program solves it:

```
LD 27
AD 30
AD 31
AD 32
...
...
...
AD 2576
ST 10
```

The disadvantage of this program is that it is very long. This makes the program awkward to enter into the computer and requires a large memory space. Yet the sequence of operations is relatively very simple and repetitive: repeat the AD operation many times with different operands, stored in consecutive locations 30 to 2576. This process could be more simply implemented as follows:

> Save the starting address 30 in location S;
> While contents of S < 2576 do
> > AD value stored in the location whose ADDRESS
> > is in S;
> > Increment the address in S by 1;

The only new facility that is required is for the AD instruction to get the address of its operand from an independent memory location rather than directly from the address field of the instruction itself. In other words, we only need a new method of "addressing."

Example 7.5: Computer programs very often have to perform a certain identical sequence of operations in different places of the program and possibly with different data. An example of this is floating-point division on computers which do not have this operation implemented in hardware. One solution is to insert the sequence of instructions performing floating-point division wherever required in the program. This "brute force" solution resembles the original solution of the problem in the previous example. A more elegant and economical solution is to place the sequence into one place in the program and jump to it whenever the operation is required. The only problem is that when the operation is completed the program must continue execution from where it left off when the jump to the floating-point division was made. This position varies during the execution of the program and the destination address of the "return jump" with it.

An instruction sequence of the type just described is usually called a *subroutine*, sometimes a routine or a procedure, and is a highly desirable facility. We have seen that it can be used comfortably only if special jump instructions are provided for its access which allow the automatic return to the calling program. The above examples provide only two illustrations of the need for more powerful addressing modes and instruction types. More examples will be presented later. The rest of this section deals with the typical extensions of our basic architecture found on most computers. It will become obvious that most of these additions are essential for the natural formulation of programs which is in turn, critical for the design of reliably working programs and is an economic necessity.

7.9.1 Memory Addressing

Most instructions perform operations on one or two operands. The CPU must know the locations of the operands and also where to store the result. To be able to proceed to the next instruction, the CPU must know where it is stored. Altogether *four* addresses are thus needed in many operations. The address takes valuable space in the instruction code, and this justifies attempts to remove as many of the required addresses from the instruction code as possible. This is generally achieved by implying some of the addresses or by the way in which they are generated. This saves memory space but at the same time reduces the flexibility and efficiency of the instruction set.

The address of the *next instruction* does not have to be stored if we assume sequential storage of instructions and provide jump instructions for situations where the next instruction is not executed in linear sequence. This approach is standard and the only place where instructions contain the address of the next instruction is in some microprogrammed control units implemented without a microprogram counter.

Three address instructions provide the address of both operands and the result. Commonly encountered instructions of this type typically address general purpose CPU registers for at least two of the three addresses. Since there are usually only a few general purpose CPU registers for storage of intermediate results, their address requires only a few bits and so the three addresses require little instruction space. Typically 8 or 16 addressable registers are provided and so only three or four bits are needed to specify one of them.

Two address instructions operating on two operands usually imply that the result will be stored in the location of one of the two operands whose original value will, of course, be replaced by the value of the result and therefore lost. This implied location is often a CPU register, but quite often it can be a main memory location.

One address instructions operating on two operands imply the location of one of the operands, and the same location is usually used to store the result. This location is usually a specific general purpose CPU register, such as the accumulator. We used this approach in our design example.

Zero address instructions operating on two operands imply addresses of both operands and the result. Designs using zero address instructions are increasingly popular not only because of the economy of instruction codes but mainly because of certain programming advantages associated with this mode of addressing. Zero address instructions generally use the concept of a *stack* and at least one of the operands is taken from it. A stack is a structure which is functionally identical to a stack of trays in a cafeteria in which only the top tray is accessible. Since a memory stack is usually stored in a standard RAM, i.e., an array-like type of storage, the address of the top of the stack must be kept in memory or a special *stack register* sometimes called a *stack pointer*. Most modern CPUs provide some form of stack addressing, usually as an alternative to the more traditional addressing modes rather than as replacement. There are, however, several *stack computers* whose design is based on the assumption that the programmer will use the stack as the main rather than auxiliary mode of storage. Stack addressing will be covered in more detail later. The most common use of the stack — in the transfer of data to and from subroutines — is covered in Chapter 8.

As an example of the compromise involved in choosing the number of explicit and implied addresses for the instruction format consider the following problem: it is desired to copy the contents of memory location A into memory location B. In a computer with single address instructions, this transfer is achieved by copying the value into AC — the implied location — and then to the desired destination:

    LOAD A
    STORE B

In a computer with two address instructions the same result can be achieved by a single instruction such as,

    MOVE A,B

Assume that both computers have a 64k addressable space which requires 16 bits to specify operand address. The single address CPU will need only 16 bits of the instruction word to specify the address; the two address CPU will need 32 bits or a similar arrangement. On the other hand, the one address CPU will need two instructions and therefore about twice as much time since two instructions will have to be fetched and executed. The two address CPU will only need one instruction for the same purpose and will, therefore, execute faster. Note that this does not imply that two address instructions are always better. In fact, in many applications moving data between memory locations without processing is not done frequently. This example shows that individual alternatives offer advantages and present problems which must be carefully weighed and tested in relation to the intended application and overall design of the computer. Note that there is also the possibility of implementing both one address and two address instructions, etc.

In addition to the question of how many addresses should be included in instruction sets for efficient and economic operation, there is also the problem of the exact meaning of the address part of the instruction. There are a number of alternatives which evolved in response to certain programming needs. Each of them has its advantages for special types of problems. Some common *addressing modes* are surveyed below. Note that many computers do not allow all the listed addressing modes and even the most powerful computers have restrictions. In addition, most computers restrict some available addressing modes only to certain categories of instructions rather than all instructions in their instruction sets.

Immediate addressing. This mode is not actually an addressing mode at all since the address part of the instruction does not contain a memory address but the value of the operand itself. In our example machine the instruction

LD 3

in the immediate mode would mean load value 3 into the accumulator.

Direct addressing is the mode we have been using in our design: the address part of the instruction directly specifies the address (*effective address*) of the operand.

Instruction

LD 3

in direct addressing means load contents of location 3 into accumulator, i.e.,

   [3] TO: AC

Indirect addressing. In this addressing mode the address part of the instruction specifies the address of the location which contains the effective address of the operand. Thus the instruction

   LD 3

in indirect addressing means load the contents of the address specified in location 3 into the accumulator, i.e.,

   [[3]] TO: AC

The steps performed in this case are:

1. Fetch the contents of location 3 and place the value into MAR since it is the effective address of the operand.
2. Fetch the contents of location [MAR] and load it into AC since this is the value of the operand.

Note that indirect addressing requires an extra memory access in comparison with direct addressing which, in turn, requires one more access than immediate addressing. Note also that since changing the address part of an instruction is not practical and is strongly discouraged, direct addressing means that the same instruction will always access the same memory location. With indirect addressing we can use the same instruction to access different memory locations since we can change the contents of the fixed location which contains the effective address. This can again be carried over to a comparison of immediate and direct addressing: in direct addressing the same instruction always accesses the same location, but its contents can change as the program executes. In immediate addressing execution of the same instruction in general provides the same value of the address for reasons stated above. We can see that various addressing modes provide various degrees of flexibility at the cost of different execution times and memory requirements. Indirect addressing could be carried to more levels of indirection which could be implemented by assigning one bit in the address to specify whether the address found at this location is an indirect one or the effective address. In practice it has been found that several levels of indirect addressing do not significantly add to programming capability, and this variation has not become common.

In conclusion of this outline of indirect addressing examine the following solution of the addition problem stated at the beginning of this section:

> Load accumulator from location 27;
> Store 30 in location S (direct);
> While [S] < = 2576 do
>   AD S (indirect);
>   Increment S by 1;
> Store accumulator in 10 (direct);

Indexed addressing. This addressing mode requires a special CPU register called the *index register* (usually denoted X). AD 100 in indexed addressing means

1. Add the *base address* given in the address part of the instruction to the index (contents of X) to obtain the effective address of the operand.
2. Perform the addition.

In our case the operation implied is [AC] + [100 + [X]] TO: AC. Our addition problem can be solved with indexed addressing as follows:

> Load 1 into X;
> Load accumulator from location 27 (direct);
> While [X] < = 2547 do
> AD 28 (indexed);
> Increment X by 1;
> Store accumulator in 10 (direct);

2547 is the total number of locations to be accessed. Note how similar the solution is to the solution using indirect addressing. Because of this similarity a number of computers implement only one of these two addressing modes. Since the index register is a CPU register, its incrementing is fast and may even be be done automatically by the CPU.

Relative addressing. The effective address is calculated relative to the current instruction's address or PC. Assume that instruction JM 30 relative is stored at location 1F30. The meaning of this instruction is "jump to location current-address + 30," i.e., jump to 1F60.

There are variations on these basic addressing modes and in addition some of them can be combined to obtain, for example, indirect indexed addressing and indexed indirect addressing. Justification of various programming modes will not be examined in this text since it is basically a programming consideration. It must be stressed, however, that flexibility of addressing is one of the basic criteria by which computers are evaluated and compared.

7.9.2 Standard Categories Of Instructions

This section contains the listing and brief description of the common categories of instructions which appear in most computers.

Data transfer instructions. These are instructions which move values between memory locations without any intermediate processing. Some computers group all these instructions under one heading, for example move. These instructions include the following:

> LOAD register from memory or another register
> STORE register in memory or another register.

Sometimes the MOVE instruction allows data transfer between two memory locations rather than between memory and register. This is, of course, practically implemented by moving data from memory to CPU and from CPU to memory. The advantage of a memory-to-memory instruction is faster execution and a shorter program since only one instruction is needed instead of two if moves are allowed only between memory and registers.

Exchange instruction. This instruction interchanges the contents of two memory locations. It is not very common.

The following two instructions in this category manipulate the stack. It has been mentioned that the stack is normally stored in the main memory and shares storage with data and instructions stored for ordinary random access. This means that the location of the stack in memory has to be remembered in one or more CPU registers. Many computers provide a special *stack pointer* register whose function it is to hold the address of the current *top of stack* or the address of the next available location, above the top of the stack. This implementation of a stack is shown in Figure 7.36.

Some computers have a CPU stack of registers. Their access is faster, but the size of this stack is very limited. Some computers provide another stack register for the identification of the bottom of the stack. The location of the stack in main memory is generally the responsibility of the programmer who can control it by special instructions which allow modification of the contents of the stack pointer and thus its initialization. The two basic stack accessing instructions are PUSH and POP:

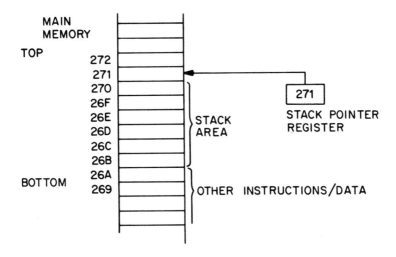

Figure 7.36   A memory stack implemented in main memory with the use of a CPU stack pointer register SP. SP "points" to the top of the imaginary stack.

PUSH is the operation which places a new item on the top of the stack. If the pushed item is taken from an implied register, then this is a zero address instruction. The PUSH instruction copies data into the first available location on the top of the stack and changes the extent of the stack. It is therefore accompanied by a change in the contents of the stack pointer whose value is automatically modified, for example incremented by 1, to point to the new top of the stack.

POP is the inverse of PUSH. It "removes" an item from the top of the stack and automatically updates the value in the stack register. Note that the original copy of the value is not actually erased from the memory. It is only made inaccessible via the stack register.

Arithmetic operations. All computers allow some arithmetic operations on integers even though even these are often limited to + and − or even only +. Integers are most commonly represented in 2's complement, sometimes 1's complement representation. Most modern computers have BCD arithmetic instructions sometimes as an option. Many computers have floating-point arithmetic which is particularly important in engineering and scientific applications. The speed of floating-point instructions is so essential in many problems that the speed of computers is sometimes measured in "flops," number of floating-point operations per second, or in megaflops. Addition and subtraction are generally standard while multiplication and division are sometimes not available in small machines because of the complexity of the corresponding ALUs.

Logic operations in a more restricted sense include AND, OR, XOR, and NOT, which is equivalent to 1's complement. Most of these operations are usually available in computers although most computers do not include all of them. These instructions are essential for convenient access to individual bits in words. We have seen an example of their importance in the extraction of status bits in interrupt-driven I/O. There are many other instances where they are very useful.

In a more general sense the following are also logic operations many of which are available on most computers.

Logical shift. This operation shifts bits in a memory location, usually a CPU register, by one or more positions left or right. One end-bit is lost and the other filled in with a 0:

original	shifted left	shifted right
010101010111	101010101110	001010101011

Arithmetic shift. This operation differs from logic shift by leaving the sign bit unchanged. This is useful for multiplication and division of sign-magnitude numbers and is usually available when these two arithmetic operations are not included in the instruction set.

Rotate register bits left or right. This operation is similar to shift except that no bits are added or deleted and the bits can be moved through another flip-flop, the carry bit of the accumulator.

ff	register	rotate left	rotate left through carry
1	00110101	1	01101010 0

Note the difference between rotate and rotate through carry flip-flop. The best visualization of the rotate operation is by viewing the register as a circular one, with the left end connected to the right end.

CLEAR register to all zeros.
SET register to all ones.

2's COMPLEMENT is the equivalent of negation when numbers are represented in fixed-point 2's complement form.

Control of flow instructions. These instructions include various forms of jump instructions. They can be generally classified as *conditional* and *unconditional.* The Boolean conditions allowed in the category of conditional instructions include mainly those which are represented by various flag bits in the status word. Typical conditions are:

Comparison of the value in a register such as $=0$, >0, <0, etc.
Overflow condition after an arithmetic operation.
Comparison of equality of two words.
Stack overflow (memory reserved for stack is filled and an attempt is made to push) or underflow (attempt to pop when stack pointer points to bottom indicating an empty stack).
Value of interrupt enabled bit.

Note that conditional jumps are in a sense logic operations.
In addition to standard JUMP instructions there are some instructions which can be interpreted as their variations. The following are very common:

SKIP is a variation of JUMP which increments PC one extra time and makes the CPU skip the next instruction, conditionally or unconditionally.
JUMP TO SUBROUTINE is an instruction which allows a temporary programmed transition to a subprogram in a controlled way, including the automatic storage of the contents of PC — the return address — and possibly other information. There are several variants of this instruction.
RETURN FROM SUBROUTINE is the inverse of a jump to subroutine and allows controlled return from a subroutine to the place where the original sequence was interrupted. It involves the restoration of PC and possibly other registers. Note the similarity between the handling of subroutines and the handling of interrupts. The major difference is that jumps to subroutines are performed as a part of the programmed sequence while jumps to interrupt subroutines are performed in response to externally generated interrupt signals arriving at random time and interrupting the normal program sequence.
RETURN FROM INTERRUPT is similar to return from subroutine. The only difference is in the exact details of restoration of registers and associated control signals.

I/O operations. We have assumed so far that I/O is memory mapped. This is not always the case, and many computers have special

I/O instructions. Their function is to communicate with I/O devices, their interfaces or controllers. This communication involves exchange of information about the type of operation required (read, write, or a more specialized I/O operation such as stop or start a tape drive, etc.), amount of data to be transferred, memory region involved in the transfer, status of the device and the CPU, etc.

Large computer systems communicate with their I/O devices via very sophisticated controllers which are, in fact, computers dedicated to I/O and responding to very general I/O requests by executing more or less complex I/O programs.

In addition to these broad categories of instructions, there are a number of minor groups including manipulation of the status word (for example setting and clearing interrupt enable bits), HALT instructions which suspend the operation of the CPU, etc. Most instruction sets involve NOP (no operation) instructions which do not perform any operation but take an exact amount of time and can be used in timing loops. They can also be used as spare codes to extend the original instruction set if needed by allocating their code to a new instruction and modifying the control unit. Certain codes are usually disallowed since they are reserved for future expansion and currently perform some obscure side-effect operations.

Most of the operations presented in this section are not implemented in exactly the same way on all computers and "low-level," language programmers — programmers writing programs on a machine or comparable level — must be very careful about the side-effects which are often different on different CPUs. As an example the LOAD instruction may be implemented to allow setting the *negative accumulator* bit in the status word in one machine and have no effect in another. Relative addressing may be relative to the address of the current instruction or to PC which contains the address of the next instruction, etc.

REFERENCES

For more detail on computer organization and architecture one should read some of the recent textbooks on these subjects: Gschwind, Hamacher, Hayes, Hill, Kuck, Peterson, Sloan, Myers, Tanenbaum, Organick, etc. There are also several texts devoted to microprogramming: Husson, Chu, Agrawalla and Raucher; computer arithmetic: Flores, Hwang, storage: Matick, etc. Up to date technical information is available in previously mentioned journals such as *CACM, IEEE Transactions on Computers, Computer, Computer Design, EDN, Digital systems, Euromicro Journal, Computers and Digital Techniques, etc.*

PROBLEMS

1. Show the parts of the control unit needed to implement the remaining basic instructions from Section 7.4.

2. Add the following instructions and modify the control sequence, ALU control, etc., accordingly:
Boolean AND, OR, NOT.
COMPARE AC and operand which sets/clears an EQUAL flip-flop.
JS—jump to subroutine. JS A stores the contents of PC at location A and changes the contents of PC to $A+1$. In other words the return address is stored at location A and the subroutine begins at the instruction stored at location $A+1$.

3. Assume that the CPU has a status word with the following bits:
$AC=0$, $AC<0$, Overflow, Interrupt enabled.
Show how the control sequence and the hardwired control unit are modified if condition checking is performed on the status flags rather than the AC, etc. Show how the change in the control sequence changes the microprogram and the microaddress generator.

4. Redesign the microprogram using the vertical microcode proposed in the text.

5. Control units of all digital devices are similar. As an illustration of this fact, design the control sequence of the interface control unit of an output device according to the following specification:

Input from data bus is parallel, eight bits at a time. The presence of a 1 on the WRITE line from the CPU accompanied by the address of the device on the address bus means that data for the device is available on the data bus and will be stable for 0.5 microsecond. Upon recognizing the address, the control unit of the interface must store the data in a data buffer register in the interface, clear its READY flip-flop to indicate to the CPU that it is processing the supplied data, and transmit data from the data buffer to the device in series at the rate of 50 kbits/sec. When transmission is complete, the control unit sets the READY bit. The block diagram of the interface is shown in Figure 7.37.

6. Design an interface similar to Problem 5 for an input device with serial input and parallel output to the data bus. Assume the input rate is 20 kbits/sec.

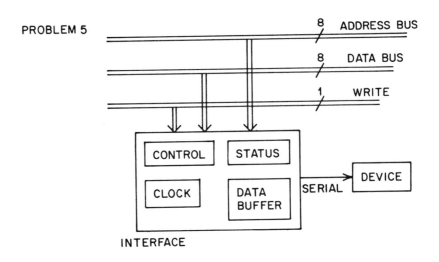

Figure 7.37   A block diagram of the interface for Problem 5.

7. Add interrupt facility to the original control sequence developed in Section 7.4. Assume that the interrupt line is to be checked before a new instruction is fetched. If an interrupt is requested and enabled, the contents of PC is to be stored at address FF — end of addressable memory — and replaced by the contents of FF-1=FE. In other words a jump is made to location FE which must contain the beginning of the interrupt routine. At the same time the IE, interrupt enable flip-flop, is cleared to 0 to prevent further interrupts. Also include a control signal for a Return from Interrupt (RI) Instruction which restores the contents of the PC.

8. Indicate which part of the control sequence does not use the memory bus and could thus be used by a DMA controller for *simultaneous DMA*.

9. Modify the CPU design in this chapter as follows: the size of the word is to be eight bits (one byte). Each opcode is one word and the addressing space is 64k. This is achieved by storing the 16-bit address in two consecutive words, following the instruction code when needed. Note that since the data bus is one byte this means that three fetches must be performed to access an instruction with a full address. The address bus is two bytes.

a. Implement the instruction set presented in Section 7.4 (hardwired or microprogrammed).

b. Implement the following additional addressing modes: indirect (with full address), relative (using ONE byte address offset), indexed (using an 8-bit index register X, an instruction to load X, include automatic incrementing of X by 1 with instructions using indexed addressing), stack addressing (add a 16-bit stack register and instructions to load its lower or upper half from the 8-bit AC).

c. Replace AC by four general-purpose registers R0 TO R3. Their function is similar to the function of AC except that none of them is implied as a source or destination of data. Access to them is only explicit via some part of the instruction code or address.

10. Control unit design.

a. Write a complete specification of a CPU patterned after suggestions from Section 7.4 or Problem 9. Include the complete instruction set, opcodes and exact function, CPU block diagram, and the complete logic diagram of a hardwired control unit.

b. Redesign the control unit as microprogrammed.

11. Design algorithms to solve the following control structures using only machine instructions presented in Section 7.9.

a. read value from location A;
if [A] > 0 then increment [A] by 1;
save [A] in location B;

b. read value from location A;
if [A] > 0 then increment [A] by 1
else decrement [A] by 1;
save [A] in location B;

c. initialize address A to value stored in S;
initialize sum to 0;
while [A] > 0 do
add [A] to sum;
add 1 to A (increment address);
save sum in location B;

d. initialize address A to value stored in S;
initialize sum to 0;
repeat
add [A] to sum;
add 1 to A;
until A = [F] (final address);
save sum in location B;

Chapter 8

SOME REAL COMPUTERS

8.1 INTRODUCTION

The discussion of basic concepts and approaches presented in Chapter 7 is an oversimplification of reality. Even the simplest computers are more complex. This chapter expands the perspective developed in the previous chapter by a more detailed description of several real computers. Before starting, it will be useful to set the framework for the subject. Computers are commonly classified by complexity as belonging to one of several common categories: microcomputers, minicomputers, medium sized computers, large computers, and supercomputers; also commonly called micros, minis, midis, mainframes and "number crunchers" or "supercomputers." In addition there are computers which use a non-standard approach and do not belong in any of these categories. The classification of a computer into one of these groups is not based on exact criteria and is often a matter of subjective judgment, or advertising.

The criteria used to distinguish between the individual categories are mainly as follows:

1. *The architecture of the computer.* This includes parameters such as word size, richness and orientation of the instruction set, number of data types available, sophistication of the ALU operations, number of programmable CPU registers, address space, I/O architecture, etc. The most quantitative of these parameters is the word size which is typically 8 bits for microcomputers, 12 or 16 bits for minicomputers, 36 bits for medium sized computers and larger, for example 64 bits, for large computers. It has to

302

be emphasized at this point that these values are subject to development: typical parameters tend to shift towards more powerful categories. As an example, several very powerful microcomputer CPUs, *microprocessors*, have recently been developed which work with a 16-bit word and other parameters until recently typical for minicomputers. This remark applies to all categories and all parameters discussed below.

2. *Physical complexity and size.* To a large extent the names micro, mini, etc. are derived from typical physical dimensions. Microcomputers typically occupy the space of a terminal and a number of them are simply built into a terminal. Even large computers are, however, becoming physically quite manageable, occupying typically the space equivalent to four lineprinters or so. This space includes all modules of the system.

3. *Cost.* Microcomputers cost from several hundred to several thousand dollars, minicomputers several tens of thousands, midis several hundred thousand, and large computers several million dollars.

4. *Typical size of installed memory.* Microcomputer systems typically have tens of kilowords; large computers have more than one megawords. It should also be realized that the word size is different and therefore the difference in memory capacity is even larger.

5. *Speed.* This parameter is determined by both the technology and the organization of the system. When measured by the typical execution time of an instruction, it varies from more than one microsecond for microcomputers to less than 10 nanoseconds for supercomputers. In this context it must be realized that in addition to the one hundred or one thousand times faster speed, instructions on large computers are often much more powerful and implement operations which require a whole sequence of microcomputer instructions. In addition, the increased complexity of a large computer system makes it possible to approach processing in a qualitatively different and much more powerful way.

6. *Organization of the CPU and the whole system.* As an example I/O operations are completely under the control of the CPU in typical microcomputers but are performed quite independently of the CPU in large computer systems.

7. *Complexity of peripheral devices.* Microcomputers typically have a CRT terminal, possibly a floppy-disk drive, and a printer.

Large computers typically have several multiple rigid disk drives, several tape drives, at least one lineprinter, card reader and card punch, a plotter, several terminals attached through telephone lines or "hardwired," etc.

8. *Complexity of software supplied by manufacturer and functions implemented in it.* Microcomputers typically come with software at least partially implemented in ROM and its size is measured in kilobytes. The functions of the software are relatively primitive as can be expected from the relative simplicity of the system and the requirement of low cost. The cost of software is typically a small fraction of the cost of hardware, usually less than 10 percent. Software sold with large computers is either sold as part of the system ("bundled") or at least partially independently ("unbundled"). The cost of even the basic software necessary to run the system represents a growing part of the total system cost (currently over 50 percent) and its size approaches one megaword.

9. *Technology employed.* The basic component of a microcomputer is the one-chip microprocessor. The technology used in its CPU and memory chips is typically the relatively slow but inexpensive and dense MOS technology. The economic factor becomes less critical in large computers where performance is the main consideration and CPUs of large computers use the fastest available components such as ECL chips for multichip CPUs and bipolar memory chips. It must be realized that building the whole computer, including main memory, with the fastest technology would be overly expensive even for very large computers. They would not only cost too much to produce, particularly because of the enormous size of the main memory, but also would be very expensive to use because of the large power consumption of the faster technologies. Fortunately, it is possible to arrange the system in such a way that its performance can approach the speed of a system built entirely from very fast components although it is actually built from less powerful components. Typical large computer systems are thus built from a combination of fast, expensive components and relatively inexpensive and less powerful ones.

In order to give a realistic picture of the wide range of actual computers, the following sections will present an in-depth description of a very elementary microcomputer, the Heathkit Micro Tutor; a less detailed description of a more typical and complex microcomputer system, the Radio Shack's TRS-80; a typical modern minicomputer, the PDP-11 minicomputer family; and two large computers, Univac 1100 and CDC Cyber 170 families. Note that none of the very popular IBM computers is discussed. This omission is intentional: IBM computers are described in almost all books on computer organization. Another description would be redundant, and the interested user will have no problem getting information on these popular computers from another source. This brief overview will allow us to get a feeling for modern approaches and typical solutions.

8.2 MICROCOMPUTERS

The microcomputer category is relatively new. Microcomputers emerged at the beginning of the 1970's when improved IC technology made it possible to put a complete simple CPU on a single chip.

The first one-chip CPU or *microprocessor* commercially available was the 4004 4-bit microprocessor made by INTEL which appeared in 1971. The 4004 was so successful that it was very soon followed by improved versions made by INTEL and other microprocessors designed by other semiconductor manufacturers. The other best known microprocessor manufacturers are Motorola, Zilog, Fairchild, Texas Instruments, Intersil, Signetics, MOS Technology, RCA, and Rockwell. It must be emphasized that the first microprocessors were not actually computers in the usual sense of the word. They were not designed for data processing, to be attached to a hardcopy device, etc. They were, in fact, the first successful answer to the search for a universal logic building block using LSI technology. In this sense they partially answered the question of a Universal Logic Module mentioned previously.

The 4004 works with 4-bit words and has 45 rather elementary instructions. It is well suited for control applications and is used as a programmable controller. A typical 4004-based controller basically consists of the CPU, a small memory which contains mainly a control program in a ROM, an I/O interface and I/O devices, typically sensors and actuators and displays. Typical application areas of control microprocessors are sophisticated home appliances, games, cash registers with special functions, traffic light controllers, intelligent computer terminals, printers, etc.

The 4004 was very successful in its control applications since it brought the advantages of programmability into the area of logic design: it allowed very flexible, modifiable, and reliable design based on a single component. This last property is particularly attractive since the existence of a universal component brings the promise of very large scale production and therefore low cost, improved design, and reliability, etc. This potential rapidly materialized, and within a few years much more sophisticated microprocessors became available at prices comparable to those of standard MSI TTL components, down to $5 and even less.

As previously stated, the 4004 was soon followed by several other 4-bit microprocessors. In two more years technology advanced to a level at which the achievable densities made it possible to put an 8-bit CPU on one chip. In 1973 INTEL produced its most popular microprocessor, the 8080. It was soon followed by a number of competitive devices, the best known among which are the 6800 made by Motorola, 6502 made by MOS Technology, and Z-80 made by Zilog. These microcomputers have features of first and second generation computers: a medium-sized set of programmable registers, fixed-point and BCD arithmetic including addition and subtraction, around 100 instructions intended for use in simple system configuration. Typical instruction times are between 1 and 10 microseconds. The use of 16-bit addressing implies a 64k byte addressable space. The design philosophy is still based on the assumption that the main application will be in controllers. There are a few exceptions to this standard; a few 12-bit and 16-bit microprocessors are available already at this stage, but they are exceptions and are not the most popular devices.

Further improvements in technology made it possible to put more components on a chip, and this led to development in two directions:

1. 8-bit *microcomputers*, rather than 8-bit microprocessors. In this context these are one-chip devices which in addition to a CPU include a small amount of memory and an I/O interface on the chip. An example is INTEL's 8748 chip which contains 1kbyte EPROM and 64 bytes of RAM. This description indicates that it is intended purely for control applications in which the control program is stored in a permanent memory and only a limited amount of data needs to be processed. The 8748 was introduced in 1976.

2. 16-bit *microprocessors* with sophisticated architectures, large address space, more sophisticated ALU with multiplication and division, and provisions for incorporation into much more sophisticated systems. The architecture and performance of these

microprocessors make it difficult or impossible to distinguish their features from those of standard "low end" minicomputers. The most often mentioned microprocessors in this category are again made by INTEL, Zilog, and Motorola. They were introduced in 1979.

We will now describe two microcomputers. The first is the very elementary Heathkit Micro Tutor and the second is Radio Shack's TRS-80.

The Micro Tutor is a system developed for self-study of microcomputers and experimentation. It is not intended for data processing in the usual sense although it can be expanded in this direction with components available from Heathkit. Its simplicity and the ease of experimentation make it ideal for our purpose since they make it possible to show in much detail how all the concepts presented previously apply to the design of a working computer.

The Micro Tutor is not a representative microcomputer system but just a vehicle to aid in understanding computers. Its rather detailed decription is therefore supplemented by an overview of the TRS-80 which is a much more sophisticated, very popular, and rather typical microcomputer. It will be described only briefly since its complexity does not lend itself to a detailed study in our text. Besides, the purpose of its description is only to show the typical configuration and features of a typical medium-sized microcomputer system rather than a detailed study of its design.

8.2.1 Heathkit Microcomputer Trainer ET-3400

The ET-3400 is available as a kit consisting of a printed circuit board, components, wires, etc. and a detailed assembly manual. The assembly is simple and requires no expertise in electronics. This "packaging" is typical for small microcomputer systems.

The Trainer is designed for individual study of computer organization and programming and is accompanied by an optional text which contains general theory of operation and a number of programming and hardware experiments.

It can be surmised even from this short description that the standard capabilities of the ET-3400 fall short of those of realistic computer systems. From the point of view of general organization, however, the system includes most basic components and is a miniature model of a full system.

8.2.1.1 Organization of the ET-3400. The detailed circuit diagram of the ET-3400 will be relatively easy to understand if it is preceded by a sequence of more general block diagrams. At the highest level of abstraction the system can be represented as shown in Figure 8.1.

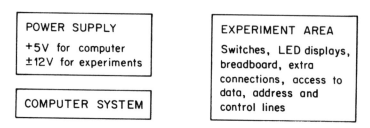

Figure 8.1   The basic structure of ET-3400.

The power supply and breadboarding facilities are not within the area of interest of this book and will not be investigated further. The relevant parts of the computer system can be broken down into more detailed descriptions as in Figure 8.2.

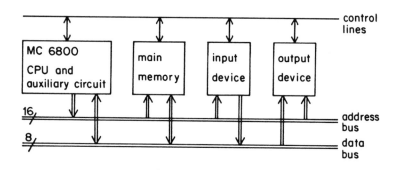

Figure 8.2   A more detailed diagram of ET-3400.

The CPU is an MC 6800 microprocessor produced by Motorola. The other parts are the main memory, an input system, an output system, and some auxiliary circuits which generate the necessary control signals. The address bus is 16 bits wide to accommodate the 16 address pins of the MC 6800. It is unidirectional and transmits the address from the CPU to memory and I/O devices. The data bus is 8-bits wide since the word size of the 6800 is eight bits. This bus is bidirectional to allow data to be transferred between CPU and memory and I/O in both directions.

The 6800 CPU chip is supported by the MC 6875 generator which is an integrated circuit designed specifically to generate timing signals with parameters required by the 6800. Its output is used by the 6800 IC. It also generates accurate control signals to control read/write operations of the system. These are closely related to the timing signal driving the CPU. The diagram in Figure 8.3 also shows tri-state buffers which provide the interface between the CPU and the data and address buses.

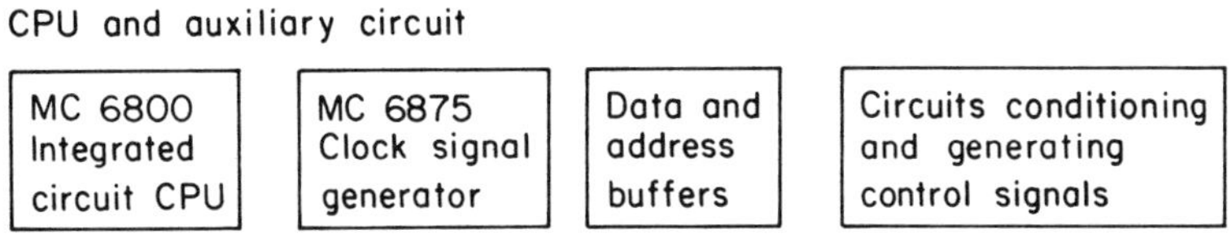

CPU and auxiliary circuit

MC 6800 Integrated circuit CPU	MC 6875 Clock signal generator	Data and address buffers	Circuits conditioning and generating control signals

Figure 8.3 CPU and auxiliary circuits of the ET-3400.

The main memory consists of a single 1k×8 ROM chip which is preprogrammed and contains a "monitor" program. Without a ROM monitor program the communication with the 6800 would be almost impossible as will become apparent later. The monitor program is especially designed for the ET-3400, its I/O configuration, and desired use. In addition to the ROM, there are a 256 byte RAM memory and sockets for additional modules of 256 bytes. The 256 byte RAM is obtained from two 256×4 RAMs connected in the usual way (Figure 8.4).

Input is by a hexadecimal (16-key) keyboard and is under the control of the monitor and the CPU; it does not use the interrupt facilities of the 6800. Output is via a set of six 7-segment LED lights and is under monitor control. Since the 6800 uses memory-mapped I/O, both the keyboard and the LEDs are assigned a range of memory addresses and are accessed through decoders, standard TTL MSI and SSI components. The organization of I/O is shown in Figure 8.5.

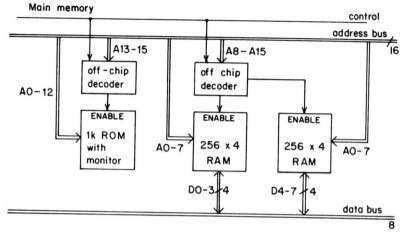

Figure 8.4   Memory structure of the ET-3400.

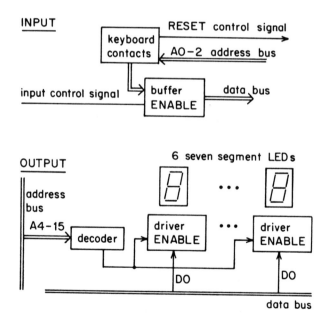

Figure 8.5   I/O organization of ET-3400.

After this breakdown into the main modules, the complete diagram is not difficult to understand (Figure 8.6).

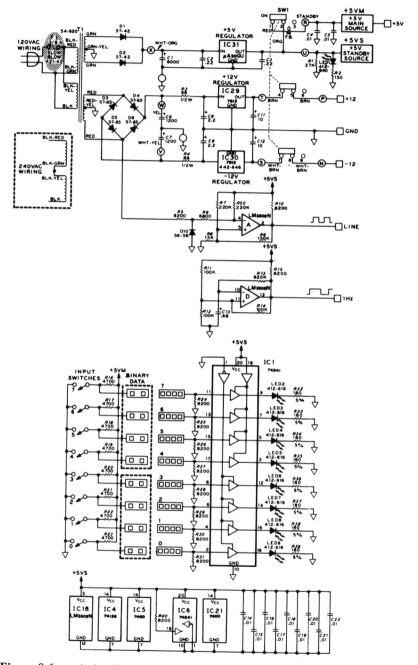

Figure 8.6 A detailed diagram of the ET-3400, modified from the Heathkit original.

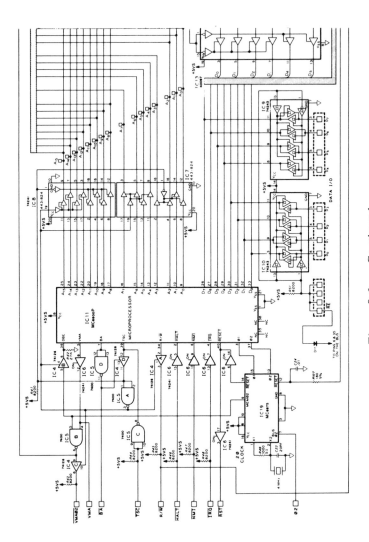

Figure 8.6 Continued.

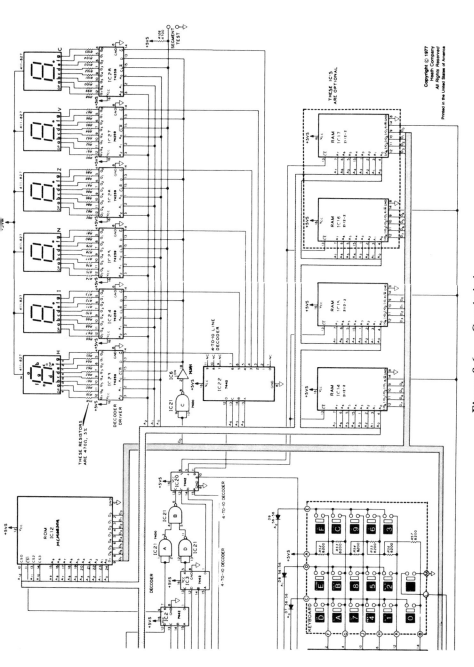

Figure 8.6 Concluded.

In order to be able to comprehend fully how the circuit works, one would need a complete understanding of all control signals that the 6800 generates and their exact timing. While these details can be easily understood with the background provided by the previous chapters, such a study will not be undertaken since it would take an unjustifiable amount of space. Instead of studying the 6800 in full detail, we will describe completely its general characteristics and then show some interesting details to demonstrate how some of the previously covered concepts are implemented and how certain processes occur at the register transfer level.

8.2.1.2 The MC 6800. As previously mentioned the 6800 microprocessor was one of the first 8-bit microprocessors and remains one of the most popular. One of the reasons for its popularity and for its use in the Trainer is the simplicity of its organization. The basic organization of the CPU is as shown in Figure 8.7.

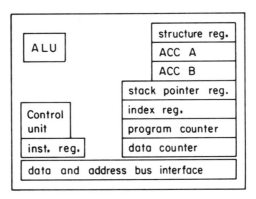

Figure 8.7   The basic structure of the MC 6800 CPU.

The CPU has two 8-bit accumulators, A and B, which have the standard accumulator functions and can be used almost interchangeably, though accumulator A has a few privileges. The stack pointer SP is a 16-bit register used to point to the top of a stack. X is a 16-bit index register which is typically used for indexed addressing but can also be used advantageously as a counter. The status register is an 8-bit register with six bits used for flags and two bits unassigned (Figure 8.8).

Figure 8.8   The status register.

The function of individual flag bits is as follows:

H (half-carry) is used in BCD arithmetic. It holds the carry from the rightmost four bits (corresponding to the less significant BCD code).

I (interrupt flag) is used to enable or disable interrupts.

N (negative accumulator) reflects the 2's complement value in the most recently used accumulator (A or B). It holds the sign bit of this accumulator.

Z (zero accumulator) is set to 1 if all bits in the most recently used accumulator are 0.

V (overflow) is set if the last 2's complement operation resulted in an overflow.

C (carry) contains the carry bit generated by the last arithmetic operation.

Data and address bus drivers amplify the signals and provide isolation between the CPU and the address and data buses. The Program Counter (PC) holds the address of the instruction to be executed; the Data Counter (DC) holds the address of the one-byte operand to be accessed; the Address Register (AR) is used for communication of an address to memory; and the Data Register is used for the transfer of data. The ALU is based on 2's complement arithmetic and is capable of addition, subtraction, and negation. It is also capable of BCD arithmetic, in an indirect way. Implemented logical operations are AND, OR, XOR, NOT. The instruction set is relatively simple but includes all essential instructions. There are 72 types of instructions, but the large number of addressing modes expands this basic set to a total of 197 instructions. Addressing modes, which will be discussed later in more detail, include immediate addressing; direct addressing with full address or only within the range of one "page"; indexed addressing; implied addressing; and relative addressing. There is no indirect addressing. The presence of the stack pointer allows stack addressing. All instructions do not work with all addressing modes, and relative addressing is available only for branch instructions, etc.

The main physical parameters of the 6800 are the following:

The 6800 uses N-MOS technology, more advanced compared to the P-MOS technology used with the earlier microprocessors. It uses a single +5 V power source (power dissipation 0.6 W). This is a significant advantage over many other microprocessors which require up to three different voltages simultaneously. The machine cycle time of the original model is one microsecond, but two more recent models allow 1.5 and two MHz clock frequency and therefore double the speed of the CPU. Instructions require one to twelve machine cycles for execution; most instructions require four or five machine cycles.

8.2.1.3 Instructions and Addressing Modes. Table 8.1 contains a summary of all instructions available on the 6800. Each instruction is listed with the following information:

1. Its mnemonic,
2. Its function and effect on individual flag bits,
3. For each addressing mode to which it is applicable the corresponding opcode (hexadecimal), number of machine cycles required for execution and number of memory locations (bytes) needed for storage of full instruction (opcode and address part).

As an example, the first instruction is Add memory to accumulator A. Its mnemonic is ADDA. In the extended addressing mode, to be explained shortly, its opcode is BB; it requires four machine cycles for execution and three bytes for storage (one for the opcode, two for the complete 16-bit address). Its function is to add the contents of the accumulator to the operand from memory and store the result in the accumulator (A). It has no effect on the Interrupt flag, but affects all other flags as described previously.

All opcodes are one byte long and therefore require one memory location. The whole instruction requires one byte for instructions with inherent addressing which require no address, two bytes for instructions which derive the effective address from a given address by adding displacement, and three bytes when the full 16-bit address accompanies the opcode.

The function of the various addressing modes is essentially as explained previously; the difference is mainly in terminology:

1. *Immediate addressing.* Value of the 8-bit operand immediately follows the opcode.

   Example: 8B 37 adds 37 to the value of accumulator A and leaves the result in the accumulator.

2. *Direct addressing.* The opcode is followed by the "low" part of the address. The "high" part is implied to be 00. Since the

"high" part determines the "page address" (a page with address XX is the addressing space XX 00 to XX FF), these instructions work with operands from page 0 (addresses 0000 to 00FF).

Example: 9B 37 adds the contents of location 0037 (i.e., location 37 on page 0) to accumulator A and stores the result in the accumulator.

The advantage of this mode is that it saves memory space since a two-byte address is fully specified by one byte and time since two bytes fetched for a complete instruction instead of three for full two-byte address instructions. Since direct addressing provides access only to the very limited amount of space available on page 0—256 bytes—this space must be used carefully, typically for the most frequently accessed data. This approach will guarantee the largest savings in execution time.

3. *Extended addressing.* The opcode is followed by the full 16-bit address of the operand. This addressing mode allows access to any location within the addressable memory space but requires three bytes, one for opcode and two for address. It is thus uneconomical and should be used only when absolutely essential. Example: BB 34 23 adds the contents of location 3423 to accumulator A and stores the result in the accumulator.

4. *Indexed addressing* uses the index register X to calculate the effective address of the operand. This is a two-byte instruction and consists of an opcode and a one-byte offset. The offset is treated as an unsigned 8-bit binary number and added to the contents of X (the base) to obtain the effective address. Since the offset is a single byte, indexed addressing allows access to within 255 locations from the base address. Typical use of indexed addressing is to process a number of contiguously stored operands such as the elements of a matrix.

Example: Consider the problem of copying a list of numbers from one part of memory to another. This can be achieved by initializing the index register to the starting address of the list, loading accumulator indexed with offset 0, and then storing it indexed with offset equal to the distance of the two memory areas. Index register is then incremented and the next number moved in the same way, etc. Note that the address parts of load indexed and store indexed instructions of this sequence remain unchanged; the offset remains constant. This is very important since it is highly desirable to write programs which do not

INSTRUCTION SET*

ACCUMULATOR AND MEMORY OPERATIONS	MNEMONIC	IMMED OP	~	#	DIRECT OP	~	#	INDEX OP	~	#	EXTND OP	~	#	INHER OP	~	#	BOOLEAN/ARITHMETIC OPERATION (All register labels refer to contents)	H (5)	I (4)	N (3)	Z (2)	V (1)	C (0)
Add	ADDA	8B	2	2	9B	3	2	AB	5	2	BB	4	3				A + M → A	↕	•	↕	↕	↕	↕
	ADDB	CB	2	2	DB	3	2	EB	5	2	FB	4	3				B + M → B	↕	•	↕	↕	↕	↕
Add Acmltrs	ABA													1B	2	1	A + B → A	↕	•	↕	↕	↕	↕
Add with Carry	ADCA	89	2	2	99	3	2	A9	5	2	B9	4	3				A + M + C → A	↕	•	↕	↕	↕	↕
	ADCB	C9	2	2	D9	3	2	E9	5	2	F9	4	3				B + M + C → B	↕	•	↕	↕	↕	↕
And	ANDA	84	2	2	94	3	2	A4	5	2	B4	4	3				A • M → A	•	•	↕	↕	R	•
	ANDB	C4	2	2	D4	3	2	E4	5	2	F4	4	3				B • M → B	•	•	↕	↕	R	•
Bit Test	BITA	85	2	2	95	3	2	A5	5	2	B5	4	3				A • M	•	•	↕	↕	R	•
	BITB	C5	2	2	D5	3	2	E5	5	2	F5	4	3				B • M	•	•	↕	↕	R	•
Clear	CLR							6F	7	2	7F	6	3				00 → M	•	•	R	S	R	R
	CLRA													4F	2	1	00 → A	•	•	R	S	R	R
	CLRB													5F	2	1	00 → B	•	•	R	S	R	R
Compare	CMPA	81	2	2	91	3	2	A1	5	2	B1	4	3				A - M	•	•	↕	↕	↕	↕
	CMPB	C1	2	2	D1	3	2	E1	5	2	F1	4	3				B - M	•	•	↕	↕	↕	↕
Compare Acmltrs	CBA													11	2	1	A - B	•	•	↕	↕	↕	↕
Complement, 1's	COM							63	7	2	73	6	3				M̄ → M	•	•	↕	↕	R	S
	COMA													43	2	1	Ā → A	•	•	↕	↕	R	S
	COMB													53	2	1	B̄ → B	•	•	↕	↕	R	S
Complement, 2's	NEG							60	7	2	70	6	3				00 - M → M	•	•	↕	↕	①	②
(Negate)	NEGA													40	2	1	00 - A → A	•	•	↕	↕	①	②
	NEGB													50	2	1	00 - B → B	•	•	↕	↕	①	②
Decimal Adjust, A	DAA													19	2	1	Converts Binary Add. of BCD Characters into BCD Format	•	•	↕	↕	↕	①
Decrement	DEC							6A	7	2	7A	6	3				M - 1 → M	•	•	↕	↕	④	•
	DECA													4A	2	1	A - 1 → A	•	•	↕	↕	④	•
	DECB													5A	2	1	B - 1 → B	•	•	↕	↕	④	•
Exclusive OR	EORA	88	2	2	98	3	2	A8	5	2	B8	4	3				A ⊕ M → A	•	•	↕	↕	R	•
	EORB	C8	2	2	D8	3	2	E8	5	2	F8	4	3				B ⊕ M → B	•	•	↕	↕	R	•
Increment	INC							6C	7	2	7C	6	3				M + 1 → M	•	•	↕	↕	⑤	•
	INCA													4C	2	1	A + 1 → A	•	•	↕	↕	⑤	•
	INCB													5C	2	1	B + 1 → B	•	•	↕	↕	⑤	•
Load Acmltr	LDAA	86	2	2	96	3	2	A6	5	2	B6	4	3				M → A	•	•	↕	↕	R	•
	LDAB	C6	2	2	D6	3	2	E6	5	2	F6	4	3				M → B	•	•	↕	↕	R	•
Or, Inclusive	ORAA	8A	2	2	9A	3	2	AA	5	2	BA	4	3				A + M → A	•	•	↕	↕	R	•
	ORAB	CA	2	2	DA	3	2	EA	5	2	FA	4	3				B + M → B	•	•	↕	↕	R	•
Push Data	PSHA													36	4	1	A → Msp, SP - 1 → SP	•	•	•	•	•	•
	PSHB													37	4	1	B → Msp, SP - 1 → SP	•	•	•	•	•	•
Pull Data	PULA													32	4	1	SP + 1 → SP, Msp → A	•	•	•	•	•	•
	PULB													33	4	1	SP + 1 → SP, Msp → B	•	•	•	•	•	•
Rotate Left	ROL							69	7	2	79	6	3				M	•	•	↕	↕	⑥	↕
	ROLA													49	2	1	A	•	•	↕	↕	⑥	↕
	ROLB													59	2	1	B	•	•	↕	↕	⑥	↕
Rotate Right	ROR							66	7	2	76	6	3				M	•	•	↕	↕	⑥	↕
	RORA													46	2	1	A	•	•	↕	↕	⑥	↕
	RORB													56	2	1	B	•	•	↕	↕	⑥	↕
Shift Left, Arithmetic	ASL							68	7	2	78	6	3				M	•	•	↕	↕	⑥	↕
	ASLA													48	2	1	A	•	•	↕	↕	⑥	↕
	ASLB													58	2	1	B	•	•	↕	↕	⑥	↕
Shift Right, Arithmetic	ASR							67	7	2	77	6	3				M	•	•	↕	↕	⑥	↕
	ASRA													47	2	1	A	•	•	↕	↕	⑥	↕
	ASRB													57	2	1	B	•	•	↕	↕	⑥	↕
Shift Right, Logic	LSR							64	7	2	74	6	3				M	•	•	R	↕	⑥	↕
	LSRA													44	2	1	A	•	•	R	↕	⑥	↕
	LSRB													54	2	1	B	•	•	R	↕	⑥	↕
Store Acmltr	STAA				97	4	2	A7	6	2	B7	5	3				A → M	•	•	↕	↕	R	•
	STAB				D7	4	2	E7	6	2	F7	5	3				B → M	•	•	↕	↕	R	•
Subtract	SUBA	80	2	2	90	3	2	A0	5	2	B0	4	3				A - M → A	•	•	↕	↕	↕	↕
	SUBB	C0	2	2	D0	3	2	E0	5	2	F0	4	3				B - M → B	•	•	↕	↕	↕	↕
Subtract Acmltrs	SBA													10	2	1	A - B → A	•	•	↕	↕	↕	↕
Subtr with Carry	SBCA	82	2	2	92	3	2	A2	5	2	B2	4	3				A - M - C → A	•	•	↕	↕	↕	↕
	SBCB	C2	2	2	D2	3	2	E2	5	2	F2	4	3				B - M - C → B	•	•	↕	↕	↕	↕
Transfer Acmltrs	TAB													16	2	1	A → B	•	•	↕	↕	R	•
	TBA													17	2	1	B → A	•	•	↕	↕	R	•
Test, Zero or Minus	TST							6D	7	2	7D	6	3				M - 00	•	•	↕	↕	R	R
	TSTA													4D	2	1	A - 00	•	•	↕	↕	R	R
	TSTB													5D	2	1	B - 00	•	•	↕	↕	R	R

*Copied with permission of Motorola.

Table 8.1   The instruction set of MC 6800.

INDEX REGISTER AND STACK POINTER OPERATIONS	MNEMONIC	IMMED OP	~	#	DIRECT OP	~	#	INDEX OP	~	#	EXTND OP	~	#	INHER OP	~	#	BOOLEAN/ARITHMETIC OPERATION	H	I	N	Z	V	C
Compare Index Reg	CPX	8C	3	3	9C	4	2	AC	6	2	BC	5	3				$(X_H/X_L) - (M/M+1)$	•	•	⑦	:	⑧	•
Decrement Index Reg	DEX													09	4	1	$X - 1 \rightarrow X$	•	•	•	:	•	•
Decrement Stack Pntr	DES													34	4	1	$SP - 1 \rightarrow SP$	•	•	•	•	•	•
Increment Index Reg	INX													08	4	1	$X + 1 \rightarrow X$	•	•	•	:	•	•
Increment Stack Pntr	INS													31	4	1	$SP + 1 \rightarrow SP$	•	•	•	•	•	•
Load Index Reg	LDX	CE	3	3	DE	4	2	EE	6	2	FE	5	3				$M \rightarrow X_H, (M+1) \rightarrow X_L$	•	•	⑨	:	R	•
Load Stack Pntr	LDS	8E	3	3	9E	4	2	AE	6	2	BE	5	3				$M \rightarrow SP_H, (M+1) \rightarrow SP_L$	•	•	⑨	:	R	•
Store Index Reg	STX				DF	5	2	EF	7	2	FF	6	3				$X_H \rightarrow M, X_L \rightarrow (M+1)$	•	•	⑨	:	R	•
Store Stack Pntr	STS				9F	5	2	AF	7	2	BF	6	3				$SP_H \rightarrow M, SP_L \rightarrow (M+1)$	•	•	⑨	:	R	•
Indx Reg → Stack Pntr	TXS													35	4	1	$X - 1 \rightarrow SP$	•	•	•	•	•	•
Stack Pntr → Indx Reg	TSX													30	4	1	$SP + 1 \rightarrow X$	•	•	•	•	•	•

JUMP AND BRANCH OPERATIONS	MNEMONIC	RELATIVE OP	~	#	INDEX OP	~	#	EXTND OP	~	#	INHER OP	~	#	BRANCH TEST	H	I	N	Z	V	C
Branch Always	BRA	20	4	2										None	•	•	•	•	•	•
Branch If Carry Clear	BCC	24	4	2										$C = 0$	•	•	•	•	•	•
Branch If Carry Set	BCS	25	4	2										$C = 1$	•	•	•	•	•	•
Branch If = Zero	BEQ	27	4	2										$Z = 1$	•	•	•	•	•	•
Branch If ≥ Zero	BGE	2C	4	2										$N \oplus V = 0$	•	•	•	•	•	•
Branch If > Zero	BGT	2E	4	2										$Z + (N \oplus V) = 0$	•	•	•	•	•	•
Branch If Higher	BHI	22	4	2										$C + Z = 0$	•	•	•	•	•	•
Branch If ≤ Zero	BLE	2F	4	2										$Z + (N \oplus V) = 1$	•	•	•	•	•	•
Branch If Lower Or Same	BLS	23	4	2										$C + Z = 1$	•	•	•	•	•	•
Branch If < Zero	BLT	2D	4	2										$N \oplus V = 1$	•	•	•	•	•	•
Branch If Minus	BMI	2B	4	2										$N = 1$	•	•	•	•	•	•
Branch If Not Equal Zero	BNE	26	4	2										$Z = 0$	•	•	•	•	•	•
Branch If Overflow Clear	BVC	28	4	2										$V = 0$	•	•	•	•	•	•
Branch If Overflow Set	BVS	29	4	2										$V = 1$	•	•	•	•	•	•
Branch If Plus	BPL	2A	4	2										$N = 0$	•	•	•	•	•	•
Branch To Subroutine	BSR	8D	8	2											•	•	•	•	•	•
Jump	JMP				6E	4	2	7E	3	3				See Special Operations	•	•	•	•	•	•
Jump To Subroutine	JSR				AD	8	2	BD	9	3					•	•	•	•	•	•
No Operation	NOP										01	2	1	Advances Prog Cntr Only	•	•	•	•	•	•
Return From Interrupt	RTI										3B	10	1		⑩					
Return From Subroutine	RTS										39	5	1	See special Operations	•	•	•	•	•	•
Software Interrupt	SWI										3F	12	1		•	S	•	•	•	•
Wait for Interrupt	WAI										3E	9	1		•	⑪	•	•	•	•

CONDITIONS CODE REGISTER OPERATIONS	MNEMONIC	INHER OP	~	#	BOOLEAN OPERATION	H	I	N	Z	V	C
Clear Carry	CLC	0C	2	1	$0 \rightarrow C$	•	•	•	•	•	R
Clear Interrupt Mask	CLI	0E	2	1	$0 \rightarrow I$	•	R	•	•	•	•
Clear Overflow	CLV	0A	2	1	$0 \rightarrow V$	•	•	•	•	R	•
Set Carry	SEC	0D	2	1	$1 \rightarrow C$	•	•	•	•	•	S
Set Interrupt Mask	SEI	0F	2	1	$1 \rightarrow I$	•	S	•	•	•	•
Set Overflow	SEV	0B	2	1	$1 \rightarrow V$	•	•	•	•	S	•
Acmltr A → CCR	TAP	06	2	1	$A \rightarrow CCR$	⑫					
CCR → Acmltr A	TPA	07	2	1	$CCR \rightarrow A$	•	•	•	•	•	•

CONDITION CODE REGISTER NOTES

(Bit set if test is true and cleared otherwise)

① (Bit V) Test Result = 10000000?
② (Bit C) Test Result = 00000000?
③ (Bit C) Test Decimal value of most significant BCD Character greater than nine? (Not cleared if previously set.)
④ (Bit V) Test Operand = 10000000 prior to execution?
⑤ (Bit V) Test Operand = 01111111 prior to execution?
⑥ (Bit V) Test Set equal to result of N⊕C after shift has occurred
⑦ (Bit N) Test Sign bit of most significant (MS) byte of result = 1?
⑧ (Bit V) Test 2's complement overflow from subtraction of LS bytes?
⑨ (Bit N) Test Result less than zero? (Bit 15 = 1)
⑩ (All) Load Condition Code Register from Stack. (See Special Operations)
⑪ (Bit I) Set when interrupt occurs. If previously set, a Non Maskable Interrupt is required to exit the wait state.
⑫ (ALL) Set according to the contents of Accumulator A.

LEGEND

OP	Operation Code (Hexadecimal)	00	Byte = Zero.
~	Number of MPU Cycles.	H	Half carry from bit 3.
#	Number of Program Bytes.	I	Interrupt mask
+	Arithmetic Plus.	N	Negative (sign bit)
-	Arithmetic Minus.	Z	Zero (byte)
•	Boolean AND.	V	Overflow 2's complement
M_{SP}	Contents of memory location pointed to be Stack Pointer.	C	Carry from bit 7
+	Boolean Inclusive OR.	R	Reset Always
⊕	Boolean Exclusive OR.	S	Set Always
M̄	Complement of M.	:	Test and set if true, cleared otherwise
→	Transfer Into.	•	Not Affected
0	Bit = Zero.	CCR	Condition Code Register
		LS	Least Significant
		MS	Most Significant

Table 8.1 Concluded.

change during execution and can be reentered and reexecuted any number of times and by different users without modification. Programs with this property are called "reentrant programs." More examples of the use of the index register are given in the Workbook.

Example: AB 34 calculates the effective address E as the sum of the contents of X and offset 34. It then adds the contents of memory location E to accumulator A and stores the result in A. Note that indexed addressing as implemented on the 6800 allows a limited offset of at most 255 locations.

5. *Inherent addressing.* Instructions using inherent addressing are one-byte instructions consisting only of the opcode.

Example: 1B is the Add accumulators instruction. It adds the contents of A and B and leaves the results in accumulator A. Note that in this instruction accumulator A has a somewhat different role from accumulator B. No address is needed because it is implied by the opcode.

6. *Relative addressing.* The effective address is obtained by adding the current contents of PC to the displacement given by the second byte of the instruction treated as a 2's complement number. Note that at the moment of addition the PC already contains the address of the NEXT instruction and so displacement is with respect to the address of the next instruction. Since the displacement is by an 8-bit 2's complement number, it is in the range -128 to $+127$. Note that although the displacement in relative addressing and the offset in indexed addressing have a somewhat similar role, the offset is treated as an unsigned, therefore non-negative, number while the displacement can be negative.

Example: Assume that instruction 20 14 is stored at locations 1225 and 1226. The instruction is jump which causes the PC contents to become $1225+2+14=122B$. $1225+2$ is the contents of PC at the time of calculation since the instruction occupies two words.

As another example, assume that the address part in the previous instruction is ED, i.e., locations 1225 and 1226 contain 20 ED. Since ED is 11101101 which represents -13 hexadecimal, the jump instruction causes PC to become $1225+2-13=1214$.

The 6800 uses relative addressing only in the category of branch instructions. All branch instructions use only relative addressing. Since this mode allows only limited displacements, there is a small additional category of jump instructions including unconditional jump and jump to subroutine which uses indexed and extended addressing and can thus be used to access any location in the addressable memory space.

The limitation of the range of relative addressing has two reasons: the large majority of branches are within a small address range, and by allowing only one byte to specify the displacement, branch instructions and their execution are shortened and memory requirements reduced. The combination of two-byte branch instructions and three-byte jump instructions makes it possible to write programs which require less memory and execute faster.

7. *Stack addressing.* This addressing mode is not provided as an alternative to other addressing modes but is simply a consequence of the existence of the stack pointer SP. It applies to two instructions (push and pull) and is very useful in conjunction with instructions operating on SP.

Note the constantly emerging concern with the efficient use of memory which is obvious in microprocessor architectures. This is typical for many computer systems. It is due to the following facts: the relatively restricted address space and the frequent use of microprocessors in controllers. In controller applications microprocessors are typically used in applications in which thousands or even millions of identical products implementing them are manufactured. In these situations the saving of even a single memory chip made possible by intelligent programming of a well-designed microprocessor can result in considerable savings.

8.2.1.4 Instructions. Most instructions perform functions described previously, and their RTL description in the table is self-explanatory. A few instructions deserve a more detailed explanation.

Decimal adjust (DAA). On the 6800, decimal operations are performed in two steps and require two instructions: the corresponding binary operation on the BCD code, which can produce an incorrect BCD result as we know from the chapter on BCD arithmetic, followed by adjustment of the code. This adjustment is performed by DAA. Note that DAA works only with accumulator A.

Add with carry. Basic addition works with one-byte operands and is of limited use since one byte can store only a very limited range of numbers. Multibyte operands can be processed by adding first the least significant bytes, then the more significant ones and carry from the first addition, etc. Addition with carry is performed by the add with carry instruction which works with both registers, ADCA and ADCB.

Shift right arithmetic. This is a shift right instruction which leaves the most significant bit of the operand in its place. It is used to perform arithmetic on signed numbers. BOOLEAN, AND, OR, XOR, NOT operate in the usual way, i.e., "bitwise." They leave the result in the accumulator. Example: B4 13 56 is ANDA with expanded addressing. If the contents of A is 00001111 and the contents of 1356 is 0101110, the result is that the contents of A changes to 00001110. There is no change in the contents of location 1356.

Bit test. Bit test instructions BITA, BITB perform essentially the same operation as ANDA, ANDB but do not change the contents of the accumulator involved in the operation. They affect only flag bits — in the same way as the AND instruction. This is very useful when it is only desired to test but not change a bit pattern. These instructions belong to a category of similar instructions which affect only flag bits and not accumulators: compare, compare accumulators, compare index register, test for zero or minus instructions. These instructions perform subtraction and update condition flags.

Increment index register (INX). This instruction is usually used to modify the base address in indexed addressing. It can, however, also be used for counting with the 16-bit index register used as a counter. This is very advantageous because the whole operation of incrementing a count in the index register requires a single one-byte instruction. The INX instruction also updates the Z flag bit. The *decrement index register* (DEX) instruction has the opposite function.

Compare index register (CPX) performs the comparison of [X] — the contents of X — with [M] + 1 where M represents the combination of the memory address specified and the immediately following address. It updates the Z flag. This instruction can be used to prepare the value in Z for a test to check whether the final address in a loop has been reached.

Branch instructions. These instructions use only relative addressing. There are one unconditional branch (BRA — branch always), and 14 conditional branches based on various tests of condition flags and a branch to subroutine. An interesting pair of branch instructions is designed to work with 2's complement representation (BGT—branch if greater than 0) or unsigned binary representation (BHI—branch if higher).

Jump instructions use indexed or extended addressing and can be used to reach any location in the address space. One of the two jump instructions is unconditional jump JMP; the other is jump to subroutine (JSR) which will be discussed in more detail later.

Other jump and branch instructions. There are four more instructions which cause the CPU to change the linear flow of instruction execution or behave abnormally. They are the return from interrupt and subroutine, software interrupt, and wait for interrupt. The first two represent two forms of return from a routine to the "main" program sequence. The software interrupt has the same effect as the hardware interrupt signal, but unlike the hardware interrupt it is performed in response to a program request. The wait instruction is essentially a halt instruction in which the CPU waits for an external interrupt to restart from a predefined point. All these instructions will be investigated later.

No operation (NOP). The only effect of this one-word instruction is that it increments the PC. It takes one machine cycle to execute. The NOP instruction is typically used in one of the following situations:

1. Assume that a long program has been developed and it was then discovered that a certain block of instructions in the program is incorrect and must be deleted. If it is not possible to rewrite the whole program, we can either bypass this block by a jump instruction or make it passive by replacing all of its instructions by NOP instructions. They have no effect on registers, memory, etc. and therefore their effect is essentially the same is if they were deleted. It must be remembered, however, that their execution consumes time.

2. In many control applications there is need for an accurately timed delay in which the control unit accurately measures a fixed amount of time but does not modify its registers and memory. This problem calls for a "timing" loop whose contents can contain NOP instructions, which do nothing but waste time, to achieve the desired delay. Programmed delays generated in this way can be very accurate because of the exact timing units one microsecond long.

Stack instructions (PSHA, PSHB, PULA, PULB). The stack is an area in the main memory accessed via the stack pointer (SP). Its location is arbitrary and under the control of the programmer who only has to make sure that the stack does not interfere with other instructions and data stored in the memory. The orientation of the stack on the 6800 is the reverse of what one would naturally expect: it is "upside down." The stack pointer points to the next available location, the empty location on the top of the stack. If SP contains 1517 the stack in the RAM is located as indicated in Figure 8.9.

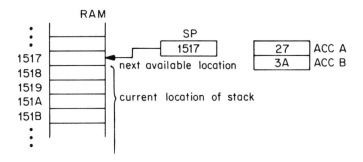

Figure 8.9   The Stack Pointer SP and the stack in RAM.

Note that addresses grow from top down: the highest address is at the bottom of the diagram, and the lowest is at the top. Assuming that the contents of accumulator A are as indicated, instruction PSHA pushes the contents of A on the top of the accumulator and updates SP to point to the next available location on the stack, i.e., DECREMENTS SP. The net effect is the new configuration shown in Figure 8.10.

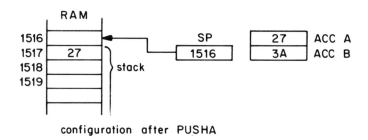

configuration after PUSHA

Figure 8.10   The new configuration of the stack after PSHA.

The "pull"—MC6800's equivalent of the more common term "pop"—instruction has the inverse effect. It modifies the SP (increments it) and copies the contents of the location pointed to into the specified register. As an example PULB would lead to the configuration shown in Figure 8.11.

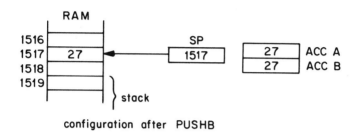

configuration after PUSHB

Figure 8.11   The new configuration of the stack after PULB.

Control over the location of the stack is via instructions which initialize the stack pointer: LDS (load stack pointer) which uses immediate, direct, indexed, and extended addressing, or TXS (transfer index register to stack pointer). The stack pointer can also be incremented or decremented and in this sense could be used as the index register. This must be done very carefully since SP has certain special uses as will be shown shortly. *Jump to subroutine* (JSR). It is very common that a sequence of instructions performing a very useful function is needed in many places of a program. An example of this is floating-point addition which must be programmed since the 6800 does not have floating-point arithmetic. This sequence could be written and repeated every time that it is needed in the program in the following manner:

$$----->\text{FPA sequence}------->\text{FPA}----->\text{FPA}------\text{ ETC.}$$

This approach wastes memory space since the sequence is always the same. A much more economical solution is to store the sequence in one place and access it when it is needed from where it is needed (Figure 8.12).

The sequence stored only once and accessed from individual places in the "calling sequence" is called a routine or a subroutine. Note that two jumps are required: one to the routine, another back to the calling sequence. The first jump is trivial if we have the starting address of the routine. The return to the calling sequence is more difficult since the return address depends upon the exact location from which the routine was called. One possibility is to modify the return address of the return jump. This could be performed by the routine itself. There are two problems with this approach: this operation would be required in each routine, and it would change the program whenever performed by changing the return address part of the return jump. This approach is highly undesirable. First generation computers handled this problem in this primitive way. All modern computers have special instructions to handle "linking" with subroutines. There are a number of variations and the 6800 uses one that is probably the most useful. Its JSR instruction is based on the use of the stack.

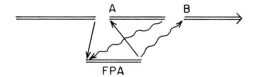

Figure 8.12   A subroutine accessed from several parts in the program.

When a JSR instruction is encountered in a program, the control unit pushes the address of the instruction following JSR on the stack and copies the address part of the JSR instruction into PC. This causes the CPU to continue with the first instruction of the subroutine; the address part of JSR is the address of the first instruction of the routine. Return from the subroutine to the calling sequence is by a *return from subroutine* (RTS) instruction. RTS pops the stack into PC and thus makes the CPU continue from where it left off. This process will work perfectly if the top of the stack still contains the return address. The subroutine must therefore guarantee that if it uses the stack, it restores the SP and the contents of the stack top to exactly what it was at the beginning of the subroutine. This is usually satisfied *almost automatically.*

Example 8.1:
Assume that in the graph in Figure 8.12
A = 1315
B = 1725
...
...
X = 7581
Y = 7796

The instruction stored in locations preceding A must be JSR 7581 (jump to subroutine starting at location 7581).
Specifically
address code
1312   BD
1313   75
1314   81
1315 corresponds to symbolic address A

After execution of JSR 7581 in the above sequence and assuming that original contents of SP is 2343 we have the situation shown in Figure 8.13.

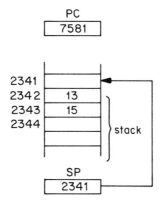

PC
| 7581 |

2341	
2342	13
2343	15
2344	

⟩ stack

SP
| 2341 |

Figure 8.13   Executing a jump to subroutine.

Note the order in which the two parts of the address are pushed on the stack. Execution now continues from 7581 until instruction RTS is encountered. This is the last instruction of the subroutine and is stored at location $Y = 7796$ according to our assumptions. Its execution leads to the configuration shown in Figure 8.14, assuming that SP and the stack contain the correct values.

Execution now continues from $A = 1315$ to the next JSR instruction which is stored as follows:

address code
1722 BD
1723 75
1724 81
1725 corresponds to symbolic address B

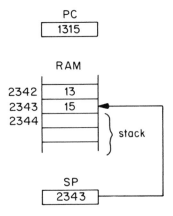

Figure 8.14   Next stage in execution.

When this JSR instruction is executed the configuration is as in Figure 8.15 (assuming, for simplicity, that SP still contains the same address; note that this is not required).

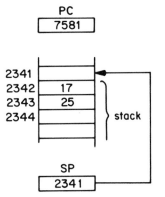

Figure 8.15   Next stage in execution.

Execution now continues from 7581, which contains the first instruction of the subroutine, to RTS stored at location $Y = 7796$. The execution of RTS, with the assumption of correct values in SP and the stack, leads to the configuration shown in Figure 8.16. Execution then continues from 1725.

In summary, the stack mechanism with the JSR and RTS instructions allows automatic implementation of linking of the calling program and the subroutine. This implementation of jumps to subroutine has one advantage and one disadvantage.

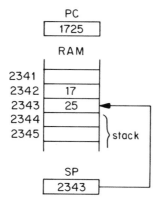

Figure 8.16 New configuration.

The disadvantage is that if the stack is not used very carefully, the JSR–RTS pairs will not work properly since RTS will cause execution to "return" to the incorrect place. It should be realized, however, that if this happens the stack is being handled incorrectly and the program would probably not work even without the problem of subroutine linkage.

The advantage by far outweighs the disadvantage: the use of stack in subroutine linkage allows subroutine jumps to be nested to any depth and even allows subroutines to call themselves, directly or indirectly, via a chain of calls to other subroutines. Calling a subroutine from itself is called a *recursive* call. The use of the stack allows automatic implementation of recursive calls with the same ease as implementation of ordinary calls. Note that return from subroutine by modification of return address in a jump instruction would make recursive calls impossible or difficult to implement. A recursive subroutine is an example of a *reentrant* subroutine—one which can be reexecuted any number of times without the need for intermediate modification. Another example of a reentrant subroutine is an interrupt subroutine which can be called in response to different interrupts with different priority levels. Such an interrupt subroutine may interrupt itself and must be capable of nested execution. Subroutine calls which are based on storing the return address in the body of the subroutine cannot be conveniently used for reentrant subroutines. In addition such subroutines are not "ROMmable"—they cannot be stored in ROMs since they need writable memory to store the return address. For all these reasons modern programming practice prefers subroutine calls based on the use of stack and this form of subroutine call is generally available on most modern computers. For more on subroutine calls see the Workbook.

Example: Assume that subroutine A is stored at locations 5566 to 5588 and subroutine B at locations 7744 to 7799. Assume that subroutine A calls subroutine B by a JSR instruction at location 5577, and the main program calls A from location 1345 and B from location 1367 Figure 8.17.

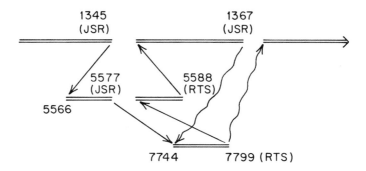

Figure 8.17   Nested subroutines.

During the execution of JSR at location 1345, the PC is first incremented to 1348 to point to the next instruction. Its value is then stored on the stack, the stack pointer updated (decremented), and PC loaded with the starting address of the subroutine (5566). Execution then continues from address 5566 until JSR 7744 is reached at location 5577. This causes the PC to be incremented to 557A and saved on the stack, on top of 1348. The stack pointer is updated and PC loaded with 7744. Execution continues with the first instruction of subroutine B. When address 7799 is reached, the RTS instruction pops the stack into PC and updates (increments) the stack pointer. The new contents of PC is thus 557A and execution continues in subroutine A. When address 5588 is reached the RTS instruction pops the stack into PC and updates SP. The new value in PC is 1348 and execution continues in the main program from address 1348. It should now be clear what will happen when the next JSR instruction is executed. The sequence described above can be illustrated by the diagram shown in Figure 8.18.

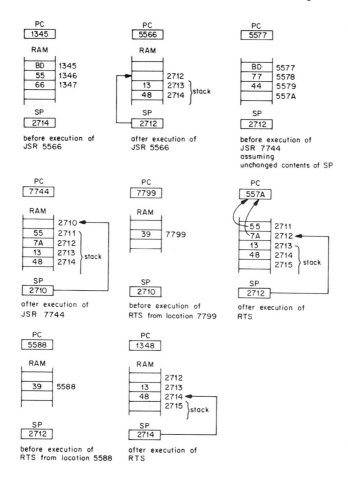

Figure 8.18 A diagram showing the sequence of multiple subroutine calls described in the text.

It is assumed that the initial contents of SP is 2219. As an example of a recursive subroutine, consider subroutine C stored at locations 4444 to 4588. Assume that the subroutine calls itself from location 4511 if accumulator A is negative. In other words, the contents of locations 4511, 4512, 4513 is JSR, 44, 45. Assume that execution reached the point at which C begins execution, i.e., the contents of PC is 4444 and the top of the stack contains the return address of the program which called C. Execution continues, and assuming that A is negative, it reaches address 4511. This location contains

JSR 4444 and so the address 4514 is placed on the top of the stack. Remember that JSR 4444 is actually stored in three locations: 4511, 4512, 4513 and the next instruction begins at location 4514. SP is updated and execution continues from 4444. Assume that this time accumulator A assumes a positive value and address 4511 is not reached. Execution continues to address 4588 which contains instruction RTS. The stack is popped into PC and SP is updated. This causes execution to continue from location 4514 in subroutine C. Assume that execution continues until 4588 is reached again. The stack is popped and loaded into PC. Execution continues from the new address which is the address of the program which called C in the first place (Figure 8.19).

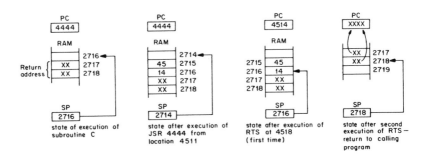

Figure 8.19   Successive configurations in a recursive call.

8.2.2   Programmed Input/Output

MC 6800 uses memory mapped I/O. Note that this is not the rule for all microprocessors — some have special I/O instructions. Programmed I/O on the 6800 is thus handled as an extension of memory (Figure 8.20).

The function of the I/O interface is to decode the address on the address bus and therefore to recognize when its I/O device is being addressed. The interface also provides a buffer to hold the data for a period of time sufficiently long for the I/O device to respond since the presence of data on the data bus is generally much too short, less than one microsecond, in duration. The interface also monitors the control lines which indicate the exact interval during which the data on the bus are valid. We will see later that this is only during a fraction of the

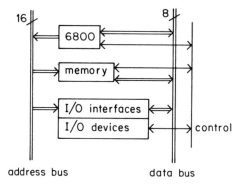

Figure 8.20   Memory-mapped I/O in MC-6800.

execution time of the instruction. Two examples of implementation of I/O are given below. Relate them to the I/O part of the diagram in Figure 8.6.

8.2.2.1 Input. Figure 8.21 shows a simplified diagram of an 8-switch input device and its interface.

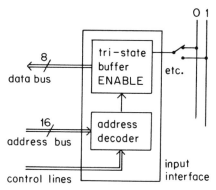

Figure 8.21   A simplified input device and its interface.

Assume that this input device is assigned address 8000. The address decoder of the interface must be designed so that when address 8000 is on the address bus, i.e., address bus contains 8000 and control lines indicate that the signals on the address bus represent a valid address, an "enable" signal is generated. The address and control signal decoder is shown in Figure 8.22.

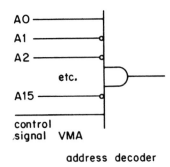

address decoder

Figure 8.22   The address and control signal decoder for address 8000.

The buffer whose output was up to this point in the high impedance state is connected to the data bus, and the 6800 can read the switch positions. All memory access instructions, such as LDAA 8000, ADDB 8000, ANDA 8000, have access to this input device in the same way as if it were a memory location. The buffer returns to the high impedance state when the enable signal is deactivated due to the change of the control signal from the CPU.

8.2.2.2 Output. Consider the output via LED lights shown in Figure 8.23.

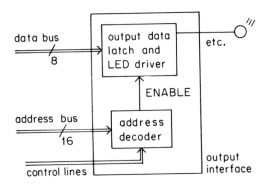

Figure 8.23   A simple output device and its interface.

If this output device is assigned address 9000, the decoder must generate an enable signal when control signals indicate a valid address on the address bus; the address bus contains 9000 and control signals indicate that valid data were placed on the data bus by the CPU, (Figure 8.24).

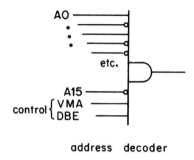

address decoder

Figure 8.24   Decoder for output device with address 9000.

The enable signal causes the register to accept the data from the data bus, and from there the value becomes available to the LEDs. The value in the register—and therefore the data displayed—remains unchanged until the CPU changes the contents of the register by another output instruction. An example of an output instruction which accesses the device in our example is STAA 9000 which stores accumulator A in location 9000 (our output device).

8.2.3 Interrupts

When an interrupt signal is generated by an external device and when an interrupt of the given category is allowed, the 6800 completes the current instruction, saves all registers (PC, X, A, B) on the stack (in this order), and loads an interrupt address into PC. The interrupt address which gives the location of the first instruction of the interrupt routine is stored in a fixed location in the memory. The interrupt flag I of the status word is disabled to prevent further interrupts of the current interrupt routine. The current interrupt routine can enable flag I if desired. Execution then continues from the starting address of the interrupt routine. The last instruction of the interrupt routine should be RTI—return from interrupt. This instruction restores all registers to their original values from the stack and in this way allows the original program to continue exactly where it left off.

There are four types of interrupts on the 6800 and each of them is assigned a fixed address in the memory to store the "interrupt vector," i.e., the address of the beginning of the interrupt routine. The assignment is as follows:

FFF8 interrupt request
FFF9
FFFA software interrupt
FFFB
FFFC non-maskable interrupt
FFFD
FFFE reset
FFFF

This assignment of addresses to interrupt vectors requires that the top of the memory be implemented in a ROM. The reason for this is that when power is applied to the CPU, this has the effect of a reset and causes the CPU to get the address of the "bootstrap" routine from locations FFFE, FFFF. This routine initializes the whole computer system, i.e., gets it ready to read keys, etc. This address and the subroutine must thus be available when power is turned on, and the only way that this can be achieved with semiconductor memories is to use a ROM. As a result, the typical memory map of a 6800-based system is as in Figure 8.25.

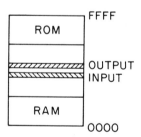

Figure 8.25   Typical memory map for an MC-6800 device The individual categories of interrupts will now be briefly examined.

Reset. This interrupt can be generated in one of two ways: when the power is turned on and reaches 4.75 V, the CPU automatically executes a reset. There is also a RESET pin which can be activated by a level signal to produce the same result. Reset is generally used to place the CPU into a well-defined initial state. This is necessary on "power-up" and also when the system starts to behave undesirably due, for example, to an error in the program. On the ET-3400 the RESET pin is connected to the RESET key. Pressing the RESET key thus has exactly the same effect as turning power on. What happens in response to a reset depends on the specific reset routine stored in the ROM. There must be a reset vector containing the address of the beginning of the reset routine, and a reset routine on every system. The reset vector is stored in FFFE, FFFF. This is not so for the other types of interrupts described below which do not have to be used in all systems. Note also that the reset interrupt is not affected by the I flag: it cannot be disabled, "masked." It is in fact one kind of a "non-maskable" interrupt. The reset is not really an interrupt in the sense that it does not cause the system to restore CPU registers. This is natural since, for example, on power-up the value of SP is unpredictable and storing accumulators on the stack is thus meaningless. The same holds for RAM. On power-up there is also no previous state to restore.

A Non-Maskable Interrupt is generated by a high-low transition on the NMI line. The address of the servicing routine is obtained from locations FFFC, FFFD. In addition to this difference between a reset and a non-maskable interrupt, there are a number of more subtle details which differentiate the two. Non-maskable interrupts are normally used to monitor certain critical conditions of the system. In a system controlling fuel injection of a motor this could be, for example, high temperature of the motor, etc. The non-maskable interrupt is not used by the ET-3400, but it is available for experimentation.

A Masked Interrupt can be generated by a level signal on the IRQ line. The interrupt will take place only if it is not masked, i.e., disallowed by the I flag. The I flag can be set or cleared by SEI and CLI instructions, and the programmer thus has a certain control over the maskable interrupt. Maskable interrupts are used to service conditions which are not critical such as requests for communication from I/O devices. The ET-3400 does not use the maskable interrupt.

Software Interrupt (SWI) is not an interrupt in the sense of being generated by an external signal. The SWI instruction produces the same sequence of operations as the masked interrupt. It can be used to simulate a hardware interrupt during the design of a 6800-based device or to allow testing of the status of the system at a specific point ("breakpoint") during the execution of a program. This is possible because the software interrupt saves the complete status information (all registers) and after examining the system via the interrupt routine, the computer can resume execution of the program in exactly the same state in which it was interrupted.

In addition to the four types of interrupts explained above, there is another function which resembles interrupts. This is the WAIt instruction which also partially implements the interrupt sequence. The "wait for interrupt" instruction saves registers in the same way as the other interrupts, but after this operation it waits for an interrupt request to appear on the IRQ or NMI lines. It also increments the PC to contain the address of the next instruction. When an interrupt signal appears, it causes the program to continue with the instruction following WAI. In other words, there is no location allocated as an interrupt vector, and in response to an interrupt signal no interrupt routine takes place. The function of the WAI instruction is similar to a HALT instruction (not available on the 6800) which stops the CPU.

Two typical uses of WAI are:

1. Wait when the CPU has nothing to do.
2. Implementation of DMA: completion of a DMA transfer can be communicated by an interrupt signal generated by the DMA controller. This use of WAI is possible because in addition to saving registers and entering the wait state, the CPU also places its pins into the high impedance (tri-state) condition. DMA can also be performed by activating the HALT line of the CPU. This signal allows the CPU to complete its current instruction and then float the bus, i.e., place it into the high impedance third state.

8.2.4   Timing Of Instruction Execution

From the perspective of modules external to the 6800, CPU instruction execution can be described as follows: the 6800 uses a two-phase clock and the relative timing of these two signals is as shown in Figure 8.26.

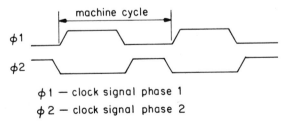

$\phi 1$ — clock signal phase 1
$\phi 2$ — clock signal phase 2

Figure 8.26   The two-phase timing signals of MC-6800.

Low-high transition of phase phi1 defines the beginning of a new machine cycle. The period of both signals is equal to the length of the machine cycle. The two signals are generated by one of the devices of the 6870 series, in our case the 6875. These are clock chips designed to produce signals satisfying the exact specifications of the 6800. The original 6800 CPUs worked with 1 MHz frequency signals; the enhanced models work also with 1.5 and 2 MHz signals.

The function of the clock signals is to provide timing for the internal operation of the control unit of the CPU. External devices use timing signals and control signals generated by the CPU to work synchronously with the CPU (Figure 8.27). The diagram does not show signals coming from external devices to the CPU such as IRQ, NMI, etc. These signals will not be discussed.

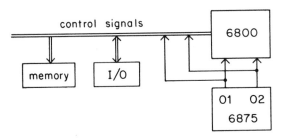

Figure 8.27   Timing signals form a part of control signals.

The basic signals are those which allow the CPU to communicate with the memory and the programmed I/O devices. This communication requires the following information:

1. Specification of the exact interval during which the address bus contains a valid address. The rest of the time signals on the address bus are of a transient character and do not represent a valid address. This information is transmitted via the VMA signal: a valid memory address is present on the bus when VMA is high.

2. What type of communication is desired, to read from memory into CPU or to write from CPU to memory? This information is present in the R/W' (Read/Write) signal. Its name implies that the level is high for read and low for write. Note that I/O devices sometimes do not need this information although they are addressed as memory since it may be clear which direction of

transfer is required. This is the case for all I/O devices on the ET-3400, and the R/W′ signal is only used to control communication with the memory.

3. Control over CPU access to the data bus: at times when the CPU performs internal operations its data pins are floated, i.e., in the high impedance state. When the CPU communicates data with external devices, its data pins are able to communicate with the data bus in the direction determined by the R/W′ signal. This control over the CPU is achieved by the data bus enable signal (DBE). Note that while the VMA and R/W′ signals are generated by the CPU, DBE is generated by external logic and synchronized with the CPU via the clock signals. In practice DBE is typically connected directly to the phi2 clock signal.

From the perspective of external devices, there are only three types of activity of the CPU: the CPU is reading or writing or performing internal operations and not communicating with the other modules. The standard READ CYCLE has the timing shown in Figure 8.28.

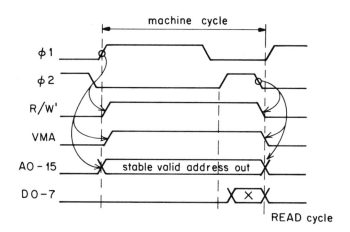

Figure 8.28   Timing of the READ cycle.

In the period labeled X (signals D0-D7), the CPU assumes that the data bus contains valid (stable) data and reads the values. This requirement must be satisfied by the parameters of the memory, I/O devices, and their interfaces. The exact beginning of interval X is given in manufacturer's data sheets. This timing diagram can be compared with the circuit diagram of the ET-3400 to see how these signals are used to control reading. The standard WRITE CYCLE has the timing shown in Figure 8.29.

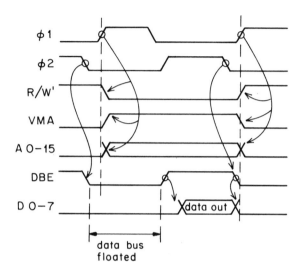

Figure 8.29 Timing of the WRITE cycle.

Note how the DBE signal controls the state (floating or data out present) of the data pins of the CPU. The basic difference between reading and timing logic is the value of the R/W' control signal. The timing is essentially the same except that the CPU which generates the data keeps the data on the data bus somewhat longer than is required for reading. This gives external devices more time to respond reliably in both read and write cycles.

Each machine instruction requires an integer number of machine cycles generally classified as read or write cycles. The following is an example of basic activities observable on individual control, data and address lines, or inside the CPU which occur during the execution of an instruction. The executed instruction is ADDA with extended addressing and has the following structure:

opcode high part of address low part of address

Machine cycle 1:
Place address of opcode (obtained from PC) on data bus, request read, get opcode from data bus at appropriate time.
VMA = 1, R/W' = 1
This is the fetch cycle and is identical for all instructions.

Machine cycle 2:
Opcode has been decoded, and it has been established that a two-byte address must be fetched from memory. PC has been incremented by 1. Operations are similar to those in cycle 1: place PC on address bus and request read to fetch the high part of the operand address. Read address from data bus at appropriate time.
VMA = 1, R/W' = 1
When data is received it is stored in the high byte of the data counter.

Machine cycle 3:
Fetch the low order byte of operand address in a way similar to cycle 2. The only difference is that when the byte is obtained from the data bus it is placed into the low order part of the data counter.

Machine cycle 4:
The one-byte operand is fetched from the memory; contents of data counter are placed on address bus and read requested, data read at appropriate time, the required addition is performed and the result stored in the appropriate accumulator. Note that for signals on control lines this cycle is identical to previous cycles: R/W' = 1, VMA = 1. It is a read machine cycle from the perspective of memory. Note how little time the CPU requires to perform the actual operation. Only the amount of time left after the operand is fetched is needed to perform the addition. The length of this cycle is the same as the length of any other read cycle. This indicates that the speed of communication with memory largely determines the length of the CPU cycle in the sense that the machine cycle length is essentially given by the speed of memory devices appropriate for the given CPU. In the case of an inexpensive microprocessor the memory is necessarily inexpensive and therefore not very fast.

The whole instruction thus executes in four machine cycles, and its exact duration is determined by the clock frequency. A 1 MHz clock produces machine cycles one microsecond long and the ADD extended would require four microseconds to execute.

As a detailed example of the changes in registers and memory locations, assume that the CPU is going to execute ADDA (opcode BB) with the operand stored at location A443 and value 25 (octal). Assume that the opcode is stored at address A312 and that accumulator A contains 13. The initial configuration is thus as follows:

IR XX (irrelevant)
PC A312
A 13
DC XX (irrelevant)
MEMORY (A312, A313, A314) BB A4 43 (instruction)
(A443) 25 (operand)

At the end of cycle 1 the state becomes
IR BB
PC A313
A 13
DC XXXX
MEMORY — unchanged

End of cycle 2:
IR BB
PC 1314
A 13
DC A4XX
MEMORY — unchanged

End of cycle 3:
IR BB
PC A315
A 13
DC A443
Complete address of operand fetched, ready to
get operand and perform addition.

End of cycle 4 (end of execution):
IR BB
PC A315 (address of next instruction)
A 38 (result of addition)
DC A443 (now irrelevant)
MEMORY — unchanged.

8.2.5   The Software of ET-3400 — The Monitor

It was stated that when the reset sequence is entered, the CPU fetches the contents of locations FFFE, FFFF into PC. The first instruction is then executed from the memory location whose address is stored in FFFE, FFFF. If, for example,

[FFFE,FFFF] = FE,00

i.e., the contents of these locations are FE,00, the first instruction executed after reset will be fetched from location FE00. The contents of the location addressed by FFFE, FFFF must therefore always have the desired value, i.e., the opcode of the first instruction, and so it must be stored in a ROM. The corresponding instruction will be the first in a sequence which prepares the computer for its regular function.

In the case of the ET-3400 (FFFE,FFFF) = FC00 and the initial sequence lead to the display of the message
  CPU UP
on the six 7-segment LEDs. The sequence does not stop here; the following instructions make the CPU scan the keyboard since it is now expecting the user to depress a key to indicate the desired next action. Each key is assigned a function in addition to its hexadecimal value such as

   display contents of accumulator A
   display contents of index register
   load data into a memory location
   read starting address of program and initiate program
   execution from this location etc.

When a key is depressed at this stage and its function recognized, a jump is made from the scanning sequence to the appropriate subroutine to execute the appropriate operations. When the subroutine is executed, a return jump is made back to the basic scanning sequence.

This whole program—implementing, the initialization, scanning, and appropriate response to key depressions—is called the *monitor*. The monitor, which includes several other subroutines written to make certain basic—but not trivial—operations automatically available to the user, is stored in a 1k ROM which occupies locations FC00 to FFFF. The reset address is FC00 because the monitor occupies 1k and thus begins at FC00. The monitor's first instruction does not have to be stored at the beginning of the ROM space but this is the natural place to locate it.

It should now be clear that the 6800 cannot function without some form of monitor program. The specific functions of the monitor differ from one computer system to another; another 6800-based computer could have a completely different monitor if its function is different or the designer of the monitor has a different taste. One feature common to all monitors, in our sense, is that they initialize the computer through a sequence evoked by reset. It should be noted that the reset function is not identical to all CPUs and that there are CPUs, such as the 1802 microprocessor produced by RCA, which theoretically do not require a ROM monitor for initialization at all.

The basic monitor functions of the ET-3400 do not require the full 1k ROM. In order to utilize the ROM more efficiently and make use of the ET-3400 easier, the basic monitor is augmented with several useful but not essential sequences. Each of them is terminated by RTS and can thus be called from any user's program and an automatic return to the calling program is guaranteed. As an example of the extra subroutines provided in the monitor, we will briefly describe subroutine OUTCH.

Subroutine OUTCH displays a character whose code is stored in accumulator A. The code is not an ASCII code but individual bits of the 8-bit code specify which segments of the 7-segment display are to be on. As an example 01001110 (the meaning of individual bits is: decimal point, segments *a, b, c, d, e, f, g*) will be displayed as capital *C*. This subroutine makes it easy to display any pattern on a 7-segment display. The starting address of this subroutine is FE3A. Access to the subroutine is thus by JSR FE 3A, i.e., BD FE 3A. Return from subroutine is automatic.

8.2.6   The Radio Shack TRS-80

The following is a brief description of the TRS-80 as an example of a more typical but also more complex microcomputer system. The basic TRS-80 consists of a power supply, a keyboard, a TV monitor, and a tape recorder.

The keyboard enclosure contains the CPU, memory and interface boards. The CPU is a Z-80 8-bit microprocessor, a successor of the 8080. It is often considered to be the most sophisticated and "computer-like" of all 8-bit microprocessors. The basic memory configuration consists of a 4k ROM and a 4k RAM. This basic system contains an interpreter (translator) of the very popular high-level programming language BASIC in its most primitive form called "level I." A more sophisticated version of the TRS-80 contains "level II"

BASIC in a 12k ROM. Memory can be expanded to 16k RAM inside the enclosure. The Z-80 CPU is capable of addressing up to 64k memory locations, and this is the maximum amount of memory that the TRS-80 can handle. Of this total addressable space, some is dedicated to the screen, some to the keyboard, and some to the monitor program and BASIC translator. It is therefore not available for storage of user written programs and data.

The TV monitor is a TV screen with better than usual frequency response which allows it to produce good quality characters and simple graphics. It can display up to 64 characters per line and 16 lines on the screen. Typical CRT terminals display 24 lines.

The tape recorder is a good quality audio recorder and uses ordinary, preferably better quality, audio tapes. Programs and data can be saved on tapes and loaded back into the computer via a single command. Communication with the tape recorder is relatively slow, 300 Baud—300 bytes per second.

The basic configuration can be expanded to include a printer, up to four floppy-disk drives, and a modem. The communication with these devices is through an expansion interface which is capable of storing additional RAM. Each diskette used with the Radio Shack system can store up to approximately 55k bytes. The system is supplied with a Radio Shack Disk Operating System (TRSDOS) which is a sophisticated analog of the monitor discussed in the previous section. TRSDOS allows among other things communication with disk drives, allowing storage and retrieval of information on diskettes.

A MODEM (abbreviation of MOdulator-DEModulator) is an interface which allows bidirectional communication of digital systems over ordinary telephone lines. Since the modem is a device with standard parameters, it is possible to use the TRS-80 as a terminal of a remote computer system.

The TRS-80 is very popular, and a large number of manufacturers produce additional or alternative devices directly compatible with the TRS-80. Some examples of these devices are:

Light Pen—provides an alternative input and allows communication with the computer via the TV screen.

Voice Synthesizer—an output device which produces artificial speech under program control.

Voice Recognizer—an input device which digitizes sound and allows speech recognition under program control. This facility has limited capabilities because of the lack of an efficient recognition algorithm.

Music Synthesizer—produces music synthesized under program control.

Various firms offer software for TRS-80 systems, including games, programming language translators (such as Pascal, FORTRAN, COBOL), business programs, etc.

Regular newsletters are published which contain descriptions of new hardware and software available for the system and new applications, and provide communication between TRS-80 users. There are also TRS-80 clubs and user groups which meet regularly and allow users to exchange information and experiences.

The TRS-80 is primarily a hobby or home computer. When expanded to include sufficient memory, disk drives, and a printer, the system becomes a respectable and relatively inexpensive system capable of supporting a small business. To satisfy larger users the Radio Shack recently developed a more powerful microcomputer system called TRS-80 Model-II.

The above description of the TRS-80 applies in its general aspects to all standard microcomputer systems of the end of the 1970's.

8.3 MINICOMPUTERS

The category of minicomputers emerged in the mid-1960's as an alternative to large and very expensive computers. These systems became possible mainly because of advances in electronic technology. Their intended application was in those areas in which the use of computers is highly desirable but not economical with large, very expensive and very sophisticated systems. Such uses include smaller scale data processing, process control, data acquisition, control of laboratory experiments, etc. The major manufacturers of minicomputers include the Digital Equipment Corporation (DEC), Hewlett-Packard (HP), and Data General. The most popular minicomputers belong to the PDP group minicomputer made by DEC, especially the PDP-8 and PDP-11 minicomputer families. We will briefly describe the architecture and organization of the PDP-11 family. It must be kept in mind that this is a modern minicomputer family in many respects significantly different from the early and unsophisticated minicomputers. The capabilities of some members of this family far surpass the capabilities of large computers of the 1950's.

8.3.1 The PDP-11

PDP-11 is not the name of a single computer but is the name of a *family* of computers, closely related to one another in organization and architecture.

The concept of a family of computers is very important and popular. Its main justifications are economic: the simpler types of a family are inexpensive and simple enough to attract and satisfy a small user. When the user's needs outgrow the small computer system — and this happens to almost every user — it can be replaced by a more powerful and expensive member of the same family without the need to make extensive program changes since the different members of the family are usually *upward compatible*. The more powerful models are capable of execution of all programs written for the less powerful models. The programs could, however, be rewritten to take advantage of the greater sophistication of the more sophisticated model. Since the cost of software generally represents the major part of the investment of the user, the elimination of the need to rewrite programs for a new computer is a major economic incentive. The user is thus attracted to computers produced in families with the prospect of easy conversion when it is needed. Compatibility and high popularity also mean that a large number of users can share programs developed at significant cost and save by avoiding the need to write programs to solve standard categories of problems Basic similarity and sharing of hardware modules present an advantage to the manufacturer who can mass-produce common modules at reduced cost and make the computer even more attractive. We will see later that the concept of a family and general continuity of design philosophy are popular even in the category of large computers. The concept was actually in use before the appearance of minicomputers. The very large computers, the "supercomputers," on the other hand, are typically designed for a specific application and often for a specific user. Only a few of the same model are typically made, and this contributes to their extremely high cost.

8.3.2 PDP-11 Organization And Architecture

The basic PDP-11 architecture is characterized by a single data bus, the UNIBUS, which allows communication between all devices connected to it (Figure 8.30). All devices can communicate without the need to use the CPU as an intermediate stage. The CPU is, of course, in overall control of all communication.

The existence of a single data bus makes the system relatively simple but also limits its speed since only one device at a time can be the source of information transmitted over the bus. Other sources must wait for the completion of communication. This applies particularly to communication between the CPU and the main memory.

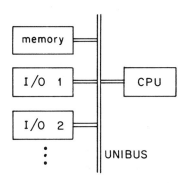

Figure 8.30   The PDP-11 system.

The CPU is based on 16-bit words and works primarily with 8 and 16-bit operands. The address is 16 bits long and the basic addressing space is thus 64k. This range can be extended by an optional memory expansion module. The CPU has eight general purpose, i.e., user programmable, registers R0, ...R7, which are essentially equivalent in their function and accessibility. One of the registers is used as the program counter. Since it is equally as accessible as other registers, it can be used to obtain several useful addressing modes. The PDP-11 includes all the addressing modes described in Chapter 7 and more.

The ALU in its basic configuration works with fixed-point 2's complement numbers. Floating-point arithmetic is available as an option via an additional hardware module.

An important part of the CPU is the Processor Status Register (PSR) (see Figure 8.31) which is basically an extended status register. It contains the standard flag bits, such as overflow, carry, zero accumulator, etc. and other more advanced information related to more sophisticated uses of the computer. All bits can be tested for conditional jumps.

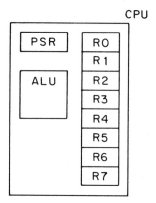

Figure 8.31   The CPU of the PDP-11.

The data types available on the PDP-11 are fixed-point, floating-point (as an option), and alphanumeric (8-bit ASCII code). Floating-point representation uses 32 bits (two words) as a basic format ("single precision"). One of the 32 bits is used for the sign of mantissa, 23 for the normalized magnitude, 8 for exponent in excess 128 representation and base 2. "Double precision" representation uses four words to represent one number. The 32 extra bits are used to increase the precision of the representation of the mantissa. The exponent is represented identically in single and double precision. The amplitude range of double precision is thus the same as that of single precision; only the number of significant digits is increased.

The basic instruction set includes all standard instructions and can be further expanded as an option. Instructions are typically one word (16 bits) long. A typical instruction consists of an opcode, the specification of one or two registers, and the specification of the addressing mode. The register can contain the address of an operand (16 bits). The combination of the register and the addressing mode determines the effective address of the operand. Some PDP-11 models are microprogrammable. Instruction sets are upward compatible between individual models which are

03 (1975), 04 (1975), 05 (1973), 20 (1970), 23, 24 (1979), 34 (1976), 40 (1972), 45 (1972), 55 (1976), 60 (1977) and VAX-II/780 (1977).

(The numbers in parentheses indicate the year in which the model was announced.)

New models in the family have been designed with the strategy typical for computer evolution: either to provide much more power for a higher cost or to provide more power for the same cost or the same power at smaller cost. The evolution is based on the evolution of technology. With these criteria in mind one can trace three evolutionary branches all starting from the original PDP-11/20.

Individual models are available in implementations using different technologies. This results in different speeds and costs. As an example, instruction ADD immediate requires 0.3 microseconds with bipolar memory, 0.5 with MOS memory, and 1.0 microseconds with core memory. These proportions are typical for the more complicated instructions since the essential operation determining execution time is memory access; as an example ADD with indirect addressing, called "deferred," is ten times slower than ADD immediate.

One of the models—the 11/03—is also known as the LSI-11. It is basically a microprocessor although not a single chip microprocessor.

The high-performance PDP/11s are so powerful that the efficient utilization of the CPU must be seriously considered. It has already been stated that typical programs execute relatively very few I/O operations. These rare I/O operations, however, require relatively very long times for their completion. The utilization of the CPU can be significantly increased by the elimination of I/O waits and the use of interrupts and DMA. During the time that I/O is being executed, the CPU could start processing another program since the current program has to wait for the completion of its I/O. This mode of operation is called *multiprogramming*. A simplified sequence in a multiprogrammed system could be as shown in Figure 8.32.

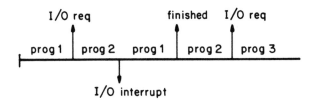

Figure 8.32   An example of the sequence of events in a multiprogramming environment.

Multiprogramming places very high requirements both on the software, which must control the proper sequences and the sharing of all "resources," and on the hardware, which may be designed to improve the efficiency of software. Typical multiprogramming environments include protection of user programs from one another and the software of the system, proper utilization of the main memory (memory management), etc.

One of the optional features available on the more powerful PDP-11 models is memory management with virtual memory. This feature allows the expansion of the addressable memory space and helps solve the problem of memory protection. It makes it seem to each individual user program that it has the full 64k addressing space just for itself, undisturbed by and inaccessible to other programs. It can be implemented as indicated in Figure 8.33.

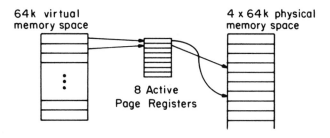

Figure 8.33   Memory management on PDP-11.

Each user's program operates with 16 address bits and addresses up to 64k memory locations, the virtual memory. The actual system memory is four times bigger and is addressed by 18-bit addresses. The 18-bit address is obtained from a set of eight Active Page Registers (APR) and the original 16-bit address. These registers calculate the physical address from the virtual address, automatically adjusting to individual user programs. Adjustment of APRs is performed by the system program via special instructions which must be inaccessible to ordinary user programs since their improper use could endanger the security of the system. For this reason the system is capable of working in a *supervisory* ("privileged") mode and the *user* ("problem") mode. Programs executing in the supervisory mode have access to the privileged instructions and all standard instructions. Programs executing in the problem mode can execute only standard instructions. The CPU must be able to recognize in which mode it is working in order to decide whether or not certain instructions should be allowed to execute. This information is stored in the Processor Status Word and is modifiable in the supervisory mode.

The last feature that will be mentioned here is the concept of the *cache memory*. This is a very fast but small memory (e.g., 2k bytes). It is inserted between the main memory and the CPU (Figure 8.34).

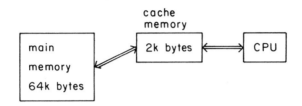

Figure 8.34   The cache memory.

All data and instructions pass through the cache memory where they are stored in the form of a pair (instruction or data item, main memory address from which it was obtained). If an address is to be accessed to obtain an instruction or to communicate data, the CPU checks the cache memory and the address part of the present pairs. If the address is found (a ''hit''), the code is accessed in the cache. If it is not found (a ''miss''), the code is fetched from main memory and replaces one of the pairs residing in it. The pair to be replaced is chosen on the basis of a more or less complex ''replacement algorithm.''

The advantage of the cache is that with an efficient replacement policy, it can speed up memory access to a point that memory accesses are almost as fast as accesses to the cache, which is built with extra fast components. As a consequence, a relatively slow, inexpensive main memory seems to function almost as fast as a very fast and expensive one. The basis of this achievement is the ''principle of locality'': most instructions and data in a typical program are arranged in such a way that access during execution is usually to nearby addresses and is repetitive. For this reason over 90 percent of accesses in a typical program are hits.

Note that there are two ways of taking advantage of the cache:

1. Use a relatively slow and inexpensive main memory and a fast cache to obtain a relatively inexpensive memory which appears to be quite fast (90 percent hits).

2. Use a fast main memory and an ultra fast cache to obtain a very fast and expensive memory with speed approaching that of the cache.

The special enhancements described in the previous paragraphs are only available on the most powerful models of the PDP-11 family. They are not available on the simpler models because they could not be justified. Enhancements are available for two reasons: to utilize the capacity of powerful CPUs efficiently and to further increase their power.

8.4 TWO LARGE COMPUTERS

8.4.1 Introduction

This section gives a brief description of the main features of two modern large computer systems, the Sperry Univac 1100/60 and the CDC Cyber 170.

The Sperry Univac 1100/60 is a system whose individual models cover the low to high power range of large computer systems. It was developed in the late 1970's and in many respects presents typical features of large computer systems. These features include:

1. A powerful and reliable CPU capable of addressing a large memory space and working at high speed. The power of the CPU can be further increased by coupling two identical CPUs together.

2. Delegation of I/O control to special processors operating under minimal CPU control. This approach is a natural consequence of the high speed of the CPU which would be very inefficiently utilized by significant involvement in I/O operations.

3. Large memory with an intermediate extra fast buffer (cache) memory of smaller size. This approach is also required to utilize fully the speed of the CPU.

4. An extensive set of secondary storage devices including disks, drums, tape drives, and paper peripheral devices.

5. Capability of participating in a network of mutually connected computers, terminals, and communication controllers exchanging information and sharing hardware and software resources.

6. Capacity of the CPU to operate in several modes ranging from the user mode with limited access to instructions and memory

on one end, to the executive mode with unlimited control of all resources at the other end. This hierarchy of modes simplifies multiprogramming and time-sharing which are common in systems of this type.
7. Software compatibility with earlier models made by the same manufacturer.

Some of these features will be illustrated on specific examples taken from the 1100/60.

The second presentation given later in this section deals with the Cyber 170 series. This family of computers is outlined to provide a complementary example illustrating alternative approaches accepted by another manufacturer in response to somewhat different requirements centered almost exclusively around the goal to provide a very powerful computer capable of very fast numeric calculations.

8.4.2   The 1100/60 System

The 1100/60 is a system which is a continuation of UNIVAC's earlier 1100 series. This means that the software of the 1100/60 system is almost fully compatible with the software of the earlier models in this series. This is an extension of the concept of a family and is typical for large general purpose computers. It has its advantages and disadvantages: it allows owners of an outdated model to transfer to a modern model with minimal conversion of existing programs. This is a strong incentive to stay with the same manufacturer. On the other hand, this philosophy forces the manufacturer to be somewhat conservative, retaining existing features, improving them, and possibly adding new ones rather than adopting completely new approaches.

The 1100/60 can be used in several configurations. The simplest is the 1100/61 system shown in Figure 8.35. It consists of a single CPU, the main storage unit (MSU), an input output unit (IOU), a system support processor (SSP), and operator's console.

The most sophisticated configuration is the 1100/62 system (Figure 8.36) which consists basically of two 1100/61s connected together and capable of working together or independently.

There are a number of possible configurations which differ in memory size, presence of buffer storage, number and complexity of IOUs, size of the instruction set, communication capabilities, etc. The essential functions and parameters of individual modules are as follows.

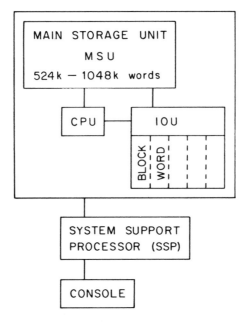

Figure 8.35   The UNIVAC 100/61 system, model C1.

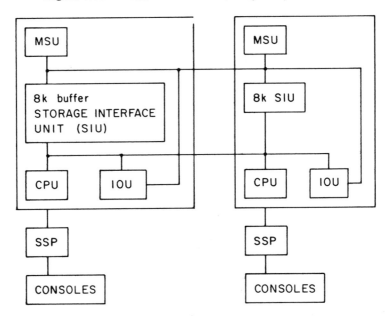

Figure 8.36   The UNIVAC 1100/62 system, model H1.

The CPU. The CPU uses the latest IC technology including an array of microprocessors. It works with a 116 nsec clock cycle. The reliability of its operation is enhanced by duplication of all operations: there are two ALUs working in parallel, and all intermediate and final results are compared. When a discrepancy is detected, the operation is automatically retried. This is normally sufficient to produce the correct result since most faults are intermittent. If the discrepancy persists, an interrupt is generated to allow further testing. An optional hardware monitor automatically collects statistics on the activity of various components of the system. This facility can be used, for example, to "tune" the system to provide the optimal service in the given environment.

The control unit is microprogrammed. It controls the execution of the instruction set which contains about 160 different types of instructions. The instruction set can be enlarged to improve the efficiency of processing particularly in business applications. The word size is 36 bits; the addressing space is 16 Mwords. Relative addressing simplifies multiprogramming.

The CPU contains 128 36-bit addressable registers. Only one-half of them are user addressable; the rest are available only to the executive system. Registers include arithmetic registers (accumulators), index registers for indexed addressing, control registers often assigned special functions, and processor registers associated mainly with interrupts. Index registers have two halves: one contains the offset and the other stores the increment which can be used to modify the offset automatically.

The instruction set includes the following types of instructions:

1. Load and store.
2. Fixed-point arithmetic, mostly with single-precision numbers, including addition, subtraction, multiplication, division, and absolute value.
3. Floating-point arithmetic providing similar operations for single and double-precision numbers. Some arithmetic operations can be performed on one-half or one-third of the word in parallel.
4. Test instructions which are essentially conditional skip instructions using conditions such as equality, etc. Search instructions are basically test instructions which can automatically test the contents of a specified area of the memory rather than a single location.
5. Shift instructions.
   Logical instructions.

Jump instructions which often have side-effects, e.g., store location and jump.

6. I/O instructions which initiate and terminate the operation and test the status of IOUs.

7. Executive system control instructions which control interrupts, set memory limits for individual users, etc.

A small group of special instructions does not fall into any of the previous categories. In addition, there are invalid codes which cause an interrupt.

The extended instruction set provides BCD arithmetic, conversion between BCD, byte and binary and bit manipulation.

Addressing modes include immediate, direct, indirect and relative. Numeric data types include fixed and floating-point representation with single or double precision. Floating-point numbers cover approximately the range 10^{**-38} to 10^{**+38} with 8-digit precision (single-precision) and 10^{**-308} to 10^{**-307} and 18-digit precision (double precision).

Main memory (MSU). Contains 524k to 1048k words per CPU. The internal size of words is 43 bits. 36 bits store data and 7 bits are used for double-error detection and single-error correction. Access times are 580 nsec for simple read/write, 625 nsec for corrected read, 928 nsec for partial word write.

Storage interface unit (SIU) is the optional 8k buffer inserted between the CPU and the main memory. When the desired address is not found in the SIU, the word is fetched from the main memory along with three consecutive words. These four words replace those four words in the SIU which were used the least recently.

The IOU is a processor which controls I/O devices and their access to the main memory (see Figure 8.35). It works under the direction of the CPU. In its basic configuration it contains one block multiplexer which operates with byte-sized data and one word channel module which is composed of four word channels working with word-sized data. Block multiplexer channels allow data transfer rates around 1.66 M byte and 1.4 M word on a word channel module (four channels).

System support processor (SSP). The SSP is a separate minicomputer which has the following main functions:

1. It allows independent diagnosis and helps in the maintenance of the main system.

2. It allows communication between the operator-controlled console and the system (see Figure 8.36).

3. It controls systems partitioning, making it possible to isolate electrically a component and controlling transition between independent and coupled operation of two CPUs in a multiprocessor (two CPUs) system.

The system console is the terminal used by the operator controlling the system. It consists of a display, keyboard, and printer.

The basic system consisting of the CPU, IOU, MSU, and SIU occupies one cabinet 30x78x64 inches, weighs 1500 pounds, and requires 7kVA. This small size, low power requirement, and thus limited air-conditioning are the consequence of the use of modern IC components.

Some of the *peripheral devices* available from the same manufacturer have the following parameters:

Disk storage:

1. Disk units with removable disks have average access time of 30 msec, capacity up to 34M words, transfer rate 179000 words/sec, speed 3600 rpm. The average access time includes arm positioning and latency.
2. Units with non-removable disks have average access time of 23 msec, transfer rate 466000 words/sec, storage capacity up to 125 M words, speed 3600 rpm.

Drum storage: Two types of drums with up to 2 M words capacity per drum, up to eight drums per subsystem, average access time 4 to 17 msec depending on model, transfer rate up to 240000 words/sec. Drum speed is 7200 rpm for the smaller drum and 1800 rpm for the larger one.

Magnetic tape drives: 7 or 9 track recording, density of recording 200 to 6250 bits per inch (bpi), transfer rate 12 to 1250k bytes/sec, tape speed 60 to 200 inches per second, maximum tape length 2400 ft.

Card reader: reads 1000 cards/min.

Card punch: punches 250 cards/min.

Line printer: prints 800 to 3000 lines per minute depending on model and number of characters in the character set (smaller character sets print faster).

We have now seen some of the ways in which the utilization of a very powerful CPU can be increased. They include the delegation of I/O to specialized processors and a modified memory organization increasing its apparent size and access speed. There are other methods, some of which will be described in the following section which deals briefly with the solution used in certain CDC (Control Data Corporation) computers. A particularly interesting feature of the CDC approach is that in one respect it goes beyond the strategies used by most large computers: it delegates not only I/O but also most of the overhead associated with the processing of multiple jobs "simultaneously." Its I/O processors are not only sophisticated I/O controllers but actual computers executing, by and large quite independently, their own programs.

8.4.3   The CDC Cyber 170 Series

We have seen that the concern to utilize efficiently the very powerful CPUs of large computer systems leads to the separation of "computation" (processing of user programs) and I/O operations. This naturally leads to allowing the CPU to switch from an uncompleted program ("job") to another if the present program requires a time-consuming I/O operation. In this environment user jobs can be submitted in a batch of unrelated programs and executed in partial overlap, seemingly simultaneously. This mode (multiprogramming) can be extended to allow the CPU to service sequentially a number of terminals in an interactive fashion ("timesharing") and even responding to other service requests in very brief intervals of time ("real-time" processing). This organization requires three types of processing: computation, I/O, and the supervision of the overall operation of the system. This last activity is performed by a very complex program—the *operating system* —typically supplied by the manufacturer of the hardware. To appreciate the complexity of the program, one should be aware that software of modern large systems costs more than hardware. The operating system has the responsibility of scheduling jobs for execution, switching between them when necessary, initiating and supervising I/O, "swapping" programs and data between the main and secondary memory, etc.

Computation, I/O, and system functions are largely independent: while the execution of a user program is in progress, the operating system may be supervising I/O, updating the queue of jobs to be executed, etc., and I/O controllers may be executing details of I/O operations, reporting on their progress to the operating system.

Note that the need to switch between programs and the separation of I/O from computation thus leads to the creation of overhead processing whose magnitude can be very significant. Multiprogramming, which is a solution of the problem of unemployed CPU, thus creates unnecessary work for the CPU and is, to some extent, counterproductive. On a properly designed and loaded system the net result is still an overall increase in "throughput" (the number of user jobs processed over a given period of time).

Most computer systems which free the CPU from I/O let the CPU execute completely the operating system. Control Data Corporation's (CDC) large computers take advantage of the basic independence of the three tasks and separate them completely. The CPU of these medium-large to very large computers is designed for extremely fast computation. Its design and the configuration of the system are such that the execution of system functions fully on the CPU would not be very efficient. The system is designed in such a way that the CPU's share in the execution of the operating system is less than 10 percent. The liberation of the CPU from anything that is unproductive is thus almost complete, and the system can use the extraordinary computational power of the CPU to its full advantage.

The whole system consists of one or more CPUs and up to 20 identical Peripheral Processors (PPs) which are essentially interchangeable minicomputers charged with I/O and the execution of system functions. PPs also execute certain frequently needed functions for users such as basic file editing, etc., and free the CPU from these trivial non-computational operations. The CPU thus gets fully prepared programs which it executes only to the point where it ceases to be efficient (i.e., when an I/O operation is desired) or until their completion.

The Cyber 170 is the latest step in a development which CDC started in 1963 by its announcement of series 6000. This series consisted of several models covering the range from medium-large to very large computers, the most powerful of its time. It was followed by the Cyber 70 series announced at the beginning of the 1970's and then by the Canadian-designed and produced Cyber 170 in the mid-1970's. The three series have basically identical organization and architecture and are upward compatible: that is, most programs written for the 6000 series work without any change on the Cyber 70 series and the Cyber 170 series. Computers in the same series are software compatible, using practically identical instruction sets. The differences between individual series are basically of two kinds:

1. Technological improvements such as the use of semiconductor

memories in place of core memories, use of the fastest ECL technology in the CPU, etc.

2. Modifications to satisfy market pressure (e.g., introduction of parity checking in the Cyber 170 which was not implemented in the previous series since CDC was confident that the reliability of memory was sufficient. Some users felt uneasy about this unusual omission.), and changes allowing further increase of the processing power, such as the addition of another memory, enlargement of the CPU instruction stack discussed below, etc.

The following is a brief description of the features of the Cyber 170 series, but most of it holds true for the earlier Cyber 70 and 6000 series. Note that all features are not available on all models in the series.

The System

Figure 8.37 shows the overall structure of a typical Cyber 170 system. Note that since there are several models in the series, there are also certain differences in the configuration. They are, however, relatively minor, such as the number of PPs, the details of the function of CPU units, etc. The basic organization is identical in all models.

CP is the Central Processor. It could almost be thought of as a very powerful ALU since it runs mostly under the full control of the PP executing the operating system. In all other respects it is, however, a true CPU. CP communication with the rest of the system is via the main memory, called also the Central Memory (CM) or Small Semiconductor Memory (SSM). This memory can act essentially as a very large cache memory. A small area in CM is reserved for communication with PPs. It is the "mailbox" in which all PPs and the CPU leave messages assigning tasks and reporting on their completion. CM is 64k to 256k 60-bit words and is thus large enough to hold large programs and sets of data. Complete programs can thus be fully executed from it without the need for swapping with the auxiliary memory. In this sense the computer does not have virtual memory. The entire contents of CM can be exchanged with a part of the much larger auxiliary memory (called the Large Core Memory— LCM —or Extended Core Storage, ECS) in a matter of microseconds. This and other features make it possible to implement extremely efficient multiprogramming. ECS is a core memory and as such is non-volatile and much faster

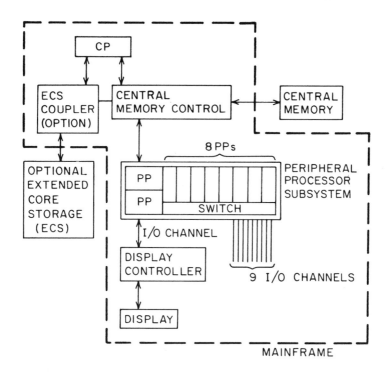

Figure 8.37   The simplified organization of a Cyber 170 series computer (Models 171 to 175 with one CP).

than secondary storage devices such as disks, etc. It is not an "executable" memory since the CPU cannot execute any instructions from it without moving them into CM first. It acts essentially as a very high speed buffer memory for intermediate storage between CM and I/O devices. Programs and data are transferred to and from it via a buffer space in CM by PPs. All PPs are identical but do not perform the same functions. They are 12-bit word minicomputers with dedicated 4k word semiconductor memories. They can independently access CM to read and write messsages and data. One of the PPs is assigned the supervisory role and controls the whole system. It determines which program the CPU excutes, assigns functions to individual PPs, etc. Another PP is permanently assigned to service the operator's console, displaying messages and data and allowing the operator to communicate with the system. All the remaining PPs are at the disposal of the system and perform I/O operations assigned to them by the operating system. I/O takes place via a number of Data Channels which connect PPs to I/O device controllers. The assignment of PPs and Channels is dynamic, is determined by the supervisory PP, and can be changed at any time.

One of the distinguishing features of the Cyber 170 series is its orientation towards computer networks. Its NOS operating system is specifically designed to allow the incorporation of the system into a network of cooperating computers. This is facilitated by the Host Communications Processor whose function is to retrieve messages from the network, send them, translate from one format into another, etc.

The CPU

It has already been mentioned that the system uses a 60-bit word. This very large size was chosen mainly to guarantee very high numerical precision to a computer whose intended application in the mid-1960's was mainly "scientific" programming involving large numbers of calculations, engineering, nuclear physics, etc. The large word size combined with the shortness of most instructions (mostly 15 or 30 bits and a few 60-bit instructions) has another benefit: a single word fetched into the memory contains several instructions, and instruction fetching is thus more efficient.

The ALU of the less powerful models (171-174) has two parts: the small arithmetic unit which operates on 18-bit operands and the large arithmetic unit which works with 60-bit operands (Figure 8.38).

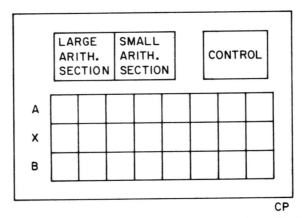

Figure 8.38   The CP of models 170 to 174 (simplified).

The ALU of the more powerful models consists of several functional units each of which performs a certain fixed operation such as one type of fixed or floating-point arithmetic or a Boolean operation (Figure 8.39).

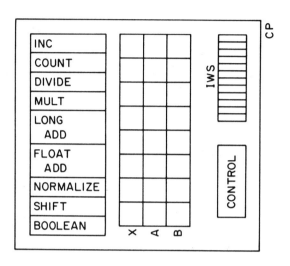

Figure 8.39   The simplified CP of models 175 and 176. Note the Instructions Word Stack (IWS) and the nine independent functional units.

The most powerful models can use any of these units simultaneously (see also parallel processing in Chapter 9) if the nature of the program allows it. Moreover, almost all of the functional units can simultaneously process a sequence of instructions (see also pipelined processing in Chapter 9). This arrangement and the use of the fastest ECL technology contribute to the extremely high speed of this computer: the most powerful model in this series can theoretically process up to 32 million instructions per second. This number would be achieved in the "streaming mode" —under ideal conditions of a program most suitable for the system structure. The instruction set consists of only 64 instructions belonging basically in eight categories. The general shortness of most instructions is due largely to the fact that most of them operate with eight CP registers (see below), each of which can be addressed by three bits. Three address instructions are very common. The purpose of the very limited number of instructions is to create a very simple and easy to use set whose small size makes it possible to use relatively short instruction formats with the advantages of reduced storage requirements and fast access pointed out above. Note that this advantage is practically eliminated by the fact that powerful instructions available on other computers have to be replaced by more or less long sequences of simpler instructions to perform the same operation. The negative consequence is the lack of certain very useful instructions such as decimal arithmetic, integer division, bit and byte manipulation, etc. This restriction is not serious for the scientific user who does not have much use for them. Other users can access the functions they need only via high-level programming languages whose compilers generate code which performs these missing functions in software. The speed of the computer is such that although this is a non-optimal solution these functions are still performed very rapidly. Execution is further speeded up by storing the instructions fetched into the CPU in a stack of 12 CPU registers—the Instruction Word Stack (IWS). This feature is only available on models 175 and 176. This greatly reduces instruction fetch time since for instructions forming shorter program loops, the entire loop can be present in the CPU during the whole length of its execution and individual instructions need not be repeatedly fetched.

The general purpose ("operating") registers are organized as follows: there are three types of programmable registers—address registers A, address modification registers B and data registers X. There are eight registers of each kind. Any change in registers A1 to A7 (under program control) automatically causes a change in the corresponding X register (e.g., automatic fetching of data into X from the new address). To prevent a "bottleneck" in the communication between the CPU and CM, five X registers are assigned for reading from CM and only two for writing into CM; most programs essentially reduce operands to results. The X0 and A0 registers have special functions. The data format of the CDC CPU is traditionally oriented towards numerical calculations. The essential unit is a floating-point number which can be single or double precision (one or two 60-bit words). Fixed-point numbers use 12 or 60 bits. Single-precision floating-point numbers use 48 bits for the mantissa in integer format and 10 bits for the magnitude of the exponent. The resulting accuracy is about 15 decimal digits. The maximum magnitude of the exponent is approximately $10^{**}300$. Double precision representation increases precision to about 29 decimal digits (the range of magnitude is unchanged). Fixed-point numbers use 18 or 60 bits with the maximum magnitude $(2^{**}59)-1$. The 18-bit format is useful for operations on addresses.

Number representation is related to 1's complement. Basic alphanumeric format is six bits in conformity with the upper-case ASCII code which was used by most computers of the 1960's. The extended character set with upper and lower case letters is represented rather inefficiently by a combination of two 6-bit codes. The whole 60-bit word can thus store only five "8-bit" ASCII characters. Two special number formats are the "infinite" and "indefinite" numbers. "Infinite" numbers are the result of overflow, "indefinite" numbers result from certain arithmetic operations (such as division) on infinite numbers. Both types are treated in a special way.

The Memory

Both memories are arranged in "phased banks," more commonly called interleaved banks; see Chapter 9. They consist of up to sixteen independent and identical modules (banks) assigned consecutive addresses: if location X is in bank 3 then location $X+1$ is in bank 4, etc. This arrangement makes it possible to access several consecutive locations simultaneously and thus to increase the transfer rate. CM can be accessed simultaneously by the CPU and several PPs if they are not attempting to access the same memory bank. Access to CM is under the control of the Central Memory Control which processes addresses, generates control signals, and resolves conflicts of attempted access to the same bank. In keeping with the subordination of everything to the utilization of the CPU, the processor has the highest priority of access.

Earlier CDC series had no error checking in CM. This was intentional since elimination of error checking speeds up processing and results in more efficient storage. Although this unusual approach seemed to work quite well, CDC introduced Single Error Correction and Double Error Detection (SECDEC) into all models of its Cyber 170 series. Each 60 bit word is augmented by 8 parity bits.

Comparison of Individual Models

The overall range of performance can be summarized by the factor 18 to 1 between the most powerful model 176 and the least powerful model 171. Some other parameters are summarized in Table 8.2.

Some peripheral devices offered with the Cyber 170 are as follows:

Disk drive model 844-21. Storage capacity 100 Mbytes, speed 3600 rpm, access time 30 milliseconds, number of platters per disk pack 11, transfer rate 0.8 Mbytes/sec.

Parameter\model	171/172/173/174	175	176
CP function	serial	parallel	parallel
Instruction stack	no	yes	yes
Central Memory	MOS	MOS	bipolar
Max CM capacity (60-bit words)	256k	256k	256k
Extended memory Capacity (maximum)	2M	2M	2M

Table 8.2   Some parameters of individual models of Cyber 170 series.

Tape drives. 7 or 9 track, 800 or 1600 bpi, speed 100 or 200 ips, length of tape 2400 ft, transfer rate 55600 to 320000 bytes per second.
Printer with output 1200 lines per minute. Card reader for 1200 cards per minute and card punch for 300 cards per minute.

8.4.4   Concluding Remarks

A student of computer organization might be misled into comparing computer systems by their hardware parameters. This would be a disastrous mistake. A computer system's power is measured by its usefulness to the user. A large computer system is a combination of complex hardware which creates a potential for a system and very complex software which makes the hardware available to the user. User communication with the system is via the software, usually provided by the manufacturer. Differences between the quality and orientation of software are surprisingly large. They include differences between the quality of translators (which determine how fast, for example, a FORTRAN program will actually execute rather than how fast it could execute given the parameters of the system) which are of obvious concern. In this respect there are differences not only between individual manufacturers but also between different products of the same manufacturer (e.g., FORTRAN and COBOL translators of the same product). The same holds true for other not so obviously important software components. For example, a text editor used to create program files may be very flexible, easy to learn and use or rather complex and inefficient, making program creation rather frustrating especially for a relatively inexperienced user.

The fact that each computer system is a collection of hardware and software must be kept in mind for comparisons between individual products.

REFERENCES

References in Chapter 7 provide a general introduction to computer architecture. The textbooks contain a few brief descriptions of selected systems. For more detailed information the reader should consult the Auerbach Reports or manufacturers' hardware manuals.

PROBLEMS

1. Consider a CPU using 16 bits for address specification. To obtain the full address in indexed addressing, at least one of the instruction fields and the index register must be 16 bits. Discuss the advantages of various combinations of sizes of the address field and the index register.

2. Give an example of a situation in which you need to test the contents of a memory location without affecting its contents.

3. Write a sequence of MC-6800 instructions to time 258 msec as accurately as possible.

4. Write a 6800 subroutine performing floating-point addition.

5. Justify the number of machine cycles required by various 6800 instructions.

6. Justify the statement that "a computer based on MC-6800 must have at least an elementary monitor program." List the desirable functions of the monitor.

7. Generate a random sequence of parameters for a sequence of jobs (independently submitted and executed programs) in a multiprogramming environment. Each job is to be characterized by the following parameters: time of submission, total CPU time required, time at which an I/O operation is requested during the execution of the job and the duration of the I/O operation. Compare the throughput (number of jobs executed in 24 hours) by simulating the processing of this sequence assuming

a. A computer system without multiprogramming which processes individual jobs in the original sequence to their full completion.

b. A multiprogramming system in which a job uses the CPU until it either fully completes execution or requests an I/O operation or exhausts the fixed amount of time allocated to it (the "time slice"). Experiment with the effect of the length of the time slice by varying it from 10 to 50 msec. Assume that overhead processing required by the operating system is five msec per time slice.

8. Multiprogramming and timesharing were introduced to improve the utilization of powerful and expensive CPUs and memories. It has recently been argued that the rapidly dropping costs of electronic components eliminate the need for multiprogramming and time-sharing in many situations.

   a. Give a qualitative justification of this claim and list some areas to which it does not apply.
   b. Give a quantitative justification assuming that a large operating system consists of about 100000 instructions, that an average programmer produces about 10 tested and documented instructions per day and is paid $15,000 per year.

9. Give an example of a situation in which it is necessary to test the contents of a memory area without modifying it.

10. Describe some situations in which a computer cannot take full advantage of its interleaved memory, its cache memory, and its parallel functional units in the ALU.

11. Prepare brief descriptions of other commercially available computers using, for example, the Auerbach reports.

12. Prepare a comparison of several commercially available computers on the basis of answers to question 14.

Chapter 9

A SURVEY OF TRENDS AND ALTERNATIVES

9.1 INTRODUCTION

This chapter presents a brief survey of concepts, alternative solutions, and trends of technical parameters which are important to provide a perspective of the recent past, the present, and an outlook for the near future in digital systems in general and computers in particular. The topics covered include:

1. Alternative approaches to processor organization and operation. This section presents the concepts of pipeline processing, multiprocessors, and computer networks. Alternative operational CPU principles such as reconfigurable computers, data base machines, high-level language architectures and fault-tolerant computers are also introduced.
2. Alternative memory organizations which include associative memories and interleaved memories in addition to the previously introduced concepts of virtual and cache memory.
3. Comparison of existing and emerging technologies, particularly in the fields of semiconductor technology and secondary storage (bubble memories, CCD and EBAM memories, and optical disk storage).

It will be seen that the main technical forces behind the exploration of alternative organizations and technologies are the search for faster processing, the need for increased storage capacities working at high speed, the requirement to improve system reliability, the increasing necessity to communicate large amounts of data at high transmission rates, the need for systems which consume less energy, and finally the pressure to adapt computer systems to more natural communication with the human user. In summary, the driving force is the need for more powerful yet affordable systems better suited for human use.

We will see that an enormous improvement in functional parameters has been achieved during the brief history of computers. At the same time it must be realized that even improvements which increase system performance by orders of magnitude are not sufficient. The generally valid observation that the appetite of a user of a system grows faster than improvements in system performance is particularly true for computer applications: computer designers will always be trailing behind the requirements of computer users and will always have to search for even better systems. This and the real potential for significant improvement are what make computer design so challenging.

9.2 PROCESSOR ORGANIZATION

There are several reasons why more and more powerful processors are needed: at any stage of development there are calculations that are too lengthy to be executable within reasonable time. Many of them are of obvious practical importance: accurate weather prediction, comfortable access to large data banks ("data base management"), applications of artificial intelligence and linguistics, real-time processing of certain types of medical data, military applications, etc. There is also the economic pressure to build a faster and more reliable processor than the competition. And then there is the natural human urge to surpass the existing limit.

There are essentially two approaches to the improvement of the speed and reliability of existing processors: to improve the building material (technology) and to improve the organization of the system. For the most powerful systems these two approaches will be combined. Developments in technology are the subject of Section 4. In the present section we will briefly present alternatives to the standard processor organizations presented in previous chapters. We will see that any of the alternatives can be applied at any level: the gate, register transfer, processor, and even system level. This should be kept in mind since only a few examples will be given.

To see how natural the alternative solutions are, consider the analogy of another processing system, a car producing factory. Assume that the company originally produces one car at a time in a workshop equipped with all the required machinery. When the demand exceeds the supply, the management has to start looking for ways to improve the production, i.e., number of cars produced in one year. Some alternatives are shown in Figure 9.1.

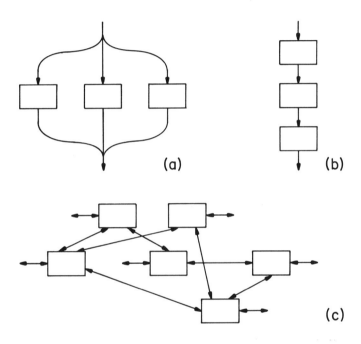

Figure 9.1   Alternative methods to increase processing power: (a) multiple parallel processing units, (b) segmentation of processing (conveyor belt or pipeline), (c) integration of processing systems (network).

1. Get more powerful machines and better qualified workers. There is a physical limit to the improvement of processing speed attainable by this approach and sooner or later other ways of improving productivity must be explored.
2. Build and equip more workshops, each of them producing one car at a time. With n workshops about n-times more cars can be produced in the same amount of time although in general the improvement will not be quite so large because of the need for coordination of individual workshops, occasional failures in the supply of materials causing stoppages in some workshops, etc.

3. The production of a single car can be broken down into a sequence of essentially independent steps, or segments, and the shop could be organized around a conveyer belt. Individual work stations would perform only a part of the process. For n equally long processing segments implemented as n consecutive work stations, productivity could improve almost n times in comparison with the original organization. n cars would be in production simultaneously at any time.

4. Considering the problem in the wider context, a car manufacturer, a truck manufacturer, and a tractor manufacturer could share some of their resources and in this way achieve higher productivity without the expense of ownership of all resources individually. The resources could include hardware (for example, the truck manufacturer could allow the car manufacturer to use the heavy press occasionally—for a fee), people (workers and engineers with special training might mutually help out), information (one could alow another access to information on suppliers, technological processes, etc.) and so on.

All these approaches can be combined if proper technology, sophisticated means of communication and management, etc., are available and economical.

Note that the alternatives can be grouped into three categories: technology, improved processor organization, and integration of independent systems.

Each of the above alternatives has its counterpart in computer design. With improving hardware and software and with decreasing cost of hardware, more and more systems incorporate these novel approaches. We will now explore the individual possibilities in our context.

1. Technological developments are the subject of Section 9.4.

2. Several processors working in parallel on a single set of data and executing the same operation constitute a *multiunit processor* or simply a *multiprocessor*. Multiprocessing can be implemented at various levels. At the gate level consider a parallel adder made of a number of identical full adders and contrast it to a serial adder made from a single full adder with a feedback. The tradeoff between speed and complexity and cost is clear. At the CPU level this approach can be implemented as several ALUs working in parallel to increase the speed of processing or to improve

the reliability of calculation. At the system level this may be implemented as several complete processors, each with its own CPU and memory, working together on the same task under the control of a central processor and sharing the same main memory. An example of a task lending itself to this type of processing is the calculation of sums of rows in a multi-row table (top of Figure 9.2). The ILLIAC IV computer with 64 parallel processors which was designed at the University of Illinois in the late 1960's is representative of this approach. It can be expected that the popularity of multiprocessing will significantly increase in the very near future, particularly with multiple inexpensive microprocessors cooperating in a single system. One major obstacle to a fast growth of multiprocessing is the problem of efficient utilization of the available hardware which is basically a software problem.

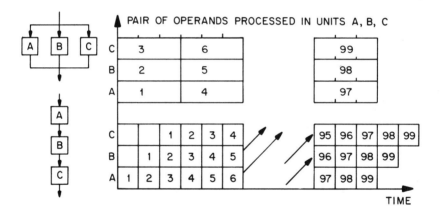

Figure 9.2   Space-time diagrams showing the processing of $x(1)+y(1)$, $x(2)+y(2)$, .. $x(99)+y(99)$ by a multiunit processor (top) and a pipelined procesor (bottom). Both processors are assumed to have three independent subunits.

3. Several processors working independently on consecutive segments of the same "macro-operation" constitute a pipeline. Pipeline organization can be used to speed up arithmetic processing (an arithmetic pipeline) or instruction execution (an instruction pipeline). As an illustration of an arithmetic pipeline,

consider a pipelined floating-point adder. Floating-point addition can be broken down for example as follows:

a. Alignment of exponent parts.
b. Addition of mantissas.
c. Normalization of the result.

Let A, B, C be the segments of the pipelined adder performing the individual operations. Assume that it is desired to perform the following operations:

$$x(1)+y(1) \ x(2)+y(2) \ \dots \ x(99)+y(99)$$

A three-unit adder can perform this sequence as in Figure 9.2 (bottom) which also shows a comparison with a three-unit parallel solution. It can be seen that the pipeline approach is slightly slower due to the need to fill the pipeline sequentially at the beginning and empty it at the end. If the number of independent operations is large, the difference is negligible. This is also the condition for the efficient use of the multi-unit adder, and the two approaches thus exhibit a similar speed improvement. The pipeline approach is more economical and therefore more popular. (Compare this with the car factory analogy.) Instruction execution can be broken down in a similar way. A typical instruction consists of

a. Instruction fetch.
b. Operand fetch.
c. Execution of operation.
c. Storage of result.

Note that there are situations in which the segmented pipeline will not work efficiently. In the case of the arithmetic pipeline, there is no improvement of speed if addition is needed rarely and only on a single pair of operands; in this case a multi-unit adder does not improve the speed either. In the instruction pipeline the smooth flow of processing is interrupted when a jump instruction is encountered or when an instruction needs the final result from the previous instruction (not yet fully executed) or when two consecutive instructions require the same resource (such as the ALU) at the same time.

In the ideal *streaming* mode of operation, the n-segment pipelined processor will operate almost n-times faster than a simple processor. This means that if the available technology limits the maximum processing speed to 10 million operations per second

(10 MOPS), a 10-segment pipeline should speed up processing to almost 100 MOPS. A similar conclusion holds for multi-unit processors. Note that while there is a limit to possible segmentation, due to the nature of the operation, and therefore the number of segments in a pipeline, there is no limit to the number of parallel units. In this sense the multi-unit approach presents the more efficient alternative, with the reservation that with the increasing number of units it is more and more difficult to find problems which will present a sufficient degree of parallelism to guarantee the efficient use of the multi-unit processor. This implies that although a multi-unit processor may theoretically offer a 100-times faster processing speed in the streaming mode, its real speed may be only twice the speed of a standard processor if the nature of the typical processed problems does not allow it to work in the streaming mode.

In the past when components constituted a major part of the cost of a computer, pipelining was implemented only in the most powerful and expensive computers. The latest advances of technology resulted in the implementation of pipelining in some form in many computers, even at the microprocessor level.

4. Individual computer systems can be connected together to form a *computer network*. In this mode users of each system may have access to all resources in the network: all programming languages, large data banks, high speed and expensive systems, specialized I/O devices, etc. This is the highest level of integration of software and hardware and presents problems, particularly in the area of software, communication between individual systems, and uniformity of sequences of control signals—*protocols*—used in the exchange of information between systems which are often produced by different manufacturers. Although several such systems have been in existence for a long time (SAGE in 1950's, SABRE, ARPANET, DECNET) the era of easy and generalized computer networking taking full advantage of all promises of the approach has not yet been reached. The topic of networks is further dealt with in a broader context in the section on distributed processing.

We will now examine some alternative solutions to computer design, some of them based on non-standard design goals.

9.2.1 Static And Dynamic Organizations, Fault Tolerance

It has been tacitly assumed that a computer system is designed to work with a fixed (static) organization. This is a natural but restrictive approach. Consider a 64-bit computer processing a typical program including arithmetic operations. Many of the arithmetic operations do not require the full 64-bit word for the processed data. This fact has been realized, and advanced computers include instructions to process partial words or multiples of the basic word size. This approach improves utilization of storage and may even improve the speed of processing. However, the data paths and other available resources are not fully utilized. A number of other examples could be given to show that the processing needs of a typical program or sequence of programs are highly variable. Yet they must typically be satisfied by a static organization. The result is inefficient use of resources, and this translates into lower speed than could be attained with full utilization of the available hardware.

A sophisticated computer system should be adaptive, capable of monitoring the requirements of the program or programs and able to adapt its configuration to the instantaneous needs. Its organization should be dynamic. The system should be able to reconfigure its organization. At one point in time a 64-bit processor could work as two independent 32-bit processors; at another it could work as sixteen 4-bit parallel units; and later it could dedicate its combined capabilities to process 64-bit words.

Reconfigurability of internal structure has been investigated for some time. The major problem is efficient adaptation of the system to the immediate needs of the situation, basically a software obstacle. At present, systems capable of reconfiguration in the general sense presented above are only the subject of research.

In a more restrictive sense computer systems which can adapt to changing conditions are already in existence. As an example one could name a number of fault-tolerant computer systems which have been designed to modify their internal structure automatically in the case of a failure of one of their modules. A well-known system of this kind which has proven the soundness of its design is the Bell No. 1 ESS (Electronic Switching System) system. This system has been designed to replace standard electromechanical switching in a large telephone exchange. This application requires very high reliability and availability which were specified as follows: the system must not be "down" for more than two hours over 40 years of operation and must be capable of unattended operation over long periods of time. This extremely high requirement is achieved by a combination of many methods which can improve reliability: the use of the most reliable components, duplication of all critical components and data paths, parallel operation, use of diagnostic software and hardware, detection circuits. The system basically consists of two parallel subsystems. One of them is "active" and performs the desired function; the other is performing the same operation in parallel but is in the "stand-by" mode. Special circuits continuously compare their operation. When a discrepancy is detected, both units automatically execute a fault recognition program which tests their function in the area in which the fault was detected. If one of the computers detects a fault in its operation, it is disconnected and repaired. The other computer then becomes the active system.

The cost of fault-tolerance is very high: highest technology components, duplication, extra checking and detection circuits, complex software, etc. It can only be used in situations in which it is essential. It is expected, however, that because of the declining cost of hardware and the growing volumes of production of complex LSI and VLSI components, some degree of fault-tolerance will be built into many computers in the near future. It is anticipated, for example, that one way to take advantage of increased density of integration will be to implement self-testing software and hardware, for example in the form of error detecting codes and circuits etc., into the more sophisticated VLSI chips.

9.2.2 Special Purpose Designs

The great majority of computers designed in the past were *general purpose computers*. These computers are designed to satisfy a very broad category of users and are suited for programs solving problems from a wide range of applications. They include all "business" and "scientific" (also called "number crunching") problems and in addition problems from the area of process control, etc. The statement of the suitability of the same system for all types of problems has to be taken with a certain reservation; most manufacturers design their computers to give particular satisfaction to either the business user or the scientific user. The differences are, however, relatively small. In particular, all general purpose computers are capable of processing all common high-level languages, although not with the same speed and ease.

The "general purpose" approach has been dictated mainly by economic considerations: the cost of hardware and design has been so high and the need for special computer organizations so limited that it has not been feasible to produce computers with specialized architectures commercially. This situation has been progressively but drastically changing with constantly decreasing costs of hardware and constantly growing need for new solutions. A number of new developments have been announced, and some of them are in the commercial domain. The new solutions are typically related to the use of microcomputers which represent the highest level of processing capability achieved so far and the least expensive processing power. In some applications microprocessors are too slow. In these situations the relatively slow operation of microprocessors is compensated for by parallel processing—a number of microprocessors working on the same problem in parallel. Some applications, such as those requiring large scale access to data, are particularly well suited for this approach.

Two of the special purpose architectures which received most attention and are already commercially available and under active development are *data base computers* and *direct execution processors*. Two examples of these organizations are given in this section.

Data Base Computers

The invasion of computers into business data processing has a long history. It started by replacing individual isolated manual operations by computerized processing and grew to the extent where almost all data is processed by computers. It became not only natural but also necessary to integrate the shared data into a single highly structured entity—a *data base*. *Data base management* is a field of computer science which deals with approaches to integrated control and access to shared data bases. The resulting systems are called *DBM systems* or *DBMS*.

The computer system of a company with up-to-date data processing facilities is capable of "ordinary" data processing, such as the calculation of payroll, plus sophisticated access to the data base. Note that tasks such as payroll calculation, etc., are themselves becoming parts of the DBM system. Access to a data base is typically content dependent: information required from memory is not defined in terms of its location in a specific region of the memory but rather in terms of its contents, such as "all employees whose salary is between $15,000 and $20,000."

Traditional computer organizations are very inefficient for this type of processing. (It should be mentioned that these organizations are called "von Neumann organizations" after one of the first pioneers of computer design who proposed them. As we know they are based on a single CPU executing sequentially a single stream of instructions and accessing memory which stores codes interpreted as instructions or data only on the basis of context, i.e., as instructions in the fetch phase and as data otherwise. Memory access is via a one-word wide bus and by memory address.) The memory-CPU bus becomes the "bottleneck" restricting the speed of processing so severely that even the most powerful traditional computers cannot achieve adequate speeds when used for accessing large data bases. The solution to this problem appears to lie in the replacement of the passive memory by an active "back-end processor" which is a combination of a processor dedicated to accessing the data base, a dedicated buffer memory, and large secondary storage for permanent storage of the data base information. The main computer (the "host processor") performs the standard processing functions and accesses the data base by issuing commands to the back-end processor and getting preprocessed information from it. The following is a description of the organization of a data base computer under development at Sperry Univac. It should be kept in mind that the intended use of the computer is not as a "stand-alone" system but in combination with a host computer. The perspective is better understood by viewing the data base computer as an active memory.

The simplified organization of the microcomputer-based data base computer (DBC) is as indicated in Figure 9.3. The function of the individual modules shown in the diagram is as follows:

DBC accepts host commands, acknowledges their completion, generates commands for microprocessors Pi, key processor KP, and MTDC. This processor can be a minicomputer, a special purpose processor or, for a smaller system and partially defeating the approach, it can be implemented in software on the host computer. The set of disk drives stores the data base information. The disks contemplated in this design have 300 Megabyte capacities and are capable of simultaneous transfer of up to nine tracks for increased transfer rate.

MTDC controls the parallel transfer between buffer memories Mi and the disks, performs error correction, etc.

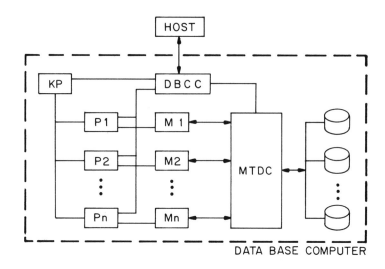

Figure 9.3   The simplified structure of a data base computer. The abbreviations have the following meaning: DBCC—DBC controller, Pi—i-th microprocessor, Mi—its buffer memory, KP—key processor, MTDC—multiple transfer disk controller.

Mi are buffer memories associated with individual microprocessors. Their sizes are chosen to match disk track sizes. After loading into Mi microprocessor Pi starts processing the loaded data. Processed data is passed to the host via DBC or to disks via MTDC depending on the operation and its result.

KP accelerates specialized data base operations. This is made possible by its several processors and memories and access to individual Pi's.

Note that the basic principle of the design is parallel access to and processing of data by individual auxiliary processors. An overall evaluation of the design on the basis of an analytical model resulted in the prediction that the system should work one or two orders of magnitude faster than the DBM system implemented on general purpose computers.

Direct Execution Processors

Writing programs in machine languages would be exceedingly complex, error prone, and uneconomical. Several hundred English-like general purpose and special purpose *High-Level Programming Languages* (HLPL) have been developed over the last twenty-five years which considerably simplify programming. Some of the most widely used languages are FORTRAN, COBOL, PL/I, APL, ALGOL, Pascal and BASIC. These languages cannot be directly executed by standard computers and have to be translated into machine language for execution. Translation adds an extra processing step and is very time consuming. In an educational environment at least 90 percent of the CPU time is spent on translation and the rest on program execution itself. Overall execution could be made more efficient and programming considerably simplified (e.g., the development of translators, etc.) if translation could be partially or completely eliminated. In addition, execution could also be made more efficient by tailoring a computer's architecture to a specific HLPL.

The topic of direct execution processors has been studied in the past and working processors built but not with commercial success, mainly for economic reasons. A partial exception to this rule are a few commercially successful computers whose architectures were designed to make it easier to develop efficient translators for certain types of languages; for example some Burroughs computers have been designed to be particularly well suited for the processing of ALGOL-like languages. The VAX computer also has instructions resembling certain common constructs of high-level languages. The situation of relative disregard for the development of software practice and theory from machine language to high-level language is now slowly changing, and the following paragraphs briefly describe a small commercial system partially belonging to the category of direct execution processsors. Note that this computer does not have a truly high-level language architecture but represents a transition between computers executing only low-level machine instructions and those processing high-level languages directly.

The *Pascal Microengine* produced by Western Digital is a microcomputer designed for use with the Pascal language. The system is not truly a direct execution processor in the sense that it does not directly execute Pascal programs. For execution on this computer, Pascal programs must first be translated into an intermediate language called the *p*-code (this translation is done on the computer) and the resulting program is then directly executed. The *p*-code is a language of higher level than a usual machine code and allows concise and efficient representation of Pascal programs at "almost" machine level. The processor is configured to execute *p*-code programs very efficiently.

The computer consists of a Computer Board, up to four disk drives, a line printer, and a standard RS 232 interface to which most standard CRT terminals can be connected. The Computer Board contains 64k RAM, I/O ports, and five chips which constitute the CPU. Three of the chips are ROMs which contain the microprogram which implements p-code execution. (The p-code is thus emulated.) The format of the ROMs is 22 bits and 512 locations.

There is generally much interest in computers and languages designed for direct execution. It should be realized, however, that direct execution of HLPLs is only the most visible manifestation of the growing influence of software on computer architecture. Traditionally, this influence has been minimal, particularly in the first phases of the development of new categories of computers: mainframes, minicomputers and microcomputers. When a computer category matures, the influence of software begins to grow. This influence began to be strongly felt particularly towards the end of the 1970's because of the growing disproportion between hardware and software costs. It is now clear that one of the tools for the reduction of the cost of software development is to design new computers with a more serious consideration of the state of understanding of the programming process. This new attitude is also economically more feasible today than a few years ago since LSI technology makes it possible to design such architectures more economically. At the same time software theory has progressed to the stage where the major trends and needs in HLPLs have become more clear. One of the major developments in the future of computer architecture can thus be expected to be a much greater respect of computer designers for the ultimate use of the computer: execution of programs developed in a high-level language.

9.2.3   Distributed Systems

During approximately the first two decades of computer development, economic considerations dictated building of increasingly powerful centralized computer facilities processing individual application programs in a way which attempted to optimize the use of the expensive hardware. In the 1960's the economic environment began to change. Hardware costs began to drop, and for a number of reasons it became feasible to give serious thought to commercial implementation of distributed computer facilities.

The idea of distributed processing in its full generality is, of course, much older. The term "distributed system" includes most of the topics covered previously in this chapter. It includes the distribution of processing elements within one processor (parallel and pipelined units), distribution of processing and storage within a localized computer system (associative memories, associative memories with block, word and bit processors, multiple processors, etc.), systems of multiple processors and multiple storage systems mutually interconnected by "switches" allowing unlimited communication and sharing of information. The most common meaning of the term is, however, the use of almost autonomous computers located at more or less distant locations and connected by a network of communication lines and controllers. These *computer networks* often employ a hierarchy of processors and *intelligent terminals*. In a typical configuration the processors would include several large computers with large storage capacities, connected to one another and to a network of smaller computers (minicomputers) and intelligent or "dumb" terminals and other I/O devices. Intelligent terminals are often standard I/O terminals equipped with a variable amount of processing power and storage — one or more microprocessors, RAM, and possibly one or more floppy-disk drives.

The concept of an intelligent terminal provides a good example of one of the motivations for distributed networks: in the past terminals were essentially passive I/O devices incapable of any complex processing. Information entered into them was coded (decoded) and transmitted to (from) the processor. Large amounts of "raw" data often had to be communicated over large distances and at large communication costs. The data had to be checked for correctness and processed — often in a very trivial way — by the very powerful central computer. Altogether, the utilization of the system was quite inefficient. In the last years of the 1970's electronic components became so inexpensive that the cost of a microprocessor and 64 kwords of RAM (the usual full addressing range of microprocessors) dropped close to the cost of a standard non-intelligent (dumb) terminal. This was the point at which the question of whether terminals should be equipped with more or less sophisticated processing capabilities and storage became economically justified. Intelligent terminals thus distribute many aspects of computing outside of the main processor. The basis of an intelligent terminal is a standard terminal augmented by some processing power and equipped with a program designed by the manufacturer or the user. The same terminal can then be tailored to perform one of a number of specialized functions or participate in data processing. It could, for example, be used in data editing (only the finalized data would be communicated to the mainframe), preprocessing (for example, calculation of summaries of data to be transmitted to the mainframe in place of the much larger set of raw data), local storage of some of the data, etc. The more powerful levels of the network can then be used for the more sophisticated types of processing, centralized storage, and access of shared data, etc. In summary, processing functions are distributed to the most appropriate processing units to make the best use of each resource. The net result is decreased cost of processing, significantly increased reliability of the processing system because of the multiplicity of functionally similar components capable of replacing one another, access to a large assortment of hardware and software resources (specialized I/O devices, compilers for uncommon programming languages, etc.), and decreased cost of communication because the information communicated is preprocessed and therefore reduced and processing is much more localized. The large processor in a computer network could have the structure shown in Figure 9.4.

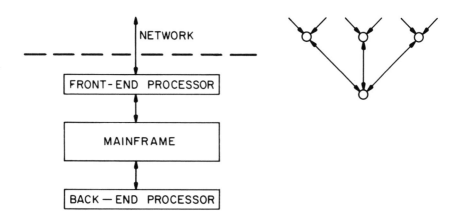

Figure 9.4   The structure of a mainframe participating in a
computer network.

The communication of this mainframe with the network and its own time-shared devices is handled by a specialized dedicated minicomputer—the *front-end* (or communication) processor. Its function is to receive, reroute, and send messages, resequence them, etc.: given the multiplicity of data paths and processors in the network, not all messages received by the front-end are addressed to its mainframe. They must be retransmitted to their true destinations. The route chosen for communication should be the best in some sense: the shortest length of communication, the least congested path, etc. The problem of routing is complex and very important. Messages received by the front-end are not necessarily received in the order in which they are to be processed. This is again due to the multiple data paths and the independent transmission of individual messages or their parts. Messages arriving at the front-end must also be stripped of their control and address information appended to them for communication purposes. This resembles the process in which a secretary removes a message from a letter, passes the message on for processing, and discards the envelope. Messages leaving the front end processor are augmented with all information required by the protocol established in the particular network, etc.

The *back-end* processor is basically a data base computer and could consist of one or more dedicated minicomputers and several banks of secondary storage containing data from a data base.

The above is only an example of a possible implementation and use of a computer network. Individual processors and terminals in various nodes of a network can be connected in several ways, with a variable number of interconnections, autonomous, or centralized control, etc. Message interchange can be organized in different ways; in particular communication protocols in different networks usually have different structure, etc. The motivation of a network usually is, at least at the beginning, to provide a large number of users with access to a large variety of hardware and software resources: I/O devices, compilers for different languages, compilers for the same languages on different computers, specialized utility programs developed at one particular center, etc. A large number of resources can thus be shared without the need for duplication. This may represent a significant cost saving. Another major incentive is reliability; a failing node of the network may be logically "masked out" and made invisible to the network while it is being repaired. Its function can be at least partially transferred to other processors and the whole system may be able to continue operation without visible degradation.

Distributed processing poses some serious problems, particularly in software. Ideally the network should be designed in such a way that the user need not be aware that the computer system being used is a network rather than a single computer: software must make the network "transparent" to the user. This requirement is combined with the need for several levels of processors to cooperate; access shared information; preserve data integrity so that information is not being modified by one processor at the same time at which it is being used by another processor, etc., and security since some users may be allowed full access to information while others may only be allowed to read it but not modify it, still others may be allowed to access only some of the information, etc.; capability of recovering from failures and reconfiguring network structure in the presence of a failure. Processors must be able to function synchronously when this is required by the task and independently in other situations. It is obvious that since a computer network is essentially a hierarchy of computer systems, the software required for a true network providing all the mentioned capabilities will be an order of magnitude more complex than software for a single computer.

Distributed processing is still very much an area of development in which practical achievements constitute a fraction of real needs and acknowledged possibilities. This is because the basic concepts of distributed processing— the distribution of processing and storage —only became economically attractive in the late 1970's. It can be expected that large scale distributed processing in the sense in which it was outlined in this section will become generally available in the second half of the 1980's. The concept of distributed processing must, however, be viewed as one of the most important concepts in computer organization since it will undoubtedly largely replace many of the current forms of information processing in the near future. The transition from isolated computer systems to cooperating and communicating nodes in a network can perhaps be likened to the transition from organic molecules to biological cells and will perhaps have a comparable impact on the relative capabilities of the corresponding systems and the processing of information in general.

9.3 MEMORY ORGANIZATION

Memory access is never fast enough to match the maximum possible speed of the CPU and in general presents the largest obstacle to faster operation of computers. A very fast memory is technologically feasible, but its cost would be prohibitive because of the enormous number of memory cells required in comparison to the complexity of the CPU. Even the fastest memories would, however, be several times slower than the fastest gates. As a consequence, access time can only be improved to match the fastest CPUs by a modified memory organization. In this sense the study of alternative memory organizations is even more important than the study of alternative CPU organizations.

The concept of a *virtual memory*, presented in Chapter 8, will now be briefly summarized in the following paragraph.

The term *virtual memory* refers to a hierarchy of main memory and secondary storage and the software/hardware techniques built into the system which make this hierarchy appear to the user as a single large homogeneous memory. The main reasons for implementing this concept are:

1. The need for a relatively large addressing space exhibited by some programs.
2. The relatively high cost of fast main memory.
3. The possibility of implementing the hierarchy in such a way that the speed of access of the virtual addressing space approaches the speed of access of its much faster and smaller component—the main memory.

The concept of a *virtual memory* is essentially a software one although the algorithms on which it is based can be implemented in hardware as well. These algorithms include in particular the conversion of virtual (logical) addresses to physical addresses and the relocation of blocks of data between the two levels of the hierarchy. In a virtual memory system these operations are typically controlled by software; and although the system appears as a large single memory space to the user program, it is treated as two levels by some system programs.

The future of virtual memories has been questioned by some designers who argue that the cost of semiconductor memories is declining so fast that it is becoming economical to design main memories large enough to match the storage requirements of even the largest programs and thus eliminate the need for virtual memory. Note that this does not imply that there will be no need for secondary storage which will still be needed to store programs and data between their execution.

The *cache memory* (introduced in Chapter 8) is basically a very high speed memory buffer inserted between the CPU and the main memory. In some situations the cache and the main memory are simultaneously accessible by the CPU. The purpose of the cache is to improve the match between the speed of a very fast CPU and the access speed of the main memory. This is not achievable economically by building a one-level high speed memory of the required very large capacity. The purpose can be achieved by using organization and techniques similar to those used by virtual memory systems. The main differences between the two concepts are in their exact role and implementation: access and manipulation of the contents of cache memories must be very fast, and the algorithms are thus implemented in hardware. The cache memory is thus inaccessible (transparent) even to system programs. The future of cache memories is in increasing their size with dropping memory costs and their access speed. A large computer system with a hierarchical memory can thus be viewed as in Figure 9.5.

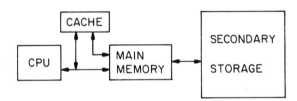

Figure 9.5   A large computer system with a cache memory which parallels the access of the CPU to a large virtual memory. The virtual memory consists of the smaller main memory and the large secondary storage. Some computers employ more than two storage levels.

The rest of this section presents two other modifications of the standard concept of memory organization: *interleaved memory* which is based on a modification of the standard physical access and *associative memory* which is based on a modification of the standard logical access. The first approach allows generally faster memory access essentially by a parallel organization. The second approach allows significantly decreased access time in those types of applications in which it is desired to access memory by the contents of memory cells rather than by the address. Access by content is needed, for example, in those cache memories in which information is stored in pairs (main memory address-value) and desired access is by the value of "main memory address." It can also be very useful in data base applications in which it is often required to locate a code exhibiting a certain pattern or contents (as indicated in the previous sections of this chapter).

9.3.1 Interleaved Memories

Memory access time limitations become especially critical when the processor is designed for very high operating speed, for example by using an instruction pipeline. Instructions and data then have to be fetched extremely quickly to match the speed of processing. The possibility of increased effective speed of memory access by using a cache memory has already been mentioned. Another approach is to use a wider word storing several instructions and fetching several instructions in one word. Instructions not immediately needed must be stored in an instruction buffer in the CPU. This approach has been demonstrated on the example of CDC computer families.

Another way to increase the speed of access is to allow access to different memory locations simultaneously or in partial overlap. Overlapped access is not possible if the memory has only one access "port" and if there is only one communication channel between the CPU and the memory. To make independent overlapped access possible, the memory must be divided into several *banks* which are independently accessible and which store non-overlapping areas of the total address space. This is particularly useful for the storage of instructions: programs mostly consist of sequentially stored and sequentially executed instructions. If the memory is divided into, for example, four independently accessible banks, the partitioning of the address space shown in Figure 9.6 will make it possible to access four consecutive instructions simultaneously which will lead to a decrease of the effective access time by a factor of four: in the amount of time that a single access can be made to a single bank, the CPU can fetch one word from each of the four banks.

bank #	addresses stored
1	0, 4, 8, 12, 16, 20, ...
2	1, 5, 9, 13, 17, 21, ...
3	2, 6, 10, 14, 18, 22, ..
4	3, 7, 11, 15, 19, 23, ..

Figure 9.6   Partitioning of the address space between four memory banks.

Note that the decision as to which memory bank is to be accessed to fetch the contents of a specified memory location is determined by the address of the location: a part of the address determines the bank;

another part the address of the memory location within the bank. The decoding process will be most efficient if there are 2**b banks since in this case the bank address can be stored in *b* bits of the address of the location, and there is no need for complex decoding.

The factor of improvement in the access time achieved by interleaving depends on the degree of sequentiality of the program. A jump instruction makes useless all the remaining prefetched instructions. Figure 9.7 shows the theoretical dependence of the average usage of the prefetched instruction sequence on the relative frequency of jump instructions in the program. This graph could be used to estimate how many banks would be needed in a particular environment (jump frequency) to achieve a desired improvement in access time.

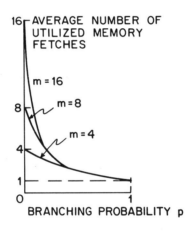

Figure 9.7   Average utilization of the prefetched instruction sequence as a function of the average frequency of jumps (denoted by *p*) and the number of interleaved banks *m*. The function is given by $(1-(1-p)**m)/m$. (Adapted from J. P. Hayes, Computer Architecture and Organization.)

9.3.2   Associative Memories

It has already been pointed out that it is sometimes preferable to specify the desired memory location by its contents rather than by its address. The need for this type of access can be found in most programs. They include most programs which work with a table. It is, of course, possible to write a program to search a table stored in a standard RAM. The disadvantage of this approach is that programmed search is typically much less efficient than hardware search, both in terms of memory space measured by the number of locations needed for the table and the program, and by the time required for the search. The possibility of replacement of software by hardware is a fact that we have already encountered. We know that any sequential operation and therefore any program can be converted into a digital hardware system performing the same function. This dedicated digital system generally works faster and does not need to store any programs in the usual sense. One of the main problems with replacement of software by hardware is that we are trading off the flexibility of a general purpose computer for the speed and complexity of a special purpose device. In general, replacement of software by hardware cannot be economically justified. Table searching and similar memory access by contents is, however, an exception because this problem is a standard part of most computer programs and in the category of data base applications it is one of the major parts of most operations. Modification of the system (its memory part) to implement this operation in hardware is thus justifiable if a suitable technology is available. Existing LSI and emerging VLSI technologies make associative access an attractive and justifiable approach.

Memory cells of associative memories must be more complex than standard RAM cells. They have to allow

1. Ordinary RAM access since access by contents does not eliminate the need for access by address, and
2. Access by contents or partial contents consisting of a comparison of the sought pattern and the contents of the cell plus the generation of a signal indicating whether a match was found or not.

An elementary content addressable memory cell consists of a flip-flop and a decoding switching circuit of about five gates. This is a significant increase in complexity when it is realized that a single memory cell of a dynamic memory consists of a single electronic component as compared to around five components for a typical gate. Associative memories—also called content addressable memories, abbreviated as CAM—are thus much more complex and costly, particularly since they are not yet in large demand. They are at present used as standard components only in some cache memories. This situation will probably change in the near future because of the progress in data base applications which work with enormous amounts of data and require very efficient access and also because of the progress in technology.

Associative memories can be combined with distributed processors (or vice versa—associative memories can be obtained from ordinary RAMs by adding dedicated processors) to provide much more sophisticated processing capabilities. Development of such *content addressable processors* has begun relatively recently.

9.4 TECHNOLOGY

This section briefly surveys a wide range of topics related to the physical principles, manufacture, parameters and their trends of commercially available technologies and promising technologies under development. It is divided into two parts: technologies related to processor and main memory components and secondary storage technologies.

The goal of this section is to help to formulate a perspective of the reality which can be used to extrapolate historical trends into the near future. Only selected topics judged as most important are considered.

9.4.1 Processor And Main Memory

9.4.1.1 Current Technologies. The integrated circuit is the basis of processor design of all modern processors and of most main memories (secondary storage will be dealt with independently). Presently available ICs in this category are all based on semiconductivity. *Semiconductor* devices act like valves controlling the passage of electronic current with a minimal dissipation of control energy. Almost all existing devices use *silicon* as the basic building element, but research into new semiconductor materials, in particular Gallium Arsenide—GaAs, has been recently quite promising and it is possible that other materials with better functional parameters—mainly speed, density, and power consumption—will start playing a more prominent role.

Presently available ICs are based on either *bipolar* devices or *MOS* devices. Broadly speaking, bipolar devices are based on the use of both positive and negative carriers of electric current while MOS devices are essentially unipolar.

Each of the two main categories has a number of subfamilies. They differ in the materials used, the basic circuit components, production processes, etc. These differences have implications for maximum attainable speeds, power dissipation, density (usually measured by the number of circuits equivalent in complexity to gates that can be placed on a chip of a given size), yield (average percentage of good chips obtained in the manufacturing process), cost (related to yield, complexity of manufacture, etc.), difficulty of electrical interfacing, noise resistance, etc. In general, the two families can be characterized as follows:

> Bipolar devices are faster, less dense, require more power and are more expensive. Representative parameters of the two families will be presented shortly in the context of memory ICs. Processor and memory technologies are basically identical.

It should be noted that this general statement applies not only to a comparison of the average parameters but also to the top representative devices. The trend is towards a decrease in the differences of parameters between the two technologies. Yet the difference is sufficiently large to lead to the use of bipolar devices only in those functions in which they can be economically justified such as in the processor and in cache memories and the use of MOS technologies where the required number of devices is too large (main memories), where density is very important (particularly very complex circuits produced on a single chip, such as advanced microprocessors), or where minimal power consumption is required.

The following is a rather detailed description of the state of semiconductor memories at the beginning of the 1980's. It is presented because of the enormous importance of memory devices in computer systems and because the state and developments in memory technologies are characteristic for the top technology semiconductor devices.

Semiconductor Memories

Memories have always been at the forefront of development in ICs. This is due to their very regular structure which makes them ideal for the full utilization of all technological advances (density and speed improvements, etc.) and also because of the unlimited need for ever increasing capacity, faster storage media, and lower cost. Memory ICs have developed as highly standardized devices; pin assignments of many established memory devices produced by different manufacturers are identical, and different ICs electrically interchangeable. Memories are truly universal components: the same devices can be used in any application with any type of processor from micros to mainframes. The demand for memories and the competition in this field have been the major forces behind the development of IC technologies. The recent progress has been such that several experts have predicted that semiconductor memories will soon become competitive even with secondary storage devices in certain applications.

Two major problems with semiconductor memories have been their cost (otherwise there would be no need for secondary storage) and their volatility. The cost factor improved very quickly, and semiconductor memories started to become standard in main memories around 1970, replacing the then standard core technology. Reduction of the cost per bit of storage continues at a constant rate.

The volatility problem has been attacked by developing two types of semiconductor memories: read/write volatile RAMs and read only non-volatile ROMs.

ROMs were originally programmable only by the manufacturer, and the writing of permanent information was a part of the manufacturing process. The abbreviation ROM is still used in this restrictive sense. Unchangeability—the unpleasant restriction of ROMs—and the persistence of a need for a non-volatile read/write device led to the development of several new categories of memory devices intermediate between ROMs and RAMs. The present commercially available types include the following:

1. ROMs as defined above. They are typically produced from the fast and power dissipating bipolar technology. The typical parameters at the beginning of the 1980's, as the other parameters in this section, are: access times 25 to 100 nsec for sizes 8k to 16k bits, power consumption around 800 mW.

    It is expected that this category of ROMs, will be replaced by MOS ROMs, whose speed parameters are beginning to approach speeds of bipolar devices; MOS ROMs with access times 80 nsec are available—and programmable ROMs discussed below. The reason for this is the large difference in power requirements and cost, high density and reprogrammability. MOS ROMs have reached 64k bit densities at the time when bipolar ROMs reached 16k. The upcoming 256k devices are seen as strong competitors of disk and tape and especially CCD devices in some applications.

    ROMs are generally memory devices with the largest capacity. ROM densities are typically three or four years ahead of RAM densities. This is due to the simplicity of the ROM storage cell which is essentially just a connection between the address decoder and the output.

2. PROMs are user programmable ROMs which cannot be reprogrammed. Progress in this category is fast. Parameters of ROMs and PROMs are comparable except for their density; ROMs are denser because they do not require selective programming of a finished chip. Densities of PROMs are about one half the densities of ROMs. Typical uses of fast bipolar PROMs with access times around 25 nsec are in fast control stores. MOS ROMs with competitive speeds but higher densities, smaller power consumption, and lower cost are beginning to penetrate even into this application.

3. Reprogrammable PROMs are commercially available in three types which differ in their physical principle and the way in which they are reprogrammed. They are all MOS devices since the principle of rewriting conflicts with some basic properties of bipolar devices.

UVEPROMs (ultraviolet light erasable PROMs) can be programmed electrically and erased by ultraviolet light. The operation can be repeated any number of times. The disadvantage of this category is the partial volatility—ultraviolet light from any source (e.g., the sun) in sufficient quantity erases the stored information. These devices remain very popular because they are well suited to most applications in which information has to be changed from time to time and in the development of new products. The 1980 top density is 32k bits with 64k bit devices just becoming available. Power consumption is lower as in all MOS devices—around 500 mW in active use and around 100 mW in the standby mode. CMOS devices use especially little power, typically around 1 mW. They are very well suited for applications requiring the use of small batteries, etc. CMOS is presently lacking in other parameters—speed, density, and cost—but the predictions are very good.

EAROMs are electrically alterable ROMs which can be altered in the circuit without removal and UV light. Alteration can be selective; individual words or even bits can be modified selectively. These devices are not so sensitive to environment and are ideal for applications in inaccessible areas where maintenance is difficult or impossible. The drawback of this category in its prospective use as a non-volatile read/write device is its limited access speed; writing is several orders of magnitude slower than reading which has access times around one microsecond. The cost of EAROMs is also relatively high.

EEROMs are electrically erasable ROMs. They are similar to EAROMs but cannot be altered in the circuit. They are typically about four times faster than EAROMs. Their densities are comparable—8 to 16k bits at the beginning of 1980's.

RAM integrated circuits are also bipolar or MOS.

Bipolar RAMs are faster but consume more power, are less dense and more expensive. The two currently most popular bipolar families which differ in the structure of their basic circuit are TTL and ECL. TTL devices are slower, and MOS devices are approaching their speed while providing better values of other parameters. The consequence is a shift from TTL to the faster ECL which is expensive and consumes even more power. ECL is the fastest commercially available technology with access times around 10 nsec for 1k bit devices and 35 nsec for 16k bit devices. The future of bipolar memories is in ECL devices for very high speed systems such as sets of CPU registers and cache memories.

MOS technologies are developing faster than bipolar and are at the center of semiconductor development. The two basic kinds—static and dynamic—are getting closer in their parameters with static devices being faster (access times below 100 nsec), requiring less support (no refresh), and being less sensitive to noise. Dynamic memories are around four times denser because their storage cell is much simpler: the cell of a dynamic memory uses a single transistor and a capacitor to store a charge while static storage uses a more complex transistor-based flip-flop. Dynamic memories achieve the top densities, 64k bits at the end of the 1970's. This density is just at the boundary between LSI and VLSI technologies. The next stage (256k devices) will bring new improvement in overall parameters and further reduce the cost per bit of memory assemblies since it will cause a four-fold decrease of size and complexity and a 50 percent reduction in power requirements. It will also lead to further improvement of reliability. Dynamic memories also use less power than static memories. New static memories are approaching dynamic memories in power consumption, around four times less than TTL and five times less than ECL. Because of their high speeds (top devices approaching TTL speeds), they are replacing TTL memories in some high speed applications. An interesting development in the rich assortment of organizations is the production of 9-bit memory cells with the ninth bit intended for parity.

A rapidly growing technology is CMOS. Its major advantage is very low power consumption during active use and almost zero consumption in standby mode. It is expected that CMOS will develop into one of the fastest and most attractive memory technologies, mainly due to its very low power consumption: bipolar and n-MOS technologies are quickly approaching their "thermal barrier." The power dissipated by the most advanced devices in these families approaches the limit of dissipation per unit of area that can be handled in normal situations without critical overheating which would lead to decrease of speed and eventual destruction. CMOS technologies can progress a long way from their present minimum line width before reaching this limit since their power consumption is 10 to 100 times less than that of MOS devices. As a consequence, only CMOS can comfortably support significant increases of density. And increased density is the main tool in achieving higher speed, reliability, etc. Because of this and other prospective advantages CMOS has been called the LSI process of the eighties. It will be particularly in the LSI and VLSI devices where its advantages will be determining.

Another promising memory technology which does not directly belong in the previous group is EBAM (Electron Beam Addressable Memory). It is a developing category which can be loosely classified as a semiconductor technology since it uses MOS semiconductor areas for storage. Data is stored as charges in microscopic MOS capacitors, whose diameter is around 1 micron. The charge is created or modified by a beam of electrons; the passage of a single electron generates a charge equivalent to several thousand electron charges. To achieve reading, the electron beam modifies the elementary charge, and the change in charge is locally amplified and transmitted to the output of the device. EBAM systems consist of subassemblies resembling CRT tubes (oscilloscopes and TV sets) consisting of a source of the beam of electrons, the focusing circuits and plates, and the target area which stores the information. At the end of the 1970's capacities reached about 1 Mbyte/tube with systems consisting of over 20 tubes and achieving access times around 10 microseconds and transfer rates around 1 Mbyte/second. EBAM developers predict that storage capacities of many billion bits per tube will be achieved and that cost of storage will drop to millicents/bit. EBAMs are non-volatile. With these parameters EBAMs could become the memory technology to bridge the gap between relatively expensive semiconductor main memories and the relatively slow secondary storage memories if the predictions of the late 1970's materialize.

Figure 9.8 compares speed and power parameters of the most promising semiconductor technologies. It can be seen that the best parameters in most respects are offered by the GaAs technology. This technology is, however, only in the development stage, and its manufacturing process presents some problems in comparison to silicon-based processes. No GaAs digital devices were commercially available at the beginning of the 1980's although MSI devices were produced experimentally. Expectations are high especially for LSI and eventually VLSI components.

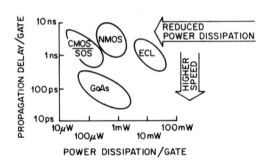

Figure 9.8   Speed/power parameters of IC technologies at the end of the 1970's. (From "Semiconductor Memory Update"—Part 3 by E. Hnatek, *Computer Design*, February 1980).

After this examination of various aspects of semiconductor memories, let us survey the typical manufacturing sequence of a semiconductor device. The *manufacturing process* is sufficiently similar for all families so that it can be justifiably termed semiconductor technology. The manufacture of a typical semiconductor IC consists of the following sequence of steps:

1. A 3-inch diameter cylinder of extremely pure crystalline silicon is produced.
2. The cylinder is cut into hair-thin (about one-fourth of a millimeter) circular "wafers" which form the basis (substrate) of the IC chip. Many identical chips are produced from one wafer in one manufacturing sequence. The exact number and size depend on the density and complexity of the circuit, the purity of the silicon crystal, the level of technology, etc.
3. The following sequence is repeated several times to obtain a multilayer chip. The individual layers (typically five to ten on each chip) serve as electronic elements with different roles: connectors, isolators, etc.

a. The wafer is coated with a light-sensitive material.
b. As many copies of a "mask" of the given layer as there are chips to be produced from one wafer are copied onto the surface in a photographic-like process referred to as lithography. Each layer has its own mask which has been obtained as a result of a lengthy design process which constitutes the main factor in the final cost of the IC. It has been estimated that the cost of the design of the most advanced ICs is around $100/gate implemented.
c. Photographic-like development removes the exposed coating, creating multiple copies of the mask. It should be noted that the process is operating with microscopic dimensions. The current minimum width of a line is just above 1 micron (0.001 mm), and is thus extremely sensitive to the accuracy of alignment of successive layers, microscopic dust, purity of the substrate and the atmospheric environment, resolution of the mask, etc. All these factors critically affect the production yield.
d. The exposed surface is modified in the desired way, by introducing new materials into the exposed surface to create the desired physical properties.
e. The rest of the protective coating is removed. The result is that the surface is in the original condition except for those parts of the material which were modified in step d.

4. Individual chips are rigorously tested. This process is particularly complicated and lengthy for the most advanced chips which are tested on computer-controlled testing machines in a process which may require over 100 testing steps. The goal of testing is not only to eliminate faulty chips but also to detect those which would not guarantee the extremely high required reliability (as high as the average of at most 30 failures/billion hours of operation in some applications) and help to locate sources of problems which will serve to improve the manufacturing process and design.
5. The wafer is cut into individual chips.
6. Good chips are packaged. With increasing chip densities and growing difficulty of providing connections to other chips and satisfactory removal of dissipated heat, this step in the sequence is gaining growing importance. New techniques are under development (e.g., ceramic chip carriers capable of holding over 100

chips, QUIPs—similar to "dual-in-line-packages," DIPs, but using four rows of contact pins instead of two—are already used, etc.) which reduce the problem of insufficient number of pins for interchip connections. Typical ICs are packaged as follows:

a. Chips are placed on a base which has pins attached to it.
b. Contact areas on the chip are connected to the pins, under microscope.
c. The package is sealed by having a top bounded to the base. The packaging material is usually plastic, sometimes porcelain. UV erasable ROMs have the memory part exposed through a quartz window which allows penetration of ultraviolet light for erasure and provides mechanical and electrical protection.

It can be seen that the process is very complex and highly automated. It poses very stringent requirements on the purity of materials and the working atmosphere: the previously used standard "at most 100 airborn particles of 0.5 micron size in one cubic foot" was found insufficient. The necessary accuracy of the optical process is extremely high. As an example, alignment of successive layers requires about four times higher accuracy than the minimum line width used. The equipment is very expensive; its design as well as the design of the chip culminating in the design of masks requires highly skilled engineers. The time required for design is very lengthy, for the most complex chips around one year. The required reliability may be very high, and this requires very thorough testing. Testing of VLSI components has to be considered during the design of the chip; very complex circuits will not be testable if special testing circuits and test points are not provided.

9.4.1.2 Trends Of Parameters. IC technologies became available in the early 1960's and have since undergone an enormous progress which is summarized in Figure 9.9.

The progress is related to a number of factors some of which are observable in the graphs:

1. The development of better circuits which tends to improve the density and/or speed of the device. As an example, original memory ICs used six elements/cell, some of the modern devices use only one. The modern memory IC thus has higher density and speed and lower power consumption. It has been observed

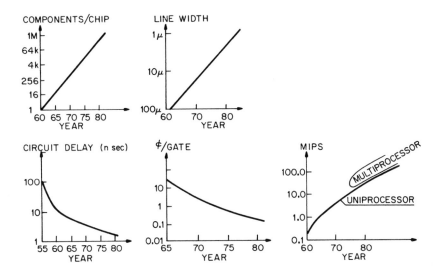

Figure 9.9   Aproximate trends of the top values of some IC and related parameters.

that reliability depends relatively little on chip complexity. This implies higher reliability per function for more complex chips.

2. Manufacture: The achievable purity of the basic silicon material has increased by several orders of magnitude. This has led to much improved production yields and thus reduced cost of the final product. This can be seen from the fact that the cost of a finished IC is largely independent of its complexity if a large quantity is produced. This implies that complex components are relatively less expensive since they require fewer ICs. As an example, the cost per bit of memory elements tends to be smaller for larger chips and moreover declines in time. A similar observation holds for reliability.

The lithographic process used in the transposition of masks on the chip became much more accurate, and the minimum width achievable with traditional optical lithographic techniques approached the physical limit of 1 micron: the same order of magnitude as the wavelength of the light used in the process. For a comparison note that a common living cell has a diameter of about 10 microns. Note that the typical values of line widths used in commercially produced ICs are about four times bigger.

Increased resolution means that denser chips can be produced. Further progress can be achieved only by using new principles rather than by improving parameters of existing technologies. X-ray and electron beam techniques working with radiation of higher frequency and therefore allowing better resolution (0.1 micron for X-ray lithography) are being explored, and several devices based on these techniques have been manufactured at very high costs. The absolute physical limit of possible reductions of geometry has been estimated to be about 0.25 micron. At this dimension microscopic electrical phenomena make further progress very doubtful. It should be noted that further progress does not depend only on obtaining high resolution manufacturing devices but also on the mastering of the other steps of the manufacturing process which also happen to require new methods for sub-micron line width, solution of the problem of power dissipation (higher densities result in higher power dissipation by the same chip area), solution of problems associated with the higher order phenomena (physical processes negligible on the macroscopic level but significant at the sub-micron level), etc. Existence of these problems is known, and their solutions in principle are possible. They do, however, require further development.

An example of a problem associated with the increasing density is the "soft error." Soft errors are transient errors that were first observed towards the end of the 1970's. They appear only in dense memories, such as the new 64k bit RAMs and the 256k bit CCD chips. They manifest themselves as relatively very infrequent distortions of individual isolated bits in the chip. Their cause can be understood by comparing the amount of the electrical charge used in the storage of a single bit in these memory chips (which is basically a function of the area of one memory cell—about 100 square microns for the 64k RAMs—and the technology and circuit used) and the amount of spurious charge generated by the passage of, for example, a cosmic ray or a similar high energy particle through the silicon material. The particle generates about six times more elementary charges than the total used for the storage of a single bit in a CCD cell and can, therefore, modify the stored information. These high energy disturbances come either from the packaging material itself (trace amounts of uranium, etc.) or from the atmosphere. There does not seem to be any way of preventing this phenomenon by shielding of the chip and further purification of the packaging material. The only solution appears to be the use of error-checking and error-detecting codes. Note that in this sense, development of higher density chips is somewhat counter-productive since one of the reasons for high density is to reduce the cost of memory and the use of error correcting/detecting codes requires extra memory. The rate of occurrence of soft errors in a single chip is relatively low; it has been estimated at seven soft errors/million hours of operation for a 64k bit RAMs and 3000/million hours for the 256k CCDs. These numbers have to be judged in the light of memories consisting of a large number of chips and working in systems often requiring very high reliabilities.

3. Transition to new principles which make it possible to achieve better parameters within the same families. These developments are often related to progress in technology. As an example, the P-MOS technology was mastered earlier than the N-MOS technology, but once the more powerful N-MOS circuit technology was made commercially feasible, it replaced almost completely the older P-MOS technology.

It has already been indicated that progress often brings new problems: sub-micron densities require transition to new manufacturing principles, the need to consider phenomena insignificant at lower densities, the problem of power dissipation, etc. Some other factors which emerge as obstacles to further increase in device density and speed are:

1. Speeds of the fastest devices are approaching values comparable to the speed of light. The speed of light is the speed of propagation of electromagnetic signals. It makes no economic sense to produce devices which work so fast that they can use their speed only 10 percent of the time and have to wait for the signal to propagate most of the remaining time. In other words, there is little advantage to increasing speed beyond a point where the speed of the system is determined mainly by the length of connecting cables.

Consider a hypothetical gate with a propagation time of one nanosecond. The operating speed of this device corresponds to the time required by an electromagnetic signal to travel about 30 centimeters. As a rule of thumb, one could conclude that the CPU, memory, and I/O interface should be designed into a

30×30×30 centimeter cube. Note that a partial solution to this problem is to increase densities even further and so reduce the length of signal paths to a microscopic (intra-chip) level. We have seen that this poses other problems. Furthermore, it is anticipated that new technologies now under development (the Josephson junction described in the following section) will work at picosecond speeds, i.e., 100 to 1000 times faster than the current fastest technologies. At these speeds, gate delays correspond to signal path lengths of the order of one millimeter. Fortunately, these devices will probably be packed much closer than current ICs because of their very low power dissipation. Yet the basic dilemma remains: are ultra fast devices economically desirable when the speed improvement impacts on packaging and interconnection restrictions? The answer lies in the development of new technologies partially removing physical obstacles and improved organizations minimizing the effect of physical restrictions on overall system performance.

2. Very high density is desirable when it can be used to produce devices which take full advantage of the improved physical parameters and offer significant economic and parametric improvement. There is no point in improving achievable densities ten times if there is no device that one might desire to put on a single chip of this complexity and if its manufacture and use are not economical. Note that this implies the solution of a number of problems related to design: how to improve the efficiency of the design process, how to make it faster, cheaper, and error-free. This problem requires the development of algorithms for automatic circuit generation, automatic mask generation, etc. At present there are several computer programs that have been used to automate individual steps in the design process in commercial environments. The usefulness of existing algorithms is somewhat limited because they produce results much less efficient than those obtained by "manual" design. As an example, the topologies of circuits obtained automatically use the chip area only about 25 percent as economically. However, given the fact that the design of a sophisticated microprocessor at the end of the 1970's required about sixty man-years and the debugging another sixty and also the state of art of the manufacturing process which allows extremely high levels of compaction of the circuit on the chip, even this performance may be economically very attractive in specific situations. In spite of this achievement, the present state of Computer Aided Design (CAD) in digital

electronics is lacking, and much work is needed before an automatic translation from a logic description into a finalized and tested chip layout by a "silicon compiler" reaches a satisfactory level.

3. Another problem is how to make the resulting circuit testable. A very complex device has an enormous number of possible modes of operations. How can the manufacturer prove that each shipped chip performs faultlessly all the functions for which it was designed? How can the manufacturer design an automatic testing machine and test sequences, preferably automatically? Which of the multitudes of functions should be tested and which tests should be bypassed? How should the designer include the requirement of testability into the design of the chip? An extremely complex but untestable device is useless.

4. There is also the economic uncertainty of the balance between supply and demand for semiconductor components. It has been estimated that if the present trends of improvement of parameters and growth of production (production volume growth about 50 percent per year) continue then by 1985, there will be so many digital ICs in the world that they will be equivalent to two mainframe computers for each inhabitant of the Earth. Is this situation economically feasible? Semiconductor manufacturers feel that it is if new applications are found for digital systems and they are confident that they will be found.

5. Another difficulty is the problem of the cost of continued research and development. It has been estimated that the cost of development of the 16-bit microprocessors of the late 1970's was between 10 and 30 million dollars—much of this is the cost of software for these ICs. The cost of the production equipment for these ICs and the latest 64k bit RAMs has been estimated at 50 million dollars. Research and development costs in the semiconductor industry grew from about 25 million dollars in 1960 to about 250 million in 1980. It is clear that in the future even the largest manufacturers will have to combine their resources, cooperate with governments, and develop methods of reducing the cost of development.

9.4.1.3 Parameter Perspectives For The Near Future. There are essentially two ways in which physical parameters of devices can be improved:

1. Find and/or develop principles which have not yet been implemented.
2. Improve existing technologies.

The following is a brief overview of what can be predicted for the next decade or so on the basis of extrapolations of past progress, of current research and development, and in the light of physical limitations.

1. It has been estimated that if the parameters of *semiconductor* devices continue to develop at a rate comparable to the present trends, then the progress over the next fifteen years will result in the following situation:

   An eight-fold increase in density (memory sizes increased to 1Mbit/chip) with access time reduced to 20 nsec, reduction of gate delays from between 1 and 10 nsec to between 100 psec and 1 nsec and unchanged power requirements for the increased complexity chip.

   This prediction is considered to be rather conservative and has been carefully justified on physical and technological grounds: it was shown that the physical limits of miniaturization, which is the basis of improvement of all essential physical parameters of computer systems, will not be reached within fifteen years at the current rate of progress. It was also shown that the technological problems do not represent new questions to be solved but rather the introduction into production of processing methods mostly already known and tested in laboratories.

   Some experts, however, have argued that the obstacles to continued development will be growing and that present trends should not be automatically extrapolated into the future. The anticipated problems are of two kinds: technological and economic.

   Technological problems arise because the new stage (sub-micron technologies) presents a qualitatively new situation whereas the last two decades presented essentially only problems of improvements of parameters of existing technologies. In the present situation completely new methods have to be developed and new physical problems—conductivity, insulation, heat dissipation, etc.—have to be surmounted.

   The economic problems have already been outlined. They include the creation of an economically justified need for huge amounts of extremely complex ICs and the very high cost of progress.

   Given the conflicting predictions (most of which are very optimistic), one should perhaps assume a cautiously optimistic attitude: progress in parameters is certainly possible and will doubtlessly occur. It will perhaps take somewhat longer than some experts predict, particularly if viewed as a simultaneous progress in all parameters. As an example, it is possible that the recent observation that the pair speed-power dissipation does not develop in the predicted harmony will become more generalized.

Another word of caution is in place for the interpretation of the impact of progress in electronics on the world of computers: it has been observed that it usually takes about five years between the commercial availability and the implementation of a new technology into commercial computers. This means that the technology available in 1985 components will become common in commercial computers only around 1990. It must also be realized that the parameters cited in connection with the latest technologies are the top values reachable in circuits with ideally regular structures. Typical parameters of more common components are much less impressive: the highest densities are achieved only on homogeneous components such as RAMs. Parameters (particularly component density) of less ideal systems such as microprocessors are significantly lower since much of the area of the chip (typically 80 percent) is occupied by passive connections between the active parts of the circuit.

2. At least one *new technology* seems to be very attractive for use in processor and fast memory systems. It is based on a discovery made by Josephson in 1962 which has not yet been exploited commercially but is presently under intensive investigation. This principle is known as the *Josephson junction*. Its operation is based on a combination of super-conductivity (the property of several materials to lose electrical resistance at temperatures around 4 degrees Kelvin, i.e. −269 degrees C, the temperature of liquid helium), semiconductivity and electromagnetism. The principle potentially allows extremely high speeds (psec delays) and extremely low power consumption (due to the disappearance of a resistance). The manufacturing process can be derived from IC technologies and because of the very low power dissipation it would allow chip densities much higher than attainable with standard semiconductor ICs. One of the problems facing this technology is cost: systems working with Josephson junctions would require a supercooler to hold liquid helium and maintain it at the required very low temperature.

At present only gate level experimental circuits have been designed and successfully tested. It is expected that another five to ten years will be required just to prove or disprove the viability of this technology. Available results indicate that the Josephson junction has potential. It has been argued that it may prove to be less expensive than generally predicted, particularly with developments in cooling technology. Researchers state that Josephson junction computers may prove to be not merely the only solution where extremely high processing powers are needed but may also become economically competitive down to the level of medium-sized computer systems. It should be noted that no further major discoveries are needed to allow implementation of this new technology, only refinement of existing technological processes and solution of non-critical problems are needed.

The following example gives an indication of the possible parameters of Josephson junction based systems:

It has been conservatively estimated that a computer with parameters exceeding those of one of the largest mainframes—the IBM 370/168 whose CPU and I/O channels comprise around 120000 logic circuits—could be implemented with Josephson junction devices as follows:

The CPU with 16 Mbytes of main memory (around three times more than IBM 370/168), 32 kbytes cache memory, and I/O channel logic could be placed into a box 15×15×15 centimeters. It would require about 7W of power to operate: a standard light bulb requires 60W. It would operate about 20 times faster than the IBM system, at 70 M instructions/second (MIPS), about one million times faster than a typical microcomputer. Improved parameters and multiprocessing could bring the rate to over one Gigainstructions/second (1 Giga = 1 billion). The system is expected to be extremely reliable.

The described Josephson module would have to be placed in liquid helium to maintain its low temperature and provide cooling. This requires a cooling system which has been estimated as a cylinder 120×70 cm. The cooling compressor would require about 15 kW (Figure 9.10). In this light the very low power consumption of the processor is not too important in most applications.

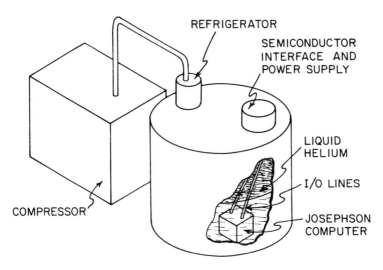

REFRIGERATOR

SEMICONDUCTOR
INTERFACE AND
POWER SUPPLY

LIQUID
HELIUM

I/O LINES

COMPRESSOR

JOSEPHSON
COMPUTER

Figure 9.10   The physical configuration of a hypothetical supercomputer based on a Josephson junction CPU and main memory. (Adapted from "Computing at 4 degrees Kelvin," W. Anacker, IEEE Spectrum 1979).

Note that the example is purely hypothetical since only the first exploratory steps have been made so far. Only time will tell whether the technology is viable. Yet this approach opens a very serious alternative particularly for very powerful computers. It could make possible calculations which are prohibitively long for today's computer systems.

9.4.1.4 VLSI Devices. There are a number of reasons why the highest density available should be used as much as possible. Some of them are:

1. High density leads to higher speeds at system level. This is because interdevice connections are replaced by microscopic connections between areas on the chip implementing the modules of the system. The system is compressed from the multi-IC level to the chip level.
2. Overall power consumption is reduced for similar reasons, but the problem of cooling becomes more serious.
3. Reliability of the system is increased, mainly because a large number of macroscopic connections are eliminated.

4. The physical size of the complete system may be considerably reduced.

5. A system based on VLSI components may be much cheaper than the same system built with smaller scale integration modules. This is because the cost of a chip is relatively independent of its complexity and the cost of connections, mounting boards, etc., is significant. Reducing a system from the size of 1000 chips to a single chip can thus reduce the cost in a comparable proportion. A similar reasoning partially justifies improved reliability.

6. Maintenance of the system is simplified. This is because of the reduction of the apparent complexity of the system and its increased reliability. It has been stated that modern computers would not be possible with old technologies since extremely high reliabilities are essential to guarantee acceptable reliability of the modern, very complex systems.

The problem with VLSI devices is that they are very expensive to design, get ready for production, and test. Their production cannot be justified unless there are very good economic reasons. This means that any device contemplated for VLSI implementation must have a sufficiently large universal appeal to guarantee production in very large quantities, or ways must be found allowing economical design of "custom chips" to be produced in limited quantities.

There are several categories of devices that satisfy the condition of general appeal. The first category includes very regular circuits whose density can be increased and the demand remains. The typical component in this category is the RAM chip. Another category includes existing popular devices enhanced by additional capabilities. As an example, one could consider devices which are almost always connected to other ICs, such as registers. These standard companion functions can be placed on the same chip. This will make the new device even more attractive than the old IC already known to be popular. As another possibility, one can consider adding various testing and self-testing features to complicated ICs, such as microprocessors. An interesting enhancement is the addition of error checking circuitry to memory chips, enhancement of arithmetic functions of the device, enhancement of CPU organization such as a pipeline, etc. Another approach is to use high density to enhance the yield of production: Bell Laboratories announced a "desensitized" 64k RAM. This is a 64k chip with 5 percent more memory cells than needed.

During wafer testing the partially faulty chips can have their non-working areas disconnected and replaced by the spare memory cells. Connections are broken and made by a laser beam. The sensitivity of the manufacturing process to defects limiting yields is thus reduced. We will see that this strategy is common in magnetic bubble memories which are covered later in this chapter.

The third category includes devices which can be economically used in many different applications and which can be made to perform various functions depending on the application. In other words, devices which can be programmed in one way or another. Some candidates are as follows:

Switching circuits are arrays of AND and OR gates, often functioning as multiplexers. VLSI integration makes it possible to enhance the complexity of MSI and LSI devices such as PLAs and multiplexers.

An example of the possible direction of evolution based on standard MSI devices is the 29693 Field Programmable Multiplexer (PMUX) produced by Raytheon. This device is equivalent to four 8-to-1 multiplexers such as the standard 74151 and contains some additional input circuitry (Figure 9.11).

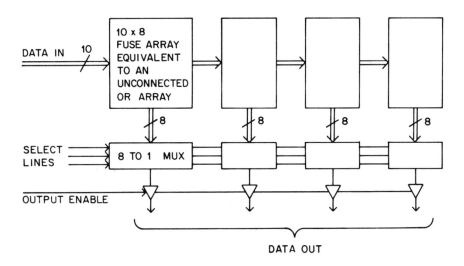

Figure 9.11   The basic internal structure of the 29693 PMUX. The device is equivalent to four 74151 multiplexers plus extra decoding circuitry.

Other examples include the "fuse array" which has the function of an array of OR gates whose connections can be electrically destroyed to obtain the desired logical function, and Field Programmable Gate Arrays (FPGA)—arrays of programmable AND gates with electrically programmable input connections.

In most applications gate arrays need to be connected to flip-flops to form more or less complicated sequential circuits. This need can be satisfied by enhancing PLAs with flip-flops, programmable feedback connections, tri-state outputs, etc. (such circuits are known as programmable Array Logic—PAL, and Storage/Logic Arrays—SLA). Some of these devices are commercially available; others are under development.

The need for LSI and VLSI programmable logic arrays arises since in the majority of sophisticated digital devices the circuit consists of a few LSI and VLSI devices such as microprocessors, memory chips, and I/O interface chips and a large number of SSI chips which condition and generate control signals, etc. SSI and MSI chips typically account for up to 50 percent of the board area and the complex interconnection pattern on the board. Devices such as PMUX, PALs, and others could substantially reduce the complexity of the device by replacing the majority of the SSI and MSI devices implementing "random logic" functions which cannot be economically implemented as special purpose ICs because of the relatively low volume of the specific random application.

Another example is Motorola's Macrocell Array. Its basic structure is a large number of unconnected components—an Uncommitted Logic Array (ULA)—which is completed according to customer's specification into a circuit of up to 1200 gates.

Another category includes devices which can support widely used components and extend their basic capabilities. An example is Intel's 8087 "coprocessor" which is a programmable IC designed to strengthen arithmetic capabilities of the 16-bit 8086 microprocessor.

Those LSI and VLSI devices which prove to be popular will become relatively very cheap. They will offer very effective digital design solutions with all the advantages of programmable logic discussed previously and extremely cheap computing power but relatively expensive development of software. This is of particular interest to computer scientists who will have to reverse completely their thinking about computer systems: present treatment of computer systems is based on the premise that the CPU and memory are very expensive facilities which must be used very efficiently, very carefully and expensively programmed for optimal utilization. This situation is drastically changing with the perspective of very inexpensive computing power at almost unlimited speeds and with a large variety of possible operations, with much larger memory space than common today. This technological progress will be reflected in more powerful organizations, particularly the growth of distributed processing. The progress in hardware technology and the decline of hardware costs have to be contrasted with the slowly developing situation in software and the growing cost of its development. To appreciate the impact of the changes in digital technology, one should think of the historical analogy of the transition to mass production of automobiles and how it changed the world.

9.4.2 Secondary Storage

Disk, drum, and tape drives have one common disadvantage: the mechanical motion of the storage medium. Mechanical motion imposes limitations on access speed, reliability, possible reductions in physical size, and power consumption, etc. The mechanical principle can be partially blamed for the enormous gap between access times for electronic memories and those for secondary storage devices. This gap is clearly visible in the graph shown in Figure 9.12. It should be pointed out that diagrams of this type have to be interpreted very carefully. As an example of their potentially misleading character consider the parameters of floppy disks. They are inferior to the corresponding parameters of comparable devices, and one might conclude that they are of little practical interest. This would be quite false since floppy disks are produced with small storage capacities; and although their cost per bit is higher, their absolute cost is considerably smaller than that of "hard disks." They are thus very popular in applications requiring limited storage capacity. This conclusion cannot be deduced from the graph in Figure 9.12 since only two of a number of important parameters are presented in it.

Two relatively recent developments—magnetic bubble memories and CCD memories—offer commercially available electronic alternatives to mechanical secondary storage devices, sometimes referred to as "solid state disks." Another category of promising secondary storage devices—the optical storage device—is a possible solution to another problem, the limited storage capacities due to limits on achievable storage density. These three new varieties of secondary storage are briefly surveyed below. The EBAM technology described in a previous section can also be included into the category of semiconductor storage devices. The presentation of semiconductor secondary storage technologies is followed by the description of trends in traditional secondary storage devices.

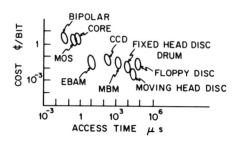

Figure 9.12   The cost/speed diagram of main and secondary storage technologies. (Adapted from "Semiconductor Memory Update," Part 3 by E. Hnatek, *Computer Design*, February 1980).

9.4.2.1 Magnetic Bubble Memories (MBM). These devices are based on the principle that strong magnetic fields can make certain materials form controllable microscopic magnetic domains (bubbles) polarized in one of two directions. The information stored in this way can be maintained permanently by a permanent magnetic field, the "bias field." Maintenance of information does not require external power; storage is non-volatile. There are no moving mechanical parts; the bubbles are accessed at fixed locations to which they are moved by an external electromagnetic field, the "drive field." At these fixed locations bubbles can be read and rewritten, i.e., modified. The production technology is closely related to standard IC technology and the achievable densities comparable to those of standard semiconductor ICs.

It can be seen from this brief description that MBMs are sequential access devices. Their speeds are therefore in the range of sequential devices—access times around 10 msec and maximum transfer rates 100kbits/sec—and they belong into the category of secondary storage. This is also justified by their storage capacities. One Mbit chips were the largest commercially available in 1979, but capacities up to 10 Mbit/chip are expected by 1985. This improvement will be achieved by reducing the size of the bubble below one micron.

The most popular organization of an MBM device is the major-minor loop shown in Figure 9.13. In this organization information is maintained in a number of minor loops. It is transported to the fixed access locations by a major loop from which it is returned to its original minor loop, possibly modified by a write operation. MBM chips are manufactured with extra (redundant) minor loops which can be used to substitute malfunctioning regular minor loops. Access to the chip is under the control of an MBM controller.

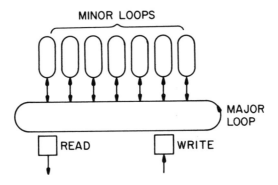

MINOR LOOPS

MAJOR LOOP

READ   WRITE

Figure 9.13   The most common organization of MBMs, the major-minor loop structure.

MBM devices began to be available commercially at the end of the 1970's. Their parameters—speed of access, storage capacity, cost, etc.—are expected to undergo a dramatic improvement in the early 1980's. They are expected to become very serious competitors to disk storage. Because of their very small size and insensivity to environment (dust and vibrations) they will find applications in many situations in which disk drives are not feasible, such as terminals, microcomputers, control of industrial processes, etc. MBM power requirements are much smaller, around 1W for a 1 Mbit chip.

It should not be concluded that MBMs will totally displace disks. Disk storage has at least two advantages at this point of development: the fastest disk systems have faster access times and the storage medium is removable, at least in some disk drive categories. This means that a single disk drive can be used to access an unlimited amount of information stored inexpensively on a number of relatively cheap removable disks. This is not possible with MBMs. From the point of view of cost MBMs have the advantage of a relatively very small initial cost while disk drives represent a large investment from the start. This observation about MBMs will, in the future, probably be true even for floppy disk drives. Like all modern electronic devices, they also have the advantage of practically unlimited durability in comparison with their mechanical counterparts.

As an example of an MBM chip, consider the 7110 produced by Intel Magnetics in 1979 (Figure 9.14). It contains 256 storage loops (minor loops) with 4k-bit capacity each for a total of 1Mbits/chip. In addition it contains redundant loops for a total gross capacity of 1310720 bits and loops for storage of error correction codes related to the use of redundant loops. The DIP package contains bias magnets, coils to generate the drive field, and a protective magnetic shield. Its size is 3.5 square inches. The maximum gross data rate is 100kbits/sec. Power consumption is 1.9W in operation and 0 in the standby mode. Up to eight of these devices can be controlled by a single 7220 controller. Eight 7110's forming a 1M-byte memory device, the 7220 controller, and the required additional circuitry can be placed on a single printed circuit board which requires close to 0W in standby mode and 16W in full operation. The transfer rate of this storage module is up to 68kbytes/sec—less than the number derived from the gross transfer rate of a single 7110. This is because of a slowdown due to the presence of redundant loops. An interesting and useful new feature of MBMs is that access can be frozen at any time (by interrupting the circulation of stored bits) and resumed from the same point whenever desired.

An interesting feature of MBMs is that access (i.e., circulation of stored bits) can be frozen at any time and resumed from the same point whenever required. This very advantageous feature is not available with disk storage.

9.4.2.2 Charge Coupled Devices (CCD). CCD devices store information as positive or negative charges. Except for this difference in the physical principle and the volatility of CCD devices, they have much in common with MBM: they have very similar parameters and organization, the manufacturing process is similar (based on standard IC technologies), they are both seen as competitors to disk storage (with CCD presenting better access characteristics) with low power dissipation, significantly smaller physical size, and much higher reliability. For both CCD and MBM the cost-capacity relation is basically linear (as was indicated in the previous section) which is not the case for

Figure 9.14   Shown in actual size, is a complete one Mbit bubble memory system with support electronics. (Courtesy of Intel Magnetics.)

mechanical disk and tape storage. This makes them suitable for small secondary storage and secondary storage modifiable in small increments of capacity. CCD is expected to start filling the access time gap between semiconductor memories and secondary storage devices. The technology is at about the same stage of development as MBMs, i.e., at the beginning of commercial utilization.

Recently, the interest in CCDs seems to have diminished somewhat. This can be understood in the light of the continuous decrease of RAM costs and the increase of memory chip density. After all, the only justification for secondary storage is the high cost of main memory and its volatility. CCD memories are potentially cheaper and denser but also volatile. If the difference in access time is not balanced by a sufficiently large difference in cost, there is no justification for commercial interest in CCDs. The future of CCD depends on the success of 256k CCD chips which are expected in the first half of the 1980's. Note that MBMs are immune to this argument since they are non-volatile. An example of a commercially available CCD chip is the F 464 produced by Fairchild. It has a 64k bit capacity, 40 millisecond average access time, 5Mbit/sec transfer rate, consumes 0.34W in operation and 66 mW in standby. It has 16 pins.

9.4.2.3 Optical Recording. Unlike CCD and MBM memories which are already commercially available, optical storage is still in development. The recording technique is similar to that used in video recording. As an example of optical storage implementation, consider the system developed by the Dutch manufacturer Phillips.

The storage medium is a double-sided disk with a 12" diameter. It is coated with protective material which makes its mechanical handling very insensitive to the environment; access is optical and does not require microscopic distances between the medium and the access device as do magnetic disks. Optical access to data is through the protective layer. Information is stored by a laser beam focused very accurately on the surface of the pregrooved disk below the protective layer. Information is stored as microscopic holes one micron in diameter produced by melting the surface by the powerful laser beam. One disk can store up to 10^{10} bits. Data are read by sensing a less intense reflected laser beam which responds differently to a hole than to a smooth surface. The disk rotates at 2.5 rps (150 rpm), and the groove is tracked by an optical system positioned on a movable arm. Because of the extremely high storage density, the attainable transfer rates are around 10^{10} bits/sec. Average access time is rather slow—250 msec but can be shortened to 70 msec by increasing the speed of rotation. The existing system can only read (a "postable" medium for single writing and repetitive reading) since no suitable materials capable of modification of stored information, i.e., writing, are yet available. It is, however, expected that read/write storage media will become available within a few years.

Optical disk storage is attractive because of its very high storage density. One potential application is as an "archival storage" medium in which very large amounts of unchangeable data need to be stored over long periods of time. Another advantage of optical disks in this perspective is their relative ease of replication.

9.4.3 Traditional Secondary Storage

The outline of new secondary storage media should not be interpreted as a suggestion that disk and tape storage is becoming obsolete and that it has reached the limits of its development. This conclusion would be completely incorrect.

It is quite true that MBMs and CCDs generated a great deal of pressure on the manufacturers of disk and tape storage devices, but this pressure is very healthy and the traditional storage devices are expected to be able to face it successfully, except in some borderline areas and applications. The reason for this is that neither disk nor tape storage devices have yet approached their physical limits and there is room for higher densities and improved access speeds. Their low cost/bit has traditionally been their major advantage. In addition, both the tape and the (removable) disk storage have the advantage of interchangeability of the storage medium which MBMs and CCDs cannot provide. This means that once the relatively expensive drive is available further expansion of ("off-line") storage capacity is relatively inexpensive. This comment does not apply to non-removable disks which, however, have other advantages, in particular higher speeds.

To document the potentials of disk and tape technologies, consider the following two observations about developments in disk storage technologies which could be paralleled by similar statements about tape storage:

1. Parameters of disk storage devices have been developing for the past twenty years at the following rates: area density grew from 2000 bits/square inch in 1956 to 6000000 in the late 1970's. This led to increased capacities: from 5 Mbytes in 1956 to over 600 Mbytes in 1976, improved access times 925 msec to access 4k blocks in 1956 to 39.6 msec in 1976, and reduced cost per bit $153 per Mbyte to $2. The improvement in density has been used to liken a single "hard disk" to 10000 memory chips used as an entity. These advances were accompanied by improved reliability.

2. A new variation of disk storage appeared in the early 1970's, which was ideally matched with the emerging new category of small computers and applications of computer technology in data processing not immediately belonging to the category of computers. In 1970 IBM introduced the floppy-disk device. This floppy used a flexible diskette eight inches in diameter. Only one side of the diskette was used for recording. Very soon this device was

modified to allow double-sided recording and then recording using double storage density. At the same time a modification of this technique appeared which used a 5.25 inch diskette (the minifloppy) much more suitable for applications such as word processing in office environment, etc. Even smaller diskettes are now under development. Typical present parameters are a capacity around 1Mbyte for floppies and around 400 kbytes for minis, transfer rates around 100 kbits/sec, average access times around 100 msec, cost of disk drive around $300, and cost of diskette around $3.00. The future developments of this category will be to improve the parameters which make the floppy a very inexpensive and relatively fast secondary storage device with significant storage capacities.

9.4.4   The Impact Of Advancing Technology

In the context of this book the influence of rapidly advancing information processing technologies should be studied in at least the following categories: impact of technology development on computer design, on engineers and computer designers, and on the whole society. The following paragraphs present an attempt to evaluate briefly the implications for the named categories.

9.4.5   The Impact On Computer Design

This problem has already been implicitly raised in the preceding paragraphs. It was shown that the most desirable tendency is not only towards faster and cheaper processing power which will soon become automatically available as a result of the present technology. It is desirable to turn more attention to the easier use of computers and their increased reliability. One aspect of this trend is manifested by the increase of "intelligence" of previously non-intelligent devices such as terminals. Further progress in this direction requires the study of high-level programming languages and of ways in which computer architectures can be made more responsive to them, the study of better hardware and software interfaces between computers and their users, the study of trends of uses of computers such as the need for large and easily accessible data bases, and the study of alternative architectures of the "non-von-Neumann" category. A major consequence of the available inexpensive processing power will be a major shift to all forms of distributed processing. The center of interest of many designers will shift from the development of faster and denser chips towards computerized design and more economical ways of developing software: a microprocessor chip now costs less than a single line of a typical program. This shift has to be seen partially as a consequence of the decrease of cost of hardware.

9.4.6   The Impact On Engineers And Computer Scientists

Restricting our attention to those involved in computer design, we can characterize their future as one in which the rate of generation of new knowledge keeps growing: the development of LSI ICs took less time than the development of transistors which took less time than the development of vacuum tubes. The knowledge necessary for the participation in digital design is getting deeper and wider since overlapping specializations tend to merge. The overall role of software in digital design grows at the expense of circuit design. Design is becoming more sophisticated and requires constant study and retraining to keep up with the advancing technology.

9.4.7   The Impact On Society

Predictions in this category are the most difficult to make. Some aspects are quite obvious: the growing productivity, automation of production, the need for retraining for new and existing jobs, appearance of new jobs, and disappearance of old ones. These are all familiar appendices of technical progress. They will manifest themselves at a much higher rate when technology begins to affect information processing and control seriously. The amount of free time will increase, and its utilization will become a major question.

Beyond these obvious conclusions, much depends on the reactions of the society at a local, national, and international scale. Some predictions are very gloomy and include Orwellian Big Brother control over individuals. Others are very encouraging, predicting increasing democratization of a society in which each individual has rapid and almost complete access to all forms of information allowing much more informed decision making and control over all levels of government. This should be accompanied by increasing education via distributed networks allowing access to computer assisted educational programs, libraries, works of art, etc. Which of the two alternatives will prevail depends mainly on each individual's concern and participation and to a non-negligible extent on the general understanding of the principles, possibilities, and limitations of information processing by computers.

9.5 CONCLUDING REMARKS

This chapter summarized some of the most interesting and talked-about developments related to computer organization and technology. Many have been omitted. As an example, much is expected of the latest progress in optical communication in particular in connection with the growing importance of distributed processing. Nothing was mentioned about developments in I/O devices which underwent changes almost as impressive as traditional secondary storage but became increasingly expensive in proportion to electronic hardware components, etc.

The situation in computer systems can be summarized as follows: advances in electronics can be safely predicted to continue at about the same rate for at least another fifteen years. Electronic components will remain the driving force which other components of the system will have difficulty in matching in cost, speed, size, reliability, and power consumption. The gap is now enormous and will keep growing at the same rate. The decreasing cost of electronics is counterbalanced by the growing cost of software and the non-decreasing cost of mechanical components such as I/O devices. Concepts of computer organizations are available which make it possible to increase the speed of computer systems beyond the speed of their constituent components. Distributed processing in particular is a very promising direction. More complex organizations pose very difficult software problems. It is in this area that the future development of computers presents the most difficult problems.

REFERENCES

A growing number of books deal with various specialized and unusual approaches to computer architecture. Books by the following authors belong in this category: Doran (deals mainly with the somewhat uncommon architecture of computers produced by the Burroughs company), Myers (devoted mainly to the impact of software on computer architecture), Foster (content addressable processors), McGlynn (distributed processing), Bray and Freeman (data base computers). For an interesting and wide-ranging discussion of the perspective of computers and their influence on the society, the reader is referred to the excellent book, *The Computer Age—A Twenty Year View*, edited by Dertouzos and Moses. Most of the information summarized in this chapter has been obtained from the proceedings of various general-topic conferences such as Compcon, AFIPS, Wescon, etc. and from journals such as *Computer, Spectrum, Computer Design, EDN, Electronic Design, Computers and Digital Techniques*, etc. Particularly useful sources were Hnatek's "Semiconductor memory update," in *Computer Design* and Anacker's "Computing at 4 degrees Kelvin," in *Spectrum*. IC technology is covered in *Introduction to VLSI Systems* by Mead and Conway. A large amount of material related to data processing technology is available in Phister's book.

PROBLEMS

1. Research the state of art in one of the following fields and write a summary illustrated with graphs: semiconductor memories, LSI and VLSI components (types, speeds, densities, complexities, cost, power consumption, etc.), secondary memories (traditional and new), input/output devices (printers, display and graphics terminals, plotters), data communication, personal computers, computer aided design (particularly in logic and circuit design), cost of research and development. Use recent journals as sources.

2. Research the development of the changing influence of computers on society covering the period 1960 to present. Consider the role of computers in fields such as business data processing, engineering and scientific calculations, government use, computers in process control and manufacture, computers in appliances and other control applications, computers in education and at home, computers in art.

3. Use your research from previous questions to extrapolate present trends into the future. Correct mechanical extrapolation by considering limitations of physical parameters, limited needs, high cost of reasearch and development.

4. Compare ten-year-old predictions of the development of digital technology with reality and use your conclusions to formulate a corrective formula to judge present predictions.

5. Suggest attractive new applications for computers.

GLOSSARY

Access Time. The average time required to read a fixed amount of information, such as a word, from a storage device.

Address Space. Range of main memory addresses accessible with the given instruction set.

Addressing Mode. Method of obtaining the address of memory location at which operand is effectively stored (effective address). The common addressing modes are direct, indirect, indexed, register, inherent, relative and immediate, where the value is part of the instruction code. See also corresponding entries in the Glossary.

Alphanumeric. The class of characters including letters, digits, and certain punctuation symbols. Also called alphameric.

ALU—Arithmetic and Logic Unit. A subunit of the CPU performing arithmetic and logic operations as directed by control signals generated by the control unit of the CPU.

Analog. In a restricted and imprecise sense used as the opposite of digital. Refers to signals whose value changes in a smooth fashion and components and systems working with and sensitive to such signals.

Analysis. In the context of systems used to denote the process of deriving the description of the behavior of a system with known structure.

Archival Storage. Extended storage used for very large collections of data.

Array Processor. A special purpose processor or attachment to another processor designed to efficiently process programs for problems related to arrays or vectors of data.

427

ASCII—American Standard Code for Information Interchange. The most common coding system for the representation of characters.

Assembly Language.   Programming language of intermediate level of abstraction. Uses symbolic codes for machine codes and alleviates programming in some other respect. Programs written in an assembly language must be translated into machine language by a computer program, the assembler. Vary from one computer to another along with the machine language.

Associative Memory.   A memory whose access is based on the contents rather than the address of memory location. Also referred to as content-addressable memory.

Asynchronous.   Used to refer to systems in which transitions between internal states occur as soon as they are required by changed inputs or states, without the control of a clock signal. Opposite of synchronous.

Auxiliary Storage.   Synonym for secondary storage.

Availability.   The degree to which a system is ready when needed.

Back-End Processor.   A computer subsystem attached to a large computer (the host) to relieve it from access to secondary storage and speed this access up. It is designed to make access to data possible at a higher level (by data properties rather than by address). Typically used only in systems dedicated to data base management.

Bandwidth.   See data transfer rate.

BCD—Binary Coded Decimal.   Usually used to refer to 4-bit representation of decimal numbers and the corresponding binary representation of decimal numbers.

BCDIC—BCD Interchange Code.   A 6-bit IBM character code. Basis of EBCDIC.

Benchmark.   A program designed to evaluate the performance of a computer system.

Biased Representation.   Number representation in which the value is obtained by subtracting a fixed number from the apparent value represented by the code. Used in the representation of exponent in floating-point representation.

Binary.   Representational system based on the use of two values.

Bipolar.   A semiconductor technology based on the use of electrical elements of both polarities to propagate the signal. Characterized by relatively high speed and power consumption and relatively small packing density because of its more complicated basic circuit. Its most popular implementations are TTL and ECL which differ in the structure of their basic circuits, speed, power consumption, and cost.

Bit. Binary digit (0 or 1). Usually abbreviated as b (e.g., 64 kb).

Boolean. Used as synonymous with "logic" as in Boolean function, expression, formula, values, and variable. Relates to Boolean algebra developed by George Boole.

Bpi. Abbreviation for bits per inch, a unit of density of storage on magnetic storage media.

Bps. Abbreviation for bits per second, a unit used to measure the speed of transmission.

Breadboard. In general, an area with contacts designed for easy connections, often with a power supply, input switches, and output indicators. Intended for quick set-up of circuits for testing of systems before manufacture.

Buffer. An intermediate system whose function is to amplify a signal in the context of digital components or temporarily hold data in the context of larger systems.

Burn-In. Period of increased stress (temperature, vibrations, etc.) during component testing. Its purpose is to accelerate the appearance of faults and the discovery of marginally functioning components.

Bus. The communication channel inteconnecting several communicating devices and carrying a group of related bits (address bus, data bus, etc.). It includes components allowing control over the establishment of the path of communication and components amplifying or shaping the communicated signals.

Bus Width. Number of bits that can be transferred over the bus simultaneously.

Byte. Usually used to refer to a group of eight bits, but a few manufacturers use it to refer to a basic group of a different size such as twelve bits. Usually abbreviated as B (e.g., 64 kB).

Cache. A small, very high speed intermediate memory between the main memory and the CPU. Its function is to improve access time to main memory at a relatively low cost.

CAD—Computer Aided Design. The use of computers to speed up and decrease the cost of design. Often used in a sense restricted to the design of digital components.

Canonical Representation. In Boolean algebra used to refer to the representation of truth functions in the form of a sum of product terms or a product of sum terms, each of which contains all variables of the function.

CCD—Charge Coupled Devices. Modern technology based on semiconductor materials with a potential for becoming an important high speed secondary storage medium.

Channel. In computer architecture a specialized processor used to control I/O operations to free the main computer from this task. Also called I/O processor or peripheral processor by some manufacturers.

Character. Letter, digit, special symbol or (in an extended sense) a control symbol such as carriage return and line feed.

Characteristic. Representation of the exponent of a floating-point number in a biased format.

Chip. In a strict sense a small plate of semiconductor material implementing an integrated circuit. In a broader sense the whole component including the chip, its usually plastic packaging, and connecting pins.

Clock Skew. The lack of synchronization of the arrival of a clock signal to all components of a clocked system. Due to different delays along individual signal paths.

CMOS—Complementary MOS. An IC family whose elementary circuit is basically a combination of an N-MOS and P-MOS element. Characterized by extremely low power consumption, high noise immunity, and the capability of working with a relatively unregulated power supply. Expected to become one of the most important future semiconductor technologies.

Combinational Circuit. A circuit implementing a memoryless Boolean function.

Compiler. A computer program for the translation of a high-level "source" program into a low level "object" program.

Complement Representation. Number representation allowing efficient handling of fixed-point negative and positive numbers. Radix complement (2's complement in binary) is more common than radix-1 complement (1's complement in binary).

Computer. A digital system processing data under the control of a program. Main parts are the CPU, memory, and I/O devices.

Computer Architecture. The computer as seen by the programmer, characterized by its instruction set, data types, programmable registers, word size, etc.

Computer Organization. The computer viewed as a digital system by a digital designer.

Computer Network. See Network.

Content-Addressable. See Associative Memory.

Control Unit. A part of a system generating control signals directing other parts of the system to perform operations in the desired orderly fashion. Digital control units can be hardwired with control signals generated by sequential circuits or microprogrammed with control signals generated in response to very low-level internally stored instructions forming a microprogram).

Converter. In digital systems usually devices converting signals from analog to digital (ADC) or from digital to analog (DAC) form.

Counter. A device counting the number of occurrences of an input signal (often the clock signal) and producing a code of the count. More generally a device producing a repetitive sequence of codes.

Core. In the correct sense, the name of an older memory technology based on the use of magnetizable cores. In a generalized and incorrect sense, sometimes used to refer to the main memory of a larger computer.

Clock. A component producing regularly spaced and shaped signals used to control the function of systems with synchronous components such as the CPU.

Control Sequence. Sequence of events consisting of the generation and distribution of control signals by a control unit.

Control Unit. Sequential circuit generating control signals which enable data transfer and logical operations on data.

CPU—the Central Processing Unit. One of the major parts of a computer which controls its operations and performs its data processing functions under the control of a program stored in the memory. Its main parts are registers (programmable or hidden), ALU, and the control unit (hardwired or microprogrammed).

CRT Terminal. A display terminal based on the Cathode Ray Tube (similar to standard TV display). The most common type of display terminal.

Cryogenics. Technologies taking advantage of unusual behavior of materials at temperatures approaching absolute zero.

Cycle Stealing. A method of DMA in which data transfer is made at the expense of the CPU which is frozen in an inactive state for one or more machine cycles.

Cycle Time. Minimum time between successive accesses to a memory device. Compare with access time.

Data Base. A collection of data serving a related purpose, accessed, and stored together. Often used only in the context of Data Base Management Systems.

Data Base Management System—DBMS. A software system allowing high-level contents-oriented access to a data base.

Data Selector. See Multiplexer.

Data Transfer Rate. Maximum number of bits per second (bauds) or other units that can be transferred over a given communication channel. Synonymous with bandwidth.

Data Type. In computer architecture, used to refer to types of data that can be processed by the given instruction set. Includes floating and fixed-point numbers, BCD, single and double precision, etc.

Decoder. A device converting a code, such as the BCD code, to a less encoded signal, such as a Boolean value on one of ten output lines.

Deterministic. Governed by a fixed rule, usually used as opposite of random.

Demultiplexer. The opposite of a multiplexer. Can direct an input signal to one of a number of outputs.

Development System. A system designed for orderly design of a new product, usually a computer-based digital system. Typically includes a CPU, main and auxiliary memory, a terminal, and special purpose components and programs to simplify and speed up design.

Diagnostic. Used to refer to a set of signals or programs designed for efficient testing of a system.

Digital. Refers to signals representing data codes and systems based on them. Digital signals are often described as those based on discretely rather than smoothly varying values. In electronic design used as the opposite of analog.

DIL—Dual In Line Package. Standard packaging of integrated circuits with two rows of pins extending from the base of the plastic or ceramic housing of an integrated circuit.

Direct Access. Synonymous with semirandom access (see sequential access).

Direct Addressing. Effective address forms address part of instruction code.

Direct Execution. Used to refer to computer designs implementing direct execution of higher-level languages without intermediate translation.

Disk Storage. Form of secondary storage in which information is stored on magnetizable surfaces of rotating rigid (''hard'') or flexible disks.

Distributed Processing. In general, a system in which processing and storage are distributed among several components of more or less independent systems. In the most common sense, a data processing system with processing, storage and I/O facilities connected by communication lines and capable of accessing one another.

DMA—Direct Memory Access. The fastest method of communication between an I/O device and memory bypassing the CPU. Controlled by a DMA controller and implemented as Cycle Stealing or Simultaneous DMA.

Don't Care.   A condition in which the Boolean value of a function for a given combination of input values is irrelevant to the function of the device that it represents.

Drum Storage.   An alternative to disk storage. Information is stored on the surface of a rotating cylindrical body.

Dumb Terminal.   A terminal with only minimal processing and storage capabilities. Opposite of intelligent terminal.

Dynamic Memory.   Type of semiconductor memory requiring periodic refresh of stored information. Opposite of static memory. Advantage is high storage density.

EBAM—Electron Beam Addressable Memory.   A developing memory technology showing promise as a secondary storage medium.

EBCDIC—Extended Binary Coded Decimal Interchange Code.   An 8-bit character code developed by IBM and used in IBM and several other computers.

ECL—Emitter-Coupled-Logic.   One of the most successful and expensive bipolar families with the highest speed among semiconductor devices. Characterized by gate propagation delays under 10 nanoseconds.

Edge-Triggered.   Responding to a change in the level of a signal rather than to the level itself.

Effective Address.   The address of the memory location to be actually accessed to fetch or store an operand. See also Indirect Addressing, etc.

Electron Beam Lithography.   One of the most advanced lithographic methods in IC production. Capable of reducing line width under one micron, the limit attainable with traditional optical lithography.

Emulation.   Execution of programs written for another computer by modifying the instruction set of the given computer. Can be relatively easily implemented on microprogrammable computers.

Encoder.   Basically, a device converting a message such as a Boolean value on one of ten lines into a code, in this case possibly the BCD code.

Excitation Table.   A truth table or its variation showing inputs of a memory device for all possible combinations of system inputs and internal states. Can also be given in the form of an excitation function.

Execute Phase.   That part of the execution of an instruction in which the required operation is performed. Follows the fetch phase.

Family.   In semiconductor technology used to refer to all devices produced on the basis of the same physical principle, basic circuit and manufacturing process, such as bipolar, MOS, and their subfamilies.

In the context of computer systems used to refer to a series of computers designed by one manufacturer and related to one another by a more or less close compatibility of instruction sets, system structure, and components.

Fail-Safe.   Method of design based on the strategy that a partial system failure should lead to a safe state of the system, such as a traffic light controller turning all lights to red or orange when it fails.

Failure Rate.   Usually the percentage of components failed per 1000 hours.

Fan-In.   The number of unit loads represented by the input of a given elementary digital component. See also Fan-Out.

Fan-Out.   The maximum number of unit loads that can be connected to the output of a given elementary digital component without overloading it so that its proper function can be guaranteed.

Fault.   The cause of a discrepancy between the actual and the expected behavior of a system.

Fault-Tolerance.   System's ability to function properly even in the presence of certain faults.

Fetch Phase.   The first phase of instruction execution during which the code of the next instruction is fetched from the memory. Followed by the execute phase.

Fixed-Point Representation.   Representation of numbers using a fixed number of digits and position of the radix point. Most common forms are integer (radix point follows least significant digit) and fractional (point precedes the most significant digit).

Flip-Flop.   An elementary memory component capable of storing one bit. Basic types of flip-flops include RS, JK, D, and T flip-flops. Depending on sensitivity to clock signal classified as level-sensitive, edge-sensitive, and master-slave flip-flops.

Floating-Point Representation.   Number representation based on the use of the magnitude (mantissa) and a scaling factor obtained as the power of a fixed base. Each number is represented by its mantissa and the exponent of the scaling factor.

Floppy Disk.   Secondary storage device used mainly in small systems employing an intechangeable flexible disk coated with magnetizable material as storage medium.

Flops.   Number of floating point operations executed per second. A unit sometimes used to measure the speed of a processor.

Flow Table.   Table showing next states of an asynchronous system as a function of present states and inputs.

Front-End Processor. A system responsible for the communication of a large computer with a group of its I/O devices (such as terminals and communication lines). Performs some preprocessing to increase the efficiency of utilization of the host computer. Often implemented by a minicomputer.

Gate. An elementary combinational device implementing a Boolean function. Also used as a verb to denote control of a signal path by a gate.

Gate Equivalent. A circuit of complexity comparable to that of a simple gate. Used as a measure of complexity of an IC. See SSI, MSI, LSI, and VLSI.

Giga. Prefix meaning $10**9$ (billion).

Glitch. A malfunction in the form of a brief pulse usually caused by inconsistent timing.

Graceful Degradation. Strategy of system design in which a partially faulty system maintains at least some essential capabilities.

Handshaking. A sequence of interlocked signals initiating or completing communication between two systems.

Hardcopy Terminal. Terminal with a printer producing a permanent copy of the terminal communication with the system.

Hardware. The collection of physical components of a digital system, particularly a computer. The complement of software.

Hardwired Control Unit. Control unit implemented by a sequential circuit which does not use an internally stored program to generate control signals.

Hazard. A malfunction of a digital system due to unbalanced path delays of propagating signals.

Hexadecimal Representation. Positional representation of numbers using base 16.

High-Level Language. Programming language in which programs can be written at a relatively high level of abstraction and without regard for the details of the architecture of the used computer. Almost identically defined on different computers. In this respect the anti-pole of machine language. Programs written in a high-level language must be converted into machine language before execution by a compiler or an interpreter.

IC. Abbreviation for Integrated Circuit.

IIL—Integrated Injection Logic. A bipolar technology which allows relatively high circuit density.

I/O. Abbreviation for Input/Output.

I/O Communication. Method of transfer of data between I/O devices and the memory. The main I/O methods are programmed, interrupt-driven and DMA. Large computers use special I/O processors to perform their I/O.

Immediate Addressing. Address part of instruction is the value of the operand.

Implied Addressing. See Inherent Addressing.

Indexed Addressing. Effective address is the sum of the address part of the instruction and the contents of a special register (the index register).

Indirect Addressing. Address part of instruction contains the direct or indirect address of the location holding the effective address.

Inherent Addressing. Operand location is implied by the instruction code (e.g., shift accumulator left when there is only one accumulator). Also called implied addressing.

Instruction. In a computer a code specifying an operation to be performed.

Instruction Cycle. The sequence of elementary operations consisting of fetching of an instruction code and the execution of the required operation.

Instruction Set. The set of instructions of a computer.

Intelligent Terminal. Terminal with built-in processing power and memory. Typically capable of limited editing and storage of data. Also called smart terminal. Opposite of dumb terminal.

Integrated Circuit (IC). A digital circuit implemented on a single chip of semiconductor material. Depending on the complexity of implemented circuit the level of integration is classified as small scale, medium scale, large scale or very large scale (SSI, MSI, LSI, VLSI). Also used in the same sense as chip.

Interface. A system inserted between two larger communicating systems which generates, partially processes and stores signals required for the communication.

Interleaved Memory. Refers to an implementation of main memory in which independently accessible modules (banks) share the computer's full address space in such a way as to make it possible to access several locations containing a sequence of consecutive instructions or data items simultaneously. Allows faster access by the CPU.

Interpreter. A computer program translating and immediately executing a high-level programming language.

Interrupt. A signal usually generated by an I/O device to notify the CPU of the occurrence of an event which requires CPU's response. In the context of higher-level programming, often used in a more general sense.

Interrupt-Driven I/O. I/O performed in response to an interrupt signal usually generated by an I/O device. I/O is performed by executing an interrupt routine from which an automatic return is made to the program whose execution was temporarily interrupted. The efficiency of this mode of I/O is intermediate between programmed I/O and DMA.

Interrupt Routine. Subroutine executed in response to an interrupt signal. Its execution is followed by an automatic return to the interrupted program and restoration of its data.

Josephson Junction. The basis of a developing technology showing promise as a future substitute for present semiconductor technologies in applications requiring the highest speeds. Operates at temperatures around 4 degrees Kelvin. Expected to allow speeds corresponding to 10 picosecond gate delays.

Karnaugh Map. A variation of a truth table used in the design of simpler combinational circuits. Allows circuit minimization by visual inspection of the recorded binary pattern.

Kilo. In data processing used as a prefix representing 1024 ($2**10$).

Latency Time. Used to refer to the average time needed for a cell on the surface of a magnetic disk to reach the read-write head.

LCD. Liquid crystal display. A display technology.

Life Cycle. For a product such as an IC refers to individual stages of the life of a specific design: product introduction, its maturity, and obsolescence.

Lithography. In Integrated Circuit technology the transfer of the drawing of a circuit (the mask) to the chip.

LSI—Large Scale Integration. Level of integration characterized by 100 to 1000 gate equivalents per chip. Examples are high capacity memory and microprocessor chips.

Machine Cycle. Usually the length of time assigned for the transmission of data between the CPU and the main memory. For a CPU with a given control sequence determines the speed of the CPU.

Machine Language. Programming language consisting of codes of instructions of the given computer. Differs from one computer to another.

Magnetic Bubble Memory—MBM. A relatively new and promising secondary storage technology. Based on semiconductor manufacturing processes. Stores data as movable microscopic magnetized domains.

Main Memory. Fast access memory accessed by instructions from the CPU.

Maintainability.   The ease of maintaining a system.

Mantissa.   Accompanies the exponent of the scaling factor in floating-point representation of numbers.

Mask.   In IC manufacture a partially transparent material carrying the copy of a pattern to be transposed on the surface of the wafer. In programming a group of bits used to access a part of a word via logic instructionss.

Memory Cycle Time.   Time in which a new access to the same memory device is permissible. Since some memories require rewriting of retrieved or previously stored data, memory cycle time may be longer than memory access time.

Micro.   Often used as a prefix denoting $10^{**}(-6)$.

Microinstruction.   An instruction in a microprogram. Its execution usually results in the generation of a set of CPU control signals.

Micron.   One millionth of a meter, i.e., one thousandth of a millimeter.

Microprogram.   A program consisting of microinstructions. Determines the function of a microprogrammed control unit.

Microprogrammed Control Unit.   A control unit generating control signals under the direction of a (micro)program stored in a special memory.

Modem—MOdulator-DEModulator.   A device converting a digital signal to an analog signal for long distance transmission and back to digital at the end of the line. The term data set is used in related meaning.

MOS—Metal-Oxide-Silicon (or Semiconductor).   The rival of bipolar technology using only one type of charge carrier— positive in the older p-MOS technology and negative in the faster n-MOS technology. One of the main advantages of the MOS technology is the possibility of packing devices close together on the chip and the relatively low power consumption. Typical gate delays are under 100 nanoseconds.

MSI—Medium Scale Integration.   Level of integration characterized by 12 to 100 gate equivalents per chip. Examples are multiplexers, counters, and registers.

MTBF—Mean Time Between Failures.   A statistical measure of the reliability of a system. Corresponds to the calculated or measured mean length of time between consecutive failures of a system.

MTTR—Mean Time To Repair.   Mean time required to repair.

Multiplexer.   Usually an IC whose function is to allow the selection of one of a number of inputs under the control of address or control signals. Also called the data selector.

Multiprocessor. A computer in which several CPU's or complete computer systems are closely connected together and more or less closely cooperate. Usually under the control of a single operating system.

Multiprogramming. Mode of operation allowing a computer system to interleave the execution of several independent programs.

Nano. Prefix used to represent $10^{**}(-9)$.

Negative Logic. Convention to consider high voltage level as logic zero and low level as logic one. Opposite of positive logic.

Network. A system of interconnected independent computer systems and I/O devices with hardware and software mutually accessible within the constraints of the imposed hierarchy.

Nibble. A group of four bits.

Noise. Undesirable signal added to the useful signal, usually by electrical interference.

Noise Immunity. Ability of a component to function correctly even in the presence of noise.

Object Program. The output of a compiler. Translated from a source program written in a high-level language.

Octal Representation. Base 8 positional representation.

1's Complement. See Complement Representation.

Opcode. Part of instruction code specifying the operation to be performed. Usually accompanied by the address part stored in the address field.

Open Collector Device. A digital IC with a modified circuit allowing direct connection of outputs of several such devices. Now largely replaced by tri-state devices.

Operating System. Software which makes it possible to interact with a computer system on a relatively high level. Performs tasks such as I/O control, scheduling of jobs, etc. Usually supplied by the manufacturer of the computer.

Optical Disk. A developing storage technology expected to play an important role in large capacity secondary storage. Based on principles similar to video recording.

Optical Lithography. Lithographic method based on the use of visible light. Its utmost resolution of one micron given by the wavelength of light has been attained. For the production of VLSI systems being replaced by Electron Beam and X-ray lithography.

Overflow. Situation arising when an arithmetic operation produces a result whose value cannot be represented by the available codes and cannot be stored.

Page. A fixed number (e.g., 256 words) of memory locations. The whole address space is usually divided into individual pages to simplify and speed up memory access.

Parallel Processor. A processor capable of simultaneous (parallel) execution of several operations of the same kind.

Parity. Remainder of division by two. Odd and even parities are used for simple error detection in coding.

Perfect Induction. Method of proving or disproving the identity of two Boolean expressions on the basis of the comparison of their truth tables.

Peripheral Device. Synonym for I/O device.

Phase. In the execution of an instruction, a sequence of operations performing a related function: the fetch and execute phase.

Pico. Prefix used to represent $10**(-12)$.

Pipeline. An alternative to a single-module implementation of a processor based on the division of an operation into a sequence of sub-operations which can be executed independently.

Port. Usually used to refer to the connection between a device and an I/O bus.

Positional Representation. Number representation in which each position in the codeword has a fixed weight. Examples are standard decimal, binary, octal, and hexadecimal notations.

Positive Logic. Convention to consider high voltage level logic one and low voltage level logic zero. Opposite of negative logic.

PLA—Programmable Logic Array. A circuit (normally an IC) containing a number of gates with some interconnections left uncompleted to allow users to partially modify the device to suit their needs.

Program. A sequence of instructions to solve a given problem.

Programmed I/O. Method of I/O in which the CPU repeatedly checks the state of an I/O device awaiting its availability for the desired operation. Results in very inefficient utilization of the CPU and slow I/O.

Propagation Delay. Time needed for the output of a device to stabilize its response to a change in an input signal.

Protocol. The set of rules governing the interchange of signals establishing or completing the communication between two autonomous systems.

Race. The largely unpredictable response of an asynchronous sequential circuit in a situation requiring the simultaneous change of values of several state variables.

RAM—Random Access Memory. Used as a synonym for a read/write memory in which the duration of access to any location is independent of the address. Compare with sequential access.

Raster Scan. The principle of CRT displays in which the screen is scanned by the electron beam line by line.

Recursive. Used to refer to a subroutine which calls itself, directly or indirectly via other subroutines.

Redundancy. In digital design use of multiple circuits or data paths to improve the reliability of a system.

Refresh. Reading and rewriting of stored information which has to be performed periodically on dynamic memories to prevent the loss of stored data. Typical refresh period is measured in milliseconds.

Register. In the design of digital circuits, a memory device capable of storing a group of several bits related by their function. It is often capable of simple logic operations such as shifting. In computer architecture often used to refer to addressable CPU registers, also called programmable registers.

Relative Addressing. Addressing mode in which the effective address is obtained as the sum of the address in the program counter and the offset in the address part of the instruction.

Relay. An electromechanical device in which electric current controls the closing or opening of contacts.

Reliability. System's ability to perform the desired function over a period of time.

Reliable Design. Strategy of design aimed at achieving exceptionally high reliability, usually by using redundant components.

Resolution. The smallest possible increment of a value.

ROM—Read Only Memory. Used to refer to random access memory devices with only read capability. Information is stored (written) into them permanently or semipermanently.

RTL—Register Transfer Level. Used to refer to the description of digital systems at the level of transmission of codes (groups of bits) between registers. Also used to refer to formal languages used for such descriptions.

Secondary Memory. Slower large capacity and less expensive memory not directly accessible by instructions. Serves as an extension of the storage of a computer system. Data from secondary memory must be transferred to the main memory for processing. Usually implemented by magnetic disk and magnetic tape devices.

Seek Time. Time required to move read-write heads of a disk drive from one track to another.

Self-Repairing System. A system which detects its malfunction, identifies the faulty module, disconnects it, and replaces it with a properly functioning spare module.

Self-Testing System. One which permanently or periodically tests its essential functions and notifies the operator and possibly repairs itself when it detects a malfunction.

Semiconductor. Material which exhibits different electrical resistance in two directions. Semiconductors form the basis of modern electronic devices. The most successful ones are Si, Ge, GaAs.

Sequential Access Storage. Storage medium on which information can only be accessed in the same order in which it is physically stored, such as magnetic tape. Also called serial access storage. Disk and drum storage are examples of semisequential (also called semirandom or direct) access devices on which access is partially sequential (access to data on the track) and partially random (tracks can be read in any order).

Sequential Circuit. A digital circuit whose response to an input is related to the sequence of previous inputs.

Sign-Magnitude Representation. Number representation based on positional representation of magnitude and a sign bit.

Simulation. The representation of essential features of a system by more easily accessible parameters of another system. In the past mainly based on analog computers now increasingly implemented by computer programs.

Simultaneous DMA. DMA performed by utilizing the bus when it is not needed by the CPU. Does not cause any slow-down of the CPU.

Software. Programs available on a given computer. In a more restrictive sense (system software) programs shared by all users of the system and largely supplied by its manufacturer.

SOS—Silicon On Sapphire. The fastest and most promising form of CMOS technology. Uses silicon deposited on insulating sapphire.

Source Program. Input of a compiler, translated into object program.

SSI—Small Scale Integration. The lowest level of integration characterized by circuits with up to 12 gates per chip. Examples are gate and flip-flop chips.

Stack. Used to refer to a model of storage in which only the data item most recently placed ("pushed") on the stack can be read and removed ("popped").

Stack Computer. A computer using the stack as the main storage structure.

State. Combination of values fully describing the present condition of a system. Includes input, internal, and output states.

Static Memory. Semiconductor RAM which does not require refresh. Opposite of dynamic memory.

Status Register. A CPU register dedicated to the storage of information about the status of the CPU—the status word. The status word consists of bits ("flags") indicating whether the last arithmetic operation produced an overflow, a zero result, etc., whether interrupts are enabled or not, etc.

Streaming. The ideal situation in which a parallel or pipelined processor is executing a program taking full advantage of its modular design.

Strobe. Usually used as a verb to denote gating of a signal into a device.

Subroutine. A sequence of instructions accessible from any program which is implemented in such a way that its access from the "calling" sequence guarantees the storage of all information necessary for an automatic return when the execution of the subroutine is completed. Also called a procedure.

Synchronous. Used to refer to a system in which transitions are controlled by a single signal usually generated by a clock.

Synthesis. In digital design, synonymous with design— formulation of a structural description of a physical circuit implementing the given functional description.

Terminal. An I/O device used for communication with a computer. Usually includes a keyboard for input and a display screen or printer for output. See also Dumb and Intelligent Terminal.

Test Set. A set of signal combinations designed to test a circuit for the presence of specific faults.

Throughput. Number of results obtained per unit of time (e.g., the number of programs executed per 24 hours).

Time-Sharing. A mode of operation in which a computer system allows interleaved execution of several programs or similar processes. In a more restrictive sense, a mode of operation allowing several users to interleave their interactive access to a computer system.

TMR—Triple Modular Redundancy. A method of reliable design using triple redundancy and majority vote.

Transducer. A device converting energy from one form to another.

Transfer Rate. See Data Transfer Rate.

Transistor. An elementary semiconductor component which forms the basis of semiconductor circuits. Its basic function is the electronic control of a current path with a minimum amount of energy and delay.

Transition Table. A table describing transitions between internal states of a sequential circuit in response to input signals.

Tri-State Device. An IC device whose output can be connected to outputs of other tri-state devices. Its output can assume the normal Boolean values or a high impedance state equivalent to removing the output connection of the device to the rest of the circuit. Controlled by an "enable" signal.

Truth Table. A tabular representation of a Boolean function specifying the value of the function for each combination of values of its variables.

TTL—Transistor-Transistor-Logic. One of the most successful bipolar logic families. Typical gate delays are around 10 nanoseconds.

2's Complement. See Complement Representation.

Underflow. Situation which arises when the magnitude of the result of an arithmetic operation is too small to be representable in the given floating-point format, i.e. with a normalized mantissa and exponent in the available representation.

Vacuum Tube. A tube in which the flow of electrons in the vacuum between electrodes is controlled by an electric field generated by one or more charged grids. In digital circuits now completely replaced by semiconductor devices.

VDU—Video Display Unit. Terminal with a non-permanent display of output. Opposite of hardcopy terminal.

Virtual Memory. An implementation of the addressing space of a computer in which the ("logical") address space is not directly related to the physical size of the main memory. Uses a function mapping the address space into the secondary storage.

Virtual Processor. A fictitious machine implemented by software in order to simplify programming.

Volatility. The property of some storage devices (semiconductors and CCDs) to lose stored information when the source of power is disconnected.

VLSI—Very Large Scale Integration. Integration achieving the equivalent of over 1000 gates per chip. 64kb semiconductor RAMs are on the lower limit of this level of integration.

Wafer. A circular slice usually made of very pure silicon which is the basis of the manufacture of integrated circuits. In a sequence of steps its surface is covered with several layers of material forming several copies of the same circuit. The individual copies are tested, separated and packaged.

Word. A group of bits of a size which is convenient to consider as an entity (often defined to be equal to the memory data bus width).

X-Ray Lithography. A prospective tool in IC manufacture replacing optical lithography for the production of masks of very complex VLSI chips. Its parameters are similar to those of electron beam lithography.

BIBLIOGRAPHY

Books:

Abramson, Norman. *Information theory and coding.* New York: McGraw-Hill, 1963.

Agrawalla, Ashok K. and Rauscher, Tomlinson G. *Foundations of microprogramming: Architecture, software and applications.* New York: Academic Press, 1976.

Aspinall, D. and Dagless, E.L., eds. *Introduction to microprocessors.* London: Pitman Publishing, 1977.

Bell, Gordon C.; Mudge, Craig J.; McNamara, John E. *Computer Engineering: A DEC view of hardware systems design.* Bedford, Mass.: Digital Press, 1978.

Bishop, Ron. *Basic microprocessors and the 6800.* Rochelle Park, N.J.: Hayden Book Co., 1979.

Blakeslee, Thomas R. *Digital design with standard MSI and LSI.* 2nd ed. New York: John Wiley and Sons, 1979.

Bray, O.H. and Freeman, H.A. *Data base computers.* Lexington, Mass.: Lexington Books, 1979.

Breuer, Melvin A., ed. *Design automation of digital systems.* Theory and techniques, Vol. 1. Englewood Cliffs, N.J.: Prentice-Hall, 1972.

Breuer, Melvin A., ed. *Digital systems design automation: Languages, simulation and database.* Rockville, Md.: Computer Science Press, Inc., 1975.

Breuer, Melvin A. and Friedman, Arthur D. *Diagnosis and reliable design of digital systems.* Rockville, Md.: Computer Science Press, Inc., 1976.

Brzozowski, Janusz A. and Yoeli, Michael. *Digital networks.* Englewood Cliffs, N.J.: Prentice-Hall, 1976.

Chu, Yaohan. *Computer organization and microprogramming.* Englewood Cliffs, N.J.: Prentice-Hall, 1972.

Clare, Christopher R. *Designing logic systems using state machines.* New York: McGraw-Hill, 1973.

Control Data Corporation. *CDC Cyber 170, Hardware Reference Manual.*

Dertouzos, Michael L. and Moses, Joel, eds. *The computer age: A twenty-year view.* Cambridge, Mass.: MIT Press, 1979.

Doran, R.W. *Computer architecture: A structured approach.* New York: Academic Press, 1979.

Flores, Ivan. *The logic of computer arithmetic.* Englewood Cliffs, N.J.: Prentice-Hall, 1963.

Foster, Caxton C. *Content addressable parallel processors.* New York: van Nostrand Reinhold Co., 1976.

Gear, William C. *Computer organization and programming.* 3rd ed. New York: McGraw-Hill, 1980.

Grishman, Ralph. *Assembly language programming for the CDC 6000 series and the Cyber 70 series.* New York: Algorithmic Press, 1974.

Gschwind, Hans W. and McCluskey, Edward J. *Design of digital computers.* New York: Springer-Verlag, 1975.

Hamacher, V. Carl; Vranesic, Zvonko G.; and Zaky, Safwat G. *Computer organization.* New York: McGraw-Hill, 1978.

Hayes, John P. *Computer architecture and organization.* New York: McGraw-Hill, 1978.

Hill, Frederick J.; Peterson, J.; Gerald, R. *Digital systems: Hardware organization and design.* 2nd ed. New York: John Wiley and Sons, 1978.

Husson, Sarnir S. *Microprogramming: Principles and practices.* Englewood Cliffs, N.J.: Prentice-Hall, 1970.

Hwang, Kai. *Computer arithmetic: Principles, architecture and design.* New York: John Wiley and Sons, 1979.

Kohavi, Zvi. *Switching and finite automata theory.* 2nd ed. New York: McGraw-Hill, 1978.

Kuck, David J. *The structure of computers and computations.* Vol. 1. New York: John Wiley and Sons, 1978.

Lancaster, Don. *TTL cookbook.* Indianapolis, Ind.: Howard W. Sams and Co., 1974.

Lancaster, Don. *TV typewriter cookboook.* Indianapolis, Ind.: Howard W. Sams and Co., 1976.

Lancaster, Don. *CMOS cookbook.* Indianapolis, Ind.: Howard W. Sams and Co., 1977.

MacKenzie, Charles E. *Coded character sets: History and development.* Reading, Mass.: Addison-Wesley, 1980.

Matick, Richard B. *Computer storage systems and technology.* New York: John Wiley and Sons, 1977.

McGlynn, Daniel R. *Distributed processing and data communication.* New York: John Wiley and Sons, 1978.

McGlynn, Daniel R. *Microprocessors.* New York: John Wiley and Sons, 1976.

Mead, Carver and Conway, Lynn. *Introduction to VLSI systems.* Reading, Mass.: Addison-Wesley, 1980.

Mowle, Frederick J. *A systematic approach to digital logic design.* Reading, Mass.: Addison-Wesley, 1977.

Myers, Glenford J. *Advances in computer architecture.* New York: John Wiley and Sons, 1978.

Organick, Elliot I. *Computer system organization: The B-5700, B-6700 series.* New York: Academic Press, 1973.

Osborne, Adam. *An introduction to microcomputers.* Vols. 0-2. Berkeley, Ca.: Adam Osborne and Associates, 1977, 1976, 1976.

Osborne Adam. *6800 programming for logic design.* Berkeley, Ca.: Adam Osborne and Associates, 1977.

Peterson, James I. *Computer organization and assembly language programming.* New York: Academic Press, 1978.

Phister, Montgomery Jr. *Data processing technology and economics.* 2nd ed. Bedford, Mass.: Digital Press, 1979.

Roth, Charles H. *Fundamentals of logic design.* 2nd ed. St. Paul, Minn.: West Publishing Co., 1979.

Sandige, Richard S. *Digital concepts using standard integrated circuits.* New York: McGraw-Hill, 1978.

Sawin, Dwight H. *Microprocesssors and microcomputer systems.* New York: D. C. Heath and Co., 1977.

Sloan, Martha E. *Computer hardware and organization.* Chicago: SRA, 1976.

Svoboda, Antonin and White, Donnamaie E. *Advanced logical circuit design techniques.* New York: Garland Publishing, Inc., 1979.

Swartzlander, Earl E. *Computer design development: Principal papers.* Rochelle Park, N.J.: Hayden Book Co., 1975.

Stone, Harold S., ed. *Introduction to computer architecture.* Chicago, SRA, 1975.

Tanenbaum, Andrew S. *Structured computer organization.* Englewood Cliffs, N.J.: Prentice-Hall, 1976.

Texas Instruments, Inc. *The TTL data book for design engineers.* 2nd ed. 1976.

The Oregon Report. *Proceedings of the Conference on Computing in the 1980's.* IEEE Computer Society, 1978.

Tokheim, Roger L. *Schaum's outline of digital principles.* New York: McGraw-Hill, 1980.

van Cleemput, W. M., ed. *Computer-aided design tools for digital systems.* 2nd ed. IEEE Computer Society, 1979.

van Cleemput, W. M. *Computer aided design of digital systems—A bibliography.* Vols. 1-4. Rockville Md.: Computer Science Press, Inc., 1976, 1978, 1979.

Wakerly, John F. *Error correcting codes, self-checking circuits and applications.* New York: North Holland, 1963.

Wiatrowski, Claude A. and House, Charles H. *Logic circuits and microcomputer systems.* New York: McGraw-Hill, 1980.

Williams, Gerald E. *Digital technology.* Chicago: SRA, 1977.

Zaks, Rodnay. *Microprocessors from chips to systems.* Berkeley, Ca.: Sybex Inc., 1977.

Zissos, D. *Problems and solutions in logic design.* London: Oxford University Press, 1976.

Periodical Publications:

Auerbach Reports
Annual International Symposium on Fault tolerant computing
ACM Computing surveys
Byte
Communications of ACM
Computer
Computer design
Computer world
Computers and digital techniques
Compcon digest of papers
Design Automation Conference
Digital design
EDN
Electronics
Euromicro journal
IEEE Transactions on computers
International symposium on computer hardware description
    languages and their applications
Interface age
Kilobaud microcomputing
NCC proceedings

INDEX

PROM - see programmable ROM
propagation delay - see delay
protocol, 277, 377
prototype, 97
push on stack, 294

race
  critical, 143
  -free assignment, 143
  non-critical, 143
Radio Shack TRS-80, 305, 345
radix - see also base
  -complement, 200
random access memory, 226, 396
RAM - see random access memory
read cycle, 340
read-only-memory, 57, 70, 396
real-time processing, 360
redundancy, 88
register, 144, 153, 224, 349, 357, 365
  shift, 154
  transfer, 164
relative addressing, 293
relay, 9, 33
reliable design, 88
reliability, 88
replacement algorithm, 353
reset input, 125
return from subroutine, 326
retry, 357
ripple counter, 145
rotate instruction, 296
rounding, 196
RS, 232
ROM - see read-only-memory

Schmitt action, 123
secondary memory, 266, 381, 390, 415
seek delay, 269
self-repairing system, 91
semiconductor, 10, 394
  manufacture, 400
  memory, 260
sequential circuit, 15, 110
  analysis, 129

sequentiality of program, 392
seven-segment display, 110
shift register, 154
  design, 135
sign-magnitude representation, 197
silicon, 394
simulation, 97, 156
  language, 100
simultaneous DMA, 283
small scale integration, 39
soft error, 404
software, 1, 244, 304
SSI - see small scale integration
stack, 290
  computer, 290, 294
  instructions, 294, 323
  pointer, 290, 294, 314
stable state, 141
state, 15, 110
  assignment, 118
  graph, 113
  map, 114
  next, 111
  present, 111
  table, 113
  unstable, 141
static
  memory, 261
  organization, 378
status
  bit, 276, 314
  register, 249, 275, 280, 314
  word, 275, 280
streaming mode, 365, 376
stuck-at, 83
subroutine, 289, 297, 325
  call, 325
  nesting, 330
  recursive, 329
subtraction, 191
sum of products, 30
supercomputer, 302
supervisory mode, 352
switching circuit - see combinational
  circuit